Management Consulting Services

Sam W. Barcus III, Editor

Partner
Barcus Nugent Group
Brentwood, Tennessee

Joseph W. Wilkinson, Editor

Professor of Accounting
Arizona State University
Tempe, Arizona

McGraw-Hill Book Company

New York   St. Louis   San Francisco   Auckland
Bogotá   Hamburg   Johannesburg   London   Madrid
Mexico   Montreal   New Delhi   Panama   Paris
São Paulo   Singapore   Sydney   Tokyo   Toronto

Library of Congress Cataloging-in-Publication Data
Main entry under title:

Handbook of management consulting services.

Bibliography: p.
Includes index.
1. Business consultants—Addresses, essays, lectures.
I. Barcus, Sam W.   II. Wilkinson, Joseph W.
HD69.C6H36 1986   658.4'6   85-23144
ISBN 0-07-003658-6

  234567890   DOC/DOC   89321087

ISBN 0-07-003658-6

The editors for this book were Martha Jewett and Esther Gelatt,
the designer was Mark E. Safran, and the production supervisor
was Thomas G. Kowalczyk. It was set in Melior by Saybrook Press.

Printed and bound by R. R. Donnelley & Sons, Inc.

Contents

iii

Contributors

Sam W. Barcus is a partner in the Barcus Nugent Group, a management consulting firm located in Nashville, Tennessee. He received his BBA from the University of Texas at Arlington and his MBA from the University of Houston. He started his career in data processing as a programmer/analyst with Texas Instruments in Dallas, Texas. In 1976, he joined Price Waterhouse in Memphis, Tennessee, as a computer consultant and was later transferred—to build a consulting practice in Nashville, Tennessee. During the next 5 years, he expanded the practice, developing for Price Waterhouse a reputation as the premier computer consulting firm in the community. In 1983, Barcus joined Touche Ross & Co. in Nashville as director of Microcomputer Consulting Services. He formed Barcus Nugent in 1983 to provide management consulting services to professionals and small business executives. He is a Certified Public Accountant, has a Certificate in Data Processing, and is a Certified Management Consultant. He has held leadership positions in a number of professional organizations, including the Tennessee Society of CPAs, the Planning Executives Institute, and the Association of Systems Management. He serves on the board of Public Radio and is chairman of the Financial Review Committee of United Way. He has written numerous articles, conducted workshops, and presented seminars on topics related to the personal computer industry.

James L. Buck is president of James L. Buck and Company, a management consulting firm headquartered in Nashville, Tennessee. Buck spent 7 years in manufacturing with Gifford-Hill Corporation prior to establishing his own consulting firm in 1978. The firm specializes in executive skill and human resource development. Clients include major corporations as well as small businesses. James Buck has been active in public and government affairs, having served as chairman of a Governor's Special Task Force on Small Business in 1983, member of the Tennessee Industrial and Agricultural Commission, a delegate to the 1984 National Small Business Issues Conference in Washington, D.C. He serves as vice chairman of Growth Enterprise Nashville, Inc., member of the board and treasurer of the Nashville Rotary Club. He personally consults with presidents and CEOs who want to practice participative management, develop a more cohesive team-style management, or improve their corporate culture.

J. Owen Cherrington is professor of accounting at Brigham Young University. He earned his Ph.D. in accounting at the University of Minnesota in 1972. Prior to his present position, Dr. Cherrington served as assistant professor at Pennsylvania State University and associate professor at Utah State University. He is the author of several textbooks and journal articles. He also serves as consultant for several business organizations. He holds memberships in the American Accounting Association, American Institute of Certified Public Accountants, and Utah Association of Certified Public Accountants.

Michael Eugene Davis is manager of human resources and productivity development at Avco Aerostructures Division. He earned his Ph.D. in psychology at the University of Tennessee in 1976. Prior to his present position, Dr. Davis served as vice president of organizational development for James L. Buck and Company, Inc., management consultants, from 1982 to 1983. He was also president and owner of Davis and Associates, management and psychological consultants, from 1977 to 1982, and staff psychologist and adjunct professor at Middle Tenessee State University. Dr. Davis holds membership in the President's Advisory Council, Nashville State Technical Institute, and is on the Board of Directors, Mid-Cumberland Council on Alcohol and Drugs.

Myron A. Friedman, CPA., has been involved as a financial management consultant for the past 6½ years through his own consulting firm. Prior to that time, he was a partner with Alexander Grant & Company, an international firm of certified public accountants, involved with both internal management responsibility and management of client responsibilities for over 20 years. He has had extensive experience both as a consultant and in working with other consultants, and his consulting practice specializes in providing services to consulting businesses.

Friedman has been an active member of the Ohio and California State Societies of CPAs and a member of the American Institute of CPAs. He has also been Los Angeles Chapter president as well as a member of the International Board of Directors of both the Planning Executives Institute and the North American Society for Corporate Planners.

Steven P. Golen is associate professor of general business at Arizona State University. He earned his DBA in general business from Arizona State University in 1979. Prior to his present position, Dr. Golen served as chairman and associate professor at Louisiana State University. He is coauthor of the following textbooks: *Report Writing for Business and Industry,* 1985; *Principles of Business Communication: Theory, Application, and Technology,* 1984; *Business Communications Basics: Application and Technology,* 1984; and *Readings and Cases in Business Communication,* 1984. All of these textbooks were published by John Wiley & Sons. He holds memberships in the American Accounting Association, Institute of Internal Auditors, Association for Business Communication, Society of Data Educators, and Academy of Management.

Jane Graham, CDP, is vice president for customer support for Endata, Inc., a computer services company providing information processing systems and software nationwide. Graham's areas of responsibilities include customer training, documentation, on-site support, telephone response center support, and product quality assurance. She was previously a partner in Graham-Hune Associates, a data processing consulting firm. Her consulting engagements included selection and implementation of computer systems for clients in a wide variety of industries. The firm also specialized in training computer users. Graham has had extensive experience in project management, both from a practical standpoint, and as a consultant to software development organizations. She has conducted seminars nationally on project management, systems analysis, and software development methodologies. A graduate of Vanderbilt University, Graham has been active in the Association for Systems Management and the Independent Computer Consultants Association.

Gary M. Grudnitski is associate professor of accounting at the University of Texas at Austin. He earned his Ph.D. at the University of Massachusetts in 1975. Prior to his present position, Dr. Grudnitski held positions as systems analyst with Bell Telephone (Canada) and the Government of Saskatchewan from 1965 to 1970, and as assistant professor and chairman of the Department of Information Processing at the West Virginia Institute of Technology from 1970 to 1972. He has served as instructor in a variety of professional programs, including the AICPA

National MAS Training Program and the University Education for Management Consulting. He has also served on such professional committees as the MAS Committee of the Texas Society of Certified Public Accountants and the Computer Technology Research Committee of the American Accounting Association. He is coauthor of *Information Systems: Theory and Practice*, third edition, published in 1983 by John Wiley & Sons. He has also published articles in a variety of journals. He holds membership in the American Accounting Association, EDP Auditors Association, American Institute of Decision Sciences, and Society for Management Information Systems.

George Hill has been partner-in-charge of the management information and consulting (MIC) division of Arthur Andersen & Co., Phoenix, since 1977. Hill earned his BS in accounting from Kansas State University in 1960. He joined Arthur Andersen & Co. in the audit division, where he served for 2 years. He then transferred to the MIC division, where he became manager in 1965 and partner in 1971. For several years he served as the division head for the transportation industry.

Charlotte A. Jenkins is a manager within the management consulting services area of Price Waterhouse. Jenkins has worked with Price Waterhouse since 1980. She recently transferred from the Nashville office to Los Angeles, where she will specialize in health care consulting. Her background and experience have been with information systems, procedures, and organization analysis. Some specific projects that she has conducted and managed address: business planning; information system feasibility studies; computer system hardware and software evaluation, selection, and implementation; productivity improvement studies and procedures; job descriptions and specifications; and organization reviews.

James C. Kinard is associate professor of accounting at The Ohio State University. He earned his Ph.D. in accounting from Stanford University in 1969. Prior to accepting his present position in 1972, Dr. Kinard served as assistant professor of accounting and management information systems at Cornell University from 1968 to 1972. He has served with three different public accounting firms. He has also held positions as director for the AICPA National MAS training program and member of the AICPA EDP Technology Research Subcommittee. He has published articles in several academic journals. He holds memberships in the American Accounting Association, Institute of Management Sciences, American Institute for Decision Sciences, and Association for Computing Machinery.

Lynn J. McKell is a professor of accounting at Brigham Young University. He earned his Ph.D. in Management Science at Purdue University in 1973. Prior to his present position, Dr. McKell served as visiting professor of management science and information systems at the University of Minnesota. He also held several positions in private industry. Currently, he is a member of the board of directors of the Sterling Wentworth Corporation of Provo, Utah. Dr. McKell has also served as the principal investigator for the MASPACK 85 study conducted under the auspices of the American Institute of Certified Public Accountants, as well as chairman of the MAS section of the American Accounting Association and member of the MAS Education and Professional Development Subcommittee of the AICPA. He has received a patent for an improvement on a signal generator and has published articles in a variety of professional journals. He holds memberships in the Institute of Management Science, American Institute for Decision Sciences, American Accounting Association, and International Association for Financial Planning.

Albert M. Miller, Jr., CPA, has spent 30 years in the field of public accounting. From 1956 through 1963 he was employed by Price Waterhouse & Co., and was with Miller and Miller, CPAs in Knoxville, Tennessee, until 1984 serving as managing partner. He has specialized in management advisory services and in practice development. In mid-1984 he became the president of Apple Restaurants, Inc., a franchise in Jacksonville, Florida, of the D'Lites of America, Inc., restaurant chain. He is a graduate of the University of Tennessee and a member of the American Society of CPAs and the Tennessee Chapter of the AICPA.

Terrance L. Nugent is a consulting manager in the Nashville office of Touche Ross & Co. His specialties include microcomputer systems and office productivity. He has worked extensively with forecasting, planning, and budgeting systems in small to medium-sized businesses. His industry skills include professional firms, banking, and manaufacturing. Prior to joining Touche Ross & Co., Nugent was a manager in the consulting division of Arthur Andersen & Co. He received an MBA from Vanderbilt's Executive Program and a BS in engineering from Case Institute of Technology. He is a member of the Association for Systems Management and the American Production and Inventory Control Society.

Timothy J. O'Shea is a cofounder and chairman of SEAMARK Consulting Group, Inc., in Long Beach, California. Prior to founding SEAMARK in 1981, he held management positions with several large corporations, and was west coast manager of operations consulting for an international professional firm. He concentrates his practice in the area of business computers and office automation, particularly in the area of human and organizational behavior in automated work environments.

Edward L. Summers is the Arthur Young professor of accounting at the University of Texas at Austin. He earned his Ph.D. at the University of Texas at Austin in 1965. Prior to accepting a position at the University of Texas, Dr. Summers served as assistant professor of accounting at Rice University from 1965 to 1968. He was chairman of the accounting department at the Unversity of Texas from 1975 to 1980. He has also held positions as director of the MAS Bodies of Knowledge and Experience Project, sponsored by the American Institute of Certified Public Accountants; as vice president of the Texas CPA Society; as president of the MAS section of the American Accounting Association; as graduate advisor to the University of Texas Graduate Studies in Accounting; and as director of the University Federal Credit Union. He holds memberships in the American Institute of Certified Public Accountants, Financial Executives Institute, American Accounting Association, Texas Society of CPAs, and Texas Association of College Teachers.

Larry White is the founder and president of Services Rating Organization (SRO), a management consulting firm founder in 1975 that provides syndicated and custom market research to professional service firms in over 70 markets in the United States and Canada. SRO also provides help to professional service firms in areas such as business development strategies, communications, professional selling skills, marketing management, and implementation. SRO recently became part of the Kluwer Organization—a publicly held Dutch corporation—the largest publisher of materials for the legal profession in Europe. Prior to founding SRO, White served as director of Practice Development in the midwest region of a Big Eight accounting firm, chairman of the Department of Communication Studies at the University of Detriot, and director of Media Development at St. Mary's College/Notre Dame University. His doctoral course work is in communications at the University of Michigan. He earned an MBA in marketing from the University of Detroit, an MA in communications from Northwestern University, and a BA in communications from the University of Michigan. He is a past treasurer and board member of the American Marketing Association and has spoken at numerous professional groups.

Joseph W. Wilkinson is professor of accounting at Arizona State University. He earned his doctorate at the University of Oregon in 1966. For approximately 10 years before entering the teaching profession, Dr. Wilkinson held positions as engineer, systems analyst, and accountant in such organizations as Price Waterhouse & Co., Rural Electrification Administration, and Hughes Aircraft Co. He has authored or coauthored three textbooks: *Accounting and Information Systems*, Wiley, 1982 and 1986, *Computer Programming for Business and Social Science*, Irwin, 1970, and *Accounting with the Computer*, Irwin, 1969, 1972, 1975. He holds memberships in the American Accounting Association, National Association of Accountants, and Association of Systems Management.

Preface

Management advisory and consulting services are in great demand among business, not-for-profit, and governmental organizations. Every year many individuals join the management consulting profession to provide such services. Perhaps you have taken this step or are planning to do so in the near future. If so, this handbook is intended to help you succeed in this most demanding profession.

The handbook consists of many parts. The first introduces you to consulting and the consulting profession. It also describes the attributes and skills that you need as a consultant, such as the ability to communicate effectively. The second part clearly outlines the major phases of the consulting process, including problem definition, fact finding and analysis, solution development, and implementation. The third part describes the administrative aspects of consulting, including proposal preparation, engagement planning and documentation, and the presentation of results. The fourth part discusses matters concerning the management of a consulting practice. Among the matters discussed are practice planning and administration, marketing of professional services, selection and development of staff, and economics of the practice. The final part is an appendix of eighteen checklists and work plans in key practice areas, each of which contains important, relevant points and suggestions for the professional consultant. Taken together, these checklists and work plans survey most of the service areas encountered by management consultants. At the end of the handbook is a bibliography of the better references in the management consulting field.

Even from this brief summary of the handbook's contents, you can comprehend its broad scope and direct relevance to the world of mangement consulting. We believe that it can serve you as both (1) a tutor and (2) a reference work. We also believe that you will find its contents especially useful if you perform management advisory and consulting services as:

1. A member of a local or regional public accounting firm
2. A member of a small to medium-sized management consulting firm
3. An individual practitioner

It can also be useful if you are a university student or working professional who has an interest in a management consulting career.

We wish to acknowledge the numerous contributors, who are listed in the pages preceding this preface. Their efforts and expertise have provided the main value of this handbook. In addition, we want to express appreciation for the support and guidance provided by two McGraw-Hill editors, Martha Jewett and Bonnie Binkert. Their contributions have also been considerable.

In conclusion, we hope that this handbook will help in some small way to further the practice of management consulting.

SAM W. BARCUS III
Nashville, Tennessee

JOSEPH W. WILKINSON
Tempe, Arizona

PART 1

Introduction to the Management Consulting Profession

What Is Management Consulting?

JOSEPH W. WILKINSON
Department of Accounting
Arizona State University
Tempe, Arizona

Management consulting is a profession whose members provide extremely useful services to managers. In fact, many of its practitioners are called management advisory services specialists. The profession of management consulting is growing at an accelerating rate, and the end of this growth trend is not in sight. Every day new organizations join the ranks of management consulting clients. The overwhelming majority of these organizations appear to be satisfied with the range of services that they receive.

This introductory chapter explores the meanings of management consulting, the reasons for using management consultants and the roles that they perform, and the types of organizations that draw upon the services of management consultants. It also reviews the history and evolution of the management consulting profession, as well as the relationships and responsibilities of management consultants to a variety of parties. The chapter concludes by discussing the pros and cons of a management consulting career.

DEFINITION OF MANAGEMENT CONSULTING

Defining management consulting is an elusive process. The term is so broad that its definition has defied the efforts of experienced management consultants themselves. In fact, a committee of management consultants, formed under the auspices of the Arizona Society of Certified Public Accountants, recently concluded that the term cannot be defined. In spite of this pessimistic conclusion, however, a wide variety of authors and other authorities have offered their interpretations of the term. Thus, we suggest the following definition, based on the deliberations of another group of consultants:

> Management consulting is an independent and objective advisory service provided by qualified persons to clients in order to help them identify and analyze management problems or opportunities. Management consultants also recommend solutions or suggested actions with respect to these issues and help, when requested, in their implementation. In essence, management consultants help to effect constructive change in private or public sector organizations through the sound application of substantive and process skills.[1]

The stock-in-trade of a management consultant is:

> . . . advice and technical assistance, where the primary purpose is to help the client improve the use of its capabilities and resources to achieve its objectives. For the purpose of illustration, "helping the client improve the use of its capabilities and resources" may involve activities such as*
>
> a. Counseling management in its analysis, planning, organizing, operating, and controlling functions
> b. Conducting special studies, preparing recommendations, proposing plans and programs, and providing advice and technical assistance in their implementation
> c. Reviewing and suggesting improvement of policies, procedures, systems, methods, and organization relationships
> d. Introducing new ideas, concepts, and methods to management[2]

These activities of management consultants involve two types of encounters with clients: consultations and engagements.

A *consultation* normally consists of providing advice and information during a short time frame. This advice and/or information is provided orally during one or more discussions with the client. Sometimes the

---

*Material from the AICPA Statement on Standards for Management Advisory Services, no. 1, *Definitions and Standards for MAS Practice,* copyright © 1981 by the American Institute of Certified Public Accountants, Inc., is reprinted with permission.

advice and/or information will be represented as definitive by the consultant, as when he or she is fully aware of the situation and possesses sufficient expertise to require no recourse to references. Often, however, such advice and/or information will be qualified by stated limitations. These limitations may be due to lack of first-hand observation of the problem situation, to lack of familiarity with underlying technical aspects, and so on.

An *engagement* consists of that form of management advisory or consulting service

> . . . in which an analytical approach and process is applied in a study or project. It typically involves more than an incidental effort devoted to some combination of activities relating to determination of client objectives, fact-finding, opportunity or problem definition, evaluation of alternatives, formulation of proposed action, communication of results, implementation, and follow-up.[3]

REASONS FOR USING CONSULTANTS

Management consultants are generally engaged by key managers and administrators of client organizations. Why do such managers and administrators need the services of consultants? Consultants, after all, cannot be expected to be as familiar with the organizations as are the managers and administrators. Also, consultants are generally much more costly for each day of service than would be a newly hired manager or employee.

Benefits Provided by Consultants

A management consultant can provide at least three valuable benefits:

1. *Independent viewpoint:* Precisely because a management consultant is *not* a member of the organization, he or she brings objectivity and detachment to problems faced by the organization. That is, the consultant is sufficiently removed to see the true nature of the problems and to distinguish between feasible and infeasible solutions. In addition, an experienced consultant can introduce new ideas into the organization that were gleaned from other engagements. Also, because the consultant is customarily neither involved in the internal politics nor associated with cliques within the informal organization, his or her suggestions tend to be accepted as unbiased.

2. *Special qualifications:* An experienced management consultant possesses special knowledge, skills, and a variety of personal attri-

butes. These qualifications tend to establish the consultant as the most desirable candidate to undertake an engagement involving his or her area of expertise. While success in any engagement cannot be guaranteed, the consultant with the most suitable qualifications should have the greatest chance of achieving a successful conclusion.

3. *Temporary professional service:* Organizations sometimes find themselves short of critical professional resources. For instance, a manager may have an accident or take a short leave of absence to attend a graduate management program. Alternatively, a short-term problem may arise, such as the need to train managers in computer modeling, and there may be no one available in the organization to provide the instruction. In such cases management consultants can fill in as temporary professional help. The use of consultants will probably be less expensive in the long run than hiring new managers or employees.

Management consultants are sometimes engaged for other, less justifiable reasons. For instance, a manager may be involved in a struggle with another manager in the organization over the best course of action. The first manager may engage a consultant to prepare a report supporting his or her point of view. If the consultant is expected to prepare the report solely on the basis of that manager's conclusions, and is not given the opportunity to form objective views, then the engagement is not professional in nature.

Roles Performed by Consultants

In providing the above-mentioned services to clients, consultants can be seen to perform the following roles:

1. *Professional advisor and counselor:*   A consultant is a professional, in that he or she meets the standards of a profession. That is, the consultant has mastered an established body of knowledge, has completed educational requirements, and is governed by a code of conduct. (While in reality not all practicing management consultants currently meet these standards, in our view only those consultants who do so are worthy of the name.)

   In addition to being a professional, a management consultant provides management advisory and consulting services. These services are rendered to managers and are intended to assist in the management and administration of organizations.

2. *Qualified resource:*   A management consultant is a resource upon which managers and administrators of organizations can draw as needed. In this sense the management consultant is akin to a vendor

of a computer system. However, the management consultant provides services consisting of advice and managerial consulting assistance.

3. *Change agent:* A management consultant is a catalyst for change. In the process of solving problems for clients, the consultant must consider means by which solutions can be effected. These solutions often consist of changes within the context of organizations. For instance, changes may be made to the organizational structures, to procedures, and to job responsibilities. Unless these changes are understood and accepted by the affected employees and managers, the recommendations of the consultant will have little value.

Roles to be Approached with Caution

While all consultants would probably agree on the above roles, other less clear-cut roles are sometimes performed by some members of the consulting profession. Among these latter roles are the following:

1. *Decision maker:* A management consultant provides management advice and consulting services. Often these services consist of recommending preferable courses of action. However, most consultants stop short of actually making the decisions for managers of client organizations. The moment a consultant assumes authority for making and implementing decisions, he or she ceases to provide a truly independent viewpoint.

2. *Salesperson of proprietary products:* As noted above, the stock-in-trade of a management consultant is management advisory and consulting services. Some consultants offer, as an adjunct to such services, proprietary products. For instance, certain public accounting firms (large as well as small) espouse specific computer hardware and software products. While such consultants believe that these computer-related products will improve the clients' information systems, a question arises concerning the independence of the consultant. If the consultant receives monetary benefits from the manufacturers of such products, the client may have concerns about the fairness of the evaluation. Even if the consultant can in fact perform a fair evaluation, the appearance of bias might possibly undermine the value of the consulting service.

3. *Packager of standard services:* Management consulting services are professional in nature. A question may be raised with respect to "prepackaged" services, such as 1-day packaged seminars on data base software systems or 1-week installations of spreadsheet software systems. While consultants may legitimately be involved in training programs and system installations, such projects normally involve

analytical and creative activities. Once a training program or installation has become so standardized that the analytical and creative aspects no longer exist, it is generally viewed as no longer being a consulting service. A consultant who insists upon handling such packaged services is not likely to be viewed as serving a consultant role during such activities.

TYPES OF CLIENTS SERVED

Who uses the services of management consultants? While the mix of clients will vary from one consultant to another, the types of clients served by the management consulting profession as a whole include:

1. *Privately owned business firms:*   Every firm organized for the purpose of earning profits through commerce and industry is a potential client. Thus, as a consultant you might expect to have clients that are involved in merchandising, manufacturing, banking, transportation, insurance, food services, education, and other industries. These firms will exhibit such varied characteristics as:

    a. Major activities consisting of providing products or services to others

    b. Ownership structures consisting of single proprietors, partners, or stockholders

    c. Organizational sizes ranging from a few employees to many thousand employees

    d. Physical sizes ranging from a single building in one location to numerous buildings in scattered geographical locations

    e. Organizational structures ranging from a high degree of centralization to a high degree of decentralization

    f. Resource structures ranging from labor-intensive requirements to capital-intensive requirements

2. *Governmental agencies and organizations:*   Most if not all governmental organizations engage management consultants at one time or another. In many such engagements the clients are government agencies at either the local, state, national, or international level. For instance, management consultants have been engaged by the:

    a. Parks and Recreation Department, city of Mesa, Arizona

    b. Department of Transportation, state of Arizona

    c. Rural Electrification Administration, Department of Agriculture, United States of America

    d. International Labor Organization, United Nations

Management consultants also on occasion are engaged directly by countries. For instance, consultants have been engaged by such countries as Venezuela and Egypt to aid in their economic planning and development.

3. *Not-for-profit nongovernmental organizations:* Organizations such as hospitals, universities, research institutes, and charitable institutions are increasingly using management advisory and consulting services. While many such organizations are operated by governments, many others are under private ownership. In recent years the latter have been faced with problems of raising funds and revenues while reducing costs; in attempting to solve such problems, they often turn to consultants for advice and assistance.

4. *Professional associations:* Modern industrial societies spawn numerous groups and associations of persons who provide professional service. Many of these groups and associations are private and organized for profit, e.g., medical, legal, accounting, and engineering practices. Others are not-for-profit, e.g., National Association of Accountants, American Medical Association. While such groups and associations generally include highly trained and skilled persons, they often need advice and assistance with respect to management and organizational problems.

5. *Other types:* Although every potential client will probably fit into one of the above categories, it is useful to include a catchall category. This category might contain such groups as labor unions, sports organizations, and religious organizations.

HISTORY AND EVOLUTION OF MANAGEMENT CONSULTING

Management consulting has its origins in biblical times. However, the modern-day origins began two centuries ago. This section traces the history and evolution of management consulting since that time. Our focus will be upon the evolutionary thread that weaves through the accounting profession.

Pre-Twentieth Century

As far as we know, management advisory and consulting services were applied for the first time by an English accountant in 1744. In that year Alexander Chalmers prepared an interest table and planned the keeping of books for the Fund of Widows and Orphans. In 1788 a Scottish merchant asked his accountant to provide advice concerning business matters. Otherwise, the eighteenth century and much of the nineteenth century found British accountants generally performing bookkeeping tasks.

The English corporation laws (i.e., the Companies Act of 1879 and the Bankruptcy Act of 1883) changed the dominant role of professional accountants from bookkeepers to auditors. However, in the United States accountants still served primarily as bookkeepers until the first decade of the twentieth century.

1900—1918

The role of accountants in the United States shifted during the first decade of the twentieth century from bookkeepers to auditors. With the passage of the income tax laws in 1913, accountants also began to provide tax services. On the other hand, very few management advisory and consulting services were provided. Perhaps the most prominent engagement involved the survey of Westinghouse's East Pittsburgh plant by the public accounting firm of Marwick and Mitchell in 1910. This survey consisted of reviews of the organization, cost and general accounting system, production methods, and premium pay scales.

Science and engineering also contributed to the development of management consulting methods during the early years of the century. Perhaps the best-known pioneer from this era was Frederick Taylor, who applied the scientific method to the solving of production problems. By careful observation and study of every step and operation in a manufacturing process, followed by correlation and analysis of the data, he was able to establish fair work standards for workers and machines. His achievements laid the foundations for methods analysis, work simplification, and time and motion studies. Other men such as H. L. Gantt, Frank Gilbreth, and Harrison Emerson continued Taylor's efforts and achievements.

1919—1945

Income tax rates increased after World War I; consequently, the role of the accountant as tax advisor grew accordingly. Tax services, together with auditing services, effectively occupied most of the professional accountants' attention.

In the meantime, however, management consulting firms were beginning to flourish. These firms generally had an engineering orientation that dated back to the work of the pioneers in scientific management and industrial engineering. However, they also tended to be broader-gauged, since business firms were becoming larger and more complex. Men such as Ed Booz, George Fry, and Carl Hamilton, among others, recognized the importance of the human resource in the organization. Thus, their consulting firm led the way with a "people-oriented" approach, focusing upon such areas as organization planning, management development and training, administrative policies, and personnel administration.

As the movement toward general business management consulting intensified, American public accounting firms awoke to the potentialities of management advisory and consulting services. They realized that such consulting was within the capabilities of accountants, especially with respect to such areas as financial management and control. They also recognized that accountants who perform audits possess important advantages when undertaking consulting engagements: (1) Auditors already have a familiarity with the clients and their organizations, operations, and problems. (2) Auditors maintain continued contact with the clients, thereby providing warranties (in effect) for the clients. (3) Auditors function in accordance with professional rules of conduct, thus helping them assure the clients of quality work and ethical conduct.

Just as public accounting firms began to move diligently into management advisory and consulting services, events conspired to derail temporarily their expansion. The depression of the 1930s reduced the ability of clients to purchase such services, and World War II depleted the accounting firms of consulting employees.

However, World War II showed public accounting firms that the demand for consulting services was strong and apt to grow. Numerous firms in war industries employed those accountants who were available and qualified to develop cost accounting systems and to perform other related services.

Post World War II

In the years since World War II the management consulting profession has mushroomed and matured. A number of management consulting firms have been formed and have grown immensely. Among the nonaccounting consulting firms are Booz, Allen & Hamilton; McKinsey & Company; Cresap, McCormick & Paget; and Theodore Barry & Associates. These firms vary widely in the services that they emphasize, though all stress the primacy of providing personalized management advisory and consulting services.

The postwar history of the public accounting firms reflects the severity of the changes that have taken place throughout the management consulting profession. Shortly after the war the firms formally acknowledged the growing importance of management advisory and consulting services. Nearly every large firm established a separate division, on an equal standing with the audit and tax divisions, for management advisory services. Large firms also began to perform consulting engagements that were completely separated from the audit and tax engagements.

In addition to these organizational steps, the firms considered the services that they would provide. The American Institute of Certified Public Accountants (AICPA) published a list in 1946 of services that were reasonable for public accounting firms to provide, and many firms included some or all of these services. Among the services included were operational budgeting, forecasting, and cost controls.

During the remainder of the 1940s and into the 1950s, the firms continued to add services. Certain of these services, such as computer systems analysis and inventory management, were added in response to developments in information and computer technology. Other services, such as capital budgeting and computer system auditing and acquisition analysis, were added in response to the demands of clients. As the services expanded beyond the areas of basic accounting competence, the firms began to employ nonaccountants. Thus, computer system analysts, programmers, and management scientists began to intermingle with auditing and tax specialists.

Management advisory and consulting services have grown at an ever-increasing rate during the 1960s, the 1970s, and into the 1980s. At present the management advisory and consulting services division of the typical large public accounting firm, and of many smaller local accounting firms, is growing more rapidly than the audit and tax divisions. In some firms small business and/or microcomputer service divisions have been added. These divisions are essentially offshoots of management advisory and consulting service divisions.

Developing Trends

The practice of management consulting has changed dramatically since the early days of this century. As the above history has indicated, one trend has been in the direction of greater scope and specialization of services. The "efficiency engineer" and generalist of past decades have been supplemented by multivaried specialists. Management consultants now specialize in information systems, automated offices, financial analysis and modeling, budgetary and cost controls, organizational structures, personnel compensation, strategic planning, and a host of other areas.

A second trend has been the improving quality of business education. Numerous universities throughout the United States and other developed countries are providing sound education in such fields as accounting, management, marketing, and statistics. At the graduate level many of these universities offer programs leading to the master of business administration. These quality undergraduate and graduate programs of study are producing a supply of better-trained entrants into the ranks of the management consulting profession. As a result of this infusion, management consulting is becoming a catalyst for the advancement of better management concepts and techniques.

A third trend concerns the changing management culture. Before World War II many business firms were relatively small family-owned enterprises managed by individuals with extensive experience and limited education. Since World War II managers, like management consultants, have become more educated. More managers are employed by large or moderate-sized firms and organizations. These managers tend to view themselves as members of a profession. Consequently, they exhibit a decreasing degree of loyalty to individual firms and an increasing degree of mobility between firms. They also are showing an increasing understanding of the roles and benefits of management consultants in the business world.

A related trend is the growth in size and complexity of institutions that function in the business world. Many business firms have become conglomerates. A firm that some years ago might have been called a chemistry company is now an energy complex. Many not-for-profit organizations have also become large and diversified. For instance, some hospitals have become nationwide health-care chains. Furthermore, an increasing number of firms and organizations have become multinational in nature.

On the other hand, there has been a concurrent upward trend in the number of new business start-ups each year. Most of these new start-ups are small business firms in a service or high-technology area.

A final trend pertains to modern technology. Technological developments have occurred at a breathtaking pace in such areas as information sciences and decision sciences. Computer hardware and software, together with data communications and robotics, represent powerful tools for business management. These tools are spawning automated offices, superproductive factories, real-time information systems, and interactive decision support systems. Managers now have the means to control far-flung operations, to develop sounder plans, and to make faster decisions than ever before.

Future Prospects

What do these trends portend for the future of management consulting? A veteran management consultant makes the following predictions.[4]

First, management consulting will become even more specialized. Consulting specialists will need to be ever-diligent to avoid obsolescence. Consulting firms will need to continually add new specialties, just as producing firms add new products.

Several areas of specialization have been developed or strengthened in recent years by a number of firms. One area is financial modeling, using spreadsheet software packages on microcomputers. Another area is "one-stop-shop" service for small business firms. This service, which often is administered by a separate division in the consulting firm, involves the assignment of a single consultant to each small business client. This single consultant provides advice across the entire array of the client's activities. In effect, the consultant becomes almost a member of the client's management team. A third area is assistance on large projects involving perhaps a year or longer. A typical project is the design and implementation of a complex computer-based information system.

Second, practicing consultants will interact more closely with the faculties of business schools. They will draw upon the results of research performed at such academic institutions. In turn they will provide academic researchers with the materials for performing research and preparing case studies.

Third, management consulting firms will tend either to remain small or to become quite large. Small practitioner firms will prosper by focusing upon narrow areas of specialization. Large firms will more easily sustain the high costs of developing and offering a wide range of specialties.

Fourth, the number of internal consultants (i.e., consultants who are employees of nonconsulting firms) will continue to grow, since they provide beneficial services at less cost. However, they will never replace the external consultants, who provide an essential service through their objectivity.

Fifth, as consultants grow in number, they will develop more sophisticated means of marketing their services.

Sixth, the bright graduates of management and business schools will continue to be attracted to careers in management consulting. The reasons for this continuing interest in the profession are discussed at the end of this chapter.

RELATIONSHIPS TO OTHER PARTIES

A management consultant must maintain close relationships with a variety of parties. Here is a partial list of such parties:

1. Managers who contact the consultant on behalf of clients
2. Managers and employees of clients who will need to be interviewed and otherwise dealt with during the course of engagements
3. Employees of clients who are assigned to work under the consultant's direction

4. Managers and employees of clients who will be affected by results of consulting engagements
5. Managers of prospective clients
6. External auditors, lawyers, and other professionals who represent clients or perform services for them
7. Competing management consultants
8. Professional consulting associations, such as the Institute of Management Consultants
9. Communities within which the consultant and client reside

As a professional, the consultant must always strive to act responsibly and ethically toward all these parties. In return for the faith and trust that these parties place in the consultant, he or she accepts an obligation to behave in a manner that reflects a high level of public service.

PROS AND CONS OF MANAGEMENT CONSULTING

In concluding this opening chapter, let us consider the benefits and drawbacks of being a management consultant.

A career in management consulting offers interesting challenges. Your work assignments tend to be varied. They encourage you to employ your talents, abilities, and skills to the fullest. They often allow you to avoid the 8-to-5 routine.

Management consulting can be quite rewarding. On the one hand, you gain considerable satisfaction from helping others and solving tough problems. You enjoy seeing the fruits of your efforts emerge in the form of successful information systems or strategic plans. On the other hand, you are generally paid handsomely for your efforts. The salaries and bonuses of consultants in both large and small firms compare favorably with those of other professionals.

As a management consultant you will probably be offered one or more enticing opportunities.You may be asked to join the management team of a client, perhaps even to assume the top position in the client firm. You may see that your specialty is in such demand that you could start your own consulting practice.

The drawbacks relate primarily to the life-style and risks that face every management consultant. On occasion you must expect to endure irregular living conditions, such as lengthy workdays and stays away from home. You will sometimes be placed under tremendous job pressures and stresses. These conditions can put severe strains on your health, peace of mind, and family harmony. If you decide to go into practice on your own, you are also likely to encounter strains on your pocketbook and self-confidence while waiting for clients to appear.

If you have the personal qualities and education that a management consultant needs, as well as an intense interest in the challenge and rewards of the profession, these drawbacks need not represent insurmountable hurdles.

NOTES

1. This definition was developed by directors of the management consulting professional associations (AICPA/MAS, ACME, IMC), together with practitioners and academics, at a conference on University Education and Management Consulting, held in Salt Lake City, February 21–22, 1985.

2. Statement on Standards for Management Advisory Services no. 1, *Definitions and Standards for MAS Practice*, American Institute of Certified Public Accountants, New York, 1981, par. 4.

3. Ibid.

4. Richard M. Paget, "The Future of Management Consulting," *MAS Communication*, March 1982, pp. 59–61.

2

The Management Consulting Profession and Advisory Services

JAMES C. KINARD
Faculty of Accounting
The Ohio State University
Columbus, Ohio

The management consulting profession consists of a diverse and profuse collection of individuals, firms, and associations. All members of the profession have one common interest: to provide professional advice and assistance to clients with respect to the management of their organizations.

This chapter examines both the profession and the services that it provides. It begins by identifying the attributes that bestow the status of a profession upon management consulting. Then the chapter surveys the composition of the profession, including the major professional associations that unify and serve the member consultants and their firms. The second main portion of the chapter surveys the consulting process, as well as the types of consulting engagements and advisory services provided. It also identifies the ways in which consultants organize to effectively accommodate the varied engagements and render the specialized services.

WHY MANAGEMENT CONSULTING IS A PROFESSION

The term *profession* is defined as a calling or vocation in which members possessing certain attributes provide beneficial services to clients under strictly specified conditions. Management consulting qualifies as a profession, since its members:

1. Possess a variety of skills and qualities, the acquisition of which often requires extensive education, training, and/or experience
2. Provide services that are grounded in technical knowledge, which in turn is recorded in an appropriate body of literature
3. Abide by a code of ethics, including practice standards, in the delivery of services to clients and in relationships to competitors and to the public
4. Establish fees that are fixed with respect to amount and type of work to be performed and that are not contingent on an outcome of some event (e.g., a legal suit)

In addition, certain management consultants, such as those employed by public accounting firms within some jurisdictions, are expected to hold certificates issued by states or other governmental bodies.

COMPOSITION OF THE MANAGEMENT CONSULTING PROFESSION

The management consulting profession is growing rapidly. This growth is due in part to the intense demand for management advice and consulting services by all types and sizes of organizations. It is also due to the relatively small amount of capital needed to start a management consulting practice.

Although numbers quickly become obsolete, the overall number of full-time consultants in the United States (as of 1985) is estimated to be in the range of 60,000 to 75,000. Furthermore, there are additional thousands of part-time consultants, many of whom are university faculty members. Accurate estimates of both full-time and part-time consultants are hard to obtain, since authorities do not agree as to the boundaries of the profession.

On the other hand, the basic structural composition of the profession is readily apparent. The several categories comprising this structure are as follows:

1. *Independent management consulting firms:* This category consists of large, medium, and small firms, totaling roughly 3000 in number.

These firms range in size from several thousand consultants down to two consultants. The services they provide are extremely varied, sometimes including engineering and scientific consulting as well as management consulting. Some of the medium-sized firms in this category, plus a few large and small firms, hold memberships in the Association of Management Consulting Firms (ACME, Inc.). Examples of firms in this category are: Booz, Allen & Hamilton, Inc.; McKinsey and Company; Cresap, McCormick and Paget, Inc.; Arthur D. Little, Inc.; and Theodore Barry & Associates.

2. *Public accounting firms:* This category consists of large, medium, and small public accounting firms. It constitutes the largest identifiable segment of the management consulting profession. As many as 6000 firms can be identified. While most or all provide management advisory and consulting services, they provide these in addition to auditing and tax services. The largest firms, as well as some of the medium and small firms, maintain separate divisions for providing management advisory and consulting services (MACS). Within these divisions are housed full-time consultants, many of whom are not accountants by training. Most public accounting firms, however, do not maintain separate MACS divisions. In these firms accountants serve as part-time consultants on those occasions when clients ask for consultations or contract for consulting engagements.

   The public accounting firms that perform the largest amount of consulting work (i.e., the Big Eight) are: Price Waterhouse & Co.; Arthur Andersen & Co.; Arthur Young & Co.; Coopers & Lybrand; Touche Ross & Co.; Peat, Marwick, Mitchell & Co.; Ernst & Whinney; and Deloitte, Haskins, and Sells. The MACS divisions in these firms (though called by other names) are sufficiently large to be included in the top thirty consulting firms, when measured by size of billings.

3. *Individual practitioners:* In this category are full-time and part-time management consultants who are unaffiliated with consulting firms or who operate their own practices. These consultants, who number many thousand, perform a variety of services. Typically they provide services within limited areas for relatively small clients. Their general appeal is that they can maintain closer ties with each client and be more familiar with its situation than can the large or medium-sized consultants. Also, they tend to charge lower rates.

   This group is not homogeneous, however. For instance, many individual consultants are university professors who provide very specialized advice and consulting services to clients of all sizes.

4. *Internal consulting groups:* Consultants listed in the three above categories may be characterized as *external consultants*, since they provide services to clients who are external to their firms or practices. Consultants who are employees of a nonconsulting firm are known as

internal consultants. These consultants are typically specialists who are assigned to specific service departments, such as the industrial engineering department, the information systems department, or the long-range planning department. In some firms, however, they are attached to more broadly based consulting departments. Two examples are the Management Services Group within W. R. Grace & Company and Corporate Consulting Services within General Electric.

Internal consultants provide advice and consulting services to the other departments of the organization. While they lack the fully independent status of external consultants, they have a more thorough knowledge of the complex relationships within the organization than external consultants could reasonably hope to attain. Thus, they tend to be assigned to problem situations requiring this thorough knowledge. Since the services of internal consultants are less expensive than those of external consultants, internal consultants are also more often involved in projects that are expected to be quite lengthy and detailed. For instance, an internal consultant is more likely to be assigned to an implementation project than an external consultant, since implementation projects tend to be relatively long-lived.

On the other hand, internal consultants are less preferable than external consultants for assignments requiring (a) independent perspectives or (b) prior experiences gained from problems faced by other organizations.

Certain assignments, such as the development of new information systems, may suitably be performed jointly by internal and external consultants. Each may have specified tasks. For example, the external consultants may be assigned to define the problem, the internal consultants to gather facts and opinions from employees, and both to analyze the findings and develop feasible solutions. In some assignments the main task of internal consultants may be to observe the activities and techniques of external consultants, so that the former can complete the projects or be able to perform similar projects on later occasions.

5. *Research-oriented organizations:* This category includes a relatively few institutes and other organizations that undertake engagements looking beyond specific short-range internal problem situations. Certain organizations in this category (a) perform studies of broad economic and social problems or (b) aid in developing and implementing public-sector programs. Government agencies, the customary clients of such organizations, award contracts (often on a competitive basis) for the above-mentioned consulting services. An example of an public-sector consulting organization is Planning Resources Corporation (now known as PRC). Other organizations in this category are research institutes popularly known as "think tanks."

These institutes perform research studies and provide advice in technical, military, and economic areas. Their clients may be government agencies, business firms, industry associations, or universities. Examples of research institutes are The Rand Corporation and Stanford Research Institute (now known as SRI International).

PROFESSIONAL MANAGEMENT CONSULTING ASSOCIATIONS

Associations have been formed to provide a variety of services to the management consulting profession. Through the efforts of such associations, the management consulting industry has moved from being a heterogeneous collection of firms and individuals toward becoming a relatively cohesive profession. The major associations in the United States are:

Institute of Management Consultants (IMC)

IMC was founded in 1968 for the purpose of assuring the public "that members possess the ethical standards and the professional competence and independence" necessary to be qualified management consultants.[1] In order to achieve the first part of this purpose, IMC has established a code of ethics. To achieve the second part, it administers a certification program for management consultants. An applicant who meets the following requirements earns the coveted professional designation of Certified Management Consultant (CMC):

1. Devotes current activity (well over half of working hours) to the public practice of management consulting, serving clients on a fee basis
2. Has accumulated at least 5 years of experience in the full-time practice of management consulting, including 1 year with major responsibility for client projects
3. Possesses a bachelor's degree from an accredited college or university, or has accumulated an additional 5 years of management consulting experience
4. Submits written summaries of 5 client assignments in which a major role was played
5. Passes a qualifying interview by demonstrating professional competence in areas of specialization, application of experience, and understanding of the current state of the art
6. Obtains 6 references, 3 of them from officers or executives served during the past 5 years

Among other activities sponsored by IMC is a broad program of professional development courses, seminars, and workshops. This professional development program ranges from orientation courses for newer consultants to workshops for senior consultants on advanced consulting skills. In addition, the association was instrumental in the commencement of the *Journal of Management Consulting*, the most authoritative periodical in the field of management consulting.

Approximately 1600 consultants hold memberships in IMC. Significant minorities of this membership also are affiliated with the other two major professional associations. IMC has chapters in several larger cities.

Association of Management Consulting Firms (ACME, Inc.)

ACME is the oldest of the associations, having been organized in 1929 and incorporated in 1933. Like IMC, ACME has established a code of ethics. It enforces the code, with respect to its members, by investigating all complaints of code violation and taking disciplinary action against members whose conduct clearly falls below the standards set forth in the code. ACME also serves as a central clearing house and research center for the management consulting profession. It fulfills this purpose by maintaining a complete management consulting library (including an information bank on several hundred areas of specialization), maintaining extensive files of current information on thousands of management consulting firms, and sponsoring research (including publication of monographs and participation in seminars and professional meetings).

Membership is limited to consulting firms of a specified size. About sixty firms currently are members; however, certain large consulting firms and all of the large public accounting firms have declined membership.

American Institute of Certified Public Accountants (AICPA)

The AICPA is a professional association whose membership is open only to holders of CPA certificates in the fifty states and other jurisdictions. Many members of the AICPA (though still a minority) are accountants who practice management consulting. The Management Advisory Services (MAS) division of the AICPA administers the services pertaining to these members.

Like the IMC and ACME, the AICPA (through the MAS division executive committee) has issued codes of ethics, called standards for MAS. These standards—which were issued in statements dated 1969, 1974, 1981, and 1982—pertain to both general and technical aspects of the practice of MAS.[2] They cover all professional services provided by consultants members, consultations as well as engagements. Members who violate these standards are subject to discipline.

In addition to issuing standards, the MAS division issues a series of practice aids that provide information on specialized subjects to help consultants assist clients. Two examples of such practice aids are entitled "Assisting Clients in Obtaining Funds" and "Financial Model Preparation."

The MAS division also conducts, through a structure of subcommittees, a variety of activities and studies of interest to consultants. The committee structure for the 1984/1985 year included the Practice Standards and Administration subcommittee, the Small Business Consulting Practices subcommittee, the Education and Information subcommittee, the Technical and Industry Consulting Practices subcommittee, the Computer Applications subcommittee, and the EDP Technology Research subcommittee. As an example of subcommittee activities, the Education and Information subcommittee sponsors a National MAS conference that includes sessions on various technical topics and skills (e.g., microcomputers, practice strategies).

Association of Internal Management Consultants (AIMC)

AIMC is an association of individuals engaged in the practice of internal management consulting. In addition to promoting the role of the internal consultant, its purpose is to provide a forum for the exchange of information among members and to raise the standards of the profession. Its programs include round-table meetings, educational seminars, and research grants. It also publishes a newsletter four times yearly.

Other Relevant Associations

Three other associations deserve mention. The Association of Management Consultants (AMC) accepts medium and small consulting firms into membership. Although it has been in operation for over 20 years, it has been declining since the rise of IMC. The Association of Systems Management (ASM) is an association of information systems analysts. Although the majority of its members are employees of business firms and nonbusiness organizations, a significant number are external consultants in the area of information system analysis and design. The American Accounting Association (AAA) is an association of accountants. Most of the membership consists of university professors of accounting. However, a special section of AAA is of interest. The Information Systems/ Management Advisory Services (IS/MAS) section consists of about 700 members, one-half of whom are management advisory services practitioners (i.e., management consultants, mainly within public accounting firms). The IS/MAS section coordinates presentations of topics of interest to consultants at AAA meetings. It also publishes the *Journal of Information Systems*, which includes articles concerning research in the areas of information systems development and technology, management consulting, and IS/MAS education.

THE CONSULTING PROCESS

In performing management advisory and consulting services, a management consultant engages in a process. This process is performed for the purpose of solving a problem faced by a client. Thus, it can be labeled a problem-solving process. Since it is performed by a consultant, it can alternatively be labeled a consulting process. Both labels will be employed throughout following chapters.

A consulting (i.e., problem-solving) process has three parts: analytic, administrative, and communicative. Each is discussed below.

Analytic Elements of the Consulting Process

The analytic elements or phases of a consulting process consist of (1) identifying the objectives to be achieved, (2) defining the problem or opportunity for improvement, (3) ascertaining and then analyzing the facts, (4) determining and evaluating solution alternatives and then selecting the preferable solution, (5) implementing the solution, if appropriate.

These elements or phases may be combined, or their sequence may be altered to fit specific problem situations. All must be completed, however, for a satisfactory resolution of a problem. Because the analytic elements are so important, they are discussed extensively in Chapters 6, 7, 8, and 9.

Administrative Elements of the Consulting Process

"A consulting engagement, regardless of its technical nature, requires sound and effective managing if the engagement is to accomplish its objective."[3] Most consulting engagements include the following managing or administrative activities:

1. Engagement planning, leading to a proposal (with work plan) and letter of understanding
2. Engagement operations and control, including productively following the work plan, preparing working papers and interim reports, and controlling time and expenses

3. Engagement reporting and evaluation, including documenting the conclusions, preparing the final report, and assessing the performance of participants and effectiveness of the result

Administrative elements are discussed extensively in Chapters 10, 11, 12, and 13.

Communicative Elements of the Consulting Process

Ineffective communication during a consulting engagement can impair the final result. In fact, proficiency in communication is essential to successfully completing every phase of the consulting process. A management consultant must be able to speak, write, and listen effectively. These elements of communication are discussed in Chapter 5.

TYPES OF CONSULTING ENGAGEMENTS

Management consultants apply the consulting process to engagements having widely varying characteristics. Thus, it may be useful to classify consulting engagements according to several dimensions. Six relevant dimensions are the nature of the problem, the service delivery area, the phase(s) of the analytic process, the technical aid(s) applied, the industry (or nature of organization) to which the client belongs, and the geographical area(s) where the engagement takes place. These dimensions of an engagement are displayed in Figure 2.1.

Each dimension, and its possible categories, will be discussed separately below. However, it should be noted that every engagement in-

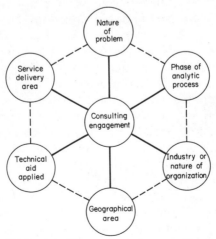

Figure 2.1 Dimensions of a consulting engagement.

volves all six dimensions. Thus, although an engagement may briefly be described as a financial management engagement (i.e., in accordance with the service delivery area), it also takes place at one or more specific locations, involves a client who is a member of a particular industry (e.g., the banking industry) or a particular organization (e.g., a corporation), and so on.

Furthermore, the categories within each dimension may be coded, so that each engagement may be concisely but fully characterized. Coding is particularly useful if a management consulting firm desires to file reports of the various engagements for later reference by staff consultants.

Nature of the Problem

Problems may be classified according to their situation as corrective, progressive, or opportunistic.

Corrective problem. A corrective problem involves a situation in which conditions have worsened. As a consultant you are expected to suggest corrective action or actions that will return the situation to its previous state. A corrective problem usually arises suddenly and demands urgent action. Essentially the process consists of "putting out a fire." Defining the problem is often much less difficult, however, than determining the preferable course of action. An example of a corrective problem is the sudden drop in productivity within a critical department.

Progressive problem. A progressive problem involves an existing situation that can be improved. While no sudden deterioration has occurred, other changes generally have taken place over a period of time. For instance, the firm may have grown appreciably while the procedures have remained unchanged. Alternatively, technology may have advanced and may have been incorporated by the firm's competitors. This situation is commonly encounterd with respect to the information system. Many firms have continued to employ manual procedures in spite of considerable growth in transactions and developments in computer technology. In such a situation you may determine that computer-based transaction processing systems are likely to provide significant improvements to the situation.

Opportunistic problem. An opportunistic problem involves a situation in which a future opportunity resides. For instance, a firm might have excessive cash and short-term investments available. The surface problem is that the funds are not earning a desirable rate of return. As a consultant your responsibility is to creatively search out and recommend opportunities for more effective long-term use of the funds. Your recommendations may range from the marketing of new products to the modernization of production plants or the training of up-and-coming managers. Obviously, opportunistic problems are likely to lead to more risky, as well as more potentially rewarding, courses of action than are corrective and progressive problems.

Service Delivery Area

Perhaps the most common means of describing engagements is in terms of the service delivery area, i.e., the function or activity in which the problem situation exists. Service delivery areas may be classified in innumerable ways. For instance, one classification plan employs the following principal service delivery areas:[4]

1.0 General management

2.0 Manufacturing

3.0 Personnel

4.0 Marketing

5.0 Finance and accounting

6.0 Procurement

7.0 Research and development

8.0 Packaging

9.0 Administration

10.0 International operations

Within each principal area are several narrower areas. Thus, under Finance and Accounting are:[5]

5.1 General accounting

5.2 Cost accounting

5.3 Long-range financial planning

5.4 Short-term planning, budgeting, and control

5.5 Credit and collections

5.6 Capital investment

5.7 Marginal income analysis

5.8 Financial information and reporting

5.9 Financial planning

5.10 Valuations and appraisals

5.11 Taxes

Another classification plan is employed in this handbook. The Appendix includes the service delivery areas listed below. While this classification plan is not highly organized or complete, it is representative of service delivery areas that are viewed as being important to present-day management consultants. The areas included are:

Business planning
Small business management analysis
Evaluating and selecting a computer system
Software package evaluation
Computer system security evaluation
Computer department effectiveness review
Office automation and automation review
Production planning and control review
Materials requirements planning
Project monitoring and control
Productivity improvement review
Personnel management review
Marketing review
Financial management review
Operations management
Operational budgets and financial reporting systems
Capital planning and budgeting systems
Merger and acquisition evaluation

Phases of the Analytic Process

As noted earlier, the analytic phases of the consulting process include identifying the objectives, defining the problem, finding out the facts, developing the solution, and implementing the solution. An engagement could involve one or more of these phases. For instance, it might focus primarily on defining the problem situation. Or it might consist of assisting in the implementation of a solution. Or it might involve all of the phases.

Generally, the phases cannot be totally isolated. For instance, defining the problem situation will probably involve identifying objectives and determining at least the pertinent facts of the problems.

The analytic phases represent the dynamic aspects of an engagement (e.g., defining, fact finding, evaluating, developing, implementing). Thus, they are employed in every engagement, whether it be a routine evaluation of operations or a special research study of customer attitudes. In fact, as the titles of the service delivery areas in the preceding discussion show, the identities of the phases (e.g., selecting, evaluating) tend to attach to the areas themselves (e.g., computer department).

Technical Aids Applied

Most engagements can be aided by technical models or methodologies. For instance, capital investment planning can be aided by a discounted cash flow model such as the present value model or the internal rate of return model. Information systems planning and design can be aided by a structured methodology. The checklists and guidelines presented in the Appendix can be viewed as structured methodologies.

An increasing number of technical aids are being incorporated into computer programs for easier and quicker use. Microcomputer spreadsheet software, such as Lotus 1-2-3, has given an impetus to this development. An illustration of the use of a computerized financial planning model is presented in Chapter 17. (The financial planning model itself, designed for use with the Lotus 1-2-3 spreadsheet software package, is maintained on a magnetic diskette that is compatible with IBM PC microcomputers.)

Industry or Nature of Organization

As described in Chapter 1, the client who is the subject of an engagement is a privately owned business firm, a government agency, a not-for-profit nongovernmental organization, a professional association, or some other type of organization.

If the client is a privately owned business firm or an industry association, it is a member of an industry group. Industries fall into the following groups: agriculture, forestry, fishing; mining; construction; manufacturing; transportation, communications, electric and gas utility, sanitary services; wholesale trade; retail trade; finance and insurance; and services. Each of these industry groups is subdivided into specific industries. For example, mining includes gold mining, bituminous coal mining, oil production, and so on.

Geographical Area

An engagement may be restricted to a single location, such as the home office of the client. Alternatively, it may involve multiple locations, such as the several production plants and warehouses of a large manufacturing firm. It may even involve locations in foreign countries.

APPROACHES TO MANAGEMENT CONSULTING PRACTICES

A variety of approaches are available to a management consultant who is establishing a practice. For instance, the consultant can be a generalist or a specialist, a process-oriented consultant or a content-oriented consultant. Each approach is best suited to certain types of problem situations. Several of the approaches are discussed below in their "pure form." It should be noted, however, that many consulting firms offer a blend of approaches, modifying each approach to suit the needs of the engagement.

Generalist Approach

The generalist approach relies upon and applies the basic principles of business management to problem situations. It maintains that these principles are equally relevant and dominant in any industry and in most if not all types of organizations. This approach is helpful in discovering and defining underlying causes of problem situations. To be soundly applied, the generalist approach requires that the consultant be trained in the principles, via either a graduate program in business management or equivalent experience.

Specialist Approach

The specialist approach has grown in importance with the growth in size and complexity of all types of organizations. Consultants have found that developing an expertise in many types of engagements and staying current in a variety of techniques and skills is too difficult. Thus, individual consultants and even consulting firms have tended to limit their services to a manageable subset of the universe of consulting services. For instance, an individual consultant might specialize in microcomputer selection and evaluation or compensation plans, while a small firm might specialize in financial planning and modeling. A medium-size or large firm would probably offer a wider, but still limited, range of services.

The practice specialization of various consulting firms differs just as the types of engagements, described earlier, differ.

Service delivery area specialization.   A firm might specialize in one or more service delivery areas. These areas often center around a function such as marketing, human resources, finance, operations, or general management.

Technical specialization.   A firm could specialize in a technical skill or methodology, such as optimization modeling, software development, financial planning and modeling, or market research methodologies.

Industry or type of organization specialization.   A third dimension of specialization relates to industries or types of organizations. For instance, a consulting firm could specialize in banking institutions, municipal governments, steel manufacturers, or educational institutions.

Geographic specialization. Many consulting firms specialize in limited geographical areas close to their offices. This type of specialization conserves resources and enables the consultants to become very familiar with local conditions, practices, and personnel.

Process-Oriented Approach

A process-oriented consultant attempts to help the client define its problems and solve these problems. In effect, this consultant conveys his or her understanding and skill in the consulting process to the client; the consultant does not recommend specific solutions. When this approach is skillfully employed, it can lead to a deeper plumbing of the problem situation and a sounder solution than the consultant could develop by himself or herself.

Content-Oriented Approach

In this approach the consultant focuses on the problem situation. While the client is questioned, the consultant relies on his or her experience to define the problem and eventually develop a recommended solution. This recommendation is presented to the client.

Many consultants blend the process- and content-oriented approaches within each engagement, with the mix dependent on the knowledge and attitude of the client personnel and the complexity of the problem.

Other Approaches

Certain consulting practices, generally the large general management consulting firms, emphasize the *diagnostic approach*. This approach focuses on the phases of the consulting process that end with a recommended solution to the problem. Advocates of the diagnostic approach believe that activity is the best use of the consultant's time and expertise. Other consulting practices, such as smaller firms and highly specialized practices, emphasize the *full-process approach*. This approach includes the implementation phase in addition to the earlier phases of the consulting process. Advocates of the latter approach believe that implementation is difficult for a client to perform alone and that the consultant has a responsibility to aid the client in effecting the change.

Still other approaches focus on the deliverables. A *customized approach* emphasizes the uniqueness of each engagement. It attempts to tailor a solution to the particular circumstances. The *packaged approach* emphasizes that each problem is similar to problems faced by other clients, i.e., that it fits into a generic category of problems. This approach attempts to apply a packaged methodology and, when suitable, a package solution that has been developed for problems in the generic category to which the problem has been assigned. While this latter approach tends to be less costly, it often does not provide the best solution.

PRACTICE MANAGEMENT BY MANAGEMENT CONSULTING FIRMS

In addition to selecting its approaches to a consulting practice and individual engagements, a management consulting firm must decide on its own management policies and procedures. Among the topics that must be considered are:

Practice planning and administration
Marketing of available professional services
Staff selection and development
Fee structuring and estimation
Financial management and budgeting

These topics are discussed extensively in Chapters 14, 15, 16, and 17.

NOTES

1. This quotation and the following requirements listed in this section are based on the brochure entitled *IMC Purposes, Programs and Benefits of Membership*, published by the Institute of Management Consultants, Inc., 19 West 44th Street, New York, NY 10036. Chapters 3 and 4 of this handbook extensively discuss the areas of knowledge and skills needed for professional competence, as well as the ethical standards and independence that should be maintained at all times by management consultants.

2. The following publications issued by the AICPA and prepared by the Management Advisory Services Executive Committee are pertinent:

    Statements on Management Advisory Services:
    No. 1, "Tentative Description of the Nature of Management Advisory Services by Independent Accounting Firms," February 1969
    No. 2, "Competence in Management Advisory Services," February 1969
    No. 3, "Role in Management Advisory Services," September 1969
    Management Advisory Services Practice Standards, January 1975
    Statements on Standards for Management Advisory Services:
    No. 1, "Definitions and Standards for MAS Practice," December 1981.
    No. 2, "MAS Engagements," November 1982
    No. 3, "MAS Consultations," November 1982

3. MAS University Education Task Force, AICPA, "University Education for Management Consulting," Exposure Draft, AICPA, New York, April 1977, p. 12.

4. Jerome H. Fuchs, *Making the Most of Management Consulting Services*, American Management Association, New York, 1975, pp. 143–46.

5. Ibid.

Competent Delivery of Consulting Services

EDWARD L. SUMMERS
Department of Accounting
The University of Texas
Austin, Texas

INTRODUCTION

Consulting competence is the ability of a consultant (e.g., management advisory services practitioner with an accounting background) to deliver specific, agreed-upon consulting services to a client on a profitable time-and-fee basis while observing high professional standards. The basic elements of competence are: practice scope, consulting knowledge, and deliverability of services to clients.

Practice Scope

The importance of practice scope can be illustrated as follows: Two practitioners with the same skills and the same skill levels may differ significantly in competence if one consistently attempts complex engagements requiring abilities not possessed while the other accepts only relatively uncomplex engagements. Similarly, two practitioners with very different levels of the same skills may both be viewed as competent if they both limit their engagements to those that are appropriate to their respective skills. Competence, therefore, also depends on a consultant's goals and his or her ability to coordinate the scope of practice with those goals.

Consultants may control the practice scope-competence relationship by either (1) limiting their practices to appropriate engagements or (2) acquiring competence to complete the engagements that they wish to accept.

Consultant Knowledge

A study conducted within the past decade—under the auspices of the American Institute of Certified Public Accountants (AICPA)—identified three major bodies of knowledge needed by consultants who provide management advisory services (MAS):[1]

1. Knowledge of the consulting art, including the public accounting profession, ethics, practice management, and engagement conduct
2. Knowledge of specific industry and public sector characteristics, similarities, and differences
3. Knowledge of organizational functions and technical disciplines, including finance, accounting, electronic data processing, management strategy and policy, operations, human resources, management science, and marketing

These bodies of knowledge are diagrammed in Figure 3.1. As the figure suggests, a consultant needs knowledge directed toward performing specific useful types of services for clients in specific industries or forms of organizations. (This use-oriented approach is in opposition to the approach taken by academicians, who organize knowledge into courses that are convenient for faculty to teach.)

The bodies of knowledge shown in Figure 3.1 do not have equal significance in every practice or engagement. In addition, no consultant can master all of them. Every consultant must resolve, however, to have sufficient understanding in at least certain relevant areas to meet the needs of clients throughout the various engagements comprising his or her practice.

Service Deliverability

A recent AICPA task force report emphasizes that a professional management consultant in public accounting practice must be able to blend the three bodies of knowledge listed above.[2] Consulting skill alone is not enough; industry/public sector knowledge alone is not enough; technical/functional expertise is not enough. Indeed, while most consultants begin as specialists in one area—such as finance, accounting, electronic data

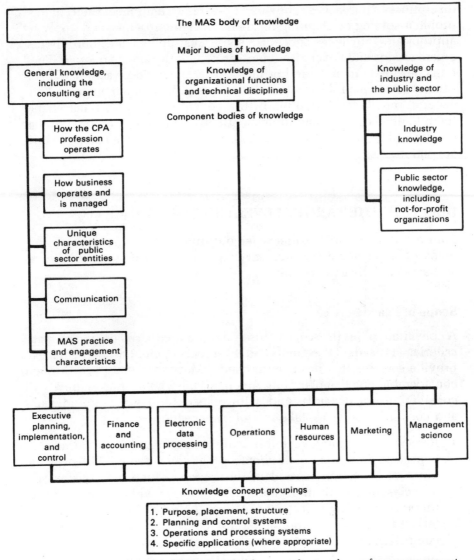

Figure 3.1 The body of knowledge needed by consultants who perform management advisory services (MAS). (*SOURCE:* Edward L. Summers and Kenneth E. Knight, *Management Advisory Services by CPAs,* American Institute of CPAs, New York, 1976, p. 82. Copyright © 1976 by the American Institute of CPAs, Inc.)

processing, management science, human resources, a specific industry—most successful consultants go beyond that specialty and acquire technical or functional expertise in a number of areas. They broaden their areas of expertise because problem-solving and planning situations are rarely restricted to single technical areas or functional disciplines.

Professional management consultants necessarily employ broad interdisciplinary approaches. They must be able to help meet their clients' problem-solving or planning needs by bringing together and applying appropriate knowledge concepts. They must understand their clients' organizations and the environments in which the clients operate. They must be able to identify and bring together the various technical disciplines that client problem situations may require. Last but not least, their general knowledge and skills in the consulting process must enable them to develop and communicate effective recommendations, so that clients will be helped to make necessary decisions and to take appropriate actions.

DEFINING THE TARGET LEVEL OF COMPETENCE

Four major factors to consider when defining the target level of competence are scope of practice area, service variety, requirements of clients, and service delivery capability.

Scope of Practice Area

A consultant plans the scope of his or her practice based on two primary criteria: (1) needs of the clients and (2) actual or potential competence to provide services that meet these needs. Most consultants go through considerable practice planning. A consultant who desires to grow will consider all practice areas and, with respect to management advisory and consulting services, take the following steps:

1. *Review the economic region in which the consulting firm draws, or expects to draw, most of its clients:* The consultant will identify the kinds of industries located in the region; which new businesses, agencies, or organizations are moving in; and which economic sectors are expanding or declining. Although this step may seem elementary, it is extremely important. Many consultants are able to deliver competent services, but not to the client base available to them!

2. *Inventory the services required by the existing clients and, in most cases, by the clients the consultant would like to add:* Client reviews performed by the consultant as part of other work (e.g., related to audits, reviews, and tax planning) should provide an excellent start for an inventory of services that the clients will potentially require.

3. *Select services from this inventory that will be provided:* A typical client base may require a larger set of services than the consultant is willing to consider providing. In that case, the consultant may consider either specialization or practice expansion. In general, the

larger the consultant's practice, the greater will be the variety of potential services that the clients will expect to be offered.

4. *Acquire the competence needed to provide the selected services:* How the consultant can acquire competence is the next concern. Although this topic is postponed until later in the chapter, there is little doubt that acquiring competence takes time and other scarce resources that must be diverted from other uses and applications. An effort to acquire competence nearly always involves a decision to forego immediate profits or practice growth in exchange for the prospect of future profit and growth.

5. *Notify clients and potential clients that the consulting firm is able and willing to perform the selected advisory and consulting services.*

Service Variety

No regulatory institute, society, or agency currently places a limit on the services that a consultant can provide. Certain consultants, however, properly exercise considerable self-restraint. For instance, consultants in public accounting firms often refrain from consulting for audit clients and avoid engagements they may not be able to complete because of a lack of required skills.

The range of services that consultants typically provide is extremely broad. Most engagements, however, would fall into one of the following major categories:

1. *Planning, control, and reporting systems:* These systems allow business firms to plan and control their activities in accordance with managerial intentions. They provide business owners or top managers with interpretations of budgets, performance reports, and financial statements. Specific examples of systems that fit into this category are financial reporting systems, fund reporting systems, general ledger systems, standard cost and performance analysis systems, management control systems, and sales forecasting systems.

2. *Operational computer system analysis, design, implementation, and evaluation:* Most organizations need computer systems to operate the planning, control, and reporting systems. This category includes basic systems, such as simple cash basis systems for small business firms; credit sales and accounts receivable, credit purchases and accounts payable, inventory, production and work scheduling, payroll, and fixed assets systems; and, in addition, specialized system design projects that may lead to new property records, redesigned forms, and revised policy and procedure manuals. The analysis and recommendations may involve complete and massive system overhauls or small-scale studies leading to minor improvements.

3. *Specialized technical services:* A third category consists of providing advice to management with respect to all the matters in which a business firm needs help. Such advice may have the purpose of enabling firms to comply with new laws, enter international markets, or keep abreast of new economic or technical developments.

Specific services that might fall into this category include acquisitions, mergers, divestments, economic and feasibility studies, equipment evaluation, financing and selecting sources of capital, goals and objectives studies, lease or buy analyses, management audits, product profitability studies, and market analyses.

Each of the above services requires that the *content* of the procedure be tailored to the particular service involved. Fortunately, however, all of the services involve the same fundamental problem-solving process.

Client Requirements

Clients of consultants have expectations concerning the extent, quality, cost, benefits, and reliability of any management advisory or consulting service for which they contract. Successful consultants reflect expertise and professional judgment in response to these expectations. However, expertise and professional judgment gained in certain areas are not easily transferable. For instance, accountants often have difficulty in transferring knowledge and judgment concerning taxes and traditional accounting areas to areas involving management advisory and consulting services.

A checklist such as the one that follows can aid consultants in reviewing client requirements:

- Will the service be provided on a "turnkey" basis? That is, will a fully implemented service (e.g., a system or recommendation) be turned over to the client ready for use? (Turnkey services require more care, organization, and attention to detail than other services.)

- Will the service require changes or adaptations by the client? (Such changes or adaptations may relate to the organization structure, human resources, level of management control, or specific operations. If they are required, the client must be told explicitly what to do in order to realize the service benefits.)

- Does the client belong to an industry with special characteristics or problems? (If so, the service must be designed to produce satisfaction in such situations.)

- Does the client have special financial or growth problems? (If so, the service should not aggravate these problems or be ineffective in their presence.)

Service Delivery Capability

Service delivery is the application of consulting skill. Without consulting skill, even high levels of knowledge and understanding cannot be put to effective use for clients. Even the ability to deliver certain services does not insure that other dissimilar services can be delivered.

As noted in Chapter 2, a consulting engagement typically delivers services through several phases. These phases may be restated as:

1. Setting objectives, identifying problems and needed services, predicting specific expected benefits from these services, and gathering essential facts pertaining to the problem and means of delivering the services

2. Adapting and designing the services that are to be the principal deliverables from the engagement

3. Implementing these services to the client's satisfaction

4. Evaluating the results in operation, in order to determine the extent to which the anticipated benefits were received from the services

Note that the last phase listed above may or may not be viewed as a separate phase. It is discussed in Chapter 8 as a part of the implementation phase.

The capability of delivering services through these phases is likely to be affected by such factors as:

- Personal characteristics of the consultant
- Degree of structure inherent in the service and client engagement environment
- Degree of multidisciplinary knowledge inherent in designing and implementing the service
- Relative importance of understanding the client's industry
- Approach and philosophy of the consultant in practice management

Consideration of these and other factors leads to the following representative questions, which you as consultant should ask and answer concerning every proposed consulting service:

- What will be the most likely time frame or schedule during which the service will be implemented? In other words, how long will you have from the time the client requests the service to delivery of the service?
- What technology is required to deliver the service? For example, must you have a specific technical ability such as COBOL language familiarity, or an in-depth understanding of certain manufacturing processes?

- Is the technology of the service truly up to date? That is, will it probably have a reasonably lengthy useful life before becoming obsolete?
- Will the service be of true economic benefit to the intended client? That is, will the cost savings or extra revenue exceed your fee and other implementation costs over the useful life of the service?
- Will you be able to deliver the service profitably? There is little value in offering a service on which, after allowing for a reasonable start-up period, you cannot earn a satisfactory profit. If a service proves to be unprofitable, you should discontinue the service before you are tempted to cut corners in the delivery process in order to achieve profitability.
- Do you have sufficient resources that can be dedicated to acquiring and retaining the ability to offer the service? In other words, are you organized to deliver the service? Although many consulting services are simple, others are complex and require extended time, multiple skills, and close cooperation among several persons. You should not underestimate the complexity of a new consulting service.
- Is the prospective client base capable of accepting the service? This question becomes particularly significant when you contemplate services involving the recommendation of integrated worker-machine systems to clients unused to their detail and complexity.

If a consultant asks such questions as these during the planning period, he or she should anticipate and define most of the problem areas in which difficulties regarding competence are likely to arise.

PLANNING TO ACHIEVE A TARGET COMPETENCE LEVEL

Planning to achieve competence actually consists of planning how to acquire knowledge and skills for delivery. The previous sections explained how to define the services a consultant is to deliver and the knowledge and skills needed to offer these services competently. This section discusses how to acquire the needed knowledge and skills.

Needs Assessment

A consulting firm should periodically assess its needs with respect to in-house knowledge and skills. Upon comparing the knowledge and skills held by its current consultants against its needs, the firm can determine the extent of its deficiencies. It may determine, for instance, that deficiencies exist at all levels. Perhaps there is an insufficient number of experienced partners and managers, or perhaps most of the staff consultants lack adequate quantitative knowledge and skills.

Approaches for Acquiring Needed Knowledge and Skills

A consulting firm can remedy such deficiencies by two approaches:

1. It can employ additional consultants with adequate knowledge and skills.
2. It can undertake a variety of "staff development" activities that are intended to endow the presently employed consultants with needed knowledge and skills.

The following sections examine the use of both approaches. Before discussing the approaches, however, it is necessary to identify the various consultant levels within a firm.

Consulting Career Ladder

Full-time consultants in a consulting firm follow a career path, i.e., climb a career ladder. A typical career ladder appears in Figure 3.2. Alongside each level on the career ladder are the principal activities for which the consultants at that level are responsible. Those activities in which the current occupants are weakest should be assigned the highest priorities when recruiting tactics or staff development programs are planned.

Recruiting

Staff consultants. Most consulting firms hire only persons with several years' experience in lower and middle levels of management. They have found that inexperienced persons can perform only functions that are within the capabilities of client personnel and are thus uneconomical. Consulting knowledge and skills require maturity and judgment that generally can be gained only through responsible experience.

Normally, persons having a few years of experience will be hired at the staff consultant level and will perform engagements under the supervision of managers. Within a relatively short time, usually 3 years or less, they should be ready for promotion. (If not, they will probably be discharged.)

A few consulting firms do hire staff consultants directly from colleges and universities. Their reasoning is that they will acquire up-to-date knowledge in such areas as computer science, financial modeling, statistics, finance, information systems—areas in which the firms can

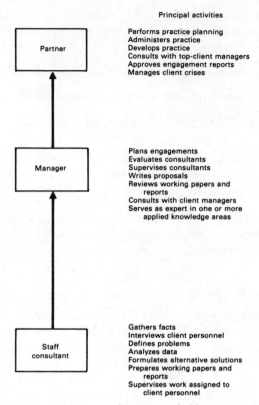

Principal activities

Partner
Performs practice planning
Administers practice
Develops practice
Consults with top-client managers
Approves engagement reports
Manages client crises

Manager
Plans engagements
Evaluates consultants
Supervises consultants
Writes proposals
Reviews working papers and
   reports
Consults with client managers
Serves as expert in one or more
   applied knowledge areas

Staff consultant
Gathers facts
Interviews client personnel
Defines problems
Analyzes data
Formulates alternative solutions
Prepares working papers and
   reports
Supervises work assigned to
   client personnel

Figure 3.2   A consulting career ladder.

serve well-defined and pressing needs. Such consulting firms are willing to trade lack of experience for this knowledge, even though they realize that the newly hired individuals will need added attention during the first few years.

A consulting firm that desires to recruit consultants directly from colleges and universities should observe the following rules:

1. Recruit only within well-defined areas of knowledge and/or skill needs.
2. Consider as sources only those higher education institutes that have solid reputations within the knowledge areas in which recruiting will occur.
3. Give preference to persons with masters' degrees.
4. Give preference to persons with management or consulting practice experience.
5. Be prepared to offer salaries higher than those offered by competing employers.

6. Contact the institutes at which recruiting will take place well in advance, to arrange dates, and participate in prescreening of candidates if possible.

7. Do not expect substantial success until the third or fourth year of recruiting.

Managers. Many consulting firms recruit for their practices mainly at the manager classification level. Their reasoning is that a manager is likely to be of worth from the beginning, since his or her personal competence will usually determine the success of individual engagements. A firm that intends to recruit a manager will probably seek the following attributes:

1. Previous successful consulting experience

2. Previous successful middle and top management experience

3. Specialized or advanced knowledge in major areas where the recruiting firm's practice has identified needs

Partners. On rare occasions a consulting firm may determine that its practice requires additional strength at the partner level. One such occasion could arise if the gap between services to be offered, and the ability to offer them, is so great that recruitment at lower levels cannot be expected to produce the desired results.

In the event that a new partner is to be recruited, the principal consideration must be the external reputation of the candidate as a highly competent consultant. The firm should proceed cautiously, since the recruiting process is extremely involved. In addition to the candidate's reputation for competency, the recruiting firm should consider his or her probable (1) remaining period of useful and productive service to the practice and (2) compatibility with the existing practice and current partners.

Work-Related Learning Experiences

Upon being recruited and hired, a consultant acquires knowledge through "staff development" activities. These activities include work-related experiences, formal training programs, and individual directed study. The first of these is discussed here. The two remaining activities are then discussed in following sections.

As in the case of other professionals, a consultant gains knowledge through on-the-job experience on varied engagements. This knowledge is transferable to other similar engagements. Moreover, the knowledge transfer can be enhanced through careful planning, counseling, supervision, and reflection.

Consultants at the manager level should assume the primary responsibility for the work-related learning of the staff consultants of a firm. The managers should counsel and guide the staff consultants, as well as evaluate their performances. A sound program that they may employ to foster work-related learning would include the following steps:

1. Anticipate engagements as far as reasonable into the future. Assign each consultant in accordance with both (a) the skills that he or she needs to improve and (b) the skills needed for each major step of the engagement. Where feasible, assign teams of consultants whose skills complement each other, so that one can observe and learn from another.

2. Review, on a quarterly basis, anticipated engagements and compare them with the description of services in the original practice plan. If necessary, discourage particular engagements that are not in line with the original plan.

3. Before each engagement, formally set out work-related learning objectives for each participating staff consultant. Involve the consultants in this process, so that each consultant understands his or her personal objectives.

4. After each engagement, or periodically, perform a "postmortem" in which the knowledge gained from the work experiences is carefully examined and recorded.

5. Maintain current competence and experience records of the staff consultants. In these records list: (a) extent of experience by year, engagement, industry, and major skills applied; (b) all training programs attended; (c) performance evaluations; and (d) knowledge and skill goals as yet unachieved. Refer to these records when contemplating staff assignments.

Formal Staff Training

Formal training is important in the development of practitioners who provide professional services to others. The importance of formal training is recognized by many states, since they require practitioners in various professions to participate in a minimum number of hours of formal training (professional development) each year to retain their licenses. For instance, public accountants in most states must participate for a specified minimum number of hours yearly in formal training courses or programs in order to retain their CPA licenses.

What is the purpose of formal training? It is to transmit needed knowledge, in an organized and usable form, during a minimum time period. It stands midway between university education and work-related learning.

A sound training program exhibits the following characteristics:

1. The training program has an applied orientation, with the clear purpose of imparting beneficial knowledge or skills concerning specific services or types of engagements.
2. Most (but not all) of the written materials are distributed in advance. From these materials the objectives, level, and content of the program should be plainly apparent.
3. Enrollment is limited to a number consistent with the nature of the materials and level of instruction. A course in financial planning, for instance, should have a lower enrollment limit than a new computer products review.
4. Instructors or discussion leaders are sponsored by a reputable organization offering quality training programs (such as a major state CPA society, a reputable business school, or a well-known private sector vendor), well-known in the subject to be taught, and highly competent teachers or course leaders.
5. A clear means of evaluating progress or learning by participants is applied. (This feature is for the benefit of the participants; no one should be misled into thinking that learning has occurred if it has not, nor should participants be allowed to underestimate what they may have gained!)

How much formal staff training is enough? As much as 20 percent of potentially billable hours may be needed during the first 5 years that a staff consultant spends in consulting practice. Thereafter, the extent of formal training may decrease and stabilize at a suggested minimum of 100 hours per year. Experienced consultants should regard such training to be a means of personal and professional enrichment, as well as an effective remedy for such problems as burnout, inflexibility, and out-of-dateness.

Figure 3.3 shows a proposed 5-year formal training schedule for a beginning consultant who has an accounting education and intends to specialize in information systems analysis and design. As is apparent, the training consists of a mixture of the consultant's specialty, the consulting firm's policies and procedures, and the basic skills of consulting. In a larger consulting firm, this training program might be provided by the firm itself, with many of the instructors being managers and partners of the firm. In a medium-sized or smaller firm, part or all of the training would probably be acquired from a professional training association or educational institution.

Individual Directed Study

In addition to work-related experiences and formal training programs, consultants can obtain knowledge in a self-directed manner from a

First year	
a. Introduction to basic management consulting policies of the consulting firm	80 hours
b. Basic consultant skills (interviewing, flowcharting, working paper organization)	40 hours
c. Specific functional and technical skill upgrades	80 hours
Total	200 hours
Second year	
a. Computer system fundamentals upgrade	80 hours
b. Business organization and control	80 hours
Total	160 hours
Third year	
a. Business planning and control systems	80 hours
b. Engagement supervision and client relations	80 hours
Total	160 hours
Fourth year	
a. Advanced information systems and databases	80 hours
b. Specialization (e.g., computer security)	40 hours
Total	120 hours
Fifth year	
a. Proposal preparation and practice administration	80 hours
b. Specialization (chosen by individual)	40 hours
Total	120 hours
Grand Total	760 hours

Figure 3.3 A suggested 5-year formal training program.

variety of sources. These sources include respected colleagues, trade journals, books, and news reports. It has been suggested that consultants could profitably spend an average of an hour a day in various forms of "self-study."

MAINTAINING CONTROLS OVER COMPETENCE AND SERVICE QUALITY

Earlier sections of this chapter have proposed that the following be established by a consulting firm:

1. An operational definition of its practice scope, including a list of services that it desires to provide

2. A clear understanding of its clients, their requirements, and the services that the firm might propose providing to each

3. The standards by which proposed services are to be evaluated with respect to their suitability for delivery

4. The criteria by which needed personnel are to be recruited

5. The programs for the achievement of needed staff development

Upon establishing the above, the consulting firm lays the foundations for the competent delivery of services through its practice. The following text offers guidance in monitoring competence, controlling the quality of services, and correcting any lapses that may occur.

Types of Controls

The items listed above represent "before-the-fact controls." In effect, they are the preventive controls that establish bench marks of expected performance, i.e., standards of comparison.

Feedback controls are "after-the-fact controls." They are generated by measuring actual performance and comparing it with the expected performance. For instance, the actual steps achieved in undertaking staff development may be compared with the planned program for staff development. Feedback controls represent the monitoring mechanisms used by consulting firms to maintain control over engagement schedules and internal administrative operations, as well as activities related to competence and service quality (e.g., staff development).

Several situations may be reflected through the use of these two types of controls. When the actual performances are in reasonable agreement with the expected performances, the activities can be viewed as proceeding according to plan. When the actual performances differ from the expected performances, but steps are promptly taken to correct detected deficiencies, the activities can be viewed as "in control." When the actual performances differ significantly from the expected performances, and the differences remain or increase over time, the activities can be generally viewed as "out of control." In some cases, however, these significant differences can indicate that the assumptions made in establishing the "before-the-fact controls" or plans are not valid in the "real world" and thus should be revised.

Steps for Maintaining Controls

Several steps may be taken by a consulting firm to ensure the maintenance of sound controls over competence and quality of services. They include service reviews, appointment of a practice director and service coordinator, engagement analysis, and staff evaluations.

Perform service reviews.   Annual service reviews should be established for the purpose of reviewing the consulting firm's objectives, offered services, and record of competence in the providing of services since the last review.

Appoint practice director.   In order to establish responsibility for practice competence and quality control, a person designated as practice director should be appointed. He or she should report annually on competence and quality control problems. He or she should also:

1. Propose practice goals and supervise the overall services planning process
2. Be responsible for practice conduct

Appoint service coordinator.   A service coordinator should be appointed to administer daily operations related to the providing of management advisory and consulting services. Responsibilities of this position relative to the competent delivery of services should be to:

1. Assign appropriate staff consultants to engagements, after consultation with managers-in-charge
2. Secure positive evidence that the delivery of services on each engagement is in accordance with firm policies
3. Identify and report knowledge or skill deficiencies and recommend staff development steps to correct them
4. Coordinate all practice development activities, including the screening of prospective engagements
5. Devise and administer a plan of staff training, consisting of both on-the-job and formal training courses

Perform engagement analysis.   The firm should keep a record of all engagements, even those that were very small or for which no fees were collected. With respect to each engagement, at least the following information should be recorded for future summation and/or reporting:

1. Client, including name, address, service location(s), client contact, referral (if applicable)
2. Other engagements with this client
3. Engagement service classification code
4. Staff consultants who were assigned to each engagement, their tasks, and hours spent on each task
5. Total engagement hours, including those not billed

6. Total hours billed, plus explanation of unbilled hours
7. Summary of other costs
8. Closing date of each engagement
9. Engagement evaluation and recommended follow-up

This information can be valuable in providing guidance during planning and operational activities. Preferably, it should be maintained in a computer-managed file, so that it can be easily and quickly rearranged, searched, and accessed. It should be reviewed frequently to be certain that it contains all required information.

Perform staff competence evaluations. The competence and related attributes of staff consultants, managers, and partners should be evaluated at least annually. In the case of staff consultants, the evaluations should take place even more often—at the end of each engagement (or at milestones if the engagements are lengthy) during the first year, and semiannually during the following 4 years.

The procedure and content of staff competence evaluations will vary from firm to firm and among staff levels. Certain steps, however, should be common to all evaluations. First, the evaluator should study the following, pertaining to the staff member to be evaluated: (1) personnel file, (2) file of engagement participation, and (3) file of competence and experience. The evaluator should make certain that the engagement file fully reflects all information concerning all engagements in which the staff member participated. Then the evaluator should complete the type of questionnaire shown in Figure 3.4, using the portion pertaining to the rank of the staff member. (Additional questions should be included as appropriate to the practice of the firm.) Finally, the evaluator should meet personally with the staff member to discuss the evaluation itself.

Staff consultant

1. Are the performance evaluations by managers and partners satisfactory?
2. Has this consultant participated in a training program?
3. Are client comments concerning this consultant favorable?
4. Is this consultant cooperative?
5. Have the knowledge and skill acquisition goals set during prior evaluations been achieved (or pursued satisfactorily)?
6. Is this consultant interested in setting high (yet achievable) learning goals?

Manager

1. Is this manager able to constructively criticize and counsel staff consultants?
2. Are client comments favorable concerning this manager?

Figure 3.4   A competency evaluation checklist for consultants.

3. Have engagements been completed on schedule?
4. Have established goals been achieved during engagements?
5. Has this manager conducted satisfactory formal training for staff consultants?
6. Is this manager able to work easily and effectively with clerical staff and client employees?
7. Is this manager developing an external reputation as a specialist?

Partner

---

1. Is this partner able to administer the practice?
2. Is this partner able to set goals for the practice?
3. Is this partner able to work with managers?
4. Is this partner able to develop new clients successfully?
5. Does this partner have an external reputation as an expert in one or more of the service areas?
6. Does this partner attract new staff consultants and managers as needed?
7. Does this partner develop and offer training programs?
8. Is this partner prominent in community service?

Figure 3.4   *(Continued)*

NOTES

1. E. L. Summers and K.E. Knight, *Management Advisory Services by Certified Public Accountants: A Study of Required Knowledge*, American Institute of Certified Public Accountants, New York, 1976.
2. Monroe S. Kuttner (ed.), prepared by AICPA University Education Task Force, *University Education for Management Consulting*, American Institute of Certified Public Accountants, New York, 1979.

4

Professional Attributes of Consultants

J. OWEN CHERRINGTON
Department of Accounting
Brigham Young University
Provo, Utah

The skills that a management consultant must possess can be classified into three broad areas: technical skills, interpersonal skills, and consulting process skills. Technical skills include both understanding and experience in a technical discipline—such as computer data processing, marketing, engineering, or organizational behavior—that qualify one to be considered an expert. Interpersonal skills include personal attributes that make an individual amiable among people and effective in accomplishing desirable objectives through people. The consulting process is the step-by-step approach used by a management consultant to (1) identify the cause of problems or inefficiencies, (2) identify alternative solutions, (3) select the most desirable alternative, and (4) implement the chosen solution. Understanding of this process and ability to use it in solving business problems constitute consulting process skills.

The objectives of this chapter are to identify the education generally required to obtain adequate technical skills, and to discuss the personal traits most commonly possessed by effective consultants. Professional ethics is one of the most important professional attributes of a consultant. Special attention will be given to the meaning of professional ethics, codes of ethics that relate to management consultants, and cases concerning the application of professional ethics.

codes of ethics that relate to management consultants, and cases concerning the application of professional ethics.

EDUCATIONAL REQUIREMENTS

The education required to obtain the necessary technical skills for management consulting depends on the area of specialization. Some generalizations can be made, however, concerning the amount of education required, the common core requirements, and the experience possessed by most consultants.

Technical Training

A consultant must bring something to the consulting process besides a likable personality and a willing pair of hands. That special "something" is obtained through education and training, experience, or some combination of the two. Generally, the combination of education and experience is an important factor in consulting success.

The following examples of successful consultants' individual career paths illustrate some of the alternatives. They also illustrate some of the technical skills that are basic to any area of consulting.

Example 1.   David Straight completed, at reputable universities, an undergraduate degree in psychology, an MBA in management, and a DBA in organizational behavior. After working for 4 years as personnel director for the manufacturing division of an international organization, David accepted employment with an international consulting organization. His primary areas of consulting are general management, leadership styles, wage and salary policies, hiring and promotion policies, and performance evaluations.

Example 2.   Mark Round had earned only a B.S. degree in political science when he became a computer company salesman. After 18 months, Mark left the company to become sales manager for the direct sales division of a cosmetic firm. This employment continued for 22 years, during which Mark attended night school, completed most of the course requirements for a master's degree in marketing, and moved up the management ladder to vice president of sales.

Because he was tired of the job and the company, he accepted an offer from an old college friend to be vice president of sales and part owner in a new electronics firm. Mark's marketing experience and business knowledge helped the company grow so that it captured a major share of the market in the short space of 4 years. The company was then sold at a substantial profit, and Mark resigned his position. Mark turned his efforts to management consulting and established a solo practice. His major areas of consulting include product packaging and pricing, distribution channels, sales force management, and sales incentive programs.

Example 3.   John Modom completed his bachelor's and master's degrees in accounting with a minor in computer science. While attending school, John worked as a part-time programmer for a local software firm. Upon graduation, John joined an international CPA firm. His initial assignments were in the areas of auditing, small business practice, and systems analysis and design for retail organizations. This industry specialization continued to develop over a 7-year period; and John is currently one of the firm's experts in the analysis and design of accounting and management information systems for retail enterprises.

Generalizations concerning the length and content of a management consultant's education can be drawn from these and similar career paths.

1. *Length of education:*   A bachelor's degree is a prerequisite, and many if not most people going into management consulting today have one or two graduate degrees.

    Education is important for many reasons. First, it is one measure of a person's intellectual ability, and intellectual ability is among the more important personal attributes in determining success as a consultant. A university degree shows evidence of ability to think. Second, the competition involved in a quality educational program develops confidence, articulation, and literacy. Third, education helps an individual mature and gain understanding of human nature. Fourth, the university education provides technical training in the chosen area of specialization.

    The better management consultants have a great deal of technical training in one area of specialization. This training includes both theory and practice. In addition, the management consultant needs a broad knowledge of business, management, economics, government, and a variety of similar topics in order to evaluate the impact of decisions in the area of specialization on the larger business and the people who work in it. Neither the extensive training required to become technically qualified as an expert in one area of specialization nor a broad general education can be obtained in an undergraduate program.

    Undergraduate programs generally teach the "how," rather than the "why." Students are trained to memorize and regurgitate, not to conceptualize and criticize. Most undergraduate programs can be criticized for their rote, cookbook approach to the business environment. Graduate programs help develop tolerance for the uncertainty and ambiguity inherent in business problems. They help increase an individual's ability to deal with frustration, to challenge the current, and to create the new.

Some of the academic subjects commonly used in management consulting engagements are only taught in graduate programs. These include many research skills, such as research design, research methodologies, and statistical analysis.

2. *Type of education:*   Educational programs usually include a technical degree and a general degree.

Whether the technical degree comes first or second does not seem to make much difference. For example, one person might obtain a general business degree at the bachelor's level and specialize in computer data processing after earning a master's and a doctoral degree in computer science and information management. Another person might do the same type of consulting with a bachelor's degree in computer science and an MBA.

Common Core Requirements

It is only natural for a major portion of an educational program to be in a desired area of specialization. A person desiring to consult in marketing, for example, would expect to devote a substantial portion of his or her program to marketing-related courses. Another person who plans to consult in systems analysis and design would expect to concentrate on courses in accounting, computer information systems, and information management.

Regardless of a person's area of specialization, however, he or she should include certain common core courses in the educational program. At a minimum, these common core courses should provide exposure to communications, mathematics and statistics, and computer data processing.

Communications.   A well-rounded education in communication is necessary. Studies to determine the time that business graduates spend on each type of communication show a fairly equal amount spent on each activity: listening, 29 percent; speaking, 26 percent; writing, 25 percent; and reading, 20 percent. The most common types of writing include: memos, 32 percent; letters, 29 percent; short form reports, 26 percent; and long form reports, 13 percent.

A management consultant must be proficient in all forms of communication. Inability to master any form of communication will inhibit the consultant's effectiveness and efficiency.

An effective consultant must be able to go one step beyond the technical aspects of communication and use it to create change in people and their organizations. For example, style, grammar, spelling, and mechanics are emphasized in most writing courses in business communications. The quality of the consultant's written communications ought to be equivalent to material published in the professional journals and magazines.

Mathematics and statistics.   Mathematical models and statistical analyses are useful in analyzing a variety of problems. A consultant may choose not to analyze a particular problem with an available mathematical model or statistical tool. But the client is short-changed if an available model or tool that will provide a better, cheaper, and faster result is not used because the consultant does not know about it.

Computer data processing.   A consultant needs to work efficiently in order to remain competitive. The development of mini- and microcomputers in recent years has made computer data processing affordable to every consultant. Applications such as word processing, spreadsheets, and data base management systems are available on most computers. Computer software provides the consultant with the capability of performing many consulting tasks more easily, more quickly, and more accurately.

Experience

Work experience, after completion of a formal education, is important for several reasons. First, it provides a track record that a consulting organization can review in evaluating the individual's potential as a consultant. Promotions achieved, interpersonal relations with others, and managerial style are all good indicators of potential success. Second, work experience that relates to an individual's area of expertise will provide added depth as well as breadth to the chosen area. Third, if the experience has been with an organization that is at the forefront of new knowledge and developments, the new consultant will bring new skills and a fresh approach to the consulting organization. Finally, work experience helps ensure credibility with clients. Credibility is important in obtaining new clients and in setting and implementing the consultant's recommendations.

In some consulting situations, experience can be combined with education. One such approach employs a relationship akin to that of a journeyman and an apprentice. The experienced consultant models his or her skills through on-the-job demonstrations, and the novice consultant learns from such modeling. This arrangement affords the novice consultant the opportunity to meld theory with practice. Programs of this type are typically offered only by large consulting firms that have well-developed practices in particular areas of specialization.

The length of experience required for entry into a consulting organization varies from almost no experience to 10 or 12 years of experience. As a general rule, people with more education require less experience. Very few people get by with less than 2 years of experience. Anyone who is hired without much experience typically must work under the close supervision of another consultant for an extended period of time. Five years of experience at a managerial level is the ideal for entry into the consulting profession.

PERSONAL TRAITS OF A MANAGEMENT CONSULTANT

Many factors other than experience and education have a bearing on the success an individual achieves in the field of management consulting. Several personal attributes are critical for success. Some of them can be learned by intelligent people through years of study and experience. Some are inherent at birth or are developed during early childhood. Unless an individual has the necessary personal attributes to meet the required high standards of competent conduct, he or she will surely fail.

A list of necessary personal attributes can be useful to those contemplating careers in management consulting and to recruiters in consulting organizations. Ideally, those who possess these attributes will be enticed to pursue management consulting and those who do not possess them will save time, money, and personal frustration by selecting alternative employment. Recruiters assist in this weeding-out process by employing only those who have the necessary skills for success.

If you are new to the consulting profession and would like to evaluate your personal attributes, complete the exercise on page 70. Completing the exercise before reading this section will make you less biased in your response. Don't give up if your score is not as high as you think it ought to be. Not all of the necessary attributes are inherent. Many can be acquired through diligent study and practice. History is replete with examples of persons who have overcome seemingly impossible odds and imposing obstacles to become successful. This exercise is primarily intended to help you identify obstacles that you need to overcome.

Inherent Attributes

A few of the personal attributes are inherent. A person either has them by birth or does not have them at all. No amount of study, experience, or perseverance can create these qualities. They are intelligence, adequate physique, and empathy.

Intelligence.   Intelligence may be defined as the capacity for reasoning, understanding, and performing other similar forms of mental activity. The limits of our capacity to learn are largely determined at birth. The best that each of us can do is to utilize our capacity to the fullest extent possible.

What level of intelligence is necessary for performing adequately as a management consultant? The most frequent answer is enough to perform adequately in a graduate program. Various tests are used to measure intelligence, and different universities and programs use different tests and minimum test scores in their screening processes. Some of the commonly used tests include:

Exam	Minimum score	Percentile
IQ test	120	90th
GMAT	500	60th

Physique. By physique we have reference to the physical body structure, organization, and development. The most significant part of one's physique that is determined by birth is the capacity to produce energy. This is largely determined by our hormonal glands and our nervous system. A high-energy level is required to support intellectual and emotional activity. It enables a person to withstand pressure, to avoid physical illnesses, and to maintain physiological equilibrium. Because of the time pressure, volume of work, problem-oriented environment, and a multitude of other frustrations, a consultant needs a high-energy level for survival.

Personal appearance, a neat look, and an attractive physique are extremely important in a consulting environment. However, only a very minor part of this is inherent. Very few people are born with physical handicaps that would impair their performance as consultants. Diet, physical activity, neatness in dress, and personal hygiene are all within our ability to control.

Empathy. Empathy is a personal trait that allows us to feel for other people. It is an intellectual identification with, or vicarious experiencing of, the feelings, thoughts, or attitudes of other people.

It is not clear whether empathy is inherent or whether it is acquired during early childhood. The exact point of its development is not really important for our purposes. Either way, it is fairly well-developed by the time an individual is old enough to consider management consulting as a profession.

Empathy, understanding, and sympathy for the feelings and desires of others make a consultant better able to identify problems and to develop solutions that are appropriate to the people affected.

Developed Attributes

The most authoritative list of essential attributes was developed by a subcommittee of the Association of Management Consulting Firms

(ACME). The nine attributes and the definitions that follow were largely identified by this committee. The definitions are, in some cases, more restrictive than would be found in general use, but they are relevant to the consulting profession.

Understanding of people (human relations):   the ability to anticipate human reactions to differing situations; to establish and maintain friendly relations and mutual confidence with people at all levels; and to recognize and respect the rights of others.

The desire and ability to understand people develops from empathy and the capacity for feeling discussed earlier. However, conscious study is required to understand how people act and react, both individually and in groups. It takes a high degree of intelligence to observe, sift, weigh, and finally evaluate the characteristics and attributes of different people.

Integrity: an abstract term describing under one head a number of attributes, such as moral and ethical soundness; fairness; equity; ability to distinguish between right and wrong; honesty; dependability; freedom from corrupting influence or practice; and strictness in the fulfillment of both the letter and the spirit of agreements made, regardless of personal considerations.

This definition contains most of the basic philosophies underlying a code of ethics. The detailed contents of professional codes of ethics relating to management consultants will be discussed in detail later in this chapter.

The main ingredients for maintaining integrity are self-confidence, intelligence, and conviction. People are apt to lose their integrity when they are anxious or unsure about their ability to face a given situation while maintaining their value system. They then shade or lose their integrity in spite of a well-developed set of ethical and moral standards. Intelligence is necessary for identifying the relationship of existing situations to ideals of honesty and equity. Too frequently people compromise their standards because they don't recognize a situation as unethical. Integrity is also contingent on the individual's convictions in a set of beliefs and principles that he or she is willing to support and from which he or she cannot be turned.

Courage: The strength of mind that enables one to encounter disagreement, difficulties, and obstructions with firmness of spirit and determination, and to consider them as challenges rather than something to be avoided and feared; the ability to stand by one's convictions regardless of pressure.

Courage in management consulting has reference to intellectual, moral, and emotional firmness. Courage causes one to support convictions that have been arrived at through intellectual conviction regarding the rightness of a situation or problem. Lack of courage is evidenced by feelings of inadequacy and dependency on others.

Objectivity: the ability to grasp and to represent facts, unbiased by prejudice.

The objectivity of the consultant is threatened when personal considerations, prejudices, and anxieties about the engagement are present. Objectivity is questioned when there is a lack of independence. In order for a consultant to be completely independent and objective, there must be both an appearance of independence and an actual state of mental independence.

Several situations can jeopardize the appearance of independence. The consultant's independence is questioned any time there is a vested interest in the outcome as a result of ownership or management responsibility. Examples of this include activities as promotor, underwriter, voting trustee, director, officer, or any capacity equivalent to that of management or employee of the company. Situations in which the consultant owns or has committed to buy an ownership interest, or where the consultant has loaned money to the company, cause a loss of the appearance of independence.

Independence and objectivity, in fact, ultimately depend upon the consultant's mental attitude. Even though a consultant may have the appearance of independence, objectivity may be lost through personal involvement. True independence and objectivity are a state of mind or a mental attitude.

Consultants must avoid situations in which they appear to lack independence and objectivity; they must maintain independent and objective attitudes. Without this, their recommendations will usually be worth very little.

Ambition: the desire and motivation to earn and obtain full recognition for the attainment of professional status.

A management consultant with too *little* ambition lacks the desire, drive, and commitment to achieve a professional status. A management consultant with too *much* ambition becomes self-centered, strives only for selfish ends, and regards the client as a pawn to be used to achieve those selfish ends. The consultant with the right amount of ambition is one who needs to accomplish to be happy, who feels a strong urge to produce concrete results, and who regards work as an important aspect of life. Without ambition, the consultant is useless; with too much ambition, he or she is unbearable.

Problem-solving ability: the degree of mental organization and development that enables one to absorb and relate facts in a logical and orderly fashion and to reason inductively and deductively.

Problem-solving ability is developed through the application of curiosity (i.e., the desire for knowledge) and imagination (i.e., the faculty that fosters creativity). It involves thorough analysis, original thinking, the synthesis of new ideas from elements experienced separately, and the development of practical solutions to complex problem situations.

Problem-solving ability is extremely important because the basic work of a consultant is to analyze and solve problems. Because time is such a factor in this competitive environment, the consultant must be able to solve problems quickly.

Judgment: the ability and reasoning power to arrive at a wise decision, a course of action, or a conclusion, especially when only meager or confused facts are available.

Problem-solving ability, discussed above, brings the consultant to a decision point. The alternative solutions have been identified and a recommendation with supporting justification must now be made as to the most desirable solution. The most successful consultants have the capability of forecasting the outcomes of each alternative and selecting the one that is most desirable.

Ease in selecting the most desirable alternative, and quality of the selection, improve significantly with practice. This is one reason why experience is a prerequisite for new management consultants.

Communication ability: the ability to use both written and spoken words to convey ideas to others.

An accurate interchange of feelings, thoughts, opinions, and information between individuals is a critical skill of the consultant. Open and active listening and responding, coupled with candidness and respect for the client, are essential. All communication messages that are sent, overt and covert, as well as verbal and nonverbal, must be recognized. Failure results from the lack of ability to communicate effectively. For most people, however, the ability to communicate easily and effectively is not a natural gift. It must be learned through study, hard work, and practice.

Psychological maturity: the ability to live life—with its frustrations, adversities and inequities—and to act with poise and control in all situations, regardless of frustrations; to refrain from any display of adverse reactions; to view situations in perspective and to take action needed on a calm and controlled basis without being diverted from a sound, logical, and ethical course by outside pressure.

Maturity is judged more by reactions to people than to things.

People are considered mature when they are capable of forgetting themselves for someone else. Psychologically mature persons:

1. Deal easily with other human beings who would be considered equals, supervisors, or inferiors. They recognize that authority is necessary and accept it in all the limits of its power, realizing that the fragile human instrument chosen to exercise the authority does not automatically become invested with natural qualities not possessed before. They see others as they are, judge situations as they are, and remain in contact with objective reality even when their emotions are aroused.

2. Integrate their emotions into their personalities, keeping them firmly under the control of reason and in contact with objective values. They have a correct assessment of their own abilities and are not thrown into total confusion by failure or by recognition of some moral, physical, or psychological defect within themselves.

Compatible Life-Style

The inherent attributes and the developed attributes discussed above are essential for achieving success as a consultant. In order to "make it" as a consultant, however, you need to enjoy the work and life-style. Travel, job pressures, and several projects in process concurrently are only a few characteristics of a consultant's life-style. In order to stay with consulting, you need to enjoy these things.

Travel. The amount of travel varies extensively among consultants. Some spend as little as 10 percent of their time away from home, others as much as 100 percent. The average is generally between 20 percent and 60 percent. The benefit of travel is that you have the opportunity to see much of our own country and perhaps several foreign countries. A disadvantage is that you lose touch with your spouse and family by being away so much. The inside of one hotel, airplane, factory, or office building is about the same as any other.

Family relationships are subject to strain when the consultant spends little time at home. Strains are particularly likely when the married consultant cannot leave the problems of work at work and convert the few hours at home into times of contentment and enjoyment.

Irregular living conditions. Most consultants have some flexibility in determining their working hours. The typical consultant needs only to fit his or her schedule to the client's schedule and complete the required work on time. However, the days may be long. When a deadline for an engagement is approaching, a day of 12 to 16 hours is not uncommon. When an engagement is away from home, the consultant must in addition live out of a suitcase, sleep in a strange bed, and try to maintain a well-balanced diet while eating out in a variety of restaurants.

Several concurrent problems.   Consulting work is frequently "feast" or "famine." When times are bad, few if any jobs are available. When times are good, the consultant may have several jobs in process concurrently and be forced to move from one job to the next in order to keep all underway and the clients satisfied. Many consultants prefer to complete one job before moving on to the next and thus find this situation frustrating.

Job pressures.   A client with a problem needs a solution today, not at some distant time in the future. The consultant who will deliver the best product in the shortest period of time is the one who will be awarded the contract. Therefore, industry pressures to work efficiently—and client pressures to solve their problems quickly—mean that the consultant constantly works under pressure. The amount of pressure may vary, but it is always there.

Staff capacity.   A consultant's work, from the client's point of view, is a staff function. Functioning in a staff capacity, the consultant does not make final decisions. He or she is limited to identifying problems, collecting and analyzing data, and recommending solutions. The decision-making function is a line function that rests with the client. The consultant must, therefore, enjoy functioning in a staff capacity if he or she is to have job satisfaction.

People.   Most of the work performed by a consultant is people-oriented. Interviews, observations, document collection, training, and other activities involve people. Because of the potential changes that may occur in their work environments, many of the people with whom a consultant interacts will hold hostile feelings toward the consultant. Thus, the consultant should enjoy working with people, so that he or she is able to tolerate such negative or hostile situations.

Problem solving.   Many people find problems depressing and frustrating; they avoid becoming involved at any cost. Consultants must be just the opposite. Their basic work is solving problems, and they need to enjoy working with problems to be successful.

Negotiation.   Consulting situations are often reduced to "either-or" or "win-lose," in which clients believe that in order to satisfy their wants (win), others must suffer (lose). This leads them to seek a stronger offense to overwhelm any resistance. A consultant must feel comfortable working in this environment. The consultant can frequently help the client by broadening the problem-solution perspective and by avoiding the "win-lose" mentality. This process requires negotiation away from "win-lose" toward "win-win" strategies. Knowing when to negotiate and being effective at it are important consulting skills.

CODES OF ETHICS FOR
MANAGEMENT CONSULTING

Every profession has a standard of professional conduct and practice. Professional codes of ethics represent a unified effort to reduce to writing some of the more obvious, definable, practicable, and enforceable rules of conduct. Codes of conduct for management consultants represent the attitudes, principles, and approaches that have been found to contribute most to success and make for equitable and satisfactory client relationships.

A professional code of ethics serves at least three useful functions. First, and perhaps most important, it has an educational effect by providing members of the profession with guides to the kind of ethical behavior that historic experience has found to attract and justify the confidence of the public. Second, it narrows the area in which a person has to struggle with doubts. Third, it serves as a visible, impersonal standard that professional men and women can use to support their decisions.

Both the client and consultant benefit from a code of ethics. The client is generally untrained in the field for which consulting services are needed. Frequently, because of the nature of the problem, the client has no choice in whether or not to hire a consultant. Just as a person who is sick must employ a doctor, a firm that is "sick" must employ the services of a consultant. Requiring the consultant's services, and being unable to evaluate those services independently, the client relies on the code of ethics to ensure fair business dealing.

Consultants also benefit from a code of ethics. In return for the faith that the public places in them, they accept certain obligations to behave in ways that are beneficial to the public. By following the code, the consultant remains relatively free from control, supervision, and evaluation of all governing bodies. The self-discipline and voluntary assumption of the obligations specified in the code of ethics place consultants above and beyond the requirements of the law.

There are three main codes of ethics that relate to management consultants. Because of the tremendous amount of consulting work that is performed by CPA firms, the code of ethics of the American Institute of Certified Public Accountants (AICPA) is relevant. The Institute of Management Consultants (IMC), the primary organization responsible for certifying management consultants, has developed a code of ethics that must be followed by all certified management consultants. The Association of Management Consulting Firms (ACME), the organization to which most major consulting organizations belong (except CPA firms, which are not allowed to join), has also developed a code of ethics.

Our objective is to summarize the principles found in these codes.

Following the summary, several short cases will be given, along with suggested solutions, to highlight certain aspects of the codes. The common principles found in these codes of ethics can be broadly classified into four areas: basic responsibilities, practice standards, fee arrangements, and business conduct.

Basic Responsibilities

Basic responsibilities cover integrity, objectivity, independence, and confidential information. The public expects a number of character traits in a management consultant, including integrity and objectivity. No matter how competent a consultant may be, recommendations will be of little value if there is lack of independence. Also, inappropriate use of confidential information is not only dishonest, but it destroys the confidence of clients and the public in the consulting profession.

Each code of ethics includes one or more statements about these principles. The statements contained in Figure 4.1 summarize the basic responsibilities and behavior required of management consultants.

Practice Standards

Practice standards may be characterized as standards pertaining to the general and technical aspects of conducting professional consulting engagements. They identify how the work is to be outlined, administered, and reported in order to provide quality services to clients. In addition, they clarify the nature of professional competence. Each code of ethics promulgated by the professional associations has several statements dealing with practice standards.

The statements in Figure 4.2 summarize the practice standards included in these three codes of ethics.

Fee Structure

Remuneration is a primary reason for entering the consulting profession. Many people are attracted to management consulting because of the perceived opportunities to earn substantial salaries or profits.

The profit motive and ethic motive must be integrated in management consulting. An adequate profit is essential for good consulting. Consultants who have been poorly paid and are hungry for work may be tempted to accept jobs for which they are only marginally qualified. As a result, the work is not performed efficiently and the consultant gets a poor return on the time invested. Also, the result is generally less than optimal so that the client is poorly served. Only by having an adequate income can the consultant afford to spend the time necessary to remain

Figure 4.1 Basic responsibilities of management consultants.

Integrity and objectivity

1. Do not knowingly misrepresent facts and never subordinate judgment to others.
2. Place the interests of clients ahead of personal interests and serve the clients with integrity.
3. Inform the clients of any special relationships, circumstances, or interests that might influence judgment or impair objectivity.
4. Do not assume the role of management or take any positions that might impair objectivity.

Independence

1. Take an independent position with the client, making certain that advice to a client is based on impartial consideration of all pertinent facts and responsible opinions.
2. Do not serve an enterprise without independence with respect to that enterprise.
3. Do not serve a client under terms or conditions that might impair objectivity, independence, or integrity. Reserve the right to withdraw if conditions develop that interfere with the successful conduct of the assignment.
4. Do not serve two or more competing clients in areas of vital interest without informing each client.

Confidential information

1. Guard as confidential all information concerning the affairs of a client that is gathered during the course of a professional assignment.
2. Do not take advantage of material or inside information resulting from a professional relationship with a client.
3. Do not disclose any confidential information obtained in the course of a professional engagement except with the client's consent.

current, and to develop new skills and new approaches to better serve clients. As a result of these activities, the clients will be more profitable, the services will be more valued, and higher fees are appropriate. This cycle continues benefiting both the client and the consultant.

Money matters are sensitive subjects to most people. Thus, each code of ethics promulgated by the associations has several statements on appropriate behavior relative to fees and commissions. These statements are summarized in Figure 4.3.

Business Conduct

Several standards included in the codes of ethics are intended to promote the highest quality of performance in the practice of management consulting. When followed they should lead to equitable and satisfactory client/consultant relationships and should contribute to success in a management consulting practice. Figure 4.4 lists these standards.

Figure 4.2   Practice standards for management consultants.

Professional competence

1. Undertake only engagements that can be completed with professional competence.
2. Accept only assignments for which the necessary qualifications are possessed.
3. Present qualifications for serving a client solely in terms of competence, experience, and standing.

Planning, supervision, and due care

1. Before accepting an assignment, confer with the client or prospective client in sufficient detail and gather sufficient facts to gain an adequate understanding of the problem, the scope of study needed to solve it, and the possible benefits that may accrue to the client.
2. Accept only assignments believed to be beneficial to the clients, and do not accept any assignment of such limited scope that the client cannot be served effectively.
3. Adequately plan and supervise an engagement.
4. Assign personnel qualified by knowledge, experience, and character to give effective service in analyzing and solving the particular problem or problems involved.
5. Provide the client with a written proposal that outlines the objectives, scope, approach, and—where possible—the estimated fee or fee basis for the proposed services, except where client relationships make it unnecessary.
6. Exercise due professional care in the performance of an engagement.
7. If conditions change during the engagement, discuss with the client any changes in the objectives, scope, and approach or other aspects of the engagement and obtain the client's agreement (preferably in writing) to such changes before taking action on them.
8. Obtain sufficient relevant data to afford a reasonable basis for conclusions or recommendations in relation to an engagement.
9. Do not knowingly without permission use proprietary data, procedures, materials, or techniques that others have developed but not released for public use.

Reporting results

1. Perform each assignment on an individualized basis and develop recommendations designed specifically for the solution of each client's problems.
2. Develop solutions that are realistic and practical and that can be implemented promptly and economically.
3. Acquaint client personnel with the principles, methods, and techniques applied, so that the improvement suggested or installed can be properly managed and continued after completion of the engagement.
4. Maintain continuity of understanding and knowledge of client's problems, and the work that has been done to solve them, by maintaining appropriate files of reports submitted to clients.
5. Do not guarantee any specific result, such as the amount of cost reduction or profit increase.
6. Do not permit your name to be used in conjunction with any forecast of future transactions in a manner that could lead to the belief that you vouch for the achievability of the forecast.

Figure 4.3   Fee-structure standards for management consultants.

1. Charge reasonable fees that are commensurate with the nature of services performed and responsibility assumed. Reasonableness is based on services performed, time required, experience, ability, reputation, responsibility assumed, and benefits that accrue to the clients.

2. Do not offer or render professional services under an arrangement whereby no fee will be charged unless a specified finding or result is obtained, or whereby the fee is otherwise contingent on the findings or results of the service.

3. Where feasible, agree with the client in advance on the fee or fee basis.

4. Do not pay a fee or commission to obtain a client or franchise a business practice; do not accept a commission, fee, or other valuable consideration for recommending products or services.

5. Do not structure pricing or charging practices in a way that impairs independence or objectivity or contributes to a conflict of interest with the client.

Figure 4.4   Business-conduct standards for management consultants.

1. Strive continuously to advance and protect the standards of the consulting profession.

2. Contribute to the development and understanding of better ways to manage corporations, governmental organizations, and other institutions in our society.

3. Share methods and techniques used in serving clients.

4. Avoid not only professional improprieties but also the appearance of improprieties, and never commit an act discreditable to the profession.

5. Do not advertise services in a manner that is false, misleading, deceptive, self-laudatory, or in any other manner derogatory to the dignity of the profession.

6. Do not concurrently engage in any business or occupation that would create a conflict of interest in rendering professional services.

7. Do not accept an assignment for a client while another management consultant is serving that client unless satisfied that any conflicts between the two engagements are recognized by, and have the consent of, the client.

8. Do not make offers of employment to consultants on the staff of another consulting firm without first informing the other firm.

9. Do not solicit employees of clients, for the purpose of employing them, except with the client's consent.

10. Do not associate, in a responsible capacity respecting client work, with any consultant who does not adhere to the code of professional ethics.

Conclusion

Every management consultant benefits from the codes of ethics. The solid reputation now enjoyed by the management consulting profession has developed over the years as a result of obedience to these concepts and principles. Each consultant has a responsibility to himself or herself, and to the profession, to live by these codes of ethics and to encourage others to do the same. Enforcement of the codes is everyone's responsibility.

EXERCISE AND CASES

Exercise—Evaluation of Professional Attributes

This exercise is intended to help you evaluate your personal attributes relative to those that are commonly possessed by successful consultants. For each statement that follows, indicate on a scale of 1 to 5, where 1 represents strongly disagree and 5 represents strongly agree, how you feel.

Instructions for scoring are given at the end of the exercise.

Strongly disagree		Neutral		Strongly agree		
1	2	3	4	5	**1.**	My home life as a child was full of love and affection from parents and brothers and sisters.
1	2	3	4	5	**2.**	Physically and mentally, I feel terrible on less than 7½ hours sleep per night.
1	2	3	4	5	**3.**	My IQ and GMAT scores (or similiar test scores) would easily qualify me for admittance to a graduate program at a quality university.
1	2	3	4	5	**4.**	I have a hard time understanding why other people feel the way they do.
1	2	3	4	5	**5.**	I work effectively under job-related pressure.
1	2	3	4	5	**6.**	Frequently, I have trouble explaining difficult concepts to other people.
1	2	3	4	5	**7.**	I would rather provide information and alternative courses of action to other people, and let them make the decisions, than make the decisions myself.
1	2	3	4	5	**8.**	It takes me longer than most people to establish my credibility and gain confidence and respect from others.
1	2	3	4	5	**9.**	I am totally honest and ethical in dealings with my fellow humans.
1	2	3	4	5	**10.**	I dislike and avoid conflict with other people, even when I am confident I am right.
1	2	3	4	5	**11.**	I enjoy solving a complex problem even if it requires me to dig through mounds of data.
1	2	3	4	5	**12.**	I dislike travel and an irregular work schedule.
1	2	3	4	5	**13.**	My career path to this point has always been well defined, with little time and energy wasted in abandoned objectives.

Strongly disagree		Neutral		Strongly agree		
1	2	3	4	5	**14.**	I frequently have difficulty in interacting with my boss or supervisor.
1	2	3	4	5	**15.**	I enjoy writing, and my writing style is both clear and concise.
1	2	3	4	5	**16.**	It is difficult for me to distinguish between relevant and irrelevant facts when I am faced with a problem situation.
1	2	3	4	5	**17.**	I frequently think about becoming rich and famous and imagine myself accomplishing things that would make other people say I am a great person.
1	2	3	4	5	**18.**	I am opinionated and don't like to be bothered with other people's prejudices or views on a situation.
1	2	3	4	5	**19.**	I am the kind of person other people like to be around.
1	2	3	4	5	**20.**	My family life is disrupted when I am traveling in connection with work or when I come home from work late at night.

Scoring. Add your responses to the even-numbered questions, subtract the sum from 60, and add the result to the total of your responses to the odd-numbered questions. The range of scores is from 20 to 100. Scores between 85 and 100 are good scores that indicate high potential for success in the consulting profession. Scores between 60 and 85 would be considered marginal; improvement or change needs to be made in some of your personal attributes to be a successful consultant. Scores below 60 indicate a poor fit with management consulting.

Ethics Cases

Several cases dealing with ethical issues are described below. A suggested solution to each case is provided at the end of this chapter.

Case 4.1. During the course of an engagement, you and a junior consultant discover illegal payments, fraud, and other questionable management practices. The client is a large publicly held corporation. Shortly after the discovery, the junior consultant makes the following comment:

> We're here as confidential counselors and have been made privy to innermost secrets by a client who has been completely open. What right do we have to tell him what's right and wrong? Do we have to be policemen as well as father confessors?

What response should you make to this comment?

Case 4.2.   Your firm is employed by the president of a company to make an overall policy study of the business and its organizational structure to determine what actions should be taken to improve efficiency. After an exhaustive study, you come to the conclusion that the president should be removed from his position. What action should you take?

Case 4.3.   As a consultant, you are at a critical point in your review of the client's financial control system. You find the procedures clearly antiquated; and data going into the annual report include grounds for serious challenges by a dissident stockholder. The trouble is that the president himself designed the system while he was controller. He is bound to be upset at what is more than occasional criticism of his work. Volatile as he is, he might even persuade the board of directors to discharge you. This has been and will continue to be an extremely profitable client. Should you tell it as it is or should you soft-pedal the subject?

Case 4.4.   You serve as both a director and a consultant for a medium-sized, publicly held company. In reviewing your plans for the next few months, you go through the following thought process.

> As a director I'm supposed to represent the stockholders, but I wouldn't be here unless our firm had been doing a lot of good consulting work for management. I know, too, that we've got a couple of darn good consultants coming off a long assignment next month, and so far there's no new assignment for them. The president has been thinking about applying some sophisticated planning techniques to replace the current, old-fashioned forecasts. Now might be the time to do it. Frankly, I don't think a company this size has to get so fancy, but if he wants it, and considering keeping those two good staffers at full billing . . . I think I'd better have Charlie bring it up at the next director's meeting. I'll refrain from voting, so there should be no question. . . .

Discuss the ethics of the consultant-director's position and thought process.

Case 4.5.   Your firm has been invited by a hospital to perform a feasibility study concerning a new wing for the hospital. Your firm has an outstanding reputation in this area, and the hospital feels that a positive recommendation from your firm would help it sell the bonds to provide the needed financing. As you discuss the engagement with the client, you become aware that the decision has already been made to construct the new wing and that your study is being pursued merely as an attempt to help sell the bonds. As you contemplate the study, you conclude there is only a 50 percent chance that the results will show it to be economically desirable to pursue the expansion. However, a negative outcome would completely undermine any attempts to sell the bonds. The job is yours if you want it, and it would be a very profitable contract. What should you do?

Case 4.6. Your firm has been engaged by a manufacturing firm to make a study of top management. As the study neared completion, the president instructed you as to what she expected the recommendations and findings to be and directed you to come to this conclusion. What should be your response?

Case 4.7. As an internal consultant, you were asked to evaluate and recommend reorganization of top management. From the beginning it was apparent that you were in "over your head" in this one, and you wished they had given the job to an external management consultant. Now you're on the brink of recommending some changes that literally involve the guy who signs your paycheck. He keeps telling you to pull no punches in your report, but it's hard to believe he could be that objective. What should you do?

Case 4.8. The manager of a medium-sized city asked your firm to conduct a position evaluation program for all employees in the public works department. He indicates that he has favorable knowledge of your firm in this area but suggests that the citizens of the city, and the employees as well, have little, if any, knowledge of your firm. He therefore suggests retaining a specific public relations firm to assist in giving your organization higher visibility. He suggests that you should spend approximately 10 percent of the total fee, which would be agreed upon in advance, for this public relations effort. Is it ethical to accept this arrangement?

Case 4.9. You are the sole owner of your own management consulting practice; however, you have several consultants who work for you on a full-time basis. Your firm's specialty is marketing, and you have developed an outstanding reputation for your ability to develop marketing programs that are successful. One of the major tobacco manufacturers has recently offered you a very profitable consulting contract to develop a marketing program for the southeastern portion of the United States. Personally, you do not smoke and you feel it is wrong for other people to smoke. Is it ethical for you to accept the engagement, feeling as you do?

APPENDIX: SOLUTIONS TO ETHICS CASES

Case 4.1. Nondisclosure is not considered an acceptable alternative because it makes you an accessory to the fact. Disclosure to the offending party only—with no action—may result in the destruction of part of the evidence. Probably, the first step is to report the matter to the chairman of the board. Circumstances, however, may require that the matter be referred to an external body such as the Securities and Exchange Commission, Justice Department, Internal Revenue Service, or the shareholders.

Case 4.2.   The appropriate action depends on the type of company:

1. *Privately held company in which the president is the owner:* Discuss the matter with the president who, as owner, can make the decision.
2. *Company with several shareholders in which the president holds a controlling number of shares:*   Discuss the matter with the president. If the president accepts the recommendation and resigns, the problem is resolved. Otherwise, the matter should be discussed with the chairman of the board and the board of directors.
3. *A large publicly held company:*   The tendency here is to step over the president and go directly to the chairman of the board. This is unwise. You have a responsibility to discuss it first with the president.

Case 4.3.   The honest and ethical solution is to tell it as it is. The most tactful approach is to make a full disclosure to the president privately, pointing out the vast growth of the company and the tremendous changes in technology that have occurred since he, as controller, installed the system. If he understands the danger in which he is putting himself with regard to a possible dissident shareholder, he probably will acquiesce and agree to go forward. If he doesn't, and this is a privately held company in which he has control, you have accomplished your task. In a publicly held company, you may need to report the problem to the chairman of the board if the impact on the annual report is serious.

Case 4.4.   You are not in a good position from an ethical point of view. Your position as a director provides you with a significant influence over the direction of the company. As such, you have a responsibility to do what is best for the company. Your responsibility to the consulting firm is to secure employment to keep your people busy. By being both director and consultant for the same company, you are in a position that creates a conflict of interest, which is in violation of the code of professional ethics.

Another problem is your planned conduct in the upcoming board meeting. It is not honest and ethical for you to remain silent when you have relevant information on a decision. You have a responsibility to express your feelings about the proposed engagement even if it means losing the engagement.

The solution here is to resign from the board of directors and become an advisor to the chairman. You should point out how you feel about the installation of the sophisticated system at this time. An objective decision can then be made by the board based on all the available facts.

Case 4.5. Professional ethics requires that you accept only those engagements which are felt to be beneficial to the client. Clearly, if the results of the study are favorable, the client will be benefited. There is only a 50 percent chance, however, that this will result. The question, therefore, is whether a 50 percent chance of benefit is sufficient to pursue the study. Many consultants would answer yes to this question and accept the engagement because of the potential profit. The consultant who faced this situation declined the engagement and suggested that the client should use the money set aside for the feasibility study to employ an advertising firm to help them sell the bonds.This decision was justified by what the consultant thought was the client's best interest.

Case 4.6. Ethical conduct requires that you not misrepresent facts and never subordinate judgment to others. Further, you should not serve a client under terms or conditions that might impair objectivity, independence, or integrity, and you should reserve the right to withdraw if conditions develop that interfere with successful conduct of the assignment.

The consultant who was faced with this situation refused to follow the direction of the president, and the president refused to pay the consultant's fee. The president wanted to use the consultant as a means for firing a vice president. Ultimately, the fee was settled and no report was issued.

Case 4.7. Professional ethics require honesty, integrity, and placing the interests of the client or prospective client ahead of personal interests. The fact that this is an internal consultant, as opposed to an external consultant, makes no difference. The internal consultant wrote the report based on the available facts and was discharged.

Case 4.8. This arrangement is not acceptable under professional ethics. A consultant should not pay a fee or commission to obtain a client or franchise a business practice. The fact that the client came first and the commission came second in this case makes no difference. The commission is being paid to franchise a business practice.

The consultant who was faced with this situation accepted the engagement. After it was completed and he had paid the fee to the public relations agency, it was discovered that the city manager's brother owned the public relations agency. This disclosure was made by the Better Business Bureau in conjunction with the city's audit. The consultant willingly cooperated with the state's attorney in prosecution of the case. The matter was brought to the ethics committee and, while the consultant was in violation of the ethics code, he was discharged with a reprimand. His willingness to assist in the prosecution and the fact that he was not prosecuted in the case were significant in this decision.

Case 4.9. This is considered an ethical issue because its solution involves the future of the consultant's personal doctrine and nonprofessional associations as well as the effectiveness and integrity of the consultation process in which the consultant is about to engage. The principles involved in this case are not uncommon.

Although accepting such engagements would not be in violation of the code of ethics, acceptance would be ethical only if the consultant's relationship with the client firm were completely divorced from the consultant's personal doctrine and the client was made aware of the consultant's values. These circumstances are not likely, and the consultant would be justified in declining such an engagement because of a conflict of norms.

Effective Communications Skills

STEVEN GOLEN
Department of General Business
Arizona State University
Tempe, Arizona

An important attribute you must possess as a management consultant is the ability to communicate effectively. No matter how much technical expertise you possess, if you cannot communicate messages effectively clients will have difficulty understanding, interpreting, and relating to these messages. Not only does misunderstanding frustrate the client, but the client will also begin to question your credibility as a consultant. To be an effective communicator, therefore, you must develop interpersonal, written, and oral communication skills.

The purposes of this chapter are to discuss the principles behind effective communication of information, to identify and offer solutions to deal with or overcome barriers to effective communication, to review some guidelines and problems of written communication. It also will provide some suggestions for conducting interviews, leading problem-solving conferences, and making oral presentations.

CHARACTERISTICS OF THE COMMUNICATION PROCESS

Regardless of the types of communication that a management consultant must undertake, each type follows a predetermined process. That is, the communication flows from one individual to one or more individuals and is thus a two-way process. This physical process takes place both when a message is sent and when one is received. More specifically, however, the communication process involves more than just sending and receiving. It contains certain characteristics that are common to any oral or written communication situation. These characteristics are: (1) information source, (2) encoder, (3) transmitter, (4) channel, (5) receiver, (6) decoder, and (7) feedback.

The *information source* is a speaker or writer who develops an idea or observes some fact, object, or experience and wishes to convey this idea or experience to another individual. This idea or experience is *encoded* or translated into a message and *transmitted* or sent through a *channel* or medium, such as a spoken or written word. The message is *received* by the listener or reader and *decoded* or interpreted. Based on the interpretation, meaning is given to the message and the receiver *takes action*. The process is completed when the listener or reader provides *feedback* to the speaker or writer. A model of this communication process is illustrated in Figure 5.1.

This model can be applied to a consulting communication situation. For example, Joe Thompson, a management consultant, has been hired by a local bank to determine the parameters to be included in a request for proposal (RFP) for a new computer system. After reviewing the current system and talking to the bank officers involved with this project, he formulates in his mind the requirements that should be included in the RFP. Joe translates these requirements into a message that he places in a letter.

The letter is sent to Sandy Bell, the executive vice president of operations. Sandy receives the letter and interprets the message sent by Joe. She decides that the requirements Joe suggested for inclusion in the RFP

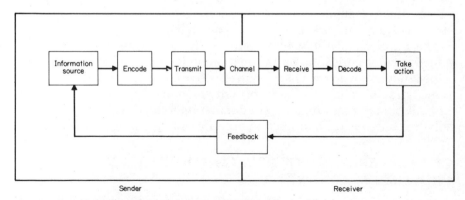

Sender   Receiver

Figure 5.1   The communication process.

are what the bank was seeking in a new system. Sandy instructs her assistant to prepare a formal RFP that includes Joe's requirements and to send it to the various vendors. Sandy calls Joe; she tells him that she agrees with his analysis and thanks him for the work he undertook for the bank.

Any communication situation will involve this process. Whether the communication consists of a letter, a report, or even a telephone conversation, the process is the same. The only difference is the time factor involved. A letter or report will take more time to travel through the channel and to complete the process than a telephone call or face-to-face conversation.

BARRIERS IN THE COMMUNICATION PROCESS

An assumption that may be drawn from the model in Figure 5.1 and the example is that there has been a free flow of information from the sender to the receiver. This assumption is not always realistic, however, since problems occur that inhibit or impede the free flow of information from the sender to the receiver. When such problems occur, message formulation and transmission—as well as message understanding and interpretation—can be affected. These problems are often described as barriers to effective communication. Figure 5.2 shows the places where potential barriers may occur in the communication process.

An important point to remember is that communication barriers may develop within the sender, within the receiver, between the sender and receiver, or in situations external to both. In other words, these barriers can be classified as intrapersonal, interpersonal, or organizational.

Intrapersonal barriers arise within the sender or receiver. For example,

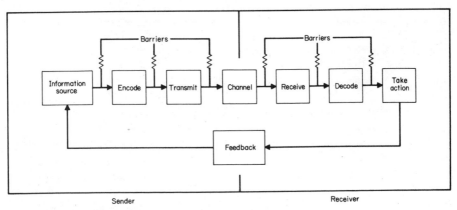

Figure 5.2   Barriers in the communication process.

the user or receiver of a consultant's report may lack adequate knowledge of systems design to understand the report.

Interpersonal barriers, however, occur because of the interaction between sender and receiver. An example of the interpersonal barrier would be the hostile attitude of a client's employee toward the consultant, arising from the possibility that the employee's job could be changed as a result of the consultant's recommendations.

On the other hand, organizational barriers develop as a result of the communication environment. This barrier may occur when a relatively new consultant meets with a corporate president. The status or position differences between the two may have an impact on the communication exchange.

BARRIERS COMMON TO CONSULTANTS

Before consultants can offer solutions to problems, they need to identify the specific problems. This is also the case when consultants face communication barriers. Consultants need to be aware of the specific types of barriers that may arise in their position before they can deal with or perhaps eliminate them. Diagnostic ability is extremely important because it allows consultants to understand the circumstances surrounding the communication situation and the pitfalls that may affect it.

Figure 5.3 lists sixteen potential barriers that may occur in a consulting situation. Each barrier will now be discussed, with suggestions for improving the communication situation. Many of these barriers can arise collectively; in other words, two or three barriers may cluster together and occur at the same time. When one of the barriers is eliminated, however, the others are usually eliminated or dealt with more easily.

Figure 5.3   Potential barriers to effective communication in a management consulting environment.

1. Know-it-all attitude	9. Resistance to change
2. Inability to understand technical language	10. Lack of credibility
3. Inadequate background or knowledge	11. Inability to understand nonverbal communication
4. Poor organization of ideas	12. Hostile attitude
5. Differences in perception	13. Lack of feedback
6. Prejudice or bias	14. Inappropriate physical appearance
7. Personality conflicts	15. Differences in status or position
8. Tendency not to listen	16. Information overload

Know-It-All Attitude

In any business situation, you are likely to encounter an individual who is a "know-it-all." Anything you say will probably be rejected by the know-it-all. This individual always perceives things in the light of his or her own interests; to reason with this individual is difficult, if not impossible, when the discussion goes contrary to his or her way of thinking. You must not try to change this individual's attitude, since it may be incapable of change. Instead, you should approach know-it-all from his or her own perspective. Try to develop a cooperative and supportive climate. Build on this individual's background and knowledge by reinforcing his or her role in a project. Use well-thought-out and logical reasoning that leads up to a particular action. By no means disagree overtly with this individual. Such action will likely dampen any future working relationship with him or her.

Inability to Understand Technical Language

Among the most common barriers you may experience is a client's inability to understand technical language. This barrier does not occur when the consultant deals with a client who is an expert in the field and is very familiar with the jargon. It may arise, however, when you interact with a nonexpert client or some of the client's employees. You should remember to use terms that are familiar to the receiver. Since various levels of understanding exist among receivers, you should exercise care when using words that may be misunderstood by the receiver.

Learn as much as you can about the receiver. It takes careful audience analysis to determine the receiver's level of understanding. More will be said about audience analysis in the written and oral communications sections of this chapter. In addition, technical terms or words may not be the only language that is misunderstood; common words can cause problems as well. For example, the 500 words most used in the English language have an average of 28 separate definitions each. You should remember, therefore, that meanings of words are not in the words themselves but in the minds of the sender and receiver of a message. Seek feedback whenever necessary, in order to ensure that the meaning the receiver gives to a word or term is what was intended by the sender.

Inadequate Background or Knowledge

Closely related to the technical language barriers are background or knowledge differences. They deal with different levels of understanding. Audience analysis is essential, especially when dealing with clients or client employees who have varied backgrounds and expertise. Remember that no two people are the same. Each individual's background is made up of various experiences, interests, values, and viewpoints that are unique to this individual. The background determines how well an individual will understand or interpret a message. You cannot always expect clients or their employees to have similar backgrounds or the same degree of understanding. Be patient and have empathy for the receiver. Provide additional information for clarification and be prepared to explain things more thoroughly to individuals who need explanation for better understanding.

Poor Organization of Ideas

Poor organization of ideas is a barrier that stems from lack of planning and preparation. Nothing is more irritating to a receiver than a message that lacks coherence and logical reasoning. When a message is poorly organized, it reflects on the sender's ability to develop and structure an idea. The receiver may question this ability and may even lose interest in the intent of the message. Generally, poor organizational skills make the sender appear to ramble without a clear purpose. Thus, the purpose should be defined clearly at the outset. Once the purpose has been established, an outline should be prepared that identifies the main points in a logical arrangement that you wish to cover. This process should be followed whether you are writing a letter or report or even preparing to make a telephone call.

Differences in Perception

Perceptual differences arise in a communication situation to which an individual brings his or her own frame of reference. Individuals' frames of reference consist of meanings they assign to people or situations. These meanings are based on their past experiences and often are related to their own interests. For example, through experience you may favor a particular microcomputer system. This predisposition may become a problem if the client or receiver has a different preference. You must attempt to see the client's point of view and to exercise an empathetic attitude. Recognize that differences will occur and take the time to listen carefully to the client's reasoning before jumping to conclusions.

Prejudice or Bias

Prejudice or bias exists when an individual has a strong opinion about something and a tendency not to change this opinion regardless of what is said. Since such individuals often encounter information that does not support their feeling or position, they establish illogical defense mechanisms. Consequently, the use of logical reasoning with these individuals is counterproductive. You should remember not to denounce overtly the position of an individual with strong prejudices. Try to explain things clearly and logically and refrain from trying to influence this individual without first trying to understand the situation from his or her perspective.

Personality Conflicts

No one will question the importance of having a pleasant personality. A good personality coupled with the ability and aptitude to complete an engagement are essential to a successful consultant. What happens when personalities differ or are in conflict? Problems can arise and communication can be affected. Conflict may be triggered because of a first impression or because of the role an individual is playing or the reputation of that individual. It is important to remember that personality differences cannot be changed. You should try to learn as much as possible about the client's personality and modify your behavior accordingly.

Tendency Not to Listen

Of all the communication activities—which include reading, writing, speaking, and listening—you will probably spend the majority of your communicating time listening. Research indicates that the typical individual after hearing a speech will forget about 50 percent of the speech by the next day. A few weeks later, that same individual will have forgotten 25 percent more. Thus, ineffective listening can have a considerable impact upon retention. Determine whether you are listening effectively by answering some questions regarding your listening skills. Figure 5.4 contains a list of questions that will provide feedback on your ability to listen effectively.

To improve your listening ability, you should listen attentively, carefully, objectively, and empathetically to the speaker. Be patient and try not to jump to conclusions. Put your emotions aside and concentrate on the message, not on the speaker's mannerisms. Encourage the speaker through actions that show you believe what the speaker has to say is important. Question the speaker or paraphrase a point for clarification. This action conveys interest on your part. A last point to remember is that you cannot listen effectively when you are talking. The role of a consultant is to gather information and seek clarification in identifying problems. What better way is there to accomplish this task than to practice effective listening skills?

Figure 5.4 List of listening effectiveness questions.

Question	Yes	No
1. Do you maintain eye contact while listening?	_____	_____
2. Do you pay attention to the speaker's feelings as well as to what is being said?	_____	_____
3. Do you lack interest in the speaker's subject?	_____	_____
4. Do you often become impatient with the speaker?	_____	_____
5. Do you overreact to certain language, such as slang or profanity?	_____	_____
6. Do you often ask questions or paraphrase for clarification?	_____	_____
7. Do you often daydream or become preoccupied with something else while listening?	_____	_____
8. Do you concentrate on the speaker's mannerisms?	_____	_____
9. Do you have a tendency to disagree or argue with the speaker?	_____	_____
10. Do you try to maintain a relaxing and agreeable environment?	_____	_____
11. Do you often jump to conclusions before the speaker has finished?	_____	_____
12. Do you often interrupt the speaker with your point of view?	_____	_____
13. Do you put yourself in the speaker's shoes (i.e., do you empathize)?	_____	_____
14. Do you often become distracted by noise from office equipment, telephones, or other conversations?	_____	_____
15. Do you try to relate to and benefit from the speaker's ideas?	_____	_____
16. Do you have difficulty reading the speaker's nonverbal cues?	_____	_____
17. Do you often listen only for details?	_____	_____
18. Do you often think of another topic because of what the speaker has said?	_____	_____
19. Do you allow your biases and prejudices to hamper your thinking while listening?	_____	_____
20. Do you often become emotional because of what the speaker has said?	_____	_____
21. Do you listen even if the subject is complex or difficult?	_____	_____
22. Do you feel that listening takes too much time?	_____	_____

Resistance to Change

To maintain a successful business firm, management must adapt continually to meet the varying needs of its customers and employees. Generating change within individuals, including concerned managers, however, is generally a difficult task. Individuals have a natural tendency to resist change when it is perceived as a threat to their work, and this tendency can affect communication. In a consulting situation, resistance to change can affect the client's managers and the employees. You should seek the support of the client and its employees and encourage their input regarding the proposed change. If change is recommended, explain it in a positive manner in order to reduce their anxieties: say clearly why the change is going to be made and how it is going to affect them individually. By being open and by encouraging participation, you will provide a better climate for implementing change.

Lack of Credibility

Credibility, or believability, is necessary to success in the consulting field. When a consultant lacks credibility, problems occur and communication can be affected. How does one establish credibility? The first way is by gaining expertise or competence in the field. Your confidence can be dampened when your ability is in doubt. Credibility can be influenced by reputation and personality. Reputation comes from experience and status, while personality can be developed. Effective consultants are likable; they get along well with people. The consultant's degree of credibility can affect the receiver's attitude or belief regarding the information conveyed in a message.

Inability to Understand Nonverbal Communication

As a consultant, you need to remember that there are other means of message communication besides the written or spoken word. The old adage that says actions speak louder than words is important in the consulting environment. If you say one thing and do something else, your words and actions are in conflict and communication can be misinterpreted. Individuals observe and pay attention to your actions, especially when they contradict what is said.

You should be aware of various nonverbal clues that, if read properly, will aid in message understanding and interpretation. Being aware of an individual's facial expressions, posture, gestures, tone of voice, eye contact, and even silence can help you to read meaning into a message. For example, you explain a particular procedure to a client and then ask the client whether he or she understands. The client shakes his or her head yes, but at the same time looks puzzled. Does the client really understand the procedure? Upon sensing this confusion, you should probe with specific questions in order to determine if the procedure is really understood.

Hostile Attitude

Clients' employees often exhibit hostility toward consultants. Bad experience with a consultant in the past could have created these hostile feelings. Or an individual may have hostile feelings toward the consultant because he or she perceives a threat: You (as the consultant) may suggest changes to the current work environment. Regardless of the reason, a hostile attitude is difficult to change. Try to approach the situation in a friendly and self-controlled manner. Do not get upset, because this reaction will only confirm the individual's suspicions and create even more hostile feelings. Convey an attitude of caring and support and encourage a cooperative environment.

Lack of Feedback

As illustrated earlier in this chapter, the feedback loop completes the communication process. Effective communication is a two-way process. Whether you are giving instructions, explaining a task, or training an employee, feedback is crucial to message understanding. Encourage feedback by asking questions that require explanation. Also ask the individual to repeat or paraphrase what was just presented so that you can determine the extent of understanding. By encouraging feedback, you will create an open and supportive climate.

Inappropriate Physical Appearance

Although sometimes taken for granted, one's physical appearance can affect communication. A well-groomed and well-dressed individual conveys an orderly and organized manner. Wearing the latest styles may not be the way to impress a client. Dress conservatively and wear clothes that convey a professional attitude.

Differences in Status or Position

Status or position differences can affect communication because the person in the inferior role usually becomes intimidated. He or she becomes nervous and reluctant to communicate. Individuals in the inferior role may fear that what they say will have a negative effect on the superior. The individual in the higher status role should try to create an atmosphere of openness by encouraging others to talk about themselves and their interests freely. If you as consultant have the higher status role, you should try to reduce the fear of those with lower status and secure their goodwill. Be friendly and cordial. This approach will open the lines of communication.

Information Overload

Any individual has a limit when dealing with information. Exceeding this limit can hamper further communication of information. You should be aware of the climate developed as a result of new job pressures and increased reporting requirements. Try to guide clients and employees by helping them manage their time, set priorities, and delegate work responsibilities to others. Do not approach anyone who for the moment appears to be overloaded with work. An idea may be rejected, no matter how ingenious it is, because it is perceived as requiring even more work for an overloaded individual. Exercise good judgment and timing when confronted with this situation.

WRITTEN COMMUNICATIONS

The ability to write effectively is an important skill for a consultant to develop. When the written word is unclear, much time and even money may be wasted. Basic principles of effective writing can be learned; all it takes is discipline and practice. Regardless of whether one is writing a letter or a report, follow these principles:

- Analyze the audience.
- Determine the purpose.
- Organize the message.
- Use a proper style.

Analyze the Audience

Consultants face a diversity of information requirements from their clients. Consequently, they often deliver information that is not exactly what the clients require. The reason for this problem is insufficient consideration of the needs and perception of the receivers. You should never lose sight of the receivers (i.e., audience), toward whom the communication should always be directed. One way of analyzing the audience is by answering several questions concerning the receivers' needs:

- Who are the receivers?
- What information do they need?
- When do they need the information?
- Where do they need the information?
- Why do they need the information?
- What are the receivers' educational levels?
- What kind of related experiences have they had?
- What are their attitudes toward the topic?

Gathering information about the audience will help in determining what content and how much detail will be needed. When writing to a lay person who may not have sufficient background in the subject, you should probably include additional information to help clarify and explain some of the topics covered. In addition, define any words or terms that may be unfamiliar to this individual. The best place to define a term is upon first use in the narrative of the message.

Determine the Purpose

Every written communication should have a definite and clear purpose statement describing what the writer intends to accomplish. This purpose statement should be appropriately limited rather than broad. In report writing, one way of limiting a purpose statement is to answer the who, what, when, where, and why of a problem. For example, assume that you were hired to determine whether a new computer system would be feasible for an automotive parts store in Los Angeles. The answers to these questions, together with a statement that can be drawn from the answers, will provide guidance and direction:

Who:	Top Quality Automotive Parts
What:	A study of a new computer system
When:	Within the next year
Where:	Los Angeles
Why:	To determine the feasibility of implementing a new computer system

Purpose statement: Is it feasible for Top Quality Automotive Parts of Los Angeles to implement a new computer within the next year?

When you are writing a letter or memorandum, you need to determine whether its purpose is to persuade or convince a client of the services a consultant offers, to request routine information, or to enumerate what was agreed to for an engagement. In other words, you need to establish what is (are) the main objective(s) of the message.

Organize the Message

Once the purpose has been identified, you need to structure the message in a logical sequence that will fulfill the purpose. One way to begin giving structure to a message is to identify certain factors, criteria, or characteristics. These factors are an extension of your purpose, and they provide the framework for an outline. This approach is particularly important in report writing.

To illustrate, assume that you are engaged in the review and evaluation of a computerized banking system. After the data collection and analysis phase, a report describing the results of the engagement is to be prepared. The following pattern could be followed in preparing this report:

I. Introduction
    A. Purpose of the project
    B. Scope of the project
    C. Methods of data collection

II. Findings
    A. User satisfaction
    B. Efficient use of computer and people resources
    C. Administrative procedures

III. Conclusions

IV. Recommendations
    A. Management controls
    B. Staff and equipment
    C. Business planning

This pattern or outline could be used first as a writing outline and eventually as paragraph headings in the final report. An important point to remember is that the findings should answer the questions posed in the purpose statement for the project. The conclusion and/or recommendations are based on the findings. Organizing a report in this manner will allow the readers to follow logically the message of the report from the introduction to the recommendations.

The pattern or plan you should follow when writing letters or memoranda depends again on the purpose or nature of the correspondence. Three plans—direct, indirect, and persuasive—can be used to cover most correspondence writing.

The direct plan is used when you want to communicate favorable news. Some examples are a routine request, a favorable response to a request, an order for goods or services, understanding or confirmation of the requirements of an engagement, and a goodwill message. When the message is favorable, use the following direct plan:

1. Come right to the point with the main message.
2. Provide supporting facts that explain any details, concerns, or circumstances that deal with the message.
3. Close with a goodwill statement.

When desiring to communicate unfavorable news, you use the indirect plan. Refusing a request for information or assistance and refusing a claim on goods or services are examples. The following plan should be used when sending an unfavorable message:

1. Open with a neutral or buffer statement that centers on something positive.
2. Give reasons for the refusal.
3. Refuse.
4. Suggest an alternative or substitute if possible.
5. Close with a goodwill statement.

If you need to persuade or convince someone about selling goods, services, or ideas, use a persuasive plan. The persuasive plan is as follows, and a letter example illustrating this plan is shown in Figure 5.5.

1. Open with an attention-getting statement.
2. Create interest in the subject.
3. Develop a desire in the subject.
4. Close with an action request.

The proposal, though usually placed in a letter format, is a persuasive report that essentially identifies problems that need to be solved and suggests ways to solve them. A possible format that can be used is:

1. Problem definition
2. Purpose of the project
3. Scope of the project
4. Role of the firm and client
5. Benefits of the engagement
6. Approach to carry out engagement
7. Interim reporting requirements (status reports)
8. Personnel
9. Fees
10. Time schedule

Because each engagement is unique, proposals will vary with respect to the number of items included and the order of their presentation. However, the above format should provide you with a guide for preparing proposals. An example of a proposal letter containing many of these items appears in Chapter 10.

Thompson & Thompson
134 Main Street
Buffalo, NY 14207

March 15, 1985

Mr. Joe Williams
Williams and Smith, P.C.
65 Court Street
Buffalo, NY 14205

Dear Joe:

With the advent of the small business computer, privately held businesses have access to computer capability unavailable a few years ago. Implementing a business computer can improve productivity and help a company address current challenges, such as competition, cash flow, government reporting requirements, and the information explosion. Companies have increasingly enhanced their effectiveness by implementing computerized accounting and operational business systems.

Small business computers today are referred to as ''microcomputers,'' ''minicomputers,'' ''home computers,'' and ''small business systems.'' The distinction among them is very blurred and there are a host of vendors offering a vast array of hardware and software products. Some of these vendors offer a genuine contribution to the industry and others simply come into existence only to disappear a few years later. For the potential computer system buyer, the end result can be confusion.

The process of acquiring and implementing an effective business computer system does not have to be a traumatic experience. By emloying a systematic and methodical approach to the evaluation, selection, and implementation of computer hardware and software, significant problems can be avoided. Thompson & Thompson has developed tools and techniques that can be of assistance when you implement a new or additional business system. I believe we are one of Buffalo's leaders in this area.

Figure 5.5 Example of a persuasive letter.

Currently, I am director of the Management Consulting department for Thompson & Thompson in Buffalo. I have extensive experience designing and implementing computer based business systems. I was with Strategic Instruments, Inc., a computer services firm, prior to joining Thompson & Thompson. I have conducted workshops for the business community to provide participants with a basic and practical background for using computers in small and medium size companies.

I have recently completed projects for a number of Buffalo companies assisting in the evaluation, selection and implementation of a business computer. The types of companies include: manufacturing, distribution, services, construction, health care, and publishing. The approach to a project usually includes:

   a) Defining information requirements
   b) Issuing a Request for Proposal to selected vendors
   c) Preparing a comparative analysis
   d) Recommending the best alternative

If you are considering acquiring a business computer or implementing a new or additional business system, I can provide professional advice. An independent, objective viewpoint combined with extensive EDP experience can ensure that you select the right business computer. Please call so that we can discuss your computer system requirements further.

Sincerely,

Peter Barber
Director, Management Consulting

Figure 5.5   *(Continued)*

Use a Proper Style

A suitable style for business writing employs short and simple words and sentences of varying lengths (with an average length of 20 words or less). The overall effect should usually be conversational, i.e., informal, in tone, though overused expressions should be avoided. In other words, you should write as you would converse, using the first and second person pronouns and easy-to-understand words. Most business situations do not require a style as formal as that employed in this handbook.

One sign of a good writing style is the avoidance of imbalanced construction, wordiness, the passive voice, and nominalization. These problems and suggestions for correcting them are presented below.

Imbalanced construction.   Thoughts and ideas appearing in consecutive phrases and not in balance with each other are poorly constructed. Ideas and thoughts, and the grammar used to express them, should be constructed in parallel (i.e., in balance with each other). Here are some examples of imbalanced and parallel construction:

Incorrect: Emphasis in the definition of requirements step will be on documentation procedures, looking for enhancements, and an assessment of where automation might be applicable.

Correct: Emphasis in the definition of requirements step will be on *documenting* procedures, *looking* for enhancements, and *assessing* where automation may be applicable.

Incorrect headings in a report:
  I.   System requirements
  II. Vendor proposal
  III. Review of final contract

Correct headings in a report:
  I.   System requirements
  II. Vendor proposal
  III. Final contract

Wordiness.   This is a problem of using too many words to express an idea when fewer words could be used without influencing the meaning. Some examples of wordiness and concise alternatives are:

Wordy	Concise
according to our records	we find
are of the opinion that	believe, think
at this point in time	now
despite the fact that	though
fully cognizant of	aware
in accordance with your request	as you requested
in the amount of	for
in view of the fact that	because, since
inquired as to	asked
pursuant to our agreement	as we agreed
with reference to	about
with respect to	about

Passive voice.   Use of passive voice dulls the verb in a sentence, and the doer of the action is usually placed in a prepositional phase. For more lively writing use the active voice, in which the doer of the action is the subject of the sentence. Passive voice is not wrong, but its overuse can make your writing less forceful. Here are some examples:

Passive: The procedures *were followed* by the clients.
Active: The clients followed the procedures.

Passive: The systems analysis *was conducted* by our firm.

Active: Our firm conducted the systems analysis.

Nominalization.   Nominalization occurs when you change a verb into its noun form. Also, such sentences often require the passive voice. Some examples of nominalization are:

Weak: *Cancellation* of the engagement was effected by the client.

Strong: The client canceled the engagement.

Weak: An *investigation* of the new system was conducted by the controller.

Strong: The controller investigated the new system.

Note that by avoiding nominalization, you use an active verb form and eliminate excess words. In addition, you might consider using personal pronouns when the doer of the action is not identified; for example:

Weak: *Completion* of the new system was accomplished.

Strong: They completed the new system.

ORAL COMMUNICATIONS

In addition to effective written communication skills, a consultant needs to develop skills in various forms of oral communication. You will be faced with many situations that require you to conduct interviews, lead problem-solving conferences, and make oral presentations.

Conducting Interviews

The first type of interview involves meeting with a prospective client and determining his or her needs prior to the engagement. The second type involves gathering necessary information from the client and his or her employees once the engagement begins. No matter what the type of interview, you need to learn as much as possible about the interviewee. In other words, you need to analyze the audience prior to the interview. This aspect begins in the preparation phase. Answer the questions posed earlier in the audience analysis section of this chapter. Try to learn as much as possible about the interviewee before the interview. This gives you a better perspective of the interviewee and serves as an excellent way to establish rapport at the beginning of the interview.

Another task to complete prior to the interview is determining the purpose for meeting with the individual. Prepare a series of questions that relate to the purpose. Answers to these questions will provide the facts necessary for your analysis. The questions should serve as a guide to keep the interview from lacking structure. Remember that they are only a guide and should not restrict the use of other related questions once the interview begins.

After learning about the interviewee, structuring questions, and arranging an interview place and time, you are ready to begin the interview. Schedule it for no more than an hour. If more time is needed, schedule a second interview. Remember to start with a friendly chat to establish a positive and cooperative atmosphere. The more comfortable the interviewee, the more open and candid he or she will be during the interview. Be sure to explain the interview's purpose, method or structure, and perhaps even expected outcome. Be tactful and objective and expect some resistance, especially from the client's employees. Be mindful of the types of barriers discussed earlier in this chapter. Listen well and empathize with the interviewee. He or she may be nervous. When taking notes during the interview, try not be obvious and do not write down everything the interviewee says. The interviewee can become cautious, suspicious, and defensive.

Once the interview is over, summarize the results. By reviewing your notes, you can clarify, check for accuracy, or even expand on some points. Remember, the interviewee will be concerned about what was written. Close on a positive note and always keep the lines of communication open; you may have to interview this individual again later in the engagement.

Leading Problem-Solving Conferences

Once all the data have been gathered and analyzed by each consultant participating in the engagement, it is likely that all the participants will meet to discuss the findings and arrive at possible solutions to the problems. To arrive at the desired end results in a conference, you need to plan and prepare carefully.

If you are serving as group leader, you need to identify the purpose(s) of the conference. Determine the points or topics that need to be covered and perhaps prepare an agenda. This agenda should be sent to the participants so they too can prepare adequately for the conference. You must direct the meeting and maintain control. You need to create an atmosphere in which each participant feels free to express his or her ideas or opinions regarding the topic. Encourage involvement by asking open and leading questions. After an idea has been presented, give proper feedback. Recognize a good idea, but also expect to give and receive constructive criticism if an idea needs improvement. Remember, the success of a conference depends on giving all the participants an opportunity to express their ideas clearly.

Listen carefully and be sure to discuss one point or topic at a time. Try to arrive at a solution to one problem before going to the next item. Summarizing what has been said after one item has been discussed is a good technique to use. This technique allows you to be sure that you understand the appropriate course of action, and it allows the participants to check the correctness of solutions. Close on a positive note by thanking all participants for their contributions.

Making Oral Presentations

Perhaps one of the tasks consultants dread most is making an oral presentation. Whether you are presenting a formal proposal or conducting a training session, the task can be made easier if you spend enough time preparing and practicing for the presentation. Therefore, the following discussion will concentrate on preparing, practicing, and giving the presentation.

The first step you need to take in the preparation stage is determining the purpose of the presentation: to propose a new system, present findings, and so forth. Your analysis of the audience is the next step in a successful presentation. Review the audience analysis questions that were listed earlier in the chapter. Note the planned date of the presentation as well as how long it should take. Once you have completed this step, gather information or review the material previously gathered at the engagement. Be sure that the information is accurate, complete, and pertinent to the audience. Prepare an outline, from introduction to conclusions and/or recommendations. If a proposal or final report has been sufficiently written, either item can often provide the structure you will follow.

The opening should be something more than, "My presentation today is about. . . . " You should capture the audience's attention. Take a possible benefit and turn it into a question for the opening. Follow with other related questions or comments. This approach will set the stage for the major points to be expanded in the body of the presentation. This section should contain all the main points and be organized with the most important items first. Plan to include transition statements; these make the presentation flow smoothly from one point to another. The conclusion should summarize and reinforce the major points.

While preparing the outline, you should also write down possible questions the audience may have about the material. Whether you decide to entertain questions during or after the presentation, having these ready beforehand will give you more confidence in handling this important part of the presentation. You might also note, on the outline, places where you may want to use a visual aid. Marking these spots clearly on the outline will remind you when to show the visuals.

Perhaps the one technique that clearly separates a good speaker from an excellent speaker is practice. If you know the material well and if you practice, you can eliminate stage fright. When practicing, try to simulate the actual presentation. Speak aloud and practice while standing. Ask a colleague to listen to the presentation, and seek his or her feedback. Try to find out the type of room you will be using. If possible, go and see it. Having this information will help you visualize the actual presentation and reduce the anxiety of speaking in an unfamiliar location.

When the time has arrived to give the presentation, approach it with confidence. Remember to define terms during the presentation that might be unfamiliar to the audience. Keep the audience feedback in mind. If people seem puzzled or confused, perhaps rephrase the points made previously. If they start to get restless, maybe it is time to take a break. When using visual aids, you should be sure that they help clarify and support the points. They should be easily read and understood and not contain too much detail. They should flow naturally during the presentation. Remember to speak toward the audience while referring to the visual: The projection of your voice will be affected if you face the visual rather than the audience.

When preparing visual aids, whether for oral or written reports, you might consider using computer graphics. Although there are several graphics packages that run on large computer systems, consider one of the many microcomputer graphics packages. A list of some popular microcomputer graphics software packages, along with their vendors, is presented in Figure 5.6. Depending upon the package, you can create virtually any type of graph: everything from the basic bar, line, or pie graph to a time or flow chart. Not only can the microcomputer prepare prints for reports or handouts, it can also generate transparencies and 35-mm slides with appropriate attachments. In addition, color and hatchings can be used to add more emphasis to the visual.

Although nothing helps a speaker more than practicing, consider the following when making an oral presentation:

- Relax.
- Be optimistic and enthusiastic.
- Speak loudly and slowly.
- Use an outline (don't read notes).
- Use a variety of sentences.
- Avoid fillers (ah, um, you know, etc.).
- Use a conversational tone.
- Use gestures for emphasis.
- Use proper body movement.
- Maintain eye contact.

- Have proper posture.
- Vary pace and volume.
- Use visual aids.
- Stop on time.

Software package	Vendor
1-2-3	Lotus Development Corp.
Accuchart	Big Tree Software
Apple III Business Graphics	Apple Computer, Inc.
BPS Business Graphics	Business and Professional Software
Business Graphics Package	Convergent Technologies
Business Graphics Systems	Peachtree Software
Chartman Series	Graphic Systems, Inc.
Chart-Master	Decision Resources
Chartstar	MicroPro
Condor Graf	Condor Computer Corp.
dGraph III	Fox & Geller, Inc.
DR Graph	Digital Research
Ener Graphics	Enertonics Research, Inc.
Fast Graphs	Innovative Software, Inc.
GL/M	Selva Systems, Inc.
Graph 'n' Calc	Desktop Computer Software, Inc.
GraphPower	Ferox Microsystems, Inc.
Graphwriter	Graphic Communication
Infographics Choice	Infographics, Inc.
MicroChart	MicroSoft
PC Illustrator	Computer Graphics Group, Inc.
PFS: Graph	Software Publishing Corp.
Prime Plotter	PrimeSoft Corp.
Visiplot, Visitrend/Plot	VisiCorp

Figure 5.6   List of microcomputer graphics software packages.

All these points are extremely important to becoming an effective speaker. There is one item that can be added to the list when applicable, and that is the use of humor. Humor is effective when used in an appropriate and timely manner. A humorous anecdote or story that relates to the material can aid in establishing rapport, in easing tensions, and in providing a more informal tone to the presentation. Humor should never be used at the expense of the audience. Never try to capitalize on something humorous that happened during the engagement if it could embarrass a member of the audience. Always remember to use good taste and common sense when considering humor in any presentation.

2

Analytical Elements of the Consulting Process

6

Problem Definition

MICHAEL E. DAVIS
Avco Aerostructures Corporation
Nashville, Tennessee

Problem definition is the first phase of the problem-solving process. Its position in the problem-solving process is well established. The term *problem definition* assumes a variety of meanings, however, since it is used by numerous persons in reference to a wide variety of problem-solving situations. Each person has his or her particular view of the manner by which problems are approached, defined, and solved. Each problem-solving situation has its particular set of conditions and constraints. Due to such differing conceptual frameworks and circumstances, our initial concern is to establish standard definitions.

DEFINITIONS

How may a problem be defined? When a system or process behaves as expected, allowing for suitable tolerances, no problem exists. A problem arises only when behavior moves out of the range that an observer would normally view as being reasonable in the circumstances. Thus, a problem may be said to exist when the observed behavior of a system or process violates the bounds of reasonable expectations.

This definition of a problem requires the presence of several factors: human awareness of the problem, predefinition of the allowable tolerances, and recognition of the established standards.

First, a problem requires that involved humans be aware of the implications of the existing situation. A system or process may be beyond the bounds of reasonable expectations; if no one recognizes this condition, however, no problem (and hence no correctable solution) is truly apparent.

Second, a problem requires that the tolerances be predefined, where tolerances are the allowed deviations or variances from the ideal situation. Unless the tolerances are predefined, no one can determine when the system or process is beyond the bounds of reasonable expectations.

The tolerances that determine the existence of a problem must be established by humans, rather than by the system or process itself. For example, consider the allowable tolerances pertaining to a machined part. They are established by humans to accord with the ultimate use of the part. If they were to be established to accommodate the capabilities of the machine on which they are processed, the resulting part might not be fit for its intended purpose. To take another example, consider the tolerances related to processes in a service-oriented organization. These tolerances should be established in accordance with client or consumer expectations, rather than by the costs of the processes or the whims of the processors. Thus, the processing of any document received by a governmental agency from an applicant should reflect, in terms of time and service, the expectations of the applicant. If the applicant perceives the processing to be slow and the service to be poor, the agency can be said to have a problem.

Establishment of suitable tolerances deserves the careful attention of judicious individuals. Sometimes tolerances can be established by clear guidelines—such as contracts with customers, engineering blueprints, or procedures manuals. Often, however, they must be established on the basis of unclear and inexact guidelines—such as fuzzily written governmental regulations or vague oral statements from top management. Also, the range of allowable tolerances may vary considerably. For instance, the allowable tolerances of machined parts for toys may be much greater than those of machined parts for spaceships.

A third factor in a problem situation concerns the recognition by observers of the tolerances, and hence the expectations or standards. Quantitative standards, such as sales quotas and budget levels, are easily recognized, as are variations of actual values from these standards. Qualitative standards are not so easily recognized, even though they are pervasive in the realms of human relationships and human-oriented processes. Qualitative standards appear as written and oral rules promulgated by official bodies, as unwritten traditions of work groups comprising informal organizations, and as observed regularities. Standards such as these, especially the observed regularities, are expressed as much by actions as by words.

PHASES OF A PROBLEM-SOLVING PROCESS

Most engagements undertaken by consultants will involve the solution of problems. Hence, a process that emphasizes the solution of problems is of great interest to a consultant. A sound problem-solving process consists of four phases: (1) the problem definition phase, (2) the fact-finding and analysis phase, (3) the solution development phase, and (4) the implementation phase. Each phase has one or more distinct purposes and occupies a separate time period within the overall process. The set of phases demonstrates a sequential and hierarchical pattern, in that (1) each phase (except the first) follows a previous phase along a time dimension and (2) each phase builds upon the results of its predecessors. Figure 6.1 depicts the four phases of the problem-solving process.

Problem Definition Phase

The problem definition phase has the purpose of fully describing the underlying problem. It begins with the initial recognition of a symptom pointing to the problem and ends with the complete problem description. Key facets of the problem description include:

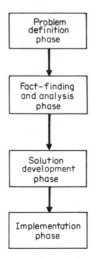

Figure 6.1   Four phases of the problem-solving process.

Identity of the problem

Objectives of the problem-solving process

Scope of the problem

Intensity of the problem

Time dimensions of the problem

Location of the problem

Human elements involved in the problem

Support system surrounding the problem

Tracking system related to the problem

Institutional process for managing the problem

Figure 6.2 shows these aspects of the problem definition phase.

Fact-Finding and Analysis Phase

The fact-finding and analysis phase has the purposes of gathering facts needed to solve the problem and analyzing these facts in order to clarify the requirements of the best solution. Often this second phase overlaps with the problem definition phase in that it helps to sort the symptoms from the underlying causes of the problem. In addition, this phase may identify the resources capable of steering the defined problem situation in the direction of a desired solution. Furthermore, it should serve as a get-acquainted period, during which the consultant can gain the cooperation and commitment of persons who are affected by the problem situation and will be affected by its solution.

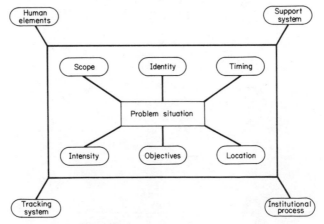

Figure 6.2   Facets of the problem-definition phase.

Solution Development Phase

The solution development phase has the purposes of selecting the optimal solution to the problem and developing a detailed plan of action. This plan of action should include the rationale for its selection, expressed in terms of benefits and advantages, the schedule for its installation, and the needed resources.

Implementation Phase

The implementation phase has the purpose of putting the detailed plan into operation. If the previous phases have been performed well, this phase should be the least difficult in logical terms. Nevertheless, it may exhibit a high degree of logistic complexity. Numerous activities may need to be meshed together smoothly. Also, minor deviations to the plan are sure to be imposed, and changed circumstances in the environment are certain to occur. In some situations, the deviations and changes may become so great that it will be necessary to recycle back to previous phases.

The second, third, and fourth phases of the problem-solving process will be discussed at length in the three following chapters.

FACETS OF THE PROBLEM DEFINITION PHASE

Now we are ready to focus in detail on the facets of the problem definition phase. Thorough attention to this phase is vital to the success of the problem-solving process. As we suggested earlier, it is the foundation upon which the following phases are built. A solid foundation is especially important if the problem situation is complex and numerous factors are interrelated.

This phase is vital for another reason. All problems cannot be solved or corrected. In some cases the cost of the solution is larger than the benefits that might reasonably be expected. In other cases the solution may create another problem. For instance, correcting the problem of high production costs may cause a problem with respect to product quality. Problems in cases such as these can only be controlled within certain limits. A thorough problem definition phase will probably detect this type of problem, thereby saving the time and expense of conducting the following phases.

Identity of the Problem

What is the problem? This should be the first question asked and last question that you, as a consultant, answer during the problem definition phase. An acceptable final answer can emerge only after the completion of two procedures: problem finding and problem stating. A comprehensive answer will incorporate the several facets to be discussed in following sections. A valid answer will avoid the variety of pitfalls that await the unwary consultant.

Problem finding.   The problem-finding procedure begins with identification of the (1) reasonable expectations pertaining to a system or process and (2) allowable tolerances from these reasonable expectations. It continues with the comparison of actual conditions against these expectations. The last step is the flagging of conditions that exceed the allowable tolerances from reasonable expectations.

An example of the problem-finding procedure, especially familiar to accountants, is the operation of a standard cost accounting system. The first step is to establish (1) standards for unit direct materials and unit direct labor costs and (2) allowable variances from these standards. Periodically, the actual unit direct materials and direct labor costs are compared with these standards. Variances that exceed the allowable ranges are flagged for the attention of production management.

As described above, problem finding is often reactive in nature. That is, it addresses problems as they are detected. Problem finding can also be opportunistic. Opportunistic scanning consists of searching for beneficial opportunities to exploit. This aggressive approach seeks to improve the system or process, thereby reaping added dividends. For example, a consultant may note that installing a computer information system could improve customer service, thus increasing sales and profits. Opportunistic scanning as well as reactive problem finding can and should be ongoing activities.

Problem stating.   As early as possible in the phase, the consultant should prepare an initial written statement of the problem. This initial statement may be relatively inexact and based on intuitive, "gut" hunches. Nevertheless, it represents a tangible starting point and should not be overlooked.

The final tangible result of the problem definition phase will be a comprehensive and, it is hoped, valid statement of the problem. It may represent an expanded and polished version of the initial statement. Alternatively, it may bear scant resemblance to the initial statement, if the initial statement is found to be faulty or superficial.

Statement content.   The final statement of the problem should contain such facets as the objectives to be achieved by the solution to the problem; the problem's scope, intensity, time dimensions, and location;

the human elements involved in the problem; the support system and tracking systems related to the problem solution; and the institutional process for managing the problem. In addition, the statement may clearly separate the symptoms from the underlying causes of the problem, identify relevant constraints, and reveal key relationships among the factors involved in the problem situation.

Pitfalls in identifying the problem. Identifying the real problem will undoubtedly require patient and exacting investigation if the problem situation is complex. Possible pitfalls include the following:

1. *Mistaking symptoms for the underlying problem:* Symptoms are the effects, rather than the causes, of the problem. While they may point to the presence of the problem, they should not be viewed as the core of the problem itself. For example, scrap from milling machine operations is a symptom. The underlying problem may be a worn cutter, a bad bearing, or an alcoholic operator. Each of these problems may, in turn, be the symptoms of deeper problems. Thus, a worn cutter or bad bearing may be the result of postponed preventive maintenance caused by budget cutbacks. You should continue searching and probing until you are satisfied that the root causes of the problem have been uncovered.

2. *Accepting without question the opinions of others concerning the problem:* A consultant will necessarily talk with various managers and employees of the client organization in order to gather facts concerning the problem. Because these managers and employees are closely involved in the situation, you may give their opinions considerable weight. However, the managers and employees may be too close to the situation to see the real problem clearly. Sometimes their biases will color their views of the problem situation. You should, therefore, suspend early judgment with respect to such opinions. You should not be in a hurry to conclude the problem-finding procedure. Instead, you should ask probing questions such as: Why do you believe that? What experiences lead you to that opinion? When did the most recent incident (accident) occur? Furthermore, you should actively search for facts that either support or deny the opinions.

3. *Assuming that the problem is a person:* Problems can be due to the behavior or nonbehavior of people, but problems are not the people themselves. It can be dangerous to personalize problems. You, as consultant, may feel obliged to make personal attacks on the individuals involved in order to support your recommendations. Actions such as these are likely to create other, equally serious, problems.

4. *"Slaying the bearer of bad news":* Another way of personalizing

problems is to confuse the messenger of news with the news itself. That is, you might view a manager who tells you of a problem to be the cause of that problem. If your questions or comments reveal this attitude, the manager is apt to "clam up." As a result, you could lose the source of vital information concerning the problem and perhaps its solution.

5. *Overlooking the multicausality of problems:* Multiple symptoms may point to a single problem. Likewise, a problem or problem situation may be due to multiple causes. For instance, declining net income is a problem that generally has more than a single cause. It might be due in part to weakening sales and in part to rising labor costs. Problems such as high employee turnover and poor customer service are also usually due to a combination of causal factors.

All the underlying causes of a problem should be isolated and clearly stated. A comprehensive statement of causes has two benefits. It provides more points of attack, so that a more effective solution is likely to be developed. Also, it may help uncover key interrelationships among the causal factors.

Objectives of the Problem-Solving Process

The objective of the problem-solving process is the desired outcome. It should be prominently expressed in the problem definition statement, generally in terms of clear-cut expectations or benefits. Preferably the objective or objectives should be expressed quantitatively and with respect to a designated time horizon. For instance, an objective might be stated as follows: "To increase the percent of on-time deliveries, so that by the end of this year 99 percent of all deliveries are made on time." Objectives expressed in this fashion should enable interested parties to evaluate the effectiveness of the problem-solving process.

The nature of the objectives depends upon the type of problem, as well as the system or process involved. Typical objectives pertaining to systems and processes in business organizations are concerned with performance, efficiency, economy, control, security, or availability of information.

Scope of the Problem

The scope of the problem pertains to the extent of its effects. Thus, when defining the problem you should ask such questions as: How widespread are the effects of the problem at the present time? Are they confined to one area in a specific department? Have they spread to proximally or functionally related areas? Have they affected the markets of the firm?

A clear statement of problem scope should suggest the extent of the needed response or solution to the problem. It might also point to the need for repackaging the consulting engagement. For instance, if the scope is discovered to be immense and to extend to a variety of activities, it may be desirable to break the engagement into a series of smaller problem areas. Each partial problem can then be solved more easily, and the solutions can be combined to attack the overall problem.

The Intensity of the Problem

Another facet of the problem is its intensity—the degree of discomfort that its adverse effects cause to interested parties. For instance, the managers of a business firm may feel very intense discomfort when a new product does much more poorly than expected in the marketplace. The level of intensity may determine the relative urgency and importance of initiating a particular problem-solving process. Thus, if the president of a firm is informed of two problems, the one that exerts the greater intensity is likely to be assigned the higher priority for solution.

The Time Dimensions of the Problem

Relevent questions.   Three questions should be answered with respect to the time dimensions of a problem:

1. How long has the problem existed?
2. How much longer is the problem likely to continue if left unattended?
3. How frequently is the problem likely to occur in the future?

Answers to these questions should be included in the final statement of the problem, since they will probably have a bearing upon the development of a solution. Let us consider the effects of certain answers.

With respect to the first question, the answer may be (a) a long time or (b) a very short time. (Of course, either answer should preferably state the exact length of time.) If the problem has been in existence a long time, its adverse effects should have become quite clear. Thus, sufficient facts should be available on which to base a sound solution. If the problem has been in existence for only a very short time, a prompt solution should minimize its adverse effects. However, adequate data may not be available to provide a clear picture. The danger in prompt action is that an inappropriate solution may be developed and implemented. To avoid this danger, you may need to delay action until the adverse effects manifest themselves in several repetitions. Alternatively, you may attempt to replicate the effects of the problem in a laboratory setting, thus reducing the delay in development of a sound solution.

With respect to the second question, the answer may be (a) a brief remaining life span or (b) a lengthy remaining life span. If the expected life span is brief, the best choice may be to tolerate the problem during its short remaining tenure. If its life span will be long, it should be attended to as soon as feasible.

With respect to the expected future appearance of the problem, the answer may be (a) very infrequent or (b) very frequent. If the problem is expected to arise only once in one thousand occurrences of a recurring circumstance, an effort to solve it may not be cost-effective. If the problem is likely to arise during every other occurrence, however, an extensive effort to solve it will most likely be worthwhile.

Relationships between frequency and intensity.   There are four ways in which the frequency and intensity of a problem may be related:

1. *Low intensity and low frequency:*   A problem exhibiting these characteristics may be viewed as inconsequential.

2. *High intensity and high frequency:*   A problem having these characteristics demands an immediate solution.

3. *High intensity and low frequency:*   A problem having these characteristics requires continual monitoring. If a solution is not viewed as being urgent, a critical level of intensity should be established. As soon as this level is reached, an "all-out" effort should be made to develop and implement an immediate solution.

    A problem that exhibits high intensity and low frequency poses agonizing dilemmas. You cannot be certain when it will recur, or even that it will recur at all. Locating the causes of such a problem can be extremely difficult, since it cannot be observed with regularity. Selecting the proper course of action can be fraught with danger. On the one hand, lack of an attempt to solve the problem can result in a costly disaster if it suddenly arises in full intensity. On the other hand, an "all-out" effort to solve the problem can be very costly and politically disastrous.

4. *Low intensity and high frequency:*   A problem having these characteristics tends to be annoying but not crippling. This type of problem is exemplified by the high rework situation. Many units of product emerging from a production operation must be reworked because key dimensions are not within the tolerance limits of the specifications. Although there may be a temptation to allow the problem situation to continue, in the hope that it will correct itself, this "do-nothing" approach is generally not a wise choice. A better choice is either to

(a) correct the problem promptly or (b) set a time limit and take corrective action if the problem has not rectified itself within the allotted time span.

The Location of the Problem

The location, or locus, of the problem is the geographic point or points where it occurs. For example, a problem may be located in the Nashville plant, building 14, northwest corner, between pillars R and S. Alternatively, it may be determined to be in the accounts payable department at the Toronto home office. While in most problem situations the location can be easily determined, in some extreme situations the location may require laborious retracings of tangled paths. In every situation, however, pinpointing the location is necessary to provide a complete description of the problem.

The Human Elements of the Problem

A problem typically is associated with a host of human-related elements. Each of these elements should be identified and assessed in the statement of the problem. Examples of such elements include:

1. The training of involved employees and managers
2. The tenure of involved employees and managers
3. The attitude of involved employees and managers with respect to such matters as loyalty to the organization
4. The personal traits of involved employees and managers, including intelligence, motivation, leadership quality, dependability, trustworthiness, and interpersonal skills

Another human-related element that may often appear in the problem statement is the prevailing political climate. You should include not only an assessment of this climate, but also an assessment of the priorities that have been established by the policy-makers. This latter assessment should be based on the priorities that have been de facto applied, rather than those that may be stated in speeches or policy statements.

The Support System Surrounding the Problem

A problem is also surrounded by elements that comprise a support system. These elements should be identified in the problem statement, together with an analysis of their functional or dysfunctional effects (if any) upon the problem. For instance, an inefficient mail room procedure may be identified as a dysfunctional element with respect to a problem involving claims processing delays. A broken crane may be identified as a dysfunctional element with respect to a problem involving delays in parts shipments, while an aggressive overtime policy may be identified as a functional element that tends to minimize these delays. In some situations a support element may be found to be the sole cause of a problem, even though the support element may be located in a separate location from the problem itself.

The Tracking System Related to the Problem

A problem is often detected by a tracking system. The problem statement should reveal:

1. How the problem was brought to light
2. Whether the problem was detected by a tracking system so designed for the purpose, or by another means (if not detected by the tracking system so designed for the purpose, why the tracking system failed)
3. Whether tracking systems other than the one designed for the purpose should have detected the problem
4. Whether tracking systems are available to monitor the situation reliably, as well as to measure the degree of improvement in the process or system due to an implemented solution

The Institutional Process for Managing the Problem

Problems in an organization are managed (i.e., defined, processed, delegated, solved) via an institutional process. The process may be informal in nature, with the management tasks being assigned quickly and with little written evidence. On the other hand, it may be quite formal, involving a chain of command and such written evidence as elaborate charts and graphs. The degree of informality or formality in the institutional process may extend outside the organization structure to encompass customers, lenders, suppliers, and consultants.

As Figure 6.2 shows, the last four facets above may be viewed apart from the earlier-listed facets of the problem. They help to establish the environment or setting of the problem, as well as to identify factors that worsen or lessen the problem.

VALIDATION OF THE STATED PROBLEM DEFINITION

As the above section amply displays, a statement of a problem may be lengthy and complex. It involves many facts and certain subjective evaluations, some of which may be contradictory. How can you, as a consultant, validate such a statement?

Perhaps the first step to undertake in the validation process is to reread the statement for internal consistency. If flagrant contradictions appear, you should recheck those sections of the statement. To do so, you might interview persons whom you have not previously seen. Or, you might review additional documents and records, observe further operations, and so on.

Another validation technique is to ask another consultant to review the statement and express his or her opinion. If another consultant is assigned to the same engagement, you could compare facts that you have gathered independently. Then you could jointly evaluate the facts and develop a common problem definition statement.

CLIENT-CONSULTANT RELATIONSHIPS DURING AN ENGAGEMENT

In an consulting engagement, the consultant must maintain two key relationships. One relationship is between the consultant and the problem-solving process. The other relationship is between the consultant and the client. A harmonious relationship with the client is generally requisite to the successful conduct of the problem-solving process.

Definition of Client

Before discussing means of maintaining harmonious relationships, we need to define the term "*client*." In the broadest sense of the term, the client is the organization that engages the services of the consultant. It might be a private business firm, a governmental agency, a hospital, or a university. In a more immediate and personal sense, however, the term client refers to the individual or individuals with whom the consultant has the initial and/or ongoing contacts. This person (or persons) discusses the engagement and its progress with the consultant and, at the conclusion of the engagement, accepts the final report from the consultant. Generally, the client will be one or more of the higher-level managers or administrators of the organization. In engagements of limited scope, however, the client may consist of middle- or lower-level managers.

Of course, a consultant will need to establish relationships with other personnel of the client's organization. Among those that you, as consultant, should expect to see during a typical engagement are:

1. Managers and employees who have facts concerning the problem situation
2. Managers and employees who are likely to be affected by an implemented solution to the problem situation

3. Managers and employees who are assigned to perform tasks under your guidance
4. Managers and employees who are assigned to serve as liaison on a daily basis between you and higher-level managers or other organizational units within the support system

Guidelines for Harmonious Relationships

From the very beginning of an engagement you should aim to develop a sense of trust and openness. Since the presence of a consultant in an organization creates widespread anxiety and even fear, it is highly desirable to take specific measures to counteract this anxiety and fear and consequent hostility. These measures should have the dual effect of introducing you to the managers and employees and answering the urgent questions that have formed in their minds.

These purposes may be achieved through both written and oral means. A written announcement, prepared jointly by the client and the consultant, should be issued as soon as the terms of the engagement are settled. The announcement should be addressed to all employees and managers within the organization who are affected by the problem situation. Oral presentations should be made at meetings. Several presentations will probably be needed, since each presentation should involve a relatively small group of employees and managers from one of the affected areas, e.g., a department. At these meetings the consultant should be introduced and should be willing to answer questions concerning the engagement. Such questions may pertain, for instance, to the likely impacts of the engagement upon the responsibilities and status of the affected employees. While certain questions may need to be shunted to organization managers attending the meetings, polite and earnest responses from the consultant can establish incipient feelings of good will.

Harmonious relations can also be established through a round of get-acquainted interviews. You should obtain appointments to meet all the managers who are affected by the problem situation. During a typical interview you should chat about the responsibilities and difficulties of the manager's position. Your main goal during this initial interview should be to establish a friendly relationship. While you may introduce the subject of the engagement, it will probably not be wise to delve into its details at this time. Instead, you might mention that you would like to return for a more in-depth discussion of the problem at a later time convenient to the manager. (Of course, if the manager insists on discussing it fully at this first interview, you should be sufficiently flexible to accommodate his or her wish.)

During the engagement you should reflect an attitude of helpfulness. This attitude may be achieved in various ways. You can maintain an "open-door" policy, welcoming the questions and communications of anyone at any time. You can also arrange meetings for discussion of the problem and provide written summaries of the meetings.

A final admonition concerns the solution to the problem. You should not directly tell the client what decision to make, i.e., how to solve the problem. Instead, you should diplomatically guide the client toward the solution. For instance, you might provide copies of articles that discuss solutions by other organizations having similar problems. You might write memoranda summarizing the key factors and relationships in the problem situation, as well as possible alternative solutions. You might chair "brainstorming" sessions concerning the problem situation.

EXAMPLE INVOLVING PROBLEM DEFINITION

An example should clarify the problem definition phase. While numerous problems would serve, let us consider a problem that is common to many business firms.

Our consulting firm is engaged by the manufacturing vice president of the ABC Company, who is concerned about the excessively high level of production costs. We begin the engagement by entering the main plant and observing the work force. We find within a short time that the employees are idle a considerable portion of the time. After random counts, we determine that certain employees are idle as much as 46 percent of their total work time.

Discussion with the manufacturing vice president reveals that the current level of idle time clearly exceeds reasonable expectations. Thus, we have established the presence of a serious problem. While we need to explore the situation more deeply, we can begin to prepare the content of the problem statement.

Our first concern is the *identity* of the problem. While idle time is the symptom or manifestation of a problem, it cannot be viewed as the underlying, root problem. To determine the underlying problem or problems, we undertake more observations. These observations point to such underlying causes as lack of orders, lack of needed raw materials, lack of proper tooling, lack of time-motion and methods studies, weak production controls, and (in some departments) poor supervisory practices.

We again discuss the excessive idle time percentage with the manufacturing vice president. He states that the *objective* that the company would like to achieve in this area is as follows: to reduce idle time to 10 percent or less of total work time by the end of this year. After noting this objective in the problem statement, we consider the scope, location, intensity, and time dimension of the problem.

The *scope* of the problem pertains to the extent of its effects. In what departments is idle time manifest? Is it worse in some departments than others? In which departments does it exceed 10 percent, 20 percent, 30 percent, 40 percent? We discover that the scope of the problem spans all production departments, except the quality control department; as we suspected, idle time is higher in some departments than others.

The *location*, or locus, of the problem seems to center on the fabrication department, which has the highest level of idle time. (Note that the location of the problem is closely related to its scope. While determining the scope we also determined the central location.)

The *intensity* of the problem first can be expressed in labor hours and then equated in dollars. We discover that 300 employees are idle part of each day. The average idle time per day is 20 percent, or 1.6 hours in an 8-hour day. If the average hourly wage (plus benefits) is $10, then an average of $16 is wasted each day by each of the above employees. The total loss per day due to idle time is therefore $4800.

The *time dimensions*, or timing aspects, of the problem can be stated as follows:

1. How long has the problem been in existence? The idle time has gradually grown to its present level from an unknown beginning date.
2. How long will it endure if left alone? There is a danger that the problem will become progressively worse and endure indefinitely.
3. How frequently does it occur? It is an everyday occurrence.

With respect to the frequency-intensity matrix, the idle time problem exhibits a high-frequency and high-intensity condition. Thus, it is sufficiently serious to warrant immediate attention.

Next we turn to the environmental facets of the problem: Its *human elements* are the idle workers, their supervisors, middle management, and possibly top management. The labor union represents an additional element. Furthermore, the human elements of supporting departments—such as production control and engineering—must be included, as well as vendors who are late in delivering raw materials.

With respect to the political situation, our observations and interviews reveal that most production supervisors, aided by a few middle managers, have been covering up the problem situation. On the other hand, a few middle managers have been advocating layoffs throughout the production function. It is expected that the union will stridently oppose any attempt to increase production quotas by reducing idle time.

The *support system* consists of the quality assurance, production control, engineering, and labor relations departments. Both the quality assurance and production control departments are impacted directly by the idleness and consequent lower productivity.

The *tracking system* includes production reports pertaining to departments and individual workers; reports concerning materials movements and work flows; and reports concerning materials replacements.

The *institutional process* consists of (a) the informal actions of suppressing information flows (i.e., the cover-up) on the part of supervisors and middle managers and (b) the sparse formal information flows via the reports listed above. The recommended process for correcting the problem is to present the data concerning idle time and its consequences directly to the production department supervisors.

7

Fact Finding and Analysis

GARY GRUDNITSKI
Department of Accounting
The University of Texas
Austin, Texas

Facts are the threads that run through the fabric of the consulting process. Facts aid the consultant in sorting out client symptoms from client problems, as well as in structuring and ordering the problems. Facts form the foundation for prospective solutions and direct the consultant to the solution ultimately rendered. Because facts serve such important functions, the consultant must be resourceful in fact gathering and skillful in fact analysis.

This chapter has the purpose of assisting the consultant in developing fact-related skills. The first section deals with fact sources. It identifies places where the consultant can look to find facts associated with the operations of a client. The second and third sections present and discuss various techniques for gathering and analyzing facts.[1]

FACT SOURCES

A wealth of internal and external fact sources are available to help you, as consultant, zero in on a client's problems. Internal and external fact sources for a typical business firm are listed in Figure 7.1. For example,

Figure 7.1 Internal and external fact sources.

Sources	Facts
Corporate planning	Corporate objectives Expansion plans
Marketing	Sales statistics Invoices and back orders Types of new products or services with market possibilities Customer response to existing products Planning and promotional campaigns Feedback from customers and sales force on product performance
Research and development	New product development schedules
Engineering	Engineering schedule for products
Data processing	Systems for organizing files and reporting operating results
Manufacturing	Inventory status
Personnel	Background on employees Salary/performance review data
Accounting	Product pricing and costing Operating expenses
External	
Industry reports	Corporate data and analysis Industry news
Competition	Products and product literature
Distributors	Market conditions Customer analysis
Customers	Profile facts Sales
State and federal statistical data and abstracts	Corporate statistical comparisons Economic/financial facts Securities and Exchange Commission facts Department of Commerce facts Bureau of Census facts
Data base retrieval systems	Product, market, and industry news and analysis Economic forecasts

the manufacturing function produces data that describe the status of inventory quantities of raw materials, work-in-process, and finished goods. Facts from these data, coupled with facts generated by the function labeled marketing, can help you separate the symptom of many cancelled orders from the problem of inadequate customer back-order procedures.

Internal Sources

The most important internal source of facts is people. The term people includes not only a client's management but also its clerical and production employees. It should be recognized, however, that the facts gathered from people may be suspect; they may be tinged with biases or colored by beliefs of what the consultant wants to hear. It is your job to unmask facts from fantasies.

A second internal source of facts is client documentation. Client documentation in most organizations can be classified according to (1) documentation that describes how the organization is structured, (2) documentation that describes what the organization is or has been doing, and (3) documentation that describes what the organization plans to do. Figure 7.2 provides a partial list, by type, of documentation typically found in a client organization.

Documentation should be used with caution as sources of facts. Certain types of documents, i.e., those identified as describing how an organization is structured and what it plans to do, *do not* necessarily reflect reality. At best, these documents serve only to give you an understanding of what client management considered its structure and direc-

Figure 7.2 Documents typically found in a client organization. (*SOURCE*: John G. Burch, Jr., Felix R. Strater, and Gary Grudnitski, *Information Systems: Theory and Practice*, 3d ed. Copyright © 1983. Reprinted by permission of John Wiley & Sons, Inc., New York City.)

Documents describing how the client's organization is run	Documents describing what the client plans to do	Documents describing what the client organization has done
Policy statements	Business plan	Annual reports
Methods and procedures manual	Budgets	Performance reports
Organization charts	Schedules and forecasts	Internal staff studies
Job descriptions	Minutes of board of directors' meeting	Legal documents, including copyrights, patents, franchises, trademarks
Performance standards		Reference documentation about customers, employees, products, vendors
Chart of accounts		

tion to be at one point in time. It is not uncommon for organizations and plans to change, while the related documentation remains unchanged.

A third internal source of facts important to a consultant can be termed as relationships. Defining the relationships among people, departments, and functions can provide you with information and insights unknown or undocumented anywhere else within the organization.

Pitfalls to Avoid

Throughout the process of internal fact gathering you must guard against overlooking the obvious. Frequently, an interview with a client employee uncovers excellent ideas unacted upon by management. Similarly, a brief analysis, based on something as simple as counting the number of times a particular event occurred, may result in the discovery of an activity not realized or understood by management. You should not overlook the opportunity to present management, at a time when its attention is focused, with your discoveries as well as the suggestions of the client's employees and operating-level managers.

External Sources

Many facts are obtained from external sources, i.e., sources outside the client organization. These sources may be several times removed from the client's operations. For example, you may gather facts from customers concerning their perceptions of the client's products as compared to those of the major competitors. Or, during an engagement involving a long-range business plan, you may test the reasonableness of internally prepared sales forecasts by comparing them to projections obtained by an econometric model of the economy.

Among the most important data obtained from external sources are economic statistics. Figure 7.3 lists thirteen annotated references containing economic statistics.

FACT-GATHERING TECHNIQUES

One of a consultant's most important tasks, especially at the beginning of an engagement, is to separate the symptoms experienced by a client from the underlying problems. As noted in the previous chapter, it is the problems, rather than the symptoms, that deserve close attention and treatment. The following techniques are available for gathering facts concerning the underlying problems.

Figure 7.3   A list of annotated references that contain economic statistics.   (*SOURCE:* R. Mayer, E. Stevens, and R. Switzer, *The Research and Report Handbook*, Chapter 29. Copyright © 1981. Used by permission of John Wiley & Sons, Inc., New York.)

1. *American Statistics Index (ASI)*, Congressional Information Service, Washington, D.C., 1972–date. Published monthly, ASI is a comprehensive indexing service for statistics gathered by the United States government. It is a guide to all statistical publications of the government. ASI identifies the statistical data by a subject, title, and agency report number index; it catalogs these data, giving full bibliographic information, and describes briefly the content of each publication. The annual compilation is usually a two-volume set: one volume is the index, and the other is the abstracting service.

2. *Barometer of Small Business*, San Diego, Accounting Corporation of America, 1950– date. A semiannual publication, the *Barometer* is a reference book of operating statistics for small business. It is indexed alphabetically by type of business.

3. *Business Conditions Digest (BCD)*, USGPO, Washington, D.C., 1961– date. Issued monthly, BCD provides a look at the economic factors useful to financial analysts and forecasters. It includes several graphs and tables indicating economic conditions and measures.

4. *Dun and Bradstreet's Key Business Ratios*, Dun and Bradstreet, New York, various dates. *Key Business Ratios* provides financial ratios for 125 retailing, wholesaling, manufacturing, and construction businesses, arranged alphabetically by industry or product line.

5. *Market Guide*, Editor & Publisher Company, New York, 1924–date. The *Market Guide* gives current data on over 1,500 newspaper markets in both the United States and Canada. Arranged alphabetically by state, then city, such information as number of banks, population, principal industries, shopping centers, newspapers, types of transportation, and retail stores is provided for each city.

6. *Predicasts*, Predicasts, Inc., Cleveland, 1960–date. Published quarterly with annual cumulations, *Predicasts* lists articles containing predictions and forecasts that have appeared in periodicals, trade journals, and newspapers. The information is indexed by subject and by Standard Industrial Classification (SIC) number.

7. *Rand McNally Co. Commerical Atlas and Marketing Guide*, Rand McNally, New York, 1911–date. Published annually, this commercial atlas gives geographic, economic, industrial, and government data on cities and states in the United States. Large maps indicating county seats, ZIP codes, trading areas, and manufacturing cities are included. Some similar information about Canada and other parts of the world is also given.

8. *Annual Statement Studies*, Robert Morris Associates, Philadelphia, 1923–date. Issued annually, this guide is quite similar in content to Leo Troy's financial ratio book, listed later. The statement studies can be used to do a financial analysis of a particular product line or industry.

9. *Sales and Marketing Mangement Survey of Buying Power*, Bill Publications, New York. This annual publication appears each summer as a supplement to an issue of *Sales and Marketing Management*. Useful to the marketing researcher, it contains data on changes in regional markets, population, number of households in each state, total dollar amount of retail, food, general merchandise, auto, drug, home furnishings sales, and so on. Each state is indexed alphabetically. Some Canadian data are given.

10. *Statistical Sources*, Paul Wasserman, editor, Gale Research Company, Detroit, 1962–date. Arranged alphabetically by subject, *Statistical Sources* is a comprehensive guide to sources of data about the United States and foreign countries. United States documents and United Nations documents are indexed. Full bibliographic information is given for all sources cited.

11. *Survey of Current Business*, U.S. Department of Commerce, Washington, D.C., 1920–date. This monthly periodical contains in-depth articles on various economic and business topics. Included are business and economic statistics, projections trends, and national income and product tables.

12. *Troy's Almanac of Business and Industrial Financial Ratios*, Prentice-Hall, Englewood Cliffs, New Jersey. Arranged by industry, *Troy's* provides financial ratios for both industry and product types. The latest edition has two tables for each industry: Table I reports the operating and financial information for corporations regardless of net profit; Table II gives this same information only for those corporations that were profitable.

13. *Value Line Investment Survey*, Arnold Bernhard Company, New York, 1943–date. Published weekly, *Value Line* gives both text materials and graphic-chart display of various products and industries. It has four parts: I, Summary and Ideas; II, Selection and Opinion; III, Ratings and Reports; and IV, Explanation of Terms. The industries represented are indexed alphabetically.

Interviews

On many engagements the best way for you to zero in on problems is to conduct a series of interviews with client personnel. In essence, an interview is the face-to-face interchange of information. It can be conducted at all levels of the client organization, from the president down to the mail clerk. Therefore, you must have the temperament to adjust to people who have differing commitments to the client's goals, as well as to many environmental variables.

Getting started.   Before embarking on a set of interviews, you should ask your client contact to issue a memorandum to persons who are to be interviewed. This memorandum should explain the purpose of the interviews and the use to which the facts obtained will be put. Before going into each interview, you should become familiar with the duties and responsibilities of the interviewee and you should also understand the working and personal relationships of the interviewee with others in the client's organization. Furthermore, you should be as aware as possible of the responses that the interviewee is apt to give.

Conducting the interview.   During the interview itself, remember to:

1. Confirm your understanding of the interviewee's job responsibilities and duties. You might use this approach: "It is my understanding that your job is . . . (a brief job description). Is this correct?"

2. To the extent possible, ask specific questions that allow quantitative responses. A typical question of this type is: "How many telephones do you now have in this department?"

3. When questions are answered vaguely, pursue them (in a pleasant way) until they are fully clarified.

4. Try to develop an awareness of the interviewee's feelings. This can best be achieved by listening well and reading the interviewee's "body language."

5. Avoid stating your own opinions or acting like a "know-it-all."

6. As the interview draws to a close, ask the interviewee if he or she has additional ideas, thoughts, or suggestions concerning the topics of discussion: "Do you have any additional suggestions or recommendations concerning the method used to calculate budget variances?"

7. On the other hand, do not allow the interview to become too lengthy. One way to keep the answers brief is to ask questions in a manner that will obtain the needed facts in the least possible time.

8. At the end of the interview summarize the main points uncovered, thank the interviewee, and indicate that you will contact him or her again if further questions are necessary.

Questionnaires

The questionnaire is a somewhat restricted channel of communication and hence should be used with great care for the purpose of fact finding. Unlike the interview, the questionnaire does not provide you an immediate opportunity to readdress comments that are vague or unclear. Moreover, comments that might well lead to additional facts or ideas cannot be followed up.

Thus, the questionnaire is best used as a fact-finding technique when the persons from whom you desire information are physically removed and travel is prohibitive, when numerous persons (e.g., all of the sales staff) are to be queried, and when the facts to be so determined are intended to verify similar facts gathered from other sources.

When one or more of the above conditions exist, and you decide to use the questionnaire approach, you should clearly identify in your mind what it is you desire to know. Then you should structure the questions that are most likely to generate the desired information, prepare the questionnaire form, and submit questionnaires to the appropriate individuals.

To be more specific, follow these guidelines:

1. Explain in an accompanying letter the purpose, use, security, and disposition of the responses generated by the questionnaire.

2. Provide detailed instructions concerning how the questions are to be completed.

3. Provide a time limit or deadline for return of the questionnaire.

4. Format questions so that responses can be tabulated mechanically or manually.

5. Ask pointed, concise questions when possible.

6. If a question cannot be answered objectively, provide an opportunity for the respondent to add a clarifying comment.

7. Provide sufficient space for complete responses.

8. Include a section in which respondents can state opinions and criticisms.

9. Identify each questionnaire by the respondent's name, job title, department, and so forth.

Observation

Observation is a third technique available to a consultant. For instance, you can gather useful facts by observing the employees of a client perform their job-related duties. The purposes of observation are to help the consultant determine (1) what is being done, (2) how it is being done, (3) who is doing it, (4) when it is being done, (5) how long it takes, (6) where it is being done, and (7) why it is being done.

Methods of observation.   One method of observing is to take a walk through an area and make notes of people, things, and activities. A second method is to observe without being observed from a fixed location. A third method is similar to the second, in that the observing is being done from a fixed point and without any interaction between you and the person being observed; however, the person being observed is fully aware that you are observing. The final method is to observe and also interact with the person (or persons) being observed. Interaction may consist of asking questions about a specific task, of requesting detailed explanations of tasks, and so forth.

The technique of observation is useful in gathering facts prior to an interview, in verifying statements made during an interview, and in ascertaining relationships between individuals.

Observation guidelines.   The usefulness of observation can be maximized by following these guidelines:

1. Before beginning, identify and define what it is that you are to observe; also estimate the length of time that the observation will entail.

2. If persons are to be aware of your observations, explain to them what will be done and why.

3. Note the time periodically while making your observations.
4. Record what is observed as specifically as possible, avoiding generalities and vague descriptions.
5. Avoid expressing value judgments when interacting with persons being observed.
6. Document all impressions and organize your notes as soon as possible after the observation period.
7. Review the facts obtained and the conclusions drawn from observations with (a) the person being observed, (b) the person's supervisor, and with (c) your own supervisor (when desirable).

Document Gathering

Another technique for gathering facts is to collect all relevant documents, i.e., source documents, work sheets, reports, and so forth. From these documents you can gain an understanding of what is presently done and how it is organized, what is not available, and perhaps what the client considers to be important. Efforts in gathering facts during interviews and observations can often be enhanced if copies of documents have been gathered and are in hand. Moreover, if you have a working understanding of the client's documents, you increase the likelihood of smooth communications with the client personnel.

Charting

Charting is a fact-gathering technique that provides a pictorial representation of a dimension of the client's organization or of its activities. This technique is highly valued, since it is also facilitates analysis, synthesis, communication, and documentation.

This section briefly describes such charts as the organization chart, data flow diagram, system flowchart, detail flowchart, and decision table.

Organization chart. The organization chart provides facts concerning reporting relationships, quantities of resources, and levels of authority and responsibility within the client's organization. It is often useful to prepare a brief narrative describing the functions and role of each manager appearing on the organization chart.

Data flow diagram. This is a logical view of data flows through a system. It clearly portrays the workings of a complex system, such as a transaction processing system. Figure 7.4 illustrates four symbols that may be used in data flow diagrams.

A square (or sometimes a rectangle) represents an external entity, a source or destination of a transaction. People (such as customers, managers, and suppliers), things (such as warehouses and main offices), or

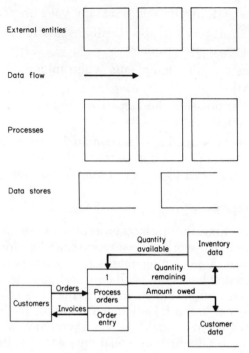

Figure 7.4 Data flow diagram symbols. (*SOURCE:* John G. Burch, Jr., Felix R. Strater, and Gary Grudnitski, *Information Systems: Theory and Practice,* 3d ed. Copyright © 1983. Reprinted by permission of John Wiley & Sons, Inc., New York.)

other systems (such as sales forecasting systems) are external entities. As such, they are outside the boundary of the system under consideration.

An arrow is the symbol for data flow. The arrowhead indicates the direction of the data flow. Each data flow arrow should be accompanied by a meaningful description of the nature of the data flow.

A segmented tall rectangle (or alternatively a circle) is the symbol for a process (i.e., an activity or task). In the standards illustrated in Figure 7.4, the rectangle is split into three areas. The top area contains an identification number. The middle area contains a description of the function performed, such as computing a sales tax or collecting a payment. The bottom area indicates how or by whom the function is to be performed.

An open-ended rectangle is the symbol for a data store, i.e., a place where data are stored between processes. Each data store symbol should contain a descriptive label, e.g., employee master file, canceled checks, purchase orders pending.

The lower part of Figure 7.4 shows a data flow diagram illustrating a sales order and invoicing system. Customers are the external entity that places orders and later receives invoices. In addition to the flows of orders and invoices just mentioned, data flows occur between the process labeled "process orders" and two data stores (inventory data and customer data).

Two points should be noted with respect to the data flow diagram illustrated in Figure 7.4. It emphasizes the logical flows of the system; thus, it does *not* specify the physical resources used in the system, such as a computer with disk files, and so on. Also, the sales order process portrayed in the figure can be "blown up" to show additional details of the processing steps.

System flowchart. A system flowchart depicts an overall view of a system in terms of major elements such as processing programs or runs, files, inputs, and outputs. It provides clear documentation of either a present system or a proposed system. Generally, it pertains to a computer-based information system. In contrast to a data flow diagram, therefore, it specifies the physical nature of the data processing and data storage. Figure 7.5 shows a system flowchart of a payroll process.

Detail flowchart. A detail flowchart graphically represents the logic of a process. Generally, it describes the logic of a computer program or run. Thus, Figure 7.6 illustrates the logic of an update program shown in the system flowchart in Figure 7.5.

Decision table. A decision table is a viable alternative to a detail flowchart, since it portrays a situation involving logic. It particularly facilitates the understanding and communication of decision processes having complex logic (i.e., multiple conditions). The format of a decision table appears in Figure 7.7. By comparing this format with the detail flowchart in Figure 7.6, you can see two major differences:

1. The decision table employs a matrix or tabular format, whereas the detail flowchart employs a diagrammatic format with standardized symbols.
2. The detail flowchart specifies a definite sequence of steps to be performed, whereas the decision table lists conditions, actions, and rules without regard to sequence.

When you examine the decision table format closely, you see that the table is divided into two parts. Its upper half contains the conditions related to a decision. These conditions are expressed in the areas labeled as stub and entry. In the stub area the conditions are expressed as "IF" phrases. In the entry area the states of the conditions (usually either YES or NO) are entered.

The lower half of the table contains the actions that are to be taken when the conditions have been satisfied. Areas within this lower half are also denoted as stub and entry. In the stub area the actions are expressed

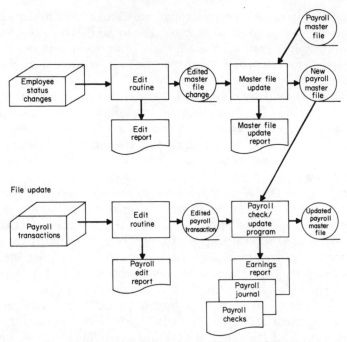

Figure 7.5   An example of a systems flowchart for a payroll process. (*SOURCE*: John G. Burch, Jr., Felix R. Strater, and Gary Grudnitski, *Information Systems: Theory and Practice*, 3d ed. Copyright © 1983. Reprinted by permission of John Wiley & Sons, Inc., New York.)

by "THEN" phrases. In the entry area the particular actions that pertain to each set of conditions are noted.

Thus, a decision table portrays sets of conditions (rules) and actions. As Figure 7.7 shows, the rules are numbered horizontally across the top of the table. In effect, a decision table states: IF this set of conditions (rule) occurs, THEN perform these marked actions. IF that set of conditions (rule) occurs, THEN perform that set of marked actions. The number of rules that may exist for a particular decision situation depends upon the number of conditions.

Each rule is reflected in a combination of YES and NO entries in a column. Each YES (Y) means that a specified condition exists, while each NO (N) means that it does not exist. (If neither is listed, then the condition does not apply.)

The example shown in Figure 7.8 should clarify the construction and use of a decision table. At the top of the figure appears a situation involving conditions and actions. Below, in the left half, is the decision table based on this situation. In the right half is a matching of possible conditions and resulting actions. Rule 1 in the decision table shows that

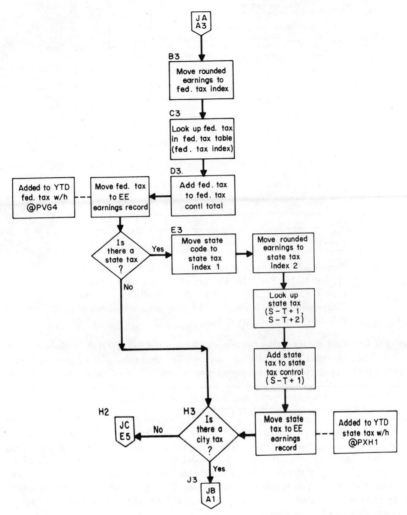

Figure 7.6   An example of a detail flowchart.   (*SOURCE:* John G. Burch, Jr., Felix R. Strater, and Gary Grudnitski, *Information Systems: Theory and Practice*, 3d ed. Copyright © 1983. Reprinted by permission of John Wiley & Sons, Inc., New York.)

IF the condition is "a record with net dollars less than zero," THEN the action to be taken by a decision maker is to classify the record as a closed order. Rule 2 in the table shows that IF the conditions are "a record with net dollars greater than zero" *and* "the shipped quantity equals the ordered quantity," THEN also classify the record as a closed order. Rule 3 in the table shows that IF the conditions are "a record with net dollars greater than zero" *and* "the shipped quantity does not equal the ordered quantity" *but* "the to-be-shipped date does equal the report

Figure 7.7 A decision table format. (*SOURCE:* John G. Burch, Jr., Felix R. Strater, and Gary Grudnitski, *Information Systems: Theory and Practice*, 3d ed. Copyright © 1983. Reprinted by permission of John Wiley & Sons, Inc., New York.)

Figure 7.8 An example involving the use of a decision table. (*SOURCE:* John G. Burch, Jr., Felix R. Strater, and Gary Grudnitski, *Information Systems: Theory and Practice*, 3d ed. Copyright © 1983. Reprinted by permission of John Wiley & Sons, Inc., New York.)

Procedure involving unfilled order file reporting

Each record on the unfilled order file must be examined and classified as either a closed order, back order, in-process order, current order, or future order. Any record which has the order quantity equal to the shipped quantity is considered closed. Any record having a to-be-shipped date earlier than the report date is a back order. A record with the to-be-shipped date equal to the report date is treated as in-process. Any record with a to-be-shipped data more than seven days later than the report date is a future order. All other records are considered current, except any record with net dollars less than zero (which are viewed as being closed.)

If	1	2	3	4	5	6	Conditions	Actions
Net \$ < 0	Y	N	N	N	N	N	The order quantity equal to	
Order qty = shipped qty		Y	N	N	N	N	the shipped quantity	Closed
							A to-be-shipped date earlier	
TBS date = rep date			Y	N	N	N	than the report date	Back order
TBS < rep date				Y	N	N	The to-be-shipped date equal	
TBS > rep date + 7					Y	N	to the report date	In-process
Then							A to-be-shipped date more	
Closed order	1	1					than seven days later than	
Back order				1			the report date	Future
In-process			1				Any record with net dollars	
Current						1	less than zero	Closed
Future					1		All other records	Current

date," THEN classify the record as an in-process order. The remaining rules require three other actions.

As this example shows, a decision table can be used to inform a "decision maker" (such as a processing clerk) about the appropriate action to take when confronted by a particular set of conditions. It may also be used to prepare a computer program, so that the computer can be instructed how to act when confronted by each set of conditions.

FACTS ANALYSIS TECHNIQUES

In most consulting engagements a consultant needs to apply a variety of fact analysis techniques. Four representative approaches to analysis— decision-level, input/output, structured, and unstructured analysis— are described below. All are useful, though consultants (like artisans) are likely to use one type more than another.

Decision-Level Analysis

Decision-level analysis has the purpose of depicting the varied inter-relationships among the decisions made throughout the segments and levels of the organization. It is useful in demonstrating to client management the variety and kinds of decisions that the organization must make.

This analytical approach begins with interviews of key client managers. During the interviews you focus on resources, since resource allocation and usage are the concern of most decisions. Your initial concern is to categorize the major tangible and intangible resources of the organization, such as inventories, plant and equipment, employee skills, and so on. After categorizing these resources, you identify the resources required at each decision level of the organization. Then you ascertain the specific items of information, as well as their sources, needed to make decisions concerning these resource requirements.

Consider the inventory resource, for instance. In a manufacturing firm the decision levels with respect to inventory include the levels of overall production scheduling, inventory stocking, stock issues, and reordering. The decisions at the production-scheduling level may be stated as follows: the quantities of each inventory item that must be put into production on each date in order to satisfy the production schedule (i.e., to meet planned shipping requirements). The decision at the inventory stocking level is: the quantity of inventory that must be stocked to accommodate all needs for production and shipments, to maintain a base stock, and to avoid excessive carrying costs. (Similar decisions could be stated for the other levels.) Information needed to make the decision at the production-scheduling level includes the quantities of products to be produced during the scheduled period, the production rate of each product, the bill of materials for each product, the expected spoilage rate, and so on. (Similar information needs can be stated for each of the other decisions.)

The interrelationships among resource decisions are illustrated by the inventory resource. Production-scheduling decisions affect stock issue and stock-level decisions, while stock-level decisions in turn affect reordering decisions.

Input/Output Analysis

A problem situation may be analyzed in terms of its inputs and outputs. Figure 7.9 illustrates the input/output approach used to analyze facts associated with the inventory function. It should be noted that while each input and output is described, nothing is included concerning the process (i.e., how the input is converted to output), the data requirements, the information flows, or the related decisions.

Structure Analysis

A fact analysis approach widely used in recent years has been the structured analysis approach. The key assumption underlying this approach is that any organization is comprised of a number of well-defined functions, which in turn are made up of a group of activities. By focusing upon these functions and supporting activities, you can gain a clear understanding of the inputs, processing, and outputs of the organization.

In performing structured analysis, the preferable procedure is to begin at the top level and then work down to the lowest activity level. Large functions can be repeatedly subdivided through several levels, until the smallest activity is isolated. The resulting structure is an upside-down treelike function diagram, similar in appearance to an organization chart. Like the organization chart, this function diagram helps you to see relationships among the activities of a function.

Consider, for example, the diagram of the inventory control function shown in Figure 7.10. From the top level, labeled "maintain inventory control," the diagram is constructed by defining all the activities (also called subfunctions) that support this function. Two levels of activities below the top are shown in the diagram. The third level shows the detailed inputs, processing steps, and outputs related to "update inventory master file." The diagram could be expanded to show a fourth level of detail for each of the third-level activities (e.g., for "determine quantity to back order") and to show a third level of detail for the other second-level activities.

Figure 7.9   An example of input/output analysis.   (*SOURCE:* John G. Burch, Jr., Felix R. Strater, and Gary Grudnitski, *Information Systems: Theory and Practice*, 3d ed. Copyright © 1983. Reprinted by permission of John Wiley & Sons, Inc., New York.)

Input/output analysis: inventory

INPUTS:

1. *Production.* Production tickets show quality, product code, product number, batch numbers, operator numbers.

2. *Scrap.* A scrap ticket is prepared as necessary, containing the same facts as production tickets but coded as scrap.

3. *Receiving.* All receipts are noted with:

   Product number
   Receipt codes
   Receiver's number
   Product quantity
   Date received
   Purchase order
   Authorization number

4. *Shipments.* Invoices are from billing, sorted by product number, including date shipped, quantity shipped, customer order number.

5. *Transfers.* Intracompany transfers are recorded with transfer code.

6. *Inventory adjustments.* Inventory adjustments entered by auditors. The adjusted amount is entered with date of physical count.

OUTPUTS:

1. *Input listing.* A listing of all inputs is prepared daily with errors in coding. This report is received by the supervisors of manufacturing, shipping, receiving, and accounting.

2. *Daily inventory status.* A daily report is prepared indicating the status of all products. Report includes opening inventory, production, shipments, transfers, adjustments, and closing inventory. Report is distributed to production scheduler, shipping supervisor, auditor, and inventory analyst.

3. *Monthly inventory status.* A monthly report is prepared with the same format as daily report, only reflecting that month's activity. This report is issued to plant manager and plant accountant, in addition to daily distribution.

4. *Monthly scrap report.* A monthly scrap report is issued showing all scrap reported lost. This report is issued to plant manager, plant accountant, supervisor of quality control, supervisor of operations.

Less-Structured Analysis

While structured analysis is useful, it has limitations. For instance, it is sometimes difficult to apply, since certain organizations are complex entities consisting of networks of people and activities, rather than

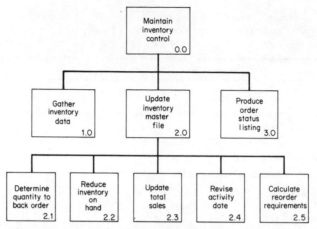

Figure 7.10   The activities of a portion of an inventory control function.   (*SOURCE:* John G. Burch, Jr., Felix R. Strater, and Gary Grudnitski, *Information Systems: Theory and Practice,* 3d ed. Copyright © 1983. Reprinted by permission of John Wiley & Sons, Inc., New York.)

clearly defined hierarchies. Also, structured analysis tends to stifle creativity.

Thus, relatively unstructured approaches to fact analysis should be employed to counteract such limitations. These alternative approaches should take advantage of the combined wisdom of many of the client's managers. Two unstructured approaches that can help extract and analyze this wisdom are the Delphi and brainstorming approaches.

Delphi approach.   This approach receives its name from the priestess of Delphi, who sent runners into the countryside to obtain opinions concerning a particular problem. A consensus of the opinions led her to a decision. This approach may be employed to obtain opinions from managers concerning impending present problems or future conditions. It is discussed further in Chapter 8.

Brainstorming.   An atmosphere conducive to the free flow of ideas is provided by the brainstorming approach. In an orgnizational setting it may be employed by gathering several managers into a group. Under the direction of a selected leader the group contributes ideas pertaining to the solution of an identified problem. Any and all ideas are received without restriction or criticism. Later the ideas are sifted to find those that are judged to be the best. This approach is also discussed further in Chapter 8.

NOTES

1. J. G. Burch, F. R. Strater, and G. Grudnitski, *Information Systems: Theory and Practice,* 3d ed., Wiley, New York, 1983, Chapter 11.

8

Solution Development

LYNN J. McKELL
Department of Accounting
Brigham Young University
Provo, Utah

Solution development is the third phase of the problem-solving process. As Figure 8.1 shows, the phase consists of several steps. These steps begin with the generation of solution alternatives and end with the presentation of a recommended solution.

The solution development phase links to the previous phases through the deliverables of those phases. Thus, it links to the problem definition phase through the objectives and other facets revealed in the statement of the problem definition. It links to the fact-finding and analysis phase through the specification of requirements and criteria. Each of the key deliverables—objectives, requirements, criteria—should therefore be established prior to the commencement of the solution development phase. As reflectors of the desired outputs, the objectives and requirements drive the problem-solving process. As evaluation instruments, the criteria point to the preferable solution.

NATURE OF THE DELIVERABLE

Throughout the problem-solving process, you should keep in mind the nature of the deliverable, i.e., the developed solution that is to be pre-

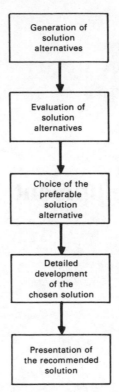

Figure 8.1 Steps in the development of a solution to a problem.

sented as the final recommended product. The following illustrate the range of deliverables that consultants may be expected to produce:

1. *Solution to specific problem:*   Many consulting engagements consist of defining a specific problem, gathering and analyzing facts concerning the problem, and developing the preferable solution to the problem. This is the "classic" problem-solving illustration. Several examples of this type of consulting engagement appear in the discussion of the problem definition phase in Chapter 6.

2. *Educational course or training program:*   Another type of consulting engagement results in the development of an educational course or a training program as the "solution." You may be expected to devise a course, for example, intended to enable employees and managers to understand the functions of computers. Alternatively, you may be expected to develop a training program that will teach employees to use a computerized transaction processing system. In some cases you may be also expected to serve as instructor in the course or training program.

3. *Designed system component:*   A third type of consulting engagement consists of developing a solution in the form of a system design.

Your assignment would be to start at the point in the process indicated by the client and to conduct the systems project within prescribed constraints. For instance, you may be given the requirements for a desired data base; your assignment may then be to develop the design specifications, determine the feasibility of the data base, and select the preferable hardware and software to implement the data base.

4. *Implemented "turnkey" system:*   A comprehensive consulting engagement consists of developing and implementing a fully operational "turnkey" system. This type of deliverable generally involves the entire system development life cycle, from definition through implementation. In most consulting cases the implemented system is an information system; however, in some cases it will be an operational system, e.g., a production system, or a management system (a management-by-objectives system, for example).

   A danger posed by this type of engagement is that the ultimate users of the system, usually the managers and employees of the client firm, will not adequately participate in its development. Certain authorities in the consulting field would contend that the consultant who performs this type of engagement has in effect become a vendor and hence has exceeded the legitimate bounds of consulting.

5. *Advice or assistance:*   In many consulting engagements a consultant is asked for advice concerning an area or methodology in which he or she has recognized expertise. Alternatively, the consultant may be engaged to provide technical assistance during the development of a system or the construction of a structure. For instance, audit consultants are often engaged to provide advice concerning internal accounting controls during the design of accounting information systems. Data-processing consultants are engaged to provide assistance during the initial selection and installation of new microcomputer-based information systems. Such advice and assistance, when provided during the various phases of the development of a system or process or structure, may be viewed as "interim" solutions to problems.

6. *Expert opinion:*   A type of consulting engagement similar to the one just described involves the consultant as an expert witness. Your professional obligation, in such an engagement, is to deliver an expert opinion that is as unbiased and accurate as possible.

GENERATION OF ALTERNATIVE SOLUTIONS

Need for Solution Alternatives

The first step in the solution development phase is to generate as many solution alternatives as feasible. This step is essential, even when time is short. Unless a thorough search for alternatives is conducted, a consultant cannot feel confident that the recommended solution to a problem is the best available. Also, the client should be given the opportunity to compare the recommended solution against the more reasonable of the alternatives. From the perspective of the client, a closely competing alternative might be more appealing than the one you recommend.

Search Approaches

Generating solution alternatives is akin to generating new ideas. The fruitfulness of such mental activity is largely a function of personal experience. As Sir Joshua Reynolds said in his *Discourses*: "Invention, strictly speaking, is little more than a new combination of those images which have been previously gathered and deposited in the memory. Nothing can be made of nothing; he who has laid up no materials can produce no combinations." Nevertheless, consultants must also employ creativity in order to devise innovative combinations. A variety of well-defined and controllable approaches that blend experience and the creative process can be identified.

Pattern recognition and matching approach. This approach emphasizes experience. In order to avoid "reinventing the wheel," the consultant can draw upon his or her own personal experience or upon the experiences of others. The experiences of others may be found in the files of the organization of which the consultant is a member, at professional conferences, or in published books and articles by consulting authorities. Successful consultants have long recognized that a definite benefit of membership in a professional organization, or attendance at a relevant conference, is the likelihood of acquiring useful ideas.

Knowledge of experiences, especially those having very similar characteristics to the problem situation being investigated, can serve as a sound starting point for solution development. By recognizing and matching the features that are common to the previous experiences and to the problem at hand, you are able to judge the applicability of the previously employed solution. If it proved to be reasonably successful, you will probably want to include it as a solution alternative.

Brainstorming approach. As Linus Pauling said: "The best way to have a good idea is to have lots of ideas." Generating a flurry of ideas is known as "divergent thinking." A widely used approach that begins with divergent thinking is described by the term brainstorming.

The first stage of brainstorming takes place in a group setting. Several people concerned with the problem situation meet in a room and contribute ideas in a freewheeling and informal manner. Every conceivable idea is encouraged, even the wildest idea imaginable. Participants are asked to suspend critical judgment. They are commended and rewarded for the sheer number of ideas that they contribute.

The beneficial result of this first stage of brainstorming is to generate the maximum number of ideas in a short time. Focusing the attention of a group on a single common problem creates a synergistic effect that causes ideas to proliferate. Each person stimulates the others in the group, and in turn each person is stimulated by the group. Encouraging the suspension of judgment creates an unguarded atmosphere that frees the mental process of each person from all constraints.

The flow of ideas during this divergent thinking process tends to follow a pattern. The most obvious and conventional ideas are suggested first. After a time these ideas tend to be exhausted, and an "idea wall" forms. With continued effort this idea wall is shattered, and less conventional ideas begin to emerge. Certain of these ideas seem to be ridiculous, even "wild and crazy." However, they generally have the positive effect of stimulating very good ideas. In other words, the best ideas tend to "piggyback" or pyramid on the foundations laid by the not-so-good ideas.

The second stage of brainstorming shifts from idea generation to idea selection and refinement. That is, it employs the activity known as "convergent thinking." In this second stage each idea is judged in the light of the objectives and requirements established earlier in the problem-solving process. Most of the ideas generated in the divergent thinking stage will be easily eliminated by this judgment process. Only a few really good ideas are likely to be identified. These good ideas should be refined, if necessary, and preserved as likely solution alternatives.

The main drawback to brainstorming is the time required to weed out the large volume of unusable ideas generated. Thus, the primary focus during the convergent thinking process is on narrowing the number of ideas or solution alternatives. The focus should not be so rigid, however, that additional new ideas are precluded from consideration. New ideas sometimes emerge, if unstifled, from the process of identifying weaknesses in the ideas generated during the first stage.

SCAMPER approach.   An approach that is more deliberate in nature than brainstorming is known by the acronynm SCAMPER, which stands for:

Substitute

Combine

Adjust (or adapt)

Magnify (or minify or modify)

Put to other uses

Eliminate (or elaborate)

Reverse (or rearrange)

This approach emphasizes the use of a systematic process to generate ideas leading to solution alternatives. Each new idea represents an evolution of a presently stated idea. Thus, one new idea may emerge from asking the question: "What is a reasonable substitute for idea A?" Another new idea may develop from the combination of ideas A and B.

Because the SCAMPER approach is more deliberate and systematic than brainstorming, it allows time for incubation. Ideas can develop and evolve in the consultant's subconscious. This incubation process can be especially fruitful if you apply the SCAMPER approach in several iterations, with time lapses between. During the first iteration you could list the more obvious solution alternatives. During the second iteration you might allot a preset period of time to substituting, combining, rearranging, and so on. Then, after a time lapse (during which you let the subconscious take over), you might allot another preset period of time to once again performing the SCAMPER functions. If it seems desirable, you might repeat the process yet another time.

A possible drawback to the SCAMPER approach is that it tends to limit the range of likely ideas. Revolutionary ideas are not likely to emerge from this evolutionary approach. Thus, it should not be viewed as a substitute for brainstorming.

Delphi approach.   This approach employs an idea-generation concept similar to brainstorming. Whereas brainstorming involves the interaction of participants in a communal setting, however, the Delphi approach insulates the participants from one another. Experts are individually polled for ideas, and these ideas are subsequently summarized and presented to each participant. After allowing time for each participant to review this feedback, the consultant again polls the experts. Presumably, each participant will adjust and revise his or her ideas in the light of the collective responses. This feedback and repolling cycle is repeated until the responses have stabilized. Then the stabilized results are summarized and presented as the refined ideas of the collective experts.

The Delphi approach should produce excellent ideas or solution alternatives, since they represent the refined views of experts. The approach is very time-consuming, however, and it tends to be better suited to problems involving forecasts than to other types of problem situations.

EVALUATION OF SOLUTION ALTERNATIVES

After the solution alternatives are sifted and refined, they must be evaluated to determine the preferable solution. This evaluation should be based upon a structured feasibility analysis that considers all relevant dimensions. Whenever possible the analysis should employ a decision model that describes the relationships and behavior of the significant factors in the problem situation. A key evaluation step is the comparison of solution alternatives by means of established criteria, where the criteria represent quantitative and/or qualitative factors chosen by the evaluators. An example of a familiar quantitative criterion is the return on assets ratio, while a qualitative criterion often employed is customer satisfaction.

Each solution alternative is evaluated, via the criteria, against all other solution alternatives. It should also be noted that each solution alternative is implicitly evaluated against the existing situation. Thus, a solution alternative that does not represent an improvement over the existing situation may immediately be eliminated.

Among the dimensions by which each solution alternative may be analyzed are economic feasibility, operational feasibility, technical feasibility, scheduling feasibility, and legal feasibility. Although certain of these dimensions may be irrelevant in particular problem situations, all of the dimensions are relevant to the domain of problems faced by modern organizations.

Economic Feasibility

Central to economic feasibility is a benefit/cost analysis. This type of analysis attempts (1) to identify and quantify all of the benefits and costs associated with a particular solution alternative and (2) to weigh these benefits and costs by means of an economically oriented criterion.

Benefits generally consist of cost avoidance, cost reduction, revenue improvement, performance improvement, and/or product quality improvement. Certain of these benefits are relatively tangible or quantifiable, while others are relatively intangible or nonquantifiable.

Costs can be categorized as development costs, implementation costs, and operating costs. Typical development/implementation costs incurred in a project to rectify a problem situation include those for: hardware (i.e., computer equipment), software (i.e., programming), documentation, personnel, and supplies. The personnel costs in turn can be classified as those incurred for: recruitment of new employees, training of both new and existing employees, learning curves of employees having new jobs, and use of consultants.* Typical operating costs include salaries for new employees, costs related to equipment replacements and new acquisitions and maintenance, costs for supplies, and so on.

---

*As new methods and procedures are incorporated into an organization, an initial drop in productivity occurs. This drop is known as the learning curve effect. It is generally attributed to a temporary drop in morale due to uncertainties associated with the adaptation to a change in the work pattern, as well as a recovery time during which the employees are learning the new method or procedure and adjusting to an efficient work pattern.

Since most of the factors are quantifiable, a variety of decision models are available for evaluating economic feasibility. Among the more commonly used models are the following:

Break-even analysis model. Cumulative benefits are compared with cumulative fixed and variable costs to determine the level of activity at which each solution alternative reaches the break-even point (i.e., the point of zero net benefits). The solution alternative that has the lowest break-even activity is the best candidate for selection, other factors being equal.

Payback model. Cumulative benefits are compared with cumulative costs to determine the point in time at which each solution alternative reaches the point of zero net benefits (and thus fully recovers the cumulative cost outlays). The solution alternative that has the shortest payback period is the best candidate for selection, other factors being equal.

Net present value model. Cumulative benefits and costs are discounted by compound interest (discount) formulas that reflect the time value of money, in order to obtain their imputed values at the present time (i.e., the time of the decision). The present value of all costs is then deducted from the present value of all benefits, in order to obtain the net present value. The solution alternative that has the greatest net present value is the best candidate for selection, other factors being equal.

Internal rate of return model. Cumulative benefits and costs are discounted by compound interest (discount) formulas, as in the case of the net present value model. However, the internal rate of return process has the purpose of determining the internal rate of return—the interest rate that causes the net present value to be zero. The solution alternative that has the highest internal rate of return is the best candidate for selection, assuming that the internal rate of return exceeds the cost of capital interest rate and that other factors are equal.

Capital budgeting model. The present value model is combined with a constrained optimization procedure, using an integer programming algorithm. The result is the selection of a portfolio of investment alternatives (solutions) that maximize the total net present value. This rather complex model is needed when budget constraints exist on the overall level of capital expenditures.

Make or buy model. Total costs to make a component are compared with total costs to buy the component from an outside vendor. The solution alternative having the lesser total costs is the better candidate for selection, other factors being equal. This model attempts to answer the question: Should the organization obtain the components externally, or is the internal solution alternative preferable? In many cases this model is rather difficult to apply, since certain additional fixed overhead costs are hard to identify.

Operational Feasibility

Operational feasibility concerns the usability of each solution alternative in the environment and by the persons for whom it is intended. Among the factors that may affect the operational feasibility of a solution alternative are the following:

1. The capability of management
2. The maturity of the organization and its planning process
3. The political environment, including the informal organization
4. The interruptions that the solution alternative may impose upon the organization
5. The requirements that the solution alternative imposes with respect to hiring and training, physical facilities, and intellectual understanding

Technical Feasibility

Technical feasibility concerns the adequacy of the existing state of technology to meet the requirements of each solution alternative. A solution alternative that imposes technical requirements near or beyond the existing state of technology carries an inherent risk. An organization must consider whether or not it has the ability to absorb the potential consequences of such a risk. Such consideration should include the following factors:

1. State of the art and availability of required hardware
2. State of the art of related software
3. Availability and capability of personnel who would be involved in the implemented system or process
4. Experience and aggressiveness of the organization

Scheduling Feasibility

Scheduling feasibility concerns the realistic likelihood that each solution alternative can be rendered operational by a specified time and/or date in order to achieve certain objectives or avoid certain consequences. An assessment of scheduling feasibility requires that the consultant carefully examine the timing of necessary activities, the precedence relationships of the various activities to each other, and the availability of necessary resources.

Legal Feasibility

Legal feasibility concerns the ability of each solution alternative to meet the legal requirements imposed by outside authorities. Legal requirements include meeting government regulations promulgated by agencies with such acronyms as SEC, EEO, OSHA, and ERISA. They also include not infringing the legal rights of other organizations with respect to patents, copyrights, and trademarks. Furthermore, they include voluntary observance of professional standards established by such associations as the American Institute of Certified Public Accountants. In ascertaining the legal feasibility of a solution alternative, you should consult attorneys or other authorities on legal matters.

Other Evaluation Considerations

Other attributes in addition to the above feasibility dimensions should be factored into the evaluation procedure. Each solution alternative should be evaluated with respect to its simplicity, flexibility, adaptability, sensitivity, reliability, and robustness. It should also be viewed in terms of the degree to which it accommodates the mind set, traditions, and morals of the employees and managers and other parties (e.g., customers) who will be affected by its implementation. All of these attributes can be important to the success or failure of a particular solution alternative.

CHOICE OF THE PREFERABLE SOLUTION ALTERNATIVE

When using a decision process, follow this general rule: Choose the solution alternative that yields the best fit or value relative to the established criteria.

Difficulties in Making the Appropriate Choice

This rule can be easily applied when all factors can be quantified and related by an explicit decision model, when a single criterion is sufficient, and when values concerning the future situation are known with complete certainty. However, these conditions usually do not exist.

In most real-world problem situations the following conditions prevail:

1. Certain important factors cannot be quantified and fitted into a known decision model. For instance, a make-or-buy decision model cannot accommodate the reputation of a vendor under consideration.

2. More than one criterion may be relevant to the decision process. Furthermore, one relevant criterion may conflict with another. For example, the criterion of high product quality conflicts with the criterion of low product price. In addition, such criteria are often not directly comparable. For instance, a financial criterion is not easily compared with a socially or environmentally oriented criterion.

3. A degree of uncertainty usually pervades the problem situation and the respective solution alternatives. This uncertainty derives in part from unknown or dimly perceived actions of competitors, employees, vendors, customers, investors, and others. It leads to uncertainty concerning the future states of nature, such as the future value (cost) of a unit of raw material or an hour of labor.

Degrees of Uncertainty

Let us focus upon uncertainty, since we have explicit ways of accommodating uncertainty in the decision process. Three degrees of uncertainty may be identified:

1. *Uncertainty,* in which the available information is limited to knowledge as to the potential states of nature; insufficient information is available, however, for assignment of probabilities to the likelihood of each state of nature occurring.

2. *Risk,* in which the future states of nature can be represented by a probability distribution.

3. Complete certainty, or simply *certainty,* in which the particular future state of nature is known (i.e., in which the probability distribution reduces to a probability of one).

Separate explicit approaches are available for each of these degrees of uncertainty. Three sets of approaches are described in the following sections. In each approach an assumption is made that all payoffs or losses are known. (That is, we assume that we know the financial consequence of choosing each solution alternative, given a specified future state of nature. This assumption may not be realistic in some or even most situations.)

Approaches in an Environment of Uncertainty

Since the environment of uncertainty does not provide sufficient information to assign probabilities to the future states of nature, the decision approaches are necessarily crude. In essence they can only reflect personal attitudes concerning the willingness to accept risk. Four approaches are maximin, minimax, maximax, and rationality.

Maximin approach.   This consists of (a) identifying the worst outcome (i.e., the minimum) that can occur for any state of nature under each of the solution alternatives and (b) choosing the solution alternative with the greatest (i.e., maximum) "worst outcome." Incorporated in the maximin approach is the cautious attitude of attaining "downside" protection to insure survival.

Minimax approach.   This consists of (a) computing the maximum opportunity loss (i.e., the regret) associated with each solution alternative for every state of nature and (b) choosing the solution alternative that minimizes the maximum summed-up opportunity cost. Reflected in this approach is an attitude of regret avoidance. If properly applied, the minimax approach provides the same decision choice as the maximin approach.

Maximax approach.   This consists of (a) identifying the best outcome (i.e., the maximum) that can occur under any state of nature for each solution alternative and (b) choosing the solution alternative with the greatest (i.e., maximum) "best outcome." Incorporated in this approach is an optimistic attitude of accepting a high degree of risk in order to "hit it big."

Rationality approach.   This begins with the assumption, in the absence of available information, that each state of nature has an equal probability of occurrence. It then consists of (a) applying these equal probabilities to the outcomes associated with the respective states of nature and (b) choosing the solution alternative having the highest expected payoff.

Approaches in a Risk Environment

In a risk environment we know the probability distributions associated with the potential states of nature. The additional information needed to develop the probability distributions is derived from historical reports, marketing studies, and other fact-finding investigations. Approaches for making decision choices in a risk environment involve expected value calculations, Monte Carlo simulations, and decision tree analyses.

Expected value calculation approach.   This consists of (a) weighting the outcomes for the states of nature by the probabilities of occurrence, (b) summing up the weighted outcomes to obtain the expected value of the payoff for each solution alternative, and (c) choosing the solution alternative having the maximum expected payoff. The drawback to this approach is that it does not consider the standard deviation associated with the expected value, thereby overlooking an important measure of risk.

Monte Carlo simulation approach.   This consists of simulating a model, usually in the form of a computer program, over one or more time periods during repeated trials or runs. The computer model incorporates one or more probability distributions to represent factors whose values are subject to variability. (These probability distributions may be based either on empirical evidence or theoretical conjecture.) During each trial or run, values for the probabilistic factors are selected randomly from the distributions. The repeated trials or runs provide results expressed in probabilistic terms (i.e., expected values and standard deviations), thus yielding information concerning the likely ranges of the payoffs for the respective solution alternatives. The Monte Carlo approach is necessary in complex situations where analytical methods cannot be applied.

Decision tree approach. Like the Monte Carlo approach, the decision tree provides probabilistic results. Instead of repeated simulation runs, however, the decision tree involves a series of computations that follow along the branches of a "tree." This approach is suitable to problem situations in which a series of sequential decisions must be made.

Other risk environment approaches. Several other probabilistic approaches are available. Two of them are based on queuing theory and game theory. Since these approaches are less often applied by managerial decision makers and consultants, they will not be discussed.

It should be noted that none of the probabilistic approaches is widely used today for choosing preferable solution alternatives. Instead, most managerial decision makers and consultants revert to the strategies associated with the environment of uncertainty and simply employ intuition. The probabilistic approaches are slowly gaining in acceptance, however, as decision makers recognize the usefulness of the added information they provide.

Approaches in an Environment of Certainty

In a certainty environment we know with certainty the values for all potential states of nature, but this environment is not completely problem-free. Most situations inhibit unrestricted decision choices because of resource shortages or other constraints. Choosing a preferable solution alternative in such situations can be a difficult evaluation task. Two approaches that have proved to be relatively useful are known as optimizing and satisficing.

Optimizing approach. This is suitable for situations in which a search can feasibly and cost-effectively lead to one best solution alternative. It typically employs one of the techniques within the mathematical programming family (e.g., linear programming, integer programming, dynamic programming). While the models incorporated in such techniques are quite elegant, the specific real-world situations in which this approach may be applied are severely limited. One reason for this limitation is the demanding nature of the information requirments: Detailed quantitative information is needed concerning both resource constraints and the objective functions. Another reason is that the simplifying assumptions imposed by most of the techniques (such as the assumption of linearity imposed by the linear programming technique) do not realistically conform to the actual complexities of real-world situations.

Satisficing approach.   This is often applied in situations for which solutions cannot be feasibly developed by the optimizing approach. It consists of a search among the solution alternatives for any solution that acceptably satisfies desired performance criteria. Once such a solution alternative is discovered, it is accepted as the choice—even though other available solution alternatives may be likely to provide higher payoffs. The satisficing approach is the most widely applied of all decision approaches because it appreciably reduces the required search time while usually providing a nearly optimal solution.

Responsibility for Making the Final Choice

Deciding upon the particular approach to apply can be quite difficult, since it forces the decision maker (e.g., a high-level manager) toward the step of choosing a particular solution alternative. While you can aid the decision maker in choosing and applying the approach that seems most appropriate in the prevailing circumstances, you cannot in your role as consultant accept responsibility for the final decision choice. The responsibility for that step must rest exclusively with the decision maker.

DETAILED DEVELOPMENT OF THE SELECTED SOLUTION

Selecting a solution is not the final step, however. The selected solution must undergo detailed design and refinement. Furthermore, its implementation must be carefully planned in order to minimize required time and costly mistakes. An important concern during this phase is the constituency of the design team. Team members should be selected on the basis of their proficiency in technical design, skill in attaining management involvement, and understanding of the users' perspective.

Typical Design Tasks

The nature of the solution will dictate the specific tasks to be performed during this detailed design and refinement step. Nevertheless, the following tasks are often involved:

1. *Designing the Outputs:*   By achieving this task you can provide the vital link to the objectives established earlier. You should be careful, therefore, to ensure that the outputs do in fact clearly reflect those objectives.

2. *Designing the Inputs:*   After designing the outputs, you are in a position to trace backwards to specify the inputs that are necessary to produce those particular outputs. In addition to establishing the content of the inputs, you should specify the means by which the inputs can be acquired in a timely and accurate fashion.

3. *Designing the Conversion Processes:*   Next you can design the methods by which the inputs are converted into outputs. Your design should incorporate the following attributes into the conversion processes: effectiveness, efficiency, simplicity, modularity, and reliability. These attributes should produce conversion processes that are useful, acceptable to users, and relatively easy to operate and maintain. They are as relevant to industrial processes involving mechanical or chemical operations as they are to financial information system processes involving paperwork or electronic processes.

4. *Designing the Resource Repositories:*   The next task is to design the repositories for the valuable resources. These repositories both insulate the respective processes and provide interfaces among the processes. If the overall design pertains to an information system, the repositories consist of data bases and the valued resources are data. If the overall design pertains to a physical system, the repositories consist of storerooms and warehouses and the valued resources are inventories.

5. *Designing the Organization:*   Finally, you should design the organizational aspects that are affected by the solution, in order that the personnel will be clearly guided concerning their activities. These aspects consist of job descriptions, including assigned responsibilities and standards. In many situations you may find it necessary to develop revised management structures and organization charts.

Management of Design Activities

During activities involved in the above design tasks you should employ sound design and project management techniques. These management techniques should ensure that the various design components are consistent with each other and with the desired objectives. They should also maintain conformance with the evaluation criteria, as well as with time and cost budgets.

Specific project management techniques are discussed in Chapter 9. Specific design management techniques that may be noted, however, are stewardship structuring and prototyping. Stewardship structuring consists of assigning clear (a) authority for making decision choices and (b) responsibility for paying allocated design-related costs to the entity (e.g., function, department) that is to benefit from the developed solution. Prototyping consists of developing a model or prototype of the selected solution, which is then tested and implemented. This model or prototype provides a concrete basis by which to judge the effectiveness of the solution; it therefore enables the organization to avoid the larger costs of a complete implementation if the solution proves to be unsatisfactory.

PRESENTATION OF THE RECOMMENDED SOLUTION

The last step in the solution development phase is to present the recommended solution to management of the client organization. You must present the recommended solution in a persuasive manner if you expect to obtain the client's acceptance of the recommendation. Gaining acceptance can best be achieved by fully justifying the recommendation. If you do not sincerely believe that a recommended solution is justifiable, you should not make a presentation in its behalf.

While the justifiable nature of a solution is of primary importance, the style of the presentation cannot be overlooked. Justifiable solutions are sometimes not accepted because the consultant's presentation style has been weak. Let us therefore consider desirable aspects of presentation style.

The presentation should normally be made orally and should be accompanied by audiovisual aids and a written report. The facts and arguments should be presented in a clear, concise, and nontechnical manner. It would be counterproductive to overwhelm the client with numerous details and arcane discussions of data analysis techniques. On the other hand, you should not attempt to hide facts or techniques. If the client asks, you should be ready to describe briefly the significance of any gathered fact and the purpose of any technique employed. Furthermore, you should volunteer information concerning the risks that a recommended solution entails and the difficulties that are expected in implementing the solution.

An important principle to remember is that the client should *never* be surprised. Interim presentations and written reports should be made throughout the solution development phase. As a minimum these presentations and reports should be offered at the completion of each step or milestone. If the client management and users have been properly involved and informed at these milestones, they should easily understand the final presentation and be open to the presented findings. The chances of embarrassment should be minimized.

GUIDELINES FOR SOLUTION DEVELOPMENT

Throughout the solution development phase you should follow several guidelines. Certain of these guidelines have already been noted; others warrant attention as this phase concludes:

1. You should be sure that the selected solution relates directly to objectives that the client desires to achieve.
2. You should maintain a comprehensive view of the problem situation and how it relates to the overall organization; at the same time, however, you should focus on the key issues or concerns.
3. As an aspect of the above, you should search for all the important relationships involved in the situation.
4. You should employ systematic procedures and methodologies while maintaining an openness to creative insights.

9

Implementation*

GEORGE HILL
Arthur Andersen & Co.
Phoenix, Arizona

Implementation is the important and lengthy phase that follows the solution development phase during a problem-solving process. A number of activities are usually involved in the implementation phase. These activities are likely to include the development of a work plan, the establishment of controls over the implementation activities, the selection and training of needed personnel, the installation of needed physical facilities, the development of standards and documentation, the testing of the solution being implemented, and the follow-up and evaluation of the implemented solution. While their sequence will vary somewhat from engagement to engagement, they are typically performed in the order listed above.

Each of the above activities is discussed in this chapter. In order to provide concreteness to the discussion, we assume that a newly redesigned information system is the "solution" being implemented. Implementation projects involving the installation of information systems are among the most frequently encountered.

*The contributor and editors wish to acknowledge the assistance of Neil Hawksworth, Neil Armstrong, John Kurkjian, Steve Tesdahl, Kathy Grove, Bob Hartmann, Mary Keller, Kirk Meighan, Joe Sykes, and Paul Harrison in the preparation of this chapter.

To be successful, implementation must be accompanied by changes on the part of those who will use the implemented solution. Therefore, the chapter contains a concluding section that discusses strategies for effecting such changes.

WORK PLAN DEVELOPMENT

The development of a sound work plan is critical to a successful implementation phase. The work plan defines what tasks are to be performed, when the tasks are to be performed, and who will perform them. Without this information the consultant and client management would have no means of measuring how well a project is progressing.

The key steps in the development of a sound work plan are:[1]

1. Define the scope of the implementation project.
2. Define the work units to be performed.
3. Identify the skill levels required by the work units.
4. Estimate the times required to complete the work units.
5. Establish milestone dates within the life of the project.
6. Develop the details of the work plan.
7. Review and approve the work plan.

A format of a work plan (also called a work program) appears in Figure 9.1. (Another example is included within a proposal.) You may want to refer to these examples during the following discussions of the seven steps.

Define the Scope of the Implementation Project

One or more problem areas were identified during the problem definition phase. At this point the scope of the implementation project must be more sharply defined. That is, you must clearly define those areas that are to be included within the implementation and those that are not. If the scope is not well defined, the project can become open-ended and it can "last forever." Furthermore, you must define the scope *before* the implementation commences. If the scope definition is delayed, the project boundaries will probably shift and thus cause confusion for the participants.

Define the Work Units to Be Performed

The next step is to identify and define the work units (i.e., tasks) to be performed. For instance, the following tasks should be included in the implementation of an information systems project:[2]

1. Organization of the project
2. Completion of the system design
3. Coding of the programs
4. Testing of the system interfaces
5. Installation of the new system

Several other tasks often included in a systems implementation project are:[3]

1. Selection and installation of hardware and system software
2. Development of the systems documentation for users, for management, and for the computer operations personnel
3. Development of the appropriate testing environment
4. Establishment of the conversion plan and procedures

The type and size of the implementation project are likely to have a significant impact on the particular tasks that need to be performed and on their relative importance. For example, a project involving the implementation of application software would probably place more emphasis on the conversion of the package to the available hardware and less emphasis on the coding and testing of programs. A large project may dictate the use of separate teams assigned to logically related tasks, with added time allowed for project administration and communication. A small project will require less time for administration and communication; because it will probably use only one project team, however, it will have less flexibility in sequencing the various tasks.

Identify the Skill Levels Required by the Work Units

For each defined work unit or task an appropriate skill level or experience level must be identified. For example, relatively experienced personnel are needed for the scope definition and system design tasks. Less experienced staff may be assigned to programming and documentation tasks. After identifying the appropriate skill level for each task, you can assign specific individuals to each task.

Estimate the Times Required to Complete the Work Units

The next step is to estimate how long each work unit or task will take. It may be possible to use estimating guidelines, such as an average number of lines coded per day. If guidelines are not available, you can draw on your past experience, the past experience of the client, or estimates provided by others (e.g., vendors in the case of application software). Regardless of the estimates' source, they should be consistent; the source should be clearly documented.

MANAGEMENT SERVICES WORK PROGRAM

CLIENT NAME
Community Services Corp.

PRELIMINARY SURVEY ☐   IMPLEMENTATION ☑   ENGAGEMENT ☐   FOLLOW-UP ☐

INFORMATION TO OBTAIN AND REVIEW PRIOR TO ACTUAL SURVEY:

ORGANIZATION CHART ☐   POSITION DESCRIPTIONS ☐   FLOW CHARTS ☐   SYSTEMS QUESTIONAIRE ☐

POLICY STATEMENTS ☐   PROCEDURES MANUAL ☐   OTHER (LIST ON REVERSE SIDE) ☐

AREAS TO BE REVIEWED (IN ORDER OF PRIORITY)

1. *Implement feasibility study*
2. *conducted as prior engagement*
3.
4.
5.
6.
7.
8.

PERSONNEL TO BE INTERVIEWED

NAME	REGARDING	WHEN
See prior engagement		

PLAN OF ACTION

ACTION STEP	TECHNIQUES TO BE USED	ASSIGNED TO *	TARGET DATES START	TARGET DATES FINISH	EST. TIME
1. PLANNING ENGAGEMENT					
2. PRELIMINARY SURVEY					
Design input-output forms		T.S.	7/27	9/18	120
Prepare detailed specs.		T.S./R.B.	7/27	10/23	560
Programming		Various	7/27	11/5	630
Write use manual		T.S.	11/13	12/18	44
System conversion		R.B.	11/13	12/18	280
Post implement support		R.B.	1/15	2/12	80
Supervision		C.S.	7/27	2/12	120
Clerical support			TOTAL		80
DAILY TOTALS					

* *Includes firm personnel only. See engagement letter for client and manufacturer's responsibilities.*

(a)

Figure 9.1*a* Example of a work plan (program). Adapted from *Documentation Guides for Administration of Management Advisory Services Engagements, MAS Guideline Series,* No. 2, 1971. Copyright © 1971 by the American Institute of Certified Public Accountants, Inc.

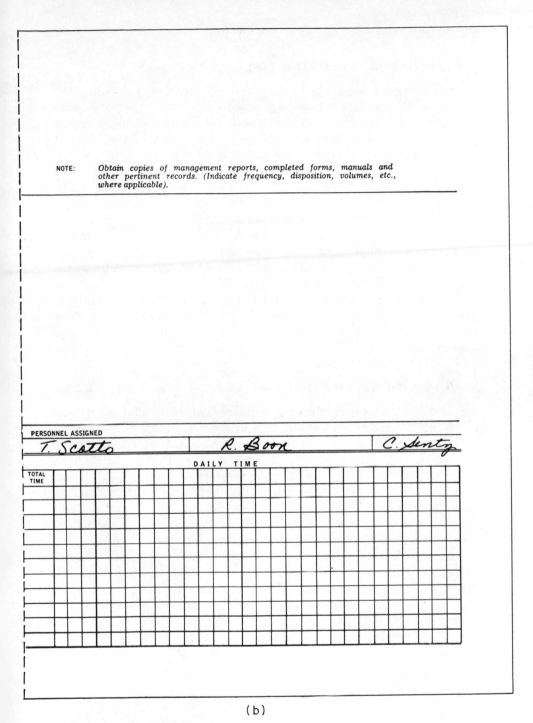

NOTE: *Obtain copies of management reports, completed forms, manuals and other pertinent records. (Indicate frequency, disposition, volumes, etc., where applicable).*

PERSONNEL ASSIGNED

T. Scotto   R. Boon   C. Senty

DAILY TIME

TOTAL TIME

(b)

Figure 9.1*b* Example of a work plan (program), continued.

Establish Milestone Dates within the Life of the Project

In order to establish milestone dates, you should first determine the project completion date. For certain projects this date is specified by an external event. In the case of an accounting system, the completion date is typically at the end of an accounting period. If the completion date cannot be tied to an external event, perhaps the beginning date can be. For instance, the beginning date may be determined by the availability of key consulting or client personnel. Then the completion date can be determined as the beginning date plus the overall project time.

Once a key date (either for beginning or completion) has been identified, the other milestone dates can be established. As the name implies, these dates should represent the completion of major work activities such as detailed testing of all programs, system test, or acceptance test of selected application software packages.

Milestone dates provide you and the client management with the means of ascertaining whether or not the project is on schedule. They also represent logical points in time at which to review the quality and scope of the project.

Develop the Details of the Work Plan

After completing the previous steps, you are ready to develop the details pertaining to the work plan or program. First you should determine all of the smaller work units (i.e., subtasks) that comprise each major work unit or task. Then prepare a network chart, such as a PERT or CPM chart. This chart should show all the milestones as well as the final completion date. Take care to sequence the tasks so that they are in proper relation to each other. When you are satisfied that the tasks are complete and properly related, sequence the smaller work units within each task. Finally, you should determine the critical path of the project.

Figure 9.2 shows a CPM chart for a system implementation project, with all the major tasks and subtasks sequenced relative to each other. The critical path begins at Task I, continues through nodes 1.1, 1.3, 1.4, 3.2, and concludes with Task VII. The estimated overall project time, as shown on the time scale, is 48 weeks. (Normally, you would also fill in the calendar scale shown at the top of the chart.)

Review and Approve the Work Plan

The final step in the development of a work plan is to review the plan with client management. At this point the client may indicate changes in the milestones or the number of client personnel who are available to be assigned to the project. If this happens, the plan should be adjusted and

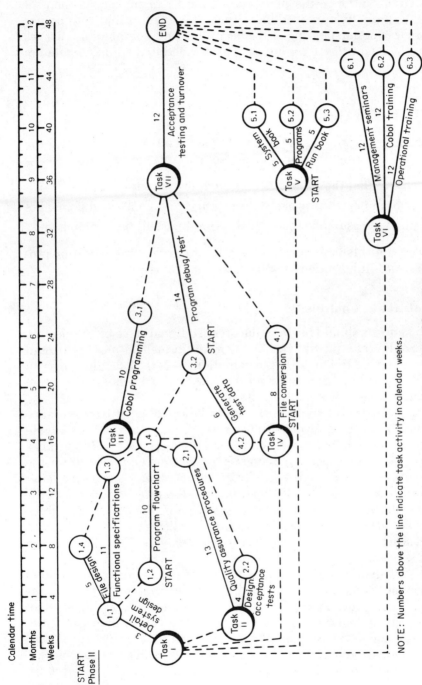

Figure 9.2 A CPM chart for a systems implementation project. Adapted from *Documentation Guides for Administration of Management Advisory Services Engagements*, MAS Guideline Series, No. 2, 1971. Copyright © 1971 by the American Institute of Certified Public Accountants, Inc.

NOTE: Numbers above the line indicate task activity in calendar weeks.

161

reviewed again. Once the plan is accepted by client management, it should be formally approved in writing. This ensures that both parties have a clear understanding of the beginning and completion dates, as well as the quantities of resources to be devoted to the implementation project.

PROJECT CONTROLS

Project controls provide the means of successfully administering the work plan. Specific objectives of project controls are:[4]

1. To ensure that the project is on schedule and within budget
2. To communicate the exact project status of all concerned personnel
3. To provide assurance that a quality product will be implemented

Project controls include administrative controls, time reporting procedures, and independent quality assurance reviews.

Administrative Controls

Project controls should begin in the organizational stage of a project. In this stage the administrative framework is formed to provide overall guidance and control to the implementation process. It should consist of individuals who have direct interest in the quality of the final product (e.g., an installed information system).

The administrative framework should be established in accordance with the size of the project and the client. The framework for a simple project and small client firm should be simple, perhaps involving only a single top-level manager. For a complex project and large client firm, the framework may be quite involved. Our description assumes the latter case. It also assumes, as stated earlier, that the project pertains to the implementation of an information system. Thus, the description given below should be scaled down to suit simpler projects and smaller firms; it should also be modified as necessary to fit other types of implementation projects.

The administrative framework should consist of one or more client management committees, with representatives from the user areas, the top (executive) management, and the information processing services department. In larger firms that have several levels of management, it may be desirable to have more than one committee. For instance, a firm might establish both a project steering committee and a management advisory committee. While each committee formed should share responsibility for controlling the project, each would have distinctive purposes:

The project steering committee would maintain direct control over the project, while the management advisory committee would coordinate the activities of the information processing services department.

Since the project steering committee is most closely involved with projects, it deserves additional attention. The committee should be comprised of senior management from each area of the client organization that is impacted by the system project. The leader of the project, as well as the manager of the information processing services department, should also be on the committee. This committee provides direct guidance over the project; thus, it has control over and is responsible for all costs and benefits pertaining to the development and operation of the system spanned by the project. In addition, the committee monitors project activities to ensure that all changes to the system design are made only with proper approval and that all policy changes are observed.

The committees hold regularly scheduled status meetings to carry out the monitoring responsibilities. In addition, ad hoc meetings are held when specific problems of significance arise.

Time Reporting Procedures

Time reporting and analysis procedures are necessary to keep the project within its time schedule and dollar budget. Specific objectives of these procedures are:[5]

1. To provide project management with information necessary for planning, administering, and controlling the project
2. To prepare and control the project work plan (program) updates
3. To assist the project leader in preparing management status reports
4. To account for all time incurred on the project by team members

Several procedures relative to time reporting should be observed. Actual time incurred on a project should be reported at the same level of detail as the budgeting of time on the work plan. Both project hours and nonproject hours should be reported by each team member. The estimated time to complete each task currently in progress should be included in the report. The upper portion of Figure 9.3 shows a time report for a job, an activity within a project.

The time reports of all team members should be reviewed for accuracy, with actual time and estimated-time-to-complete being compared to the work plan. If the client has an automated time reporting system, it should be employed by the project team when appropriate. If the client does not have an automated time reporting system, the feasibility of obtaining one for use by the project team should be studied.

JOB TIME REPORT

Herman Corporation | 4 | Design Financial & Responsibility Reports | T. Scotto

X.00/HC	T. Scotto	5/25/86 5/31/86	J.F. Pollar
RATE	NAME OF PERSON	FROM TO	PREPARED BY / APPROVED BY

PROJ. NO.	ACT. NO.	TASK NO.	DESCRIPTION	*	Actual to Date	MON	TUE	WED	THU	FRI	SAT	SUN	End Actual to Date	Earned Hours	TOTAL PLAN	Remaining to do	Check √ Complin
02	002	001	Interview Dept. Mgmt.	P		8									16		
				A	8	10	2						20				✓
02	002	002	Define Needs of Users	P			8	4	8	8					44		
				A	8		8	4	8	8	2		38			6	
01	003	001	Design Cashflow Stmt.	P				4							8		
				A	4			4					8				✓
			Total Planned	P		8	8	8	8	8					68		
			Total Actual	A	20	10	10	8	8	8	2		66			6	
			Attendance Variance	V		2	2				2						

SUMMARY

PROJ. NO.	TOTAL HOURS	TIME CHRGS	EXP	TOTAL CHRGS
01	4	X.00	X.00	XX.00
02	42	X.00	X.00	XX.00

NOTE TO PERSONNEL

The hours and expenses which appear in the summary section of this report must equal those which appear on the semi-monthly time report. Therefore, this information will be entered only on the engagement report for the week in which a semi-monthly time report is submitted.

* A = ACTUAL   P = PLANNED   V = VARIANCE

Activity Manning Sheet

Date 5/30/86

Job No. 04
Project No. 02
Activity No. 002

Page 1

Activity Name Define Resp. Report Requirements
Organization Herman Corporation

Prepared by T. Scotto
Approved by J.F. Pollar

Name		5/23	TD	5/30	TD		TD		TD		TD		TD		TD		TD		TD		TD	Total
	P	16	16	36	52																	52
Scotto	A	16	16	42	58																	58
	O	-	-	6	6																	6
	P	8	8	4	12																	12
Yalton	A	8	8	5	13																	13
	O			1	1																	1
	P																					
	A																					
	O																					
	P																					
	A																					
	O																					
	P	24	24	40	64																	64
	A	24	24	47	71																	71
Totals	V	-	-	7	7																	7
	O																					

P = Planned   A = Actual Against Plan   V = Variance
O = Actual Nonplan Other

Figure 9.3 Examples of time-related reports. Adapted from *Documentation Guides for Administration of Management Advisory Services Engagements*, MAS Guideline Series, No. 2, 1971. Copyright © 1971 by the American Institute of Certified Public Accountants, Inc.

Time reports should be summarized at a team level, activity level, or project level, depending upon the structure and size of the project. All variances between actual and budgeted time should be recorded and their causes determined. The lower portion of Figure 9.3 shows a summarized report for job no. 04, an activity in project no. 02.

Common causes of time variances include:

1. Improperly applied estimating guidelines
2. Improperly communicated task scopes and objectives
3. Inappropriately assigned personnel (people who are either over-qualified or underqualified for the assigned tasks)
4. Unexpected changes to task scopes and objectives
5. Unexpected difficulties with respect to the availability or functioning of project resources

When changes make it necessary, the project leader should revise the budgeted hours in the work plan.

Independent Quality Assurance Reviews

Quality assurance programs represent another means of control over projects. The objectives of quality assurance are:[6]

1. To ensure that the system satisfies all user requirements and is operable on a day-to-day basis without assistance
2. To ensure that the system is being developed within the time frame and cost estimates originally agreed upon
3. To ensure that the system is simple and efficient to operate, maintain, and control by client personnel
4. To ensure that the system employs satisfactory methods and techniques that are within the sphere of competence of the majority of client personnel
5. To ensure that the presentation and format of all procedures, documentation, and coding are neat, well organized, and in conformance with established client standards

Components of a quality assurance program include:

1. *Independent reviews:* These should be conducted prior to reaching implementation project milestones. They should be performed by a person who (a) is not associated with the project and (b) has a skill level at least as high as the project leader's. (On very small projects some of the review may be performed by the project leader.)

2. *Quality assurance checklists:* These contain a series of questions concerning the quality of work performed and should be (a) prepared by the project supervisor responsible for the work and (b) reviewed by both the project leader and the independent reviewer. (On very small projects, in which supervisors are not used, they would be prepared by the project leader.)

The independent reviewer should prepare written comments concerning the findings of reviews and checklists. Problems should be resolved by the project leader, if possible. Unresolvable problems should be presented to the project steering committee.

SELECTION AND TRAINING OF NEEDED PERSONNEL

Selection of Project Personnel

Skilled and experienced personnel are critical to the success of an implementation project. Thus, the selection and training of needed personnel for the project are important.

Selecting the needed personnel for a specific implementation project is often difficult. The following aspects must be considered:[7]

1. Staffing levels needed
2. Skills and experience required for project tasks
3. Past performances of available personnel
4. Availability of consulting firm personnel
5. Availability of client personnel

The first two requirements are determined during preparation of the work plan, while the third is ascertained (at least in part) by the time variances that appear on project control reports. The last two aspects are discussed below.

Availability of Consulting Personnel

Determining who is available for assignment is a fairly informal task in a small consulting firm. In larger consulting firms, however, tracking the availability of personnel requires formal procedures. On a short-term basis a daily staffing sheet may be employed. This sheet alphabetically lists each consultant's name and the project to which he or she is assigned on a particular day. On a longer-term basis a staff availability schedule is often employed. Figure 9.4 lists information that should appear on such a schedule.

Figure 9.4 A staff availability schedule.

1. Time frame for which the information is provided
2. Name of consultant
3. Employee identification number
4. Staffing level of the consultant (e.g., partner, manager, senior)
5. Availability status information:
    a. *Project to which individual is currently assigned*
    b. *Type of project (e.g., installation)*
    c. *Project scheduled starting date*
    d. *Project schedule completion date*
6. *Date the staff person becomes available for other projects*

Availability of Client Personnel

Client responsibilities must also be established. The consultant may not "exercise absolute administrative control of client personnel since he is not a member of their organization." You can, however, advise client management on the selection of qualified personnel to perform the project tasks. If a client lacks personnel who are capable of assuming responsibilities with respect to project tasks, you may recommend that the client employ additional personnel who are so qualified. "The right mixture of consultant and client personnel is a critical consideration" when planning project assignments.[8]

Criteria similar to those used to select consultants may be utilized to choose appropriate client members. Development of such criteria, however, must be based on client policies and standards.

Types of Training Methods

While personnel may be selected on the basis of skills and experience, they nevertheless need training at various times during their employment. Staff development and training is as essential to the continued well-being of the consulting firm and the projects undertaken as it is to the careers of the consultants. Chapter 16 discusses staff development and training in depth. Here, several types of training methods are considered briefly, as they bear upon the needs of implementation projects.

Formal training. Depending on the complexity of the proposed project, consulting (and perhaps client) personnel may need to attend formal training classes. For instance, if a software package is to be purchased from an outside vendor, the personnel assigned to the project may be asked to attend a vendor-sponsored school. This formal instruction will enable the project members to acquire a working knowledge of the functional and technical aspects of the package.

Another situation warranting formal training for the staff consultant is a project involving an unfamiliar technical environment. In this situation the client might offer the same training program that is attended by the client's personnel. Such training could involve reading technical manuals and attending client-instructed classes.

Ongoing training.   Every suitable consulting firm should provide ongoing training that employs a variety of educational methods and covers various subjects. This ongoing training might involve a combination of in-house and out-of-house training programs. Possible out-of-house training programs that should be considered include those offered by the National Association of Accountants and the American Institute of Certified Public Accountants.

Informal training.   Every consulting firm should maintain an assortment of periodicals, research materials, reference manuals, and past project documentation within its library and files. It should encourage its personnel to use such materials to prepare for engagements such as implementation projects. College and university libraries are also excellent sources of training materials. In addition, informal discussions with other consulting personnel having experience on similar projects can provide relevant information.

INSTALLATION OF PHYSICAL FACILITIES

The implementation of many problem situations involves installation of physical facilities. This is particularly true with respect to a newly designed information system. While the installation of physical facilities is a task that occurs mainly during the implementation phase, however, it should be considered in the context of the entire system development life cycle. Figure 9.5 shows the four phases of an information system development life cycle. In each phase certain tasks are performed and decisions are made concerning the installation of physical facilities such as computer hardware. Many of these tasks are closely related. All are influenced by existing business objectives, strategies, and policies, including those pertaining to computer hardware and software.

Let us review the impact of each phase shown in Figure 9.5 on the installation of the particular physical facilities known as computer hardware.

System Planning

If a computer hardware strategy does not already exist, it should be developed during the system planning phase. If one does exist, it should be updated as the new systems are developed. It should span several

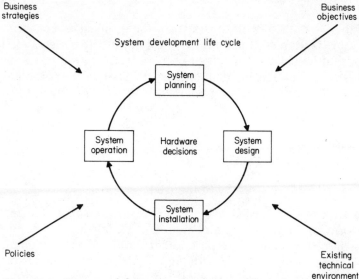

Figure 9.5   Diagram of the system development life cycle.

years into the future, taking into account all expected future development projects, as well as the changing operating and information needs of the organization.

System Design

Specific computer hardware recommendations must be made during the system design phase. Hardware selection is very important, since it has a critical impact on the overall performance of the information system. The preliminary selection should occur prior to technical design of the system, and the final selection should be completed before the implementation phase begins.

System Installation

When the implementation project schedule is prepared, it should include tasks labeled "Preparation of Physical Site" and "Installation of New Hardware." Although the vendor of the hardware may actually perform the installation, the project leader or consultant must coordinate the activity in such a way as to minimize disruption to the client firm. Numerous details may be involved, such as the installation of a special power supply and air-conditioning, plus the layout of space requirements for the equipment.

System Operation

During the operation of the installed system, a major concern is the effective utilization of the computer system and the identification of potential bottlenecks. Overutilization may indicate the need for additional hardware. Increasing maintenance costs and other problems may indicate the need for new equipment.

DEVELOPMENT OF STANDARDS
AND DOCUMENTATION

Objectives to Be Achieved by Standards

Standards are needed with respect to the solution (e.g., an improved information system) being implemented. Thus, the development of standards, followed by the preparation of standardized documentation, is a task to be performed during the implementation project. Normally, standards should be developed by the most experienced and qualified members of the implementation project team, in order that they will be as sound as possible. Establishment of sound standards should help achieve the following objectives:

1. To provide a basis for effective communication within the areas served by the implementation project
2. To improve the efficiency of installing and operating the solution, e.g., an improved information system
3. To serve as an aid in training all personnel affected by the implementation project

Well-documented, easily understandable, and strictly adhered-to standards establish an effective framework for communication. They help illustrate both concepts and specific details to all those involved with the implementation project, including client management and user personnel as well as technical experts and staff consultants. By referring to the standards, any authorized person should gain a faster and more complete comprehension of the system being implemented.

Sound standards also improve productivity and efficiency, both during the implementation project and later during the operational phase. Standards tend to reduce the possibilities of duplicated efforts and conflicting procedures. They encourage the performance of similar activities using similar techniques aimed at standardized results. Since standards help to define the procedures to be used, they make easier the activity of estimating requirements pertaining to project work units. In addition, they ensure that the maintenance of the system during the operational phase will be simple and straightforward.

The third objective relates to training. Standards should provide a common framework for familiarizing all affected persons with the environment in which they will be working. They provide guidance in training the members of the implementation project team or teams. They also facilitate the training of user personnel, such as newly hired or transferred employees who are assigned to the information systems department. By making training easier, they thereby reduce training costs.

Factors that should be considered when developing standards include the following:

1. Standards and other guidelines presently in existence
2. Relative size of the project
3. Relative complexity of the project
4. Standards, if any, that have been prepared by the vendors of the physical facilities being implemented

Standardized Documentation

Documentation of the implemented project should be developed in accordance with established standards. The purposes of standardized documentation are to:[9]

1. Record decisions
2. Communicate ideas
3. Specify procedures
4. Assign responsibilities for tasks
5. Provide a means of reviewing the quality and completeness of work performed and indicating approval or disapproval of the work performed
6. Provide historical support and backup

The documentation process is necessary to the implementation phase. It provides the following benefits:

1. A means of communicating to the client management
2. A memory aid for the designer of the project being implemented, e.g., an improved information system
3. A reference for use during the operational phase
4. A vehicle for resolving misunderstandings concerning the functioning of the implemented facilities, e.g., an information system

Figure 9.6 lists several implementation activities and the documenta-

Figure 9.6 List of implementation activities and related documentation.

Activity	Document	Description
1. Develop implementation plan	a. Program description b. File definition c. Personnel assignments d. Implementation schedule e. Hardware installation schedule f. Cost/benefit analysis—operations g. Estimate of installation costs	Abstract of logical program function, flow of control File structure diagram, data contents Chart of people and their tasks, and time estimates to complete Chart of tasks and milestones List of hardware to be installed and dates
2. Develop detailed design (if not completed during design phase)	a. Manual procedures b. Program specifications c. Test conditions d. Test data e. Expected results	Step-by-step instructions for doing tasks Program logic in narrative or diagram format or both Conditions to be tested for layout of test records Expected results of program execution
3. Estimate needs and establish controls	a. Estimates of manpower b. Approach memorandum c. Conversion schedule	Length of the conversion and who will do it Conversion files and cycle approach definitions Time when conversion tasks will take place
4. Develop security standards	a. Security memorandum	Restriction of personnel, data security, recovery from system failure, passwords IDs
5. Develop operating standards	a. User manual	Statement of exactly when and how each task is performed, brief and concise
6. Train user personnel	a. General computer concepts b. Equipment overview	User orientation to computers, if new to them User orientation to equipment and operating instructions
7. Test implemented system	a. Test data b. Actual results c. System modifications d. Resolution of system problems	Comparison of actual test results against expected results What system should do according to design request for system change, with differences well documented

tion that should be produced by each during the implementation of an information system.

A variety of standardized systems development methodologies exist to aid the documentation process, including:

1. STRADIS (STRuctured Analysis, Design and Implementation of Systems), marketed by McAuto Systems
2. PRIDE (PRofitable Information by DEsign), marketed by M. Bruce and Associates
3. 50M/70, marketed by Atlantic Software
4. METHOD/1, marketed by Arthur Andersen & Co

TESTING OF SOLUTION BEING IMPLEMENTED

Testing is an indispensable activity within the implementation phase. Thorough testing of the implemented solution can ensure that it works as designed and meets the users' needs.

The testing activity can be subdivided into three steps: unit test, string test, and system test. Each step requires considerable planning and preparation prior to actual execution of the tests.

Unit Test

This consists of testing the smallest unit of the solution being implemented. In the case of a computer-based information system, the unit is often viewed as being a computer program. The purpose of conducting a unit test is to ensure that each separate unit functions properly. The steps of a unit test consist of:

1. Identifying the test conditions
2. Preparing the test data
3. Computing the expected results
4. Performing the actual tests
5. Comparing the actual results obtained with the expected results

String Test

After unit testing has been successfully completed, string testing should begin. A string test is a test of closely related units. Its purpose is to determine that the units (e.g., computer programs) work together or interface properly. Test conditions may be created during a string test that could not be performed during a unit test. Such extra test conditions should test the design features that link the constituent programs as well as the overall design of the programs operating in combination.

System Test

This consists of testing the entire solution being implemented. In the case of an information system, the system test extends from the preparation of source documents to the distribution of outputs. A system test has the purposes of ensuring that:

1. Documentation is adequate to operate the implemented system successfully
2. User departments affected by the implementation can properly and easily prepare the necessary inputs and can use the outputs successfully
3. Overall flows through the system are in accordance with the developed solution

A system test can be subdivided into two component tests: an integration test and a user test. The integration test is performed to verify that all units in the new system communicate properly with each other. It also verifies that the new system interfaces properly with all external systems. The user test is performed to verify that the system can operate within the new environment to satisfactorily meet the needs of the users. This test should simulate as exactly as possible the actual working conditions to be faced, and in the case of a new information system it should employ live production data.

FOLLOW-UP EVALUATION OF THE IMPLEMENTED SOLUTION

Objectives of a Postimplementation Evaluation

A thorough postimplementation evaluation should be conducted shortly after the solution has been fully implemented. Reports should be prepared as written documentation of the evaluation and presented to management. The objectives of the evaluation, in the case of an information system, are to:[10]

1. Compare the actual performance of the implemented system with the expected performance
2. Compare the details of the implemented system with the documented design
3. Determine potential improvements to the new system
4. Determine means of improving the systems development methodology employed by the client firm

An early question that must be resolved concerns who is to conduct the evaluation. While the implementation team is most familiar with the implemented system, it may be viewed as biased. Therefore, it is probably better to choose qualified personnel other than members of the implementation team. Three suitable choices are:[11]

1. A special audit team selected from among the managers of the client organization
2. An internal audit team that performs operational reviews as a part of its customary duties
3. An external team of consultants

The follow-up evaluation is not a one-time process. Additional evaluations should be performed at regular intervals during the operational life of the implemented system. User needs change over time, and these changes will lead in time to the need for further improvements via future system development cycles.

Each review and evaluation should focus on three specific areas:

1. Economics
2. Operations
3. Future performance

Economic Review

The economic review should involve the comparison of (a) the actual benefits and costs of the new system with (b) the expected benefits and costs that were developed during the system design phase. Typical questions that may be asked during an economic review include:[12]

Were the development cost estimates on target?

Did the expected benefits materialize?

Were the operational costs in line with estimates?

Have significant variances occurred?

As the last question suggests, all variances should be calculated. Large variances, over or under, should be thoroughly investigated, and the reasons for their occurrences should be carefully documented. Figure 9.7 presents an analysis format that may be employed to document the benefit and cost variances. Note that it also provides space for displaying the rate of return and payback period, which can be useful to client management when making key decisions.[13]

This analysis of benefit and cost variances often yields satisfying

Figure 9.7 Format of an economic review analysis.

Benefits versus cost analysis			
Cost/benefit	Estimate	Actual	Variance
Initial cost of new system			
Site preparation cost			
System design and analysis			
Cost			
Programming costs			
Training, conversion, and			
other implementation costs			
Total one-time development costs	————	————	————
Annual operating costs			
Computer hardware and related			
equipment rental or purchase			
Software rental or purchase			
Analysis and programming			
maintenance costs			
Operating personnel costs			
Space charges, supplies, etc.	————	————	————
Total annual operating costs	————	————	————
Annual operating costs			
Reduced personnel savings			
Personnel efficiency savings	————	————	————
Total annual savings	————	————	————
Rate of return			
(Rate at which present value of			
savings equals present value of			
one-time costs)			
Payback period			
(Length of time required to			
recover one-time costs)			
Other intangible benefits			
(List)			

results. For instance, operational costs may be found to be too high or operational benefits to be missing. Upon investigation, the unsatisfactory results are attributed to improper use of the system. A relatively simple and low-cost adjustment may be the only corrective action needed to produce a significant saving in costs or an increase in benefits.

The analysis is useful even when immediate results are not likely. For example, development costs are historical in nature and thus cannot be recovered. By learning the reasons for variances in development costs, however, client management can modify the system development and thus reduce development costs in future implementations.

Operational Review

An operational review focuses on the actual use of the implemented system by the intended users. Typical questions that might be asked during an operational review include:[14]

Does the system operate successfully?

Has the system solved the organizational problems that it is intended to address?

Is the system being used or is it being resisted?

Are the automated and manual processes as efficient as intended?

An evaluation of operations after implementation should consider how well they function, with particular emphasis (in the case of an information system) on inputs, error rates, timeliness of outputs, and utilization of outputs. Various evaluation techniques may be employed. For instance, a report can be terminated for a period of time in order to determine if it is actually being used. If no one complains, the report is probably not being used. A performance monitor can be applied, in the case of an online information system, to determine the use frequency of a particular CRT screen.[15]

Future Performance Review

A future performance review identifies potential improvements to the implemented system and estimates the effort required to implement these improvements. Both benefits and costs should be considered in this review, just as they were during the planning of the currently implemented system.

Possible improvements, to be conducted by means of systems mainte-nance projects, can be subdivided into short-term attributes and long-term attributes. Client management can then prioritize the tasks, deter-mining which efforts should be undertaken immediately and which should be delayed.

EFFECTING CHANGE

Implementation leads to change. Both the client management and the direct users of an implemented solution must undergo change. Adjust-ing to change is never easy for humans. Thus, you should be aware of the three steps in a change process and the strategies by which you as consultant can successfully effect needed change in client personnel.

Change Model

According to the change model, three steps are involved:

1. Unfreezing established behavior patterns
2. Changing by moving to a new behavior pattern
3. Refreezing by firmly establishing the new behavior pattern

Strategies for Effecting Change

Each of the three steps can be achieved by positive actions on the part of a consultant.

To effect the unfreezing step, you need to create the desire for change. For instance, you might shock client management by revealing an undesirable current state of affairs (e.g., a very high unit cost of production) or current dissatisfaction (e.g., a very low level of employee morale). Once management's attention has been captured by this negative news, you can paint a positive view of improvement through specific changes. In order to create the desire for change in the client's employees, you could show that the proposed change has the support of management. Alternatively, you might show specific benefits to the employees (e.g., an easier way to get a job done).

To bring about the change, you need a commitment to action. This commitment can be achieved only by active involvement or participation. Strategies for gaining involvement include:

1. Use of brainstorming sessions or other means of soliciting ideas
2. Use of "what-if" sessions or other means of projecting views of a future that contains the change
3. Use of pilot programs in which small organizational units serve as "pioneers"
4. Use of committees to investigate the desirability of the change
5. Use of training programs in which the change is taught

To refreeze the change, you can employ such strategies as:

1. Positive individual encouragement (e.g., "You are really catching on!")
2. Well-designed training sequence, in which the change is subdivided into parts and taught in a building-up fashion and in which achievement targets are clearly established
3. Repetitive practice, i.e., many repetitions involving the change, each followed by a rest period

4. Group meetings in which achievements are displayed and the benefits of the change are repeated

5. Records of achievement in which written records are maintained to reflect performance improvements

The preparation for such activities should be undertaken as early in the planning phase as possible. In fact, as suggested above, the seeds of change are planted at the initial meeting with client management. By careful cultivation you can reap the satisfaction of fully effected changes within the client's organization.

NOTES

1. Arthur Andersen & Co., *Method/1 Information Systems Methodology*, Arthur Andersen & Co., Chicago, 1983.

2. Ibid.

3. Ibid.

4. Ibid.

5. Ibid.

6. Ibid.

7. Ibid.

8. American Institute of Certified Public Accountants, *Management Advisory Services, Guideline Series Number 1*, AICPA, New York, 1968.

9. Arthur Andersen & Co., op. cit.

10. Ibid.

11. Gordon B. Davis, *Management Information Systems: Conceptual Foundations, Structure and Development*, McGraw-Hill, New York, 1974.

12. Arthur Andersen & Co., op. cit.

13. William S. Davis, *Systems Analysis and Design*, Addison-Wesley, Reading, Massachusetts, 1983.

14. Arthur Andersen & Co., op. cit.

15. Gordon B. Davis, op. cit.

Administrative Elements of the Consulting Process

10

Proposal Process

ALBERT M. MILLER, JR., CPA
Miller and Miller, CPAs,
Knoxville, Tennessee

INTRODUCTION

The purpose of this chapter is to provide a guideline for the practitioner who is developing the proposal process within the firm. Proposal writing will be simplified and made more effective by relying on basic guidelines and by mapping out the procedures in order of priority. Practical examples are given along the way to illustrate the philosophy of the author.

By definition, a proposal is a plan and offer to be accepted or rejected. This chapter should help the consultant prepare a proposal that has a high probability of acceptance.

The proposal is the sales pitch. Whether a formal or casual proposal is made, whether it is written or verbal, getting the consulting engagement hinges on getting the potential user of consulting services to say yes to the offer. In retail and sales organizations the byword is: Nothing happens until the sale is made! This means that until a customer says yes, not much activity can occur. Consultants are in a selling game even though some may think that selling is unprofessional. The proposal is a vital piece of the total sales effort. It is the part within the process in which the prospect is asked to say yes. If he or she says no, all previous efforts end up being good experience, but no new business is created for the firm. If the answer is yes, the client receives a valuable service and the consultant wins a new project. Both parties win!

As in other sales and marketing efforts, there should be an attitude of enthusiasm. The practitioner must believe that the prospect has a real need for the service. If the consultant has approached the earlier sales efforts (which precede the preparation of a proposal) with the proper attitude, half the battle is won. The prospective client will catch the "fever of enthusiasm" and will be more eager to receive the proposal. The actual project will be much easier if the client is involved throughout the proposal effort. Building agreement along the way with the client makes it easier for the client to say yes to the final proposal.

The theme in proposal writing is to merchandise the proposal in the best, most professional manner possible. A less than superior proposal may result in a lost opportunity. This means the story has not been told properly or the proposal has not evoked the feeling of a need for the proposed service. Put forth your best effort, otherwise you may not get the project.

TYPES OF PROPOSALS

Letter of Understanding

This type of proposal is similar in style to the engagement letter accountants use to spell out other relationships with clients. A letter of understanding is not a lengthy, formal document. Like other engagement letters, the letter of understanding will help prevent misunderstanding. It will prevent ill feelings that can result from either party's being unsure of the terms of the agreement. In other words, if both sides to the engagement know exactly what is expected, there is much less chance of dissatisfaction. A clear letter of understanding is important to the success of the engagement.

The letter of understanding should set out exactly what will be involved in the engagement. The letter should summarize, as precisely as possible, the problems that the consultant is expected to solve.

The next part of the letter should explain what the client can expect the practitioner to do about the problem. It is important to state very clearly the limits within which the firm is to be held accountable. The scope of a consulting engagement should be specifically stated to protect the practitioner and prevent the client from assuming that any and all business problems will be solved. A time schedule should be a part of the letter. The letter should also state the amount of cooperation (if any) that is expected from the client's staff and a statement concerning the compensation arrangement for professional fees.

Formal Document

The formal document is the best approach when "selling" a significant engagement. Consulting work can include a myriad of services of all sizes, complexity, and fees generated. Good judgment will dictate the circumstances in which the formal document should be used as the proposal. As in most proposals, the main elements to be presented are:

1. Identification of the problem
2. Outline of the plan to solve the problem
3. A schedule of expected progress
4. Qualifications that can prevent unrealistic expectations from developing
5. Fee arrangements

It is extremely important to identify clearly the reason for the engagement: the problem the consultant has been called upon to solve. Concise but full disclosure of all elements of the client's difficulty need to be spelled out to make certain that both parties are in complete agreement on the scope of the project. A shortcut here can create a misunderstanding later on, leaving both parties dissatisfied. Reputations take a long time to build, but they can be destroyed or badly damaged almost overnight by just one unhappy client. You need to ensure that the client's expectations are fulfilled.

An outline of the work plan to solve the problem is important to client and practitioner. The work plan does not have to be in great detail, but it should give the client sufficient insight on what to expect. Properly prepared, the outline can also guide the practitioner toward an efficient and professional approach. People want to do business with the best. A professional approach helps clients believe they have gotten the best.

A brief schedule of expected progress should be contained in the formal proposal. It should include the order of steps to be undertaken and the time each step is expected to take. Once the engagement is obtained, a more detailed schedule should be given to the client and should incorporate specific dates of completion for the various steps.

Frequently, clients expect "instant wonders." Almost as frequently, the practitioner allows the client to develop unrealistic expectations about the project results. Although it is necessary to create the right impression in the eyes of the client, miracles are difficult to provide. Unrealistic promises, expressed or implied, are very risky. A distinct qualification, stating that certain situations may arise that would preclude "instant" success, should be included in the proposal. The consultant should not get painted into a corner. Include any qualifications necessary to maintain good client relations if "miracles" do not occur.

Fee arrangements should be specified in the document. If a partial fee is to be obtained before completion of the engagement, the terms should be listed. If a fixed fee is proposed, indicate when payment is due. There are many kinds of fee arrangements, and each type requires certain language. The point is: Be sure that the proposal specifies the fee arrangements.

A formal proposal can be a formal letter in which the various points are itemized, or it can be quite complex and require several pages and perhaps a table of contents. The more complex proposals will include the basic elements plus elaboration. On longer proposals the firm's background is provided. Background data can include references to clients and industries that the firm serves; such references demonstrate qualifications to do the job. A list of the types of services performed might also be included. If there is more than one office, include the other locations. Give a brief history of the firm and list any other pertinent points that will add to the prestige or strength of the proposal. Be sure to zero in on the specific experience the firm has had in serving similar clients. In a more complex proposal also include a section covering the staffing of the engagement so the client can review the backgrounds of the project team. Finally, the benefits to be derived from the completion of the engagement should be documented.

In the proposal, it is important to stress the benefits of the project rather than just explaining how the project will be completed. We have all heard the Elmer Wheeler expression, "Sell the sizzle, not the steak." The prospective client needs to understand that accepting the proposal will result in more than just a better accounts receivable or inventory system. He needs to understand that implementing the recommendations can improve cash flow or increase profits and possibly improve customer service.

Response to Request for Proposal

Accounting and consulting firms often receive requests for proposals. Obviously, responses to these requests deserve prompt attention. The best example of a request for a formal proposal is probably one from a government entity. The government request usually outlines a very specific format for the response. This means the firm's response must be constructed according to a uniform outline that will be set forth in the request for proposal (RFP) document. Deviating from the format may not be grounds for disqualification, but it may lower the "selling" impact of the response.

Requests for proposals may also be received from other entities or businesses, and some will include guidelines for the desired response. Follow the guidelines to the extent possible, but also use some imagination. By following the guidelines you flatter the prospect and demonstrate a willingness to cooperate fully in the engagement. If no guidelines are included, use this handbook as a guide to develop your response.

Unsolicited Proposal

Unsolicited proposals represent good initiative marketing. Audit and monthly write-up engagements should provide opportunities to suggest some kind of consulting service. There is almost always some type of operational problem in which the consultant can provide assistance. Alertness in this area can develop considerable consulting business. Even though the consultant may not be an expert in every field, opportunities should still be identified and the proper expertise brought in to conduct the engagement.

PROPOSAL CYCLE

Initial Opportunity

The opportunity to prepare a proposal will usually be the result of several meetings between the client and the consulting firm. Many ideas for proposals will come from regular audit or compilation work for the client. The client may have mentioned an area that needs study or review. During these meetings you should take extensive notes and define the problem and the work to be done. Ask the staff for any ideas they may have concerning additional work.

Background Research

Proposal background research is necessary in order to prepare a quality, formal document. Proper emphasis at this stage is important and should not be treated lightly. The consultant should know as much as possible about the problem to be solved and the possible approaches. Consultants should even study personalities of the people who will be involved with the project. Human relations skills are equally as important as technical skills. The consultant can have good answers to the problems, but if he or she does not understand what makes the client tick, a competitor with better people skills will win the job. The homework must be done: Make sure you understand the organization, the problem, and the employees of the client, and that knowledge will lead to a winning proposal.

Bidders' Conference

On some large prospective engagements, the client will invite a number of qualified firms to make proposals and offer solutions. Bidders' conferences are usually meetings at which all interested prospective bidders receive a short analysis of the problem from the client's perspective. Questions from bidders are answered at the conference or at a later date in writing. Smaller engagements may not have bidders' conferences though multiple firms may be asked to propose.

On-Site Fact Finding

Once background research has been completed (concerning the client's basic needs) and the problem has been determined, the consultant may need to perform on-site interviews to glean additional facts regarding the problem. This activity includes interviews with client employees working in the area where the project will take place. Ask these people what they do, hear their side of how they are handling their job, and ask them if they believe there is a better way to accomplish their responsibility. The people on the front line often have good solutions that have never surfaced or been mentioned to their employers. These people certainly have an intimate insight into the workings of the client, and are good sources of information. Be sure they understand that you are there to help, not to replace, not to destroy, but to work with them. On-site fact finding can be the key to learning more about the client and the problem leading to a responsive proposal.

Proposal Preparation

It is important to spend the proper amount of time on preparation of the proposal. The written proposal will remain in the hands of the prospect after the consultant has left, so the proposal needs to say everything that needs to be said. On a large proposal, 40-plus hours may be required to produce a quality product. A less than 100 percent effort to prepare the proposal cannot be overcome by a good personal impression or salesmanship.

Submission and Evaluation

The final part of the proposal cycle consists of submitting the written proposal plus any verbal explanation for evaluation by the prospect. You should set an appropriate time, when the client can give undivided attention, and then use the proposal as an additional component of the selling process. You should not rely on the proposal to do the whole job. The client will probably not have an immediate answer to the proposal, particularly if others have been invited to submit proposals. You should make certain the prospective client understands that your firm wants the work and will develop a solution that solves the client's problems.

Depending on the client's personality and style, you should determine the best location for submitting the proposal—your office or the client's. This consideration is important because you want to ensure the prospect's undivided attention.

PROPOSAL CONTENT

As stated by Conan D. Whiteside in the *Accountant's Guide to Profitable Management Advisory Services*, the contents of the proposal should contain:

1. Identity of document submitted to the prospect
2. Outline of the existing situation
3. Nature and scope of services to be performed—backed up by a comprehensive *action program* attached as an exhibit
4. Benefits and results to be obtained for the client
5. Statement of the time period to be covered by the assignment
6. Fee structure and billing arrangements
7. Other major considerations such as: staffing, physical facilities required, special services and supplies needed, client personnel to be assigned
8. References and personnel data sheets if requested by the client

Understanding of the Problem

To win the consulting engagement, the proposal must certainly demonstrate an understanding of the problem and should discuss precisely the degree of understanding. You should word this part of the proposal, as well as all other parts, in the language of the reader. It is in this area of the proposal process that the accountant must "get the client's attention." If you can show in simple and precise language that the problem is understood, the reader is likely to believe the proposed solution to the problem. You can bet that a prospect who doesn't think you understand the problem surely will not give your firm the job of solving it. So nothing is more important than the area of understanding, and the proposal should demonstrate the depth of that understanding.

Scope and Methodologies

It is essential to define the scope of the assignment very carefully. Careful study and questioning of the client will develop the areas that need to be included in the scope section. To avoid future misunderstandings, it is equally important to define the areas that are not to be included. To define the scope, spend time making a short preliminary study of the problem areas. This study should determine the number of people on the client's staff, the volume of work they produce, the layout of the physical facilities, the office and plant equipment in use, and even the philosophies of the client. The preliminary study will enable you to discuss the problem with the client to determine his or her objectives and the proper scope of the assignment. It will also enable you to be very specific in preparing the final proposal.

This section must outline and describe the approach to solving the problem. The outline is important because it sets the structure of the project. A potential outline for a complete study might include: analysis within the problem area, interviews with employees and staff, time and motion study, evaluation of equipment (both on-site and at vendors), and selection of the best option.

This part of the proposal also explains how the work will be conducted both at the client's premises and at the consultant's office. Often, in-depth interviews with the client's staff are required to support the fact-finding effort, but you should emphasize that you will minimize disruption of the business. Techniques such as time and motion studies should be described. If you intend to study various procedures, you should also describe the methods involved.

Staffing and Qualifications

This part of the proposal should list the selection of staff and describe very briefly their experience and how that experience relates to the project. The proposal should indicate who is responsible for the project and who represents the firm on key issues. The prospective client should be able to assess whether the appropriate people have been assigned to the project and whether they can produce the desired results on time.

Time Frame and Cost Fees

During the fact finding, the consultant should have determined the time frame necessary to complete the work. In this area of the proposal, the consultant should establish that he or she can do the work within that schedule. Specify when the project will begin and how the various phases of the work will be scheduled, from the detailed research to the final implementation of a solution. In addition to these steps, this section should include the fee arrangement. The professional fee can be based on a fixed dollar amount, a "not-to-exceed" amount, or time and out-of-pocket expenses. It is important to specify the arrangement as part of the proposal.

Benefits to the Client

Nothing in the proposal is more important than clearly expressing the benefits to be obtained from using your services. Many prospects hear proposals for services or products that would seem to benefit only the sellers. All efforts must be made to avoid creating this impression. The consultant must sincerely and clearly explain what the client is going to receive in benefits. This involves much more than saying that the efficiency of the data processing equipment will increase or the controls over inventory will improve. That may be the job the firm has been called upon to solve, but the benefits in the eyes of the client really come down to the bottom line of the income statement. You should make it clear to the client that accepting the proposal can mean more dollars to the income of the company or to the income of the individual. This is dangerous ground, but the consultant who cannot deliver should not be in the business. You should be careful about overcommitting, but the question the prospect will ask is: What am I going to get out of this project? Remember, clients are not really interested as much in inventory control as in the profit to be derived from smoother inventory control.

The contents of the proposal should be reviewed and organized into a complete and comprehensive written document. You need to demonstrate that you: understand the problem, have defined the scope and the depth of the work, have developed an approach, know whom to interview, have determined a completion date and estimated reasonable professional fees. Finally, the client should be shown in considerable detail the benefits of the engagement.

Invest the proper amount of time in the proposal effort and make sure that the preparation of the proposal is done in a professional manner. Follow the checklist below from Conan D. Whiteside.* Most proposals should address the following issues:

- What the consultant proposes to do
- What benefits the client will receive—why the consultant proposes to render the service
- How the consultant proposes to do the work; where it will be done; how many members of the consultant's staff will be needed; and what client facilities will be required
- Period of time covered by the project, from starting date to completion
- How much it will cost (including fee schedule and billing arrangements)

*Conan D. Whiteside, *Accountant's Guide to Profitable Management Advisory Services*, Prentice-Hall, 1969.

- What specific accomplishments can be expected (expressed in terms of savings, cost, reductions, benefits, increased profits, etc.)
- Why the consultant is qualified to do the work
- Planned or suggested starting date
- References that include consultant's qualifications and experience—if client has requested these data

EFFECTIVE PROPOSALS

Focus on Needs and Problems

Certainly the main emphasis in any document in which action is requested is that the needs and the problems of the client must be emphasized. You must show clearly that you understand the client's needs and problems. Not only must the client perceive that you have all of the abilities to solve the problems, you also have to demonstrate that you have a very clear view of the problem areas. The other side of this issue is not to overwhelm the prospect with excessive detail in an effort to impress.

Crisp Writing Style

Writing the proposal is going to be one of the most difficult parts of the entire consulting engagement. As in all writing, the process will require multiple passes through the document. Clients do not expect a firm submitting proposals to have a staff of journalists on hand, but it will pay dividends to be clear and precise in your writing. If no one in the firm is good at writing, you should engage someone from the local university journalism department to help polish the style and/or documents being submitted to the client. A well-written proposal enhances the possibility of winning the work.

Consistent Style Throughout

Keep in mind that consistency of style should be maintained throughout the entire document. Use uniform tenses, and remember the rules for good grammar. Inconsistent style, tenses, and a poorly prepared proposal are not likely to evoke great confidence in the firm. A crisp writing style combined with proper use of the English language can contribute to winning proposals.

Graphics and Other "Polishing" Techniques

"A picture is worth a thousand words" is a true slogan. Some say that the right picture may be worth more than a thousand words. Graphs, pictures, diagrams, flowcharts, and any other documents that help to make the proposal more understandable or more easily readable should be included. Illustrations used in a proposal do not have to be prepared by professional artists, and the increased capability of microcomputers makes graphics easier to produce. Graphics should be neat and understandable—simple ideas stand out best.

Many consulting firms today have very sophisticated graphics equipment connected to their microcomputers. These relatively inexpensive devices produce excellent and accurate graphs that demand attention. Such equipment may eliminate the need for an artist. On a single break-even graph you can show many possibilities that could not be described in regular financial statement format. Since most financial statements tend to be dry and dull, dressing up the proposal with graphs and pictures will keep the reader's attention. Color is not essential but can be a plus if used properly.

Dress up the proposal in every way possible. Polish it with graphics and other pictorial methods of showing your story. All these things help set your proposal apart from the competition.

PROPOSAL PRESENTATION

Expectations of the Client

Since the "proposal process" is really a sales effort, some of the usual elements of good salesmanship apply. With respect to client expectations, you should remember the overused but true expression that "the customer is always right." Prospective clients are customers and it's in your best interest to remember that they believe they are right about current situations. Common courtesy and good sense dictate that clients' expectations come first in the drafting of written proposals. Know what they expect and address their expectations in your proposals.

Presentation Team

In most cases the proposal will be presented to the client by one person. This person probably should be the one who has dealt with the client throughout the entire process. You may want to include an additional person who has a particular technical ability or presentation abilities. You do not want to overwhelm the client with a large team of experts; but if another person can add credence to the proposal, a team effort is appropriate. The team or person making the presentation should rehearse in the same way actors rehearse a play. Rehearse with someone playing the part of the client and have this person raise objections and questions. Try to emulate every circumstance that is likely to arise. Be prepared!

Follow-Up

If at all possible, deliver the final proposal in person. The proposal is intended to develop a clear understanding between all parties, and a one-to-one meeting will help resolve any questions that it does not answer. At the conclusion of the proposal presentation, it is appropriate to ask if the client has made the decision to accept the proposal. If the client wants more time to study, ask when the next meeting should be scheduled. The client will probably offer to call if there are any questions. If you have not heard from the client after a reasonable time, call to see if there are any questions about the proposal. The proposal has taken considerable time and expense to prepare, and lack of follow-up can render all that time and expense worthless. It is essential that the client understand all the elements of the proposal in order to make a positive response. You need to give the client every opportunity to understand the proposed work and say yes to the proposal.

APPENDIX: SAMPLE PROPOSAL

```
Mr. Samuel Smith, Administrator
County Hospital
Brown Street
Springfield, Illinois 77777


Dear Sam:

I appreciate the opportunity of meeting with you and Bruce Jones
to discuss your current computer operation and to discuss ways in
which our consulting department possibly can be of service to County
Hospital.

I understand that you have already studied the feasibility of alterna-
tive computing capability to replace your current in-house systems.
The current system is over five years old and does not provide the
desired level of support to effectively manage the hospital. Cur-
rently payroll, accounts payable, and certain portions of patient
accounting are processed on the machine. Automated insurance pro-
cessing and general ledger are not being provided. Enhancing the
current system is impractical because of the cost and, more important,
ongoing maintenance and support for the software.

The current system has limitations and does not appear capable of
meeting the changing needs of the hospital. You have added five
```

physicians this year and are opening a pediatric area. There are plans to enlarge ancillary areas and make other facility—related improvements. With the changes in place and 135—145 beds available, hopefully occupancy levels will increase. This will place an additional load on your computer system and the manual portions of the patient accounting process. This is particularly important because such a large portion of your revenues are Medicare/Medicaid based.

BENEFITS OF IMPROVED COMPUTING CAPABILITY

Recent advances in computer technology and the emphasis of many vendors on health care systems offer a wide range of options to improve your current situation. These options include in—house microcomputer systems and shared systems which provide terminals connected to a remote computer. In their simplest form these systems provide basic patient and general accounting. The more complex offer order entry, communications and specialized ancillary systems (e.g., laboratory). In addition to providing automated recordkeeping, improved computer capability can impact the following areas:

1. Productivity—Handle increased transaction volumes without adding additional clerical staff.

2. Management Reports—Provide timely accounting and operating reports on a daily, weekly, monthly, or annual basis.

3. Accountability—Enhance your control over accounting records, including patient and insurance billing.

4. Growth—Provide the capability for additional ancillary systems.

5. Accuracy—Ensure that data is valid before updating accounting records.

OUR APPROACH TO ASSISTING YOUR HOSPITAL

Senior management and the Board have the final responsibility for selecting the most cost—effective approach to fulfilling the hospital's information—processing requirements. My suggested course of action is that you utilize our technical support to review and evaluate the various hospital computer configurations that would be capable of meeting your needs. These would include both shared systems and in—house computers. In the course of our assisting other organizations facing similar decisions, we have developed techniques we believe to be essential in making an informed business decision and in successfully implementing the chosen system.

Our suggested approach to address your specific needs consists of the following three phases:

Phase I = Define Information Requirements

The purpose of this phase is to identify information needs and system objectives. System objectives include stating which systems will be automated and requirements for these systems. Interviews will be held with you and key personnel in the hospital. The major tasks in this phase include:

A. Accumulate and review existing input documents, processing steps, and out put reports.

B. Interview the administrator, the controller, and key department heads.

C. Compile and classify information requirements, including system objectives and reporting requirements.

D. Review requirements with management.

A statement of requirements for your review and approval is the product of this phase.

Phase II = Develop System Specifications

Using the information gathered in Phase I, we will develop system specifications which can be used by computer vendors to price the cost of implementing the computer programs necessary to meet your reporting needs. The major items would be:

A. An overall information flowchart

B. A list of source documents and output screens and reports

C. Data elements

D. System features and volume statistics

The product of this phase is a set of "blueprints" describing the hospital's specifications for required accounting and ancillary systems. These "blueprints" are used to develop a request for proposal (RFP) including hospital profile, system blueprints, technical hardware and software requirements, and cost schedules.

Phase III = Assist in Selection Computer Capability

The purpose of this phase is to select a computer configuration based on the requirements defined in Phase I and the RFP specifications developed in Phase II. The request for proposal is used in this phase to provide a basis for effectively evaluating alternative approaches. Major tasks in this phase include.

A. Issue the proposal to interested and qualified vendors.

B. Meet with bidders to address RFP questions.

C. Prepare an analysis of the submitted proposals.

D. Meet with management to present our report and recommenda-
    tions.

We would expect selected vendors to submit data on recommended equipment, systems, and cost. We will review and analyze the proposals
prior to meeting with you. At out meeting, we will discuss the relative merits of each proposal and recommend the proposals we believe
will best meet your computer requirements.

ANTICIPATED BENEFITS TO COUNTY HOSPITAL

I believe the aforementioned approach will maximize the benefits to
you from engaging the services of our consulting personnel. Our
assistance results in an organized and thorough approach to defining and documenting your information processing requirements.
In addition, our assistance will provide technical expertise in
the area of electronic data processing (EDP), and an independent
viewpoint based on previous experience with numerous EDP projects.
Throughout the study we will work closely with hospital personnel
in evaluating and selecting computer capability.

Most important, we believe our approach will ensure that the hospital
acquires adequate computer capability to meet current and changing
needs. Management does not want a repeat of the current situation,
and the best way to prevent this is to use professional technical
advice. Our reputation and professional standing are "on the line"
when we issue our final format report. Because of this commitment,
we have to be sure that management is able to make an informed computer system decision.

OUR FIRM

We have five consulting professionals in our office who specialize
in EDP consulting. By rendering distinguished service to a wide
variety of clients, we have increased the level of service provided
by our staff by over 300% in less than two years. We believe this
growth is the result of the satisfaction of our clients with our
services.

We believe that the wealth of our recent experience, the satisfaction of our clients, and the fact that you will be served by the
same experienced professionals who are responsible for our growth,
are all persuasive reasons why our team should be selected to perform
this project.

STAFFING AND FEES

I will have overall responsibility on the project. Susan Bauman, a Senior Consultant in our office, will assist with the project. We can begin immediately and perceive no problem in completing selection work in an eight- to ten-week time frame. Based on the accompanying work plan, we estimate the professional fees for our assistance to range from $9,000 to $12,000 plus reasonable out-of-pocket expenses. This estimate is based on an active participation in the project by you and key members of your staff. In accordance with our customary practice, our fee will be based on actual hours expended at standard hourly rates.

We look forward to working with County Hospital on this important project. We would be pleased to discuss any questions you may have regarding our proposed work.

Sincerely,

Barcus, Nugent, Steine & Co.

11

Engagement Planning

JANE GRAHAM
Endata, Inc.
Nashville, Tennessee

INTRODUCTION

"Plan the work, work the plan" is a phrase often quoted in business management circles. Yet how many of us overlook this very basic advice in our own engagements!

We all have a built-in sense of need to "get on with the work," to begin producing results as quickly as possible. To a great extent, planning does not meet this need, so we are tempted to skip it and get started.

The purpose of this chapter is to present ideas and suggestions on *how* to plan. In addition, the reader should gain an understanding of the value of careful engagement planning and be convinced of its merit and application.

THE KICKOFF MEETING

Engagement planning actually begins the first time you are contacted by a potential client, and continues in more detail as you prepare and present a project proposal. After the proposal is accepted, you turn more attention to development of a *detailed*, task-by-task work plan that will become the blueprint for the remainder of the project.

Preparation for the Meeting

The chapter will focus on the planning that takes place after the client has officially accepted a proposal for consulting work. This phase of the engagement usually begins with an engagement kickoff meeting, a key element in getting the project off to a good start.

The purpose of the kickoff meeting is to mark officially the beginning of the engagement, reestablish clearly the objectives of the work, and assign each participant's role in accomplishing the work goals.

The meeting should be attended by representatives of client management, persons who will benefit from the results of the engagement, and those who will participate in the project. As with any meeting, all the key persons should be in attendance; but keep the size of the meeting small enough to make each person feel that his or her presence is important.

Since the kickoff meeting will play a key role in establishing the tenor of the project, it should be very carefully orchestrated to cover important points in the project process. Topics to be addressed at the meeting include:

1. A review of the engagement proposal
2. Discussion of the work objectives
3. Definition of milestone points in the engagement
4. Project completion dates
5. Client participation

Before deciding on the details of the kickoff meeting, you should observe the customary rules for planning and scheduling meetings:

- Choose a time that will be convenient for the largest number of attendees.
- Schedule a meeting room, either at your office or the client's, that is large, well equipped, and away from normal office disruptions.
- Invite the participants well in advance and commit to a completion time for the meeting.
- Prepare and send out an agenda for the meeting.

The degree of formalization may vary by engagement, but the basic steps should remain the same.

The consultant responsible for the engagement should actually conduct the meeting. It helps to have something tangible for the meeting participants to see and, if possible, take with them. This might include visual aids, samples of potential project results, etc. At a minimum, applicable points of the engagement proposal should be copied and reviewed at the meeting. Long documents may need to be sent out in advance, though it is unrealistic to expect a lot of front-end preparation. A better approach is to develop summaries of the material for presentation at the meeting.

An essential, often overlooked function is taking the minutes. Since this kickoff meeting will serve as a foundation for the engagement expectations, any conclusions and agreements reached should certainly be recorded and distributed to the attendees.

Proposal Review

A good way to begin the kickoff meeting is with a review of the engagement proposal. This serves as a means of summarizing what has taken place to date and as a springboard for looking ahead to the project objectives and work required. A word of caution: This is a *review* only—you've already sold the engagement!

The proposal review should concentrate on the objectives and scope of the engagement, as well as the benefits to be realized. This is a good time to make use of visual aids, such as slides or flipcharts, to summarize clearly the work to be done. Experience shows that the client's initial perception of what the consultant will accomplish remains throughout the project, so this is a key time psychologically to establish clear expectations.

In reviewing the stated benefits, it's a good time to resolve exactly *how* and *when* achievement of the benefits will be measured. The desired objectives and benefits in the proposal should serve as the benchmark in measuring results.

The End Work Product

A logical follow-on to discussion of engagement objectives and benefits is agreement on the end results of the project. This may be the most critical agreement to be reached. What you are really trying to establish is the answer to the question: How will we know when we have finished the engagement? A clear definition of the final product must be formulated so that everyone will know when the end has been reached. You don't want this to be one of those projects that remains "90 percent complete" forever!

This end work product definition must relate to a tangible, specific event, document, or result. Work products, in addition to being observable and measurable, are related to engagement objectives. Some examples of typical work products include:

- Delivery of a request for proposal (RFP) for a new computer system to an agreed-upon number of vendors

- Publication and distribution of a policy and procedures manual to all departments of the company
- Completion of training in the use of new machinery in manufacturing
- Final executive committee approval of the strategic marketing plan for next year

Engagement Milestones

Once there is a consensus on the end work product, the meeting should turn to specification of intermediate work results.

Intermediate work results, often called engagement milestones, are important for several reasons. First, they serve as the beginning point for development of the detailed work plan that breaks up the end work product into manageable pieces. Writing a policy and procedures manual may seem like a mammoth task until you begin to think through the major work steps. Your thought process should lead to the development of intermediate work results that will help plan the work in more detail.

Second, milestones serve as measuring points for progress toward project objectives. These measuring points are critical to the consultant's project control. The client can use the milestones to review and measure project team performance.

Finally, milestones play an invaluable psychological role in an engagement. Recall the feelings you get in the middle of a long, involved project. It seems that no progress is being made and the end of the project is out of sight. When end work results are the only goals in the engagement, the satisfaction gained by completing a job is delayed for a long time. On the other hand, when intermediate work results are specified, a feeling of accomplishment is achieved. In effect, milestones serve to break the project up into miniprojects, with resulting psychological and emotional feelings of satisfaction for reaching a goal.

Establishment of milestones should follow the same guidelines as those for defining the end work product. Milestones should be specific, definable events of deliverables. The occurrence of each event should be unquestionable so that all involved will recognize that the milestone has been reached. For the end product examples mentioned, typical milestones might be:

- Publishing the system user requirements for the computer system
- Approval of the policy and procedures manual's table of contents by the personnel director
- Approval of the training course outline
- Definition of short- and long-range marketing objectives for the company

An effective use of milestones is to key them to scheduled engagement review points. An engagement review occurs when the client reviews the conduct and progress of the work at a certain point and determines if the project is on course with respect to goals, quality of work, and project schedule. Since milestones represent measurable work results, those responsible for project review will have specific events or deliverables to use in evaluation results, quality, and adherence to schedule.

Responsibility Assignments

The kickoff meeting is also the place to establish responsibility for various aspects of the project. This includes general assignment of duties for project planning and management, project task work, and review of project progress at milestone points.

All participants in the project should have a clear understanding of their roles. It's better to know on the front end if there are going to be conflicts in project team assignments, work commitments, vacation plans, availability of staff, etc. The kickoff meeting is therefore a good time to discuss what and where resources are needed and each player's general responsibility.

The most significant responsibility assignment is project manager. Assigning some project management responsibility to one of the client's staff can free the consultant to spend more time on technical issues and is a good way to ensure client involvement. This arrangement is, of course, dependent on the availability, skills, and willingness of the staff member, but it can often produce very good results.

At a minimum, agreement should be reached on using the client's staff as resources. The engagement will be successful only if the consultant has access to the persons who can provide necessary documents, background, and knowledge of client operations. An ideal arrangement would be to have one person designated as the client liaison, to serve as the central contact point for the consultant.

Review committee members should be designated at the kickoff meeting. The review group's regular participation is important to assessing the quality and completeness of project work. In addition, the group should decide on the procedure for handling changes in the scope and/or objectives of the engagement that surface at milestone review points.

Any other resources from your firm, or persons who will be used as technical resources during the engagement, should be mentioned at this point. The individual roles and responsibilities should also be covered so the client's staff will feel comfortable with each face and each resource.

Next Actions

The kickoff meeting should end with a review of the decisions and agreements reached, and a statement by the consultant that outlines the next steps to be taken in the engagement. This statement should review the general steps in the project and should focus on the development and presentation of the detailed work plan.

It is important for each participant in the kickoff meeting to understand how the engagement will proceed—to understand his or her individual responsibilities and what will happen next. The tenor of the kickoff meeting helps establish the general tone for conducting the remainder of the project.

THE DETAILED WORK PLAN

Objectives of the Plan

Other than the engagement proposal and the milestones outlined in the kickoff meeting, there is not much to show exactly how the project objectives will be accomplished. The detailed work plan fills this gap. This plan will become both the blueprint for execution of the engagement and a means by which the consultant can monitor project progress.

At this point, all those involved in the engagement are anxious to begin seeing some real progress: enough of goals and commitments; let's get on with the actual work! The consultant may be under a great deal of pressure to begin making detailed work assignments to project team members to prove that things are happening.

If you feel this pressure, and are tempted to "plunge in" before preparing a detailed work plan, ask yourself, "How do I know what tasks to assign if I haven't decided what tasks must be done?" The answer is that no work on the project should begin until the detailed work plan is complete and has been approved.

In addition to being the project blueprint, the detailed plan shows what staff will be needed to complete the project, as well as when and for how long they will be needed.

One most critical result of developing the work plan is a further clarification of how much effort will be required to deliver the end work product. Even though the news may be bad, this is the best time to acknowledge that the engagement objectives cannot be met in the anticipated time frame, staff allotment, or budget commitment. Until the work effort is planned in detail, the consultant is not really able to determine these factors. At this point, the project planner is able to illustrate to the client the extent of the work effort and can, if necessary, discuss reduced scope, increased budget, project segmenting, additional staff, and so forth.

Components of the Detailed Work Plan

The detailed work plan should consist of several parts, each serving to specify in different ways the plan for doing project work and the associated cost. These parts include:

Task identification and description

Task relationships

Task completion time estimates

Project scheduling

Project review points

Project costs

Task identification.   The steps in preparing a detailed work plan are fairly straightforward. Identifying each activity required to accomplish both intermediate and end work results is the first major step. The project planner must begin with the elements of the plan that have already been put into place: the project objectives and scope, the end work product, the milestones, the project budget (both time frame and dollars), and any other constraints that may have been placed on the engagement.

Specifying the tasks necessary to complete an engagement is a creative process that calls on the planner's imagination and experience. The best way to begin is by listing, with no concern for order or level of detail, the types of activities that must take place for the first milestone to be reached. Project plans from earlier engagements, use of standard task lists, suggestions from other professional associates and from client staff are sources for task suggestions. The objective is to include all the activities that will be required.

When the list seems relatively complete, it must be refined so that tasks of a general nature are supported by the detail activities that represent the next level of definition. Each general task category should be further refined into more specific, definable pieces of work.

Each activity in the work plan should be clearly stated and described. This one point is critical in estimating and scheduling the work effort, as well as in clear project team assignments. For example, the task "interview the controller to determine payment procedures for vendor invoices" might be taken to mean only the actual time spent in interviewing the controller. On the other hand, it might be construed to include everything related to the interview process—that is, planning for the interview, scheduling the interview, conducting the discussion, writing up notes of the interview, accumulating documents, developing a flowchart, putting together work papers to support the interview.

These two meanings are quite different—both in estimating the task and in what might be understood by the team member.

In addition to being described clearly, each task should represent a manageable, controllable amount of work. This is usually defined in terms of the number of hours or days required to complete the task. For instance, if a defined task will require 2 months to complete, there may not be any way to measure its short-term progress. As a general rule, no defined task should take longer than 2 weeks to complete. Large tasks should be broken up into smaller, more manageable pieces of work. This approach will provide much better project control as well as the team member's psychological advantage in completing a piece of work.

Each piece of work should conclude with a tangible product that can be recognized and reviewed. This means that, ideally, each activity should have some observable conclusion, such as a document, a review meeting, or a decision point. Under this arrangement, team members have no doubt as to what constitutes task completion or when they are ready to move on to the next activity.

The most difficult activities to identify are the ones toward the end of the engagement since they represent a distant time period and may depend on the results of other activities. In some cases it may be better to outline these later tasks at a general level both for the way the work will be accomplished and the scope of the work effort.

Task definition is generally not an exact science, and it calls on our experience as project team members and project managers. Remember that the purpose of a plan is to serve as a model of the way the project is expected to proceed, with the realization that changes are inevitable. The same is true when you define the tasks in a project. Outline the steps you think are required to complete the work and proceed according to this plan or "best guess." As in any other planning activity, you are projecting or forecasting into an area that is somewhat unknown. The further into the engagement you plan, the less you know. The important thing is that you have a plan in place to change; with no plan, you have nothing to follow or modify!

Task relationships.   After identifying project activities, you should determine the relationship among the tasks. Certain pieces of work can be done at any time during the project, but most tasks depend on the completion of other activities. For example, the task "proposed improvements in the accounts payable scheduling" requires that the task "interview the controller on current payment scheduling procedures" be completed first.

Determining these relationships among the tasks can best be approached as an iterative process. A graphic presentation of the tasks, to show their required execution sequence, is a useful descriptive tool.

Methods such as bubble charts, networks, PERT (performance evaluation and review techniques) charts, or other such approaches can be
helpful in illustrating these relationships.

Task relationship identification is important not only for discovering
which tasks are dependent on others, but also for pointing out which
tasks have some leeway in their performance time frame. That is, some
have no dependence on others and can be done within a general time
frame. An example of this type of task might be the ordering of forms for a
new computer system. As long as the task is done after design of the
forms and with enough lead time before the forms must be used, the task
is not related to any other tasks in the project. Tasks that can be performed independently of others are extremely valuable in the scheduling process since they allow the project planner to make optimum use of
staff time by assigning these tasks as fill-in work at slack times.

Estimating the work effort.   Of all the areas of uncertainty in developing the detailed work plan, estimating the work effort is the most
uncertain. Estimating the time required to complete a task is tough—
plus, it implies a real commitment! When you assign a certain amount of
time to complete a piece of work, you have really made a statement about
the scope and extent of the work, as well as your ability to complete the
task. You might as well recognize that some of the factors affecting and
controlling execution of project tasks are beyond your control. *Estimating the work effort is not the same as scheduling.* This is a common
mistake made by planners. Engagement planners tend to wrap up task
identification, estimating, and scheduling steps all into one, and they
quickly commit to delivering specific work results by a given calendar
date. *Estimating* includes determining how long, preferably in terms of
worker hours, each task will take. (Some consultants routinely estimate
in units of days or half-days). This estimating process has nothing to do
with which tasks will be done by whom on a certain calendar day, or
which day of the year a milestone will be reached.

By comparison, *scheduling* is the process of taking the task estimates
and dependencies, as well as the project team assignments and availability, and matching them against a calendar to determine who will
perform which task when, and when the work effort will be completed.

Each defined activity in the project should be evaluated in terms of
how many hours of a staff member's time will be required to complete
the work. This does not take into account any built-in delays, such as
delivery times. It should represent only the actual hours that must be
devoted to the task.

How does the estimator know how long a task will take? Several
estimating methods may be used, but the most successful one is probably
just plain reasoning and common sense. This is an area where experience really helps, too.

Experience is accumulated by each of us in a general but personal way. We can also develop a very specific body of experience for future estimating efforts that will be helpful to all members of the consulting firm. This approach involves keeping careful records of estimating performance on each engagement—that is, keeping track of budgeted versus actual time for the firm's project work at the milestone or even at the task level. Tracking project hours at the detail level and building a record of estimated versus actual hours can be extremely useful for evaluating your performance; it can be even more helpful for the next estimating effort.

Other estimating methods include the use of standard task tables. Some industries or professional associations may use tables of "standard estimates" during the estimating process. These can be more misleading than helpful, especially if they are not accompanied by a clear definition of what each task entails. Such guidelines can be beneficial as measuring sticks to see if your estimates are in a reasonable range.

You may want to follow an estimating technique that includes application of certain weighing factors. One such scheme involves determining a "most likely" estimate for a task and then developing both a "pessimistic" estimate and an "optimistic" estimate. The final hours recorded for the task are developed according to a formula that adds the pessimistic number of hours, the optimistic number of hours, and 4 times the most likely number of hours, then divides this total by 6.

Whatever approach is taken, any estimate of task hours should be carefully reviewed for reasonableness. Reasonableness means a judgement about whether the number of hours estimated is correct or likely and whether the investment of this many worker hours in the task is in the proper proportion to the overall project. It is a good idea to weed out or modify tasks that don't meet this criterion and figure out alternative ways of accomplishing desired results.

Project estimating can be done by an individual or by a team. The team approach can be very effective, especially if areas of the project are unfamiliar to the estimator. Whenever possible, estimates should be reviewed by someone other than the estimator—one person can easily lose sight of project goals and get too involved in details.

Scheduling tasks.   Scheduling is the step in the project plan development that shows what everyone is most anxious to know. When will the project be finished?

Unfortunately, a most common consulting practice is to quote completion dates very early in the engagement discussion process. While this is certainly a topic that should be covered in preliminary talks, no firm commitment should be made until the detailed work plan is completed. An important truism is that the first date (or first dollar amount) a client hears is the one that sticks, no matter how much effort goes into changing his or her mind. Project completion dates are a direct function of the work effort to be done, the resources available, and the quality of work, all matched against a calendar.

Engagement scheduling involves much detailed work and can be frustrating. The use of computer-aided scheduling software is a help, though much of the work still involves brainpower. Scheduling begins with matching the task list, dependency diagrams, and task completion estimates with a list of potential staff members. Staff members' skill levels and availability are also an important consideration.

Tasks should be taken, one at a time, and plotted along a time line for each prospective team member. Certain rules of scheduling should be observed:

1. Assign team members a realistic number of hours each day; you want this number to equal the actual number of productive hours available. Eight hours is the recommended maximum.

2. Plan ahead for weekends, holidays, and scheduled vacations, so that your staff availability will be realistic.

3. Try to match the skill levels required to complete a task with the appropriate team member.

4. Build in the delay factors that you know will be necessary. For example, there may be several days of delay, or wait time, between the task meeting and the task of conducting the meeting.

5. Build in time factors for any unusual elements of the project—for example, a very junior staff member assigned to a task that really requires advanced skills or a client contact person who is difficult to schedule for appointments.

6. Try to limit the number of persons who work on one task in order to simplify the work and avoid extra time spent in coordination, which can be a real time-waster.

7. Be sure to schedule time for such administrative tasks as progress meetings and for project management tasks.

Scheduling is more realistic when done at a very detailed level. The schedule developed should show the task on which each project team member will be working at any given time. However, the effort and overhead required to schedule at this level may exceed the benefit. In addition, such schedules, unless automated, are difficult to keep up-to-date to reflect changes in the project environment. An alternative approach to this detailed day-by-day scheduling is to develop a schedule for each team member for a week. While this still provides a sufficient basis for project control, it eases the difficulty of the scheduling activity and gives greater flexibility.

Determining review points.   Determining project review points was one of the topics discussed during the kickoff meeting. An effective approach is to key the review points to engagement milestones so that intermediate work products can be evaluated and the project progress can be measured.

For large engagements, it may be necessary to set up review points in addition to those keyed to milestones to provide continuity and assure that reviews occur frequently. Monthly review meetings can be scheduled regardless of other milestone review points. Review meetings should be held *regularly* because they are the most important aspect of project control.

Staffing the project.   Trying to schedule without at least an assumed knowledge of which staff members will be available and when is very difficult. As a starting point, it may be necessary to develop a tentative schedule of *needed* staff members before any one person's work schedule and availability can be assessed.

An often overlooked element of project staffing is project management. Usually, the consultant responsible for the engagement is, by default, the project manager. This may be an excellent choice, but each situation should be looked at independently. *Project management is the critical element in the success of the engagement and deserves the very best the firm can offer.* Don't make the typical mistake of assuming that the key person on the project can also be the project manager "on the side." A significant percentage of some staff member's time will be required to manage the project correctly, and you cannot treat this commitment of time and effort too lightly.

Choice of the project staff may be limited to members available at the time, or it may include options: hiring new staff; subcontracting portions of the work; using a specialized consultant as an experienced advisor to the project team for a few days; delaying the engagement until additional persons are available. Consider the possibility of using members of the client's staff as team members. Using persons outside the firm's regular staff should be viewed carefully from the standpoint of project accountability, liability, quality of work results, and control.

Project costing.   After detailed project planning, estimating, scheduling, and staffing have been completed, the planner is in a position to develop a detailed cost estimate for the engagement.

The basic approach for determining worker costs is to calculate the total number of hours scheduled for each staff member and multiply this number by the staff member's billing rate. Personnel costs for each project team member, for obtaining special outside consulting advice, and for contracting with third parties should be totaled to arrive at the project personnel costs.

Other elements of project costs should be considered, depending on the nature of the consulting arrangement. Estimate anticipated project expenses including travel, lodging, meals, telephone, copying, printing, additional clerical support, use of computer time, special equipment rental, printing expenses, and so forth. In addition, include certain other expenses such as administrative loading factors applied to direct expenses, overtime compensation, and special rates for travel time.

Detailed Work Plan Review

Presentation and review of the detailed work plan represent a critical point in the engagement. This is where client expectations come to the surface and the future success of the engagement can be affected.

Be carefully prepared for this review so that you can make all elements of the plan clear. The work plan becomes the consultant's means of explaining to the client how the project results will be accomplished. If questions arise about details of tasks, estimates, scheduling, or project team assignment, all the facts should be available.

Unfortunately, the two areas that often become problems in this plan review are the project costs and the schedule. Here is where detailed task definition, clear task results, and estimating can really pay off! When questions arise, be willing to review the elements of the plan with the client; *then ask the client to suggest which tasks can be omitted or cut back.* When the client can see the planning strategy, as well as the way the elements of the plan fit together, he or she should be able to understand the cost and target dates. Also, the client may be able to help you develop other planning and scheduling strategies to accomplish the project goals.

The realities of business and financial conditions may cause the client to refuse the detailed work plan as presented if the costs exceed earlier estimates or the projected completion date is unacceptable. In this case, it is the consultant's responsibility to present alternative strategies for continuing the engagement on a modified basis. Typical areas where modifications might be made include:

- Reduction in the scope and objectives of the project, including corresponding adjustments in the work results
- Increase in staff availability through adding members of the client's staff to the project team (beware of the increased communications problems, the possibility of lesser-skilled personnel on the project team, and the demands of these people's regular jobs)
- Breaking the project into several subengagements
- Deferring some of the work until a later time

You should not agree to cutting the cost or shortening the target dates without clear, written reduction in scope or quality.

The work plan review meeting often serves as another checkpoint for making sure that client expectations of what the project will accomplish are the same as the consultant's. Be sure that project results and milestone accomplishments are once again made clear. The work plan review should conclude with a firm agreement on the detailed plan, consent to continue funding of the engagement, commitment on the client responsibilities, and permission to begin executing the plan. It is often advisable to make this approval formal so there is no doubt that this review constitutes permission to proceed as planned.

THE PROJECT TEAM

Developing Clear Team Roles

The project team may consist of several persons, or it may be just one consultant "wearing all the hats." Regardless of the number of persons, the project leader should have thought out clearly which tasks should be assigned to whom.

If the team is small, it is tempting to overlook assignment of the project management tasks on the assumption that this function will be unnecessary. Even in a one-person project, the administrative functions are still required. If you are the manager, the librarian, the consultant, and everything else, you must realize that each "hat" (role) will require a certain amount of time and attention.

Project team chemistry can be very important to the success of the project, and the project leader must be very aware of this requirement. If there are any supervisory, technical, or specialty roles to be assumed, these should be specified. Quite often a project can benefit from having special roles preassigned.

The Briefing and Task Assignments

Before assigning the project tasks to members of the project team, hold a team briefing. The purpose of this meeting is to present team members with engagement background and objectives, and to outline clearly the roles that each person will play in the project.

The project team briefing should discuss some of the engagement's physical aspects, including:

Who will be responsible for clerical functions

Who will make travel arrangements

The availability of office or desk space at the client's office

What working hours will be observed

What are the factors or unusual aspects of working with this client

Project progress reporting

In effect, this meeting represents a statement of the ground rules, the strategy for the project, and should give each team member a chance to ask questions on these topics. The meeting should conclude with assignment of specific tasks for the first milestone segment of the project.

CONCLUSION

The engagement planning process can be seen as the strategy session period of the project. During this time frame the consultant lays out in detail the game plan for conducting the proposed work. The result of the process is a detailed specification for what will be done and by whom.

Perhaps one of the greatest benefits of presenting the plan to the client is the feeling of confidence it gives to everyone associated with the engagement. A sense of order and purpose is established, and the consultant is already on the road to developing a professional relationship that can produce work products that meet the client's expectations.

12

Engagement Documentation and Control

CHARLOTTE A. JENKINS
Price Waterhouse
Los Angeles, California

INTRODUCTION

Most successful projects are the result of well-executed and controlled project plans. The purpose of the project plan is to define the specific project tasks necessary to achieve the objectives and to identify the resources needed to accomplish these objectives. The project plan becomes the road map to all phases of project execution, while answering such critical questions as:

1. How can the objectives be accomplished?
2. What are the interrelationships of the identified tasks?
3. When should the work be completed?
4. Who is responsible for completing specific tasks?
5. Where is the work to be performed?

The documented project plan provides a basis for fee estimates and project direction and thereby becomes the schedule and key control mechanism for the engagement. All documentation, progress reports, and project revisions are based on the original project plan.

The purpose of this chapter is to describe documentation and control techniques that support the development use of the project plan as a basis for conducting a successful engagement. Figure 12.1 provides an overview of various documentation and control components needed to support engagements. Each of the areas outlined in Figure 12.1 is discussed in detail within this chapter.

The chapter is divided into three sections as outlined in Figure 12.1. The first section focuses on project control. Once an engagement has been obtained, the consultant's first priority must be to implement control mechanisms that ensure delivery of the results expected by the client.

The second section will address the what, how, when, who, and where questions as they relate to engagement documentation. Topics discussed include:

1. What documentation tools are needed to support the project plan?
2. How should documentation be prepared, obtained, and organized?
3. Why is documentation structure important?
4. Who should be responsible for engagement documentation?
5. Where should the documentation be retained, once completed?

The third section describes documenting work performed and data collected throughout each engagement. This documentation is referred to as work papers. Work papers serve as support and reference for all engagements.

Overall, this chapter focuses on fundamental engagement documentation and control techniques. By mastering an understanding of the concepts and tools described in this chapter, a consultant can learn to plan, execute, and control any engagement.

Project Management

Project management means planning, scheduling, and controlling activities to provide solutions to problems. In the consulting environment, we may solve problems, improve systems and procedures, define organization structures or any number of projects to satisfy client needs. Because fully understanding and satisfying our client's expectations is our primary business objective, we must use proven methods and techniques to ensure that our projects are successful.

Understanding and using some form of the project management tools outlined in this section is critical to continued successful consulting projects. Consistent use of these project management tools provides current information for responding to frequently asked client questions

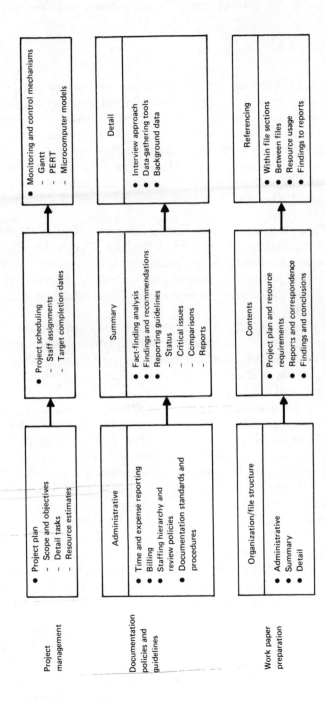

Figure 12.1 Engagement documentation and control overview. [SOURCE: Portions of this chart were adapted from the Price Waterhouse Effective Engagement Management Continuing Education course —overview block diagram of project management and delivery requirements.]

such as "What is the project status?" and "When will the tasks be completed?"

Project Plan

The first activity for a consultant, once a project has been requested, is to prepare the project plan. Project plans are divided into specific sections to categorize and analyze problems prior to providing a total solution. Major components of a good project plan include a list of tasks, estimated time to complete each task, target completion dates, and estimated resource requirements by task. Upon completion, actual resources used to accomplish tasks should be reviewed. The estimates and tasks are communicated to the client and serve as the road map for accomplishing project objectives.

The project plan is the nucleus of a consulting engagement. It serves as a guide for staff assignments and completion dates, providing the consultant with an updated status at any point during the project. In order to maintain a current status, the project plan should be updated at least weekly, providing an ongoing comparison of planned and actual resources and results.

The project plan is usually prepared using some kind of spreadsheet. Because of the frequency and importance of updates to the project plan and the need for evaluation of actual resources used at any project point, some consultants have chosen to develop microcomputer models for project planning and control.

A microcomputer-based spreadsheet software package provides a means for developing a tailored model to plan, estimate, and track projects. An example of a basic project plan format developed using spreadsheet software is provided in Figure 12.2. The objective of this model is to provide complete project information for the consultant's use; however, this level of detail should be summarized for presentation to a client. Most spreadsheet software packages will allow you to pass summarized hours and fee into another model, as illustrated in Figure 12.3.

The summary model can be updated with other data such as outputs and timetables, or it can simply outline specific tasks and hours estimated to complete each task. The summary model is most appropriate for presentation to the client.

Schedules

Once the overall project plan has been completed, schedules and target completion dates should be prepared for each person assigned to the project. The schedule should be based on specific tasks, time estimated

Figure 12.2 Detail project plan.

Last updated - 6/25/85

ENGAGEMENT PLANNING PROJECT CONTROL SAMPLE CLIENT

Staff: Billing value:	ST1 $ Bud	ST1 $ Act	MGR $ Bud	MGR $ Act	SMR $ Bud	SMR $ Act	Total hours budgeted	Total hours actual	Hours variance	Total dollars budgeted	Total dollars actual	Dollars variance
Phase I - Project Control												
A. Accumulate documentation and review	XX		XX		XX		XX			$$$$		
B. Define project control documentation			XX		XX		XX			$$$$		
C. Assign staff and target completion dates			XX				XX			$$$$		
D. Prepare final report outline			XX		XX		XX			$$$$		
E. Tailor analysis and review techniques			XX		XX		XX			$$$$		
F. Identify interviewees and schedule	XX		XX				XX			$$$$		
G. Prepare interview questions	XX		XX				XX			$$$$		
H. Prepare work paper and billing guidelines			XX				XX			$$$$		
I. Conduct client meeting - start project	XX	XX	XX		XX		XX			$$$$		
Phase I totals	XX	—	XX	—	XX	—	XX	—		$$$$		

Figure 12.3 Summary project plan.

ORGANIZATION REVIEW WORK PLAN

Task description	Resource estimate			Outputs	Target completion date
	CRD	PW hours	Fees		
PHASE III - RECOMMENDATIONS AND ACTION PLANS					
A. Prepare organization chart from director level to president		4 — 4		Organization chart	7/24/85
B. Prepare recommendations of functional responsibilities for subsidiary positions		38 — 40		Recommendations/job descriptions	7/25/85
C. Prepare suggestions for personnel qualifications for recommended positions		18 — 20		Qualifications by position	7/26/85
D. Review draft recommendations, organizition chart, and position qualification suggestions	4	12 — 16			7/29/85
E. Finalize recommendations and discuss action steps for implementing recommendations	4	10 — 10			7/31/85
Total - Phase III	8	82 — 90	$$$$$$		

to complete tasks, and critical completion dates. Figure 12.4 provides an example of a daily schedule for a consultant, outlining tasks for a specific project. The schedule should also outline tasks that can be done independently and tasks that have prerequisites for most efficiently utilizing slack time. This is further discussed in the project control section.

Project Control

The two most common graphic representations of the project plan can be prepared using a Gantt chart or a project evaluation and review technique (PERT) diagram. An example of a Gantt chart is given in Figure 12.5. The horizontal axis shows elapsed time required to complete activities and tasks that are listed vertically. This graphic representation does not show interrelationships and prerequisite tasks and is, therefore, easily understood and direct, making this method a good choice for client presentations.

Another effective project management tool is critical path scheduling. Most consultants are familiar with PERT charts, which graphically outline activities and time estimates for completing activities. The PERT method allows the consultant to chart activities using earliest and latest start and completion dates to predict the overall project completion date. Activities whose completion is critical, or prerequisite, to other activi-

Figure 12.4 Daily work schedule example.

SAMPLE CLIENT

PROJECT CONTROL PHASE

Staff assigned _____ Date last updated_____

Task description	December dates						
	22	23	27	28	29	30	31
1. Accumulate client documentation and review	X ----------X						
2. Define project control documentation	X						
3. Assign staff and target completion dates		X					
4. Prepare final report outline			X				
5. Tailor analysis and review techniques				X			
6. Identify interviewees and schedule				X ----X			
7. Prepare interview questions						X	
8. Prepare work paper and billing guidelines						X	
9. Conduct staff meeting to review project							X

Figure 12.5 Gantt chart.

SAMPLE CLIENT

Phase/task	Hours	Elapsed time in weeks									
		Week 1	2	3	4	5	6	7	8	9	10
1. Initiate project and collect preliminary data	XX	———									
2. Review background data	XX		---------								
3. Determine the effectiveness of each major software application system	XX			---------							
4. Determine the adequacy and effectiveness of the Computer Center staff in satisfying user needs in each functional area	XX				----						
5. Determine adequacy of physical facilities	XX				-------						
6. Determine adequacy of service to users	XX				---------						
7. Review provisions for acquisition, allocation, and control of computing resources	XX				-----						
8. Evaluate the effectiveness of Computer Center staff in training users	XX				-------						
9. Evaluate Computer Center personnel relative to the latest technological developments and methods	XX							---------			
10. Prepare a report of recommendations, plans, and policy guidelines	XX XX		---------								

ties can be identified, and these activities become the primary focus in charting completion dates. The set of connected lines with the greatest start-to-finish combination is known as the critical path. Other activities not on the critical path are addressed during slack time; they are secondary to critical path activities. This method provides an accurate method of depicting the importance of time and the interdependency of activities and prerequisites in accomplishing project objectives.

A basic PERT diagram uses circles for events; the circles are linked together with lines connecting associated events. PERT information is very useful in rescheduling work when additional tasks are added or target completion dates are missed. Note that in a PERT diagram, circles signify activities taken from tasks outlined in the project plan. The arrows signify the time required to complete each task (also taken from the project plan). A diagram read from left to right outlines the sequence of task performance. An example of a PERT diagram is provided in Figure 12.6. Note that PERT diagrams also help managers to control their activities on muliple-client assignments.

Microcomputer Applications

Several project management microcomputer programs are available to assist with planning, scheduling, and controlling project tasks and resources. Some common features of project management software include:

- Project plan and resource requirements model
- Project calendar
- Critical path reports
- Project summary reports
- Estimated versus actual resource usage reports

Many articles have been written comparing various project management packages. Consultants interested in project management software should research computer magazine articles or check with local computer stores for demonstrations. Microcomputer word processing packages are also invaluable tools for preparing status documentation for work papers and drafts of client reports.

To the consultant, the primary advantage in using microcomputer resources is that time is saved and control is improved. A computer can perform the calculations and repetitive tasks, allowing the consultant more time to work on specific project activities. Work smarter and more efficiently is the kind of recommendation we would make to our clients, and in this case we can follow our own advice by utilizing microcomputers.

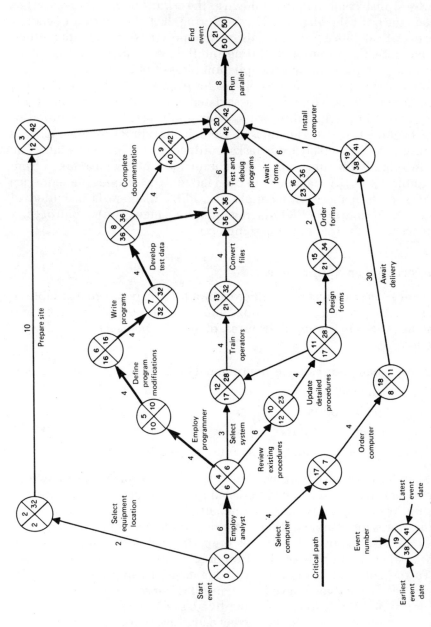

Figure 12.6 PERT diagram.

DOCUMENTATION POLICIES AND GUIDELINES

Formalized documentation policies and guidelines ensure that events and agreements affecting the project findings and conclusions are properly documented and filed. A comprehensive approach to documentation collection should include some variation of the file categories and source documents described in the work paper section. This section focuses more on some key questions that a consultant should address when establishing documentation policies and guidelines. This section also provides sample formats and guidelines for document preparation and control.

What documentation policies and guidelines should be established for internal use? Documentation policies and guidelines should address: (1) a defined structure for all documentation with sample formats; (2) timing for preparing, updating, and completing documentation; (3) procedures outlining instructions for documenting and complying with documentation policies; and (4) responsibilities for documentation and review at various project stages.

Certain documentation should have formal policies and procedures established to provide direction, communication, and control. Types of documentation that should be required and formalized include:

Documentation	Illustrated in
Project plan	Figure 12.2
Time and expense reporting	Figure 12.7
Internal status reports	Figure 12.8
Client accounting and billing	Figure 12.9

Procedures or guidelines for other documentation described in the work paper section should be considered; however, less formal guidelines are acceptable in many organizations.

How should documentation be prepared and reviewed to ensure quality control and responsibility for the documentation? Specific procedures, providing instruction to consultants using the suggested formats, should be defined for each type of documentation. Procedures should explain the format, give a complete example, and suggest situations and stages within each project where the format could best be used.

The procedures should also identify responsibilities for completing documentation. At the beginning of each project, the project manager should decide what documentation formats are most appropriate and should communicate responsibilities to other consultants working on the project.

Quality control review points should also be established by the project manager at the beginning of each project. Some organizations request

Figure 12.7 Daily time and expense log.

DAILY LOG

Client _____

Client code _____

Consultant _____

Date	W/P x-ref.	Hours	Brief description of work performed	Additional activity required problem to be resolved	Task status	Expenses

Figure 12.8 Project status reports.

PROJECT STATUS REPORT

Prepared by _____

Client _____

Project/task _____

Beginning date ___/___/___ thru

Ending Date ___/___/___

Project plan task reference	Significant activities this period	Budget hours	Actual hours this period	Total actual hours	Percent complete	Estimated completed date	Comments

Figure 12.9 Client accounting and billing analysis.

FEE ANALYSIS/BILLING SUMMARY

Client name _____   Billing period _____
Client no. _____   Prepared by _____
                                    Approved by _____

| Activity | Actual hours | Hours billed | Amounts billed | | | (Over) under budget/comments |
			Net fee	Expenses	Total	
Totals						

Decription and amounts to be shown on bill

_____
_____
_____

Mailing Instructions: ( ) Mail   ( ) Mail and send me copy   ( ) Give bill to me

Name, title _____
and address _____

Summary information

	Hours	Fees	Expenses
Original budget as of _____			
Revised budget as of _____			
Total billed as of _____			
Remainder to bill as of _____			
Variance as of _____			

Comments _____
_____

228

managers not involved in a specific project to perform periodic reviews of completed project documentation. This approach offers an objective review and ensures that all completed project documentation is in compliance with documentation policies providing complete support of recommendations presented to the client.

Documentation checklists may be established by the project manager as a required form to promote quality control reviews. The checklist provides a means of specifying documentation required for the project and staff responsible for completing the documentation. Most checklists also include columns for indication of manager review and corresponding review dates.

What documentation is needed to support conclusions? All background data, interview results, research data, and client-prepared documents should be filed and reviewed prior to preparing conclusions. These findings should be analyzed, consolidated, and cross-referenced to a summary of findings and conclusions document. Cross-referencing provides the linkage of findings to conclusions in support of recommendations. The consultant should also document (1) a statement of assumptions and alternative solutions and (2) factors influencing conclusions and recommendations. These should be cross-referenced to detail work papers and later to the draft report. These analyses and narratives help the consultant organize ideas and develop alternative solutions.

How long and where should client work papers be retained? Each client engagement should have an established retention period for work papers. The retention period should be based on internal requirements, client requirements, or legal requirements. For example, engagements involving changes to accounting policies and procedures would require work paper retention ranging from 7 to 10 years. This retention period can be determined by the number of years for which a client's accounting data would require support for audit work. Other engagements, such as hardware/software selection, may have a work paper retention of 3 to 5 years since technology advancements would significantly affect prior analyses. A statement outlining the project description, number of files, and retention period should be prepared by the project manager and included in the administrative file for each project.

Client work papers should be retained by the firm since the work papers are the support for client recommendations. Many firms use a central file room in which files are organized either in sequence (by assigned client number) or by client name. The central file room should contain the most recent engagements, i.e., engagements within the last 3 years. Work paper source documents with retention periods longer than 3 years may be archived at a location outside the central file area. If a consultant has space limitations, he or she may prefer to microfilm the source documents and discard the mass volume of paper, using this economical alternative for storing work paper files with longer retention periods.

WORK PAPERS

Purpose

The primary purpose of work papers is historical substantiation of work performed, providing a basis for developing conclusions. Work papers are a consultant's source of reference during an engagement. They also serve as support for recommendations once an engagement has been completed. Since work papers may ultimately be subpoenaed, good documentation practices—combined with explicit organization—are imperative. Good documentation records a consultant's activities and provides reference to data used for decision making and recommendations. Work paper data may be provided by the client or prepared by the consultant.

Contents

A consultant gathers background data at the beginning of each project, providing an overview of the client environment. Background data usually consist of documents provided by the client, such as financial statements and existing procedures. The consultant gathers additional data while conducting steps outlined in the project plan. The most common tools used for collecting additional information important to a particular client project are questionnaires and interviews.

The purpose of collecting information is to research, study, and analyze client problems relating to past, present, and future events that may affect recommendations. A consultant must assess various options and alternatives for satisfying the client objectives and test the possible impact of recommendations prior to issuing the client report. All alternatives, assumptions, and comparisons considered by the consultant in developing the recommended solution should be documented in the work papers.

Typically, work papers are categorized into three major sections: administrative, summary, and detail information. Further subdivision of these sections provides specific reference by data location. An example of a more detailed subdivision by section is provided in Figure 12.10.

The documents outlined within the administrative category of Figure 12.10 are usually standard forms defined by a consulting firm's documentation and quality control policies and guidelines.

Figure 12.10 Suggested work paper content by section and file category.

File cagetory	Section	Source documents
Administrative	Index	Cover page contains references to other work paper volumes and staff references Table of contents
	Checklists	Work paper contents checklist
	Controls	Project work plan revisions with explanations Time analysis by work plan task Engagement status reports Billing memoranda Work paper retention instructions
Summary	Proposal documentation	Record of inquiry Listing of key client Personnel Competitive bidding Approach Competition summary Proposal
	Report documentation	Summary and findings analysis Statement of assumptions and alternative solutions Factors influencing conclusions and recommendations Client report (draft and final)
	Correspondence	Client letters Client progress reports Memoranda documenting key events
Detail	Detail client data	Questionnaire data Interview results Client-prepared documents
	Background data	Report on client's present financial conditions Annual report Long-range plan Overview of client operations
	Research data	Documentation gathered from similar client projects Industry background and recent industry updates

The documents outlined in the summary and detail categories of Figure 12.10 may vary in format for different types of client engagements. Many of the source documents are narrative descriptions in which a standard format is not necessary. These documents include:

Record of inquiry

Listing of key client personnel

Competitive bidding approach

Competition summary (if known)

Statement of assumptions

Alternative solutions and factors influencing conclusions and recommendations

The consultant should create these documents, describing key points by listing names and sources of information, purpose of documentation, basic facts, and the opinions regarding the source and impact of the documented information.

The client proposal, the summary of findings analysis, and the client report are normally a combination of a defined format and project-related narrative. A defined format provides that framework for developing a narrative to support conclusions and recommendations resulting from the project. By defining a basic client report format, for example, the consultant can enhance the consistency and quality of all reports. The report format would include all or part of the following sections:

Statement of engagement objectives

Background information and activities conducted to analyze the client's business

Findings and conclusions

Recommendations

Benefits of implementing recommendations

Organization

Work papers should be combined using an approach that secures individual documents while providing ease of reference. Cover pages, indexes, and sectional dividers should be used to make specific document sections more identifiable. The example in Figure 12.11 illustrates the basic data and format for printed work paper cover pages.

Cross-Referencing

Cross-referencing connects data gathered at one part of an engagement with that gathered during another part. It eliminates the need for duplicating facts in several documentation sections. Cross-referencing also

Figure 12.11 Work paper cover page example.

WORK PAPER COVER PAGE

Client Name: Sample Client

Client Number: 999−99

Engagement Dates: July 1, 1985 - December 1, 1985

File Name/Number: Administrative - File A

Index to other files *for this engagement:*	*Staff Responsibility/* *Workpaper Completion Dates*	
Summary Report - File SR	James Doe	12/15/85
Detail Background Data - File B	Shirley Brown	11/30/85
	Teresa Stevens	11/30/85

provides a means of tracking pertinent information from the detail section to the final report. In addition, page numbers used in cross-referencing should link key documents within each work paper section to the table of contents.

Cross-referencing is accomplished by placing a reference number in a common location of each document filed in the work papers. The reference number is usually assigned to each page; however, further subdivision into paragraphs or specific sections within one page may be accomplished by placing a unique reference number beside each sub-division. Cross-referencing within specific sections and between the detail and administrative files can be accomplished throughout the project. Cross-referencing to report documentation within the summary file is usually addressed after the project is completed and all documents have been filed. A basic example of cross-referencing is provided in Figure 12.12. The example deals with two different documents within the same project but located in separate work paper files and sections. As illustrated in the example, a consultant could locate the associated summary of conclusion by reviewing the inverview notes on page D-21 and referring to the report file on page SR-9. Likewise, a consultant could locate the detail support for the report conclusion by referring back to interview notes.

Cross-referencing should also be used when comparing the consultant's actual time expended for each project plan activity to the project plan resource budget. Actual time used would be documented on daily time logs and summarized on the actual project plan.

Figure 12.12 Cross-referencing example.

DETAIL FILE	SUMMARY AND REPORT FILE
Detail Client Data Section	Report Documentation Section
Interview notes	*Report*
Page D-21	Page SR-9
General ledger is the client's most important system. The account structure is *XXX-XXX*, which allows account classification by cost center within the organization. This structure is important for sample client to remain consistent with other entities within the organization. SR-9.	Sample client requires a *six-digit* chart of account structure to maintain consistency with other entities within the organization. D-21

CONCLUSION

Good project management means never surprising the client with changes to the project plan projections after the changes have already occurred. The tools and guidelines outlined in this chapter provide the who, what, when, where, how, and why's to keep clients informed and to guide you through even the most difficult assignments.

Presentation of Results

TIMOTHY J. O'SHEA
Seamark Consulting Group, Inc.
Long Beach, California

INTRODUCTION

The other chapters of this handbook cover many aspects of selling, conducting, and managing consulting engagements. This chapter focuses on the last step—when you have done the work in the trenches and are ready to present your results to the client.

Every consulting engagement must include, in some form, a presentation of results to the client. I have yet to find a client who would say, "We want your firm to do a study for us, but don't bother to tell us your conclusions or recommendations." Some engagements are initiated without proposals. Some are carried out without project plans or work papers. Presenting results is a universal element of consulting work, and your success as a consultant will depend on your skill at communicating what you have done.

Importance of Communication Skills

The one universal skill of successful consultants is the ability to organize and express ideas. If you work as a file clerk or a machine operator, you don't need great communications skills to be effective. As a consultant, your effectiveness depends on your ability to reach others through the written or spoken word. Many who aspire to success in consulting start with a base of sound technical skills. Unfortunately, success often eludes even gifted technicians who lack organization and communications abilities. You may be acquainted with technical people—accountants, systems analysts, engineers—who could be successful consultants if only they could convey the elegance of their designs or the meaning of their analyses.

Why Consultants Have Difficulty Presenting Results

Many practitioners have more difficulty with presentations than with any other part of an engagement. Several factors seem to explain this.

First, presentations involve hard work. They require creativity, discipline, and intense mental effort. As an example, consider documenting and analyzing the flow of work in a customer service operation. This is a clear, step-by-step process that can be undertaken in bite-sized chunks. Drawing conclusions—identifying procedural weaknesses, specifying improvements, developing an action plan, and describing what your proposed changes will accomplish—is not a simple task.

Second, presenting results involves risks. It is normal for a consultant's anxiety factor to escalate as the end of the engagement approaches. The quiet isolation that characterizes fact gathering and analysis is different from going public with results that have to be sold to management. Several practitioners have told me they get a "bet your career" feeling every time they submit a report or make a presentation. The presentation part of an engagement is where you most visibly lay your skills, thought processes, and reputation on the line.

Third, effective communication is not a well-developed skill area for many consultants. Most of us are good technicians. We have had formal training and field experience in our technical disciplines. The skills of an effective presenter—creative analysis, clear writing, persuasive speaking, graphic communication—are seldom taught and infrequently practiced. Many of us have difficulty presenting results because we don't feel skilled at it and don't do enough presentations to become more comfortable.

This chapter is concerned with overcoming these difficulties. By understanding what to present, the types of presentations, and the techniques, you can improve your skills. When these skills are sharp, the work will seem easier and the risks will be reduced.

PREPARING TO PRESENT

There are two points you must address before you're ready to make the presentation: what to say, and how to say it.

Deciding What to Say

Experienced practitioners know that one of the most challenging parts of a consulting assignment is choosing what to say to the client at its conclusion. There are always many things you *can* say but only a few things you *should* say. Typically, consulting engagements generate a lot of data—notes, documents, sample forms, flow diagrams, and so on. You can easily spend the major part of your time simply accumulating data only to realize near the end of the project that you have few clues about what is important. The most reliable safeguard is to develop proper work papers: (1) Arrange the data as you collect them, so they are accessible and logical, and (2) identify and catalog key points as you go along.

Keeping proper work papers as the engagement proceeds is one of those things that "everyone knows" should be done; but like most things, few people do it. If you take the trouble to keep good work papers, you'll find it easy to produce superior results—results that are much better, at least, than those of your less conscientious colleagues.

Here are some ideas for identifying what is important in the data you collect:

1. Keep a log of ideas and observations as the project progresses. Review them frequently to add new information and reassess their significance. Use the list as a basis for your presentation outline.

2. Add handwritten summary or highlight points in the margins of flow diagrams and interview notes, as they are prepared. This will allow you to avoid tedious rereadings of the material weeks or months later to ferret out the key points.

3. Use the Delphi research technique with the other members of the engagement team to develop a list of important points. This approach calls for similar questions to be asked of each person, without the others being present. Frequently mentioned points may provide further material for your presentation.

4. Try to "psyche out" your client. Put yourself in the place of the key person or people in the client organization and think about what issues are most important to each of them. Then, be sure to address these issues so that your presentation is congruent with the client's mind-set.

Choosing the Method of Presentation

Having assembled the material that you will convey to your client, you move on to the second consideration in presentation of results: how to present what you want to say. In choosing your method, concentrate on one objective: to communicate effectively at a minimal cost to the client. This is easy to say but often hard to do. Effective communication can easily be confused with elaborate presentations or lengthy reports. Try not to give your client more of a presentation than is required to inform, persuade, or initiate action. Clients willingly pay for your experience, technical skills, and judgment. They are not as eager to pay for hours of drafting, editing, and copying that contribute little to the expected results.

The choice of presentation methods may not always be within your control. Circumstances may restrict your options, or the format may be specified by your agreement with the client. You should choose the presentation method carefully to the extent you can control the choice. Here is a checklist of factors to consider:

1. Purpose of the engagement (to inform, persuade, document, produce a result or product, etc.)
2. Contractual requirements or other commitments you may have made regarding reports, briefings, demonstrations, etc.
3. Time you have available to prepare
4. Size of your budget for the project
5. Type of presentation that best fits the personality of the client
6. Logistics; that is, whether the presentation must be made to one person, to several people in different cities, etc.

The correct method of presentation will vary with the type of engagement. A written report, for example, would not be sufficient if your assignment was to present a seminar to members of a client's staff. Table 13.1 shows the types of presentations that have proven effective for several common categories of consulting engagements.

WRITTEN PRESENTATION

The classical method of presenting is the written report. Many clients find written reports comfortable or simply expect them. Consultants also become attached to written reports because they look impressive and prove that something tangible was done in the client's behalf. Unfortunately, written presentations are often the most costly and least effective method of conveying results.

Types of Written Presentations

Once you have decided to prepare a written report for your client, you should determine what form it will take. The form of the report can significantly affect cost and effectiveness. There are basically six types

Table 13.1   Presentation Methods for Various Engagement Types

Engagement	Presentation type
General management/planning	Oral briefing or high-level summary
Specific studies (market research, feasibility, etc.)	Formal report with data and/or graphs
Systems design/programming	Written specifications, flowcharts, source code, system documentation
Client education	Lesson plans, visual aids, handout materials, case studies, video tapes
Litigation support	Analyses, depositions, testimony
Procedures documentation, RFP preparation	Written materials (specifications, manuals)
Management/operational reviews	Checklists, graphic evaluations, action plans
Informal management advice and counseling	Conversation, memoranda

of written reports: formal reports, informal letters and memoranda, discussion outlines, graphic summaries, charts and diagrams, and manuals.

Formal reports.   These are the classic styles of presentation. They are difficult to write, expensive to produce, and almost never read in their entirety by anyone other than the consultant's proofreader. Nevertheless, formal written reports are often required by clients, and you should develop the ability to prepare them when necessary.

Formal reports are typically divided up into major sections so that their contents will be accessible and readable. You can use the following rough guidelines for structuring formal reports. Not all reports include each section, but the headings are typical:

1. *Executive summary:*   high-level synopsis of your findings, recommendations, and benefits, which contains key information for clients who have too little time, or interest, to read the entire report

2. *Project background:*   short history of the project to help the reader understand your assignment and to place the project in perspective

3. *Objectives and scope:*   restatement of the purpose and limitations of the engagement

4. *Engagement methodology:*   description of the techniques and approaches you used in carrying out the engagement

5. *Analysis and synthesis:*   description and detailing of the analysis you undertook and the basis for major findings reached through the analysis

6. *Findings and conclusions:*   listing of your major conclusions that may also include alternatives you considered and reasons for reaching the conclusions you selected

7. *Recommendations:*   statements aimed at guiding your client toward a course of action that corresponds to the engagement's objectives and to your findings

8. *Expected benefits:*   highlights of the results that can be achieved by carrying out your recommendations

9. *Implementation guide:*   description of specific methods for implementing your recommendations, addressing sequence, timing, resources required, and constraints involved

10. *Appendixes:*   any necessary charts, exhibits, tables, or analyses related to the engagement

It is this writer's opinion that formal reports should be avoided whenever possible. This opinion is based on my observation that formal reports seldom help to achieve the most important result of the consulting engagement: constructive change that produces beneficial effects. Formal reports tend to end up on bookshelves or in file drawers.

Informal letters and memoranda.   These familiar forms of business correspondence are often used with clients who require written reports but are able to do without formality. They can be an effective means of cummunicating status, findings, and recommendations. By avoiding the pomp and flourishes of a formal report, they encourage an economical and timely flow of information between consultant and client.

Discussion outlines.   This form consists of skeletal statements that assist in conveying information to your client. They are used in conjunction with meetings or conversations at which results are explained and discussed. As such, they represent a hybrid form of the written and in-person presentations, combining some of the best elements of each. They provide a written record, to which the client can refer, while affording economy of preparation and the directness and flexibility of face-to-face communication. A useful format for the discussion outline incorporates generous spacing between points, to allow for note taking. See Figure 13.1.

Graphic summaries.   This enhanced form of the discussion outline combines highlighted wording with graphic symbols in order to convey quickly and clearly information. The graphics capability of microcomputers can be used to transmit important information vividly and rapidly to your client. This form is particularly useful for management or operational reviews, and for conceptual engagements involving marketing or strategic planning. An example of the graphic summary form of presentation is shown in Figure 13.2.

Figure 13.1   How to market the partnership.

1. Identify your contacts Segregate the field The "must" group 1st alternatives 2d alternatives	5. Anticipate questions Know what they'll ask before they ask it Prepare responses
2. Make contact Make it personal Face to face Telephone	6. Expect two-part meeting Introduction Closing 7. Suggest CPA/lawyer review
3. Know what to say Be brief Review highlights Set meeting time and place	8. Close the deal Get a commitment—one way or another Don't let it drag on Refer to the August 1 deadline
4. Know when/where to meet Meet ASAP after contact Don't meet at office during business hours Meet over lunch, dinner, drinks, etc.	

Charts, diagrams, layouts, and matrix arrays.   For some engagements, charts or diagrams constitute the entire written presentation. In data processing or methods analysis projects, flowcharts of various types may represent a complete work product for the consultant. Other examples of this form include organizational charts, facility layouts, and matrix arrays. Matrix arrays (see Figure 13.3) can be particularly useful for conveying alternatives and recommended actions to clients.

Prospectuses and manuals.   Some engagements have as their primary purpose the production of a written document. Such is the case when consultants are asked to write procedures manuals or to develop prospectuses or private placement memoranda. These represent both the work product and the presentation of results and are usually accompanied by a brief transmittal letter that records the transfer of the work product, the data transferred, and the recipient.

Planning and Developing Written Material

Choosing the type of written presentation to make is relatively easy compared to the actual writing. Many consultants fear formal writing. They "freeze up" when confronted with blank sheets of paper and a deadline. Overcoming "writer's block" is crucial to success in consulting.

Preparing to write.   The most difficult part in writing is getting started. The difficulty relates to our subconscious striving for perfection.

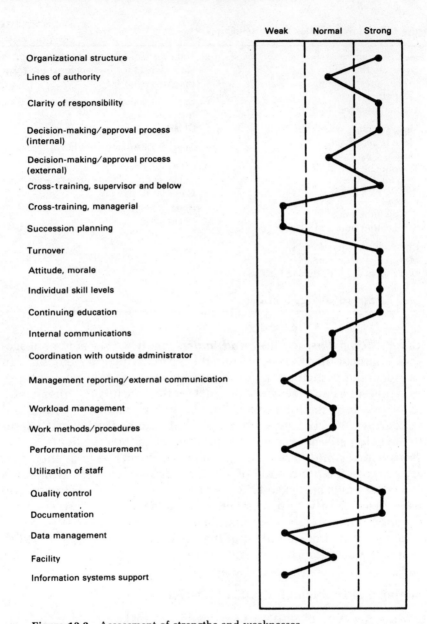

Figure 13.2 Assessment of strengths and weaknesses.

We tend unconsciously to insist that everything we put on paper be perfect. As a result our creative abilities are often stifled by our own built-in critics. Remember, there will be numerous revisions to the original version, so you do not need to create a perfect product at the outset.

Issue	Discussion	Alternatives	Recommendations

Is the current organizational structure sufficient, in light of the new automated technology being introduced into AEVS?	• No special change took place as a result of the introduction of DP technology into AEVS.
	
	• What appears to be lacking is some level of DP administrative and organizational skills to provide direction, control, and leadership in the areas of:
	
	  Definition of policy
	  Organization and execution of training programs
	  Planning and strategy
	  Implementation of controls and monitoring capabilities
	  Coordination of companywide DP activities.
	
	• This change would require some organizational restructuring but no extensive change of personnel and/or reporting relationships.
	
	• AEVS should consider organizing an "Information Resource Management" (IRM) unit.
		• Promote PGMR, and add an additional analyst/coder.
		
		• Hire an experienced DP individual who will head the new IRM group and help set direction for the integration of DP technology.
		
		• Secure temporary, outside assistance to help set up the IRM group until a qualified individual can be hired to head this group.
			Reorganize the current structure, forming a new group called "Information Resource Management," with reporting responsibility to General Manager.
			
			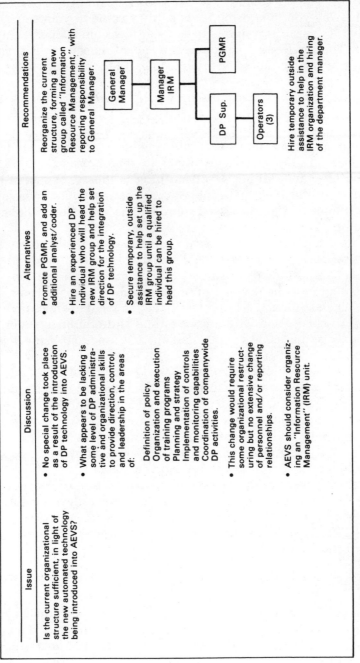
			
			Hire temporary outside assistance to help in the IRM organization and hiring of the department manager.

Figure 13.3   Matrix array.

Often, it is easier to write if you simply try to tell the reader what you want to say. You can overcome writer's block by simply preparing a first draft the way you talk, using ideas as they come to your mind. Your objective at this stage is simply to get your ideas onto paper in any way you can. There will be ample opportunity later to check words, grammar, punctuation, and sequence, in order to make the communication correct and effective.

Organizing the material.   Assuming that the data you collect during an engagement are kept in logical, retrievable form, report preparation becomes a process of editing and arranging material. Generally, you will have far more information, ideas, and conclusions than you should put in a report. The key skills involved in report preparation become wordsmithing and editing. Wordsmithing is the art of saying things properly and effectively; it touches on grammar, style, and construction. Its techniques are discussed under the heading "Enhancing Readability."

Editing means organizing material and arranging it to accomplish the writer's purpose. The key to good editing is a clear definition of purpose. Once the purpose of the writing is determined, you can define the subjects that must be covered in order to achieve that purpose in the report. When editing, it is important to define what not to cover as well as what to cover. You will conserve time and eliminate superfluous material by setting aside subjects that are not important to the objective of your report.

Another key part of organizing material is to identify your audience. The people who will read your report should be the ultimate determinants of the technical level, depth of detail, and overall content of your written presentations. In assessing your audience, consider the backgrounds, needs, and preferences of those who will read your report. Think carefully about what they know and don't know and pay special attention to how they are likely to use your report.

Enhancing readability.   Some writers can make a subject fascinating, while others can put you to sleep writing about the same thing. We can't all be great writers, but we can try to make our writing as readable as possible. Here are a few points that will help you enhance the readability of your presentations:

1. Write short reports if possible. Short reports appeal to busy clients and they also reduce the amount of preparation effort.
2. Arrange the material for emphasis. The importance of an idea is indicated by where it appears in a text. Putting the important points up front will prepare the reader's mind for what you are trying to say and will summarize your ideas for the greatest impact.
3. Avoid long, complex paragraphs and sentences. To fully appreciate

this, pick up a legal document, such as an insurance policy or loan contract. Try reading through it and see how quickly your mind wanders.

4. Avoid jargon, slang, and unnecessary technical terms. To the extent possible, use plain language, words that will be familiar to your readers. There is no harm in using long words if they are well understood. Complexity and lack of familiarity, rather than word length, make for difficult reading.

5. Use the active voice and direct, descriptive words rather than euphemisms. Action words portray the images you want better than passive ones.

6. Use pictures, graphs, and charts whenever appropriate. Well-constructed graphic material often tells more than several written pages. It provides an effective change of pace for the reader and can help ensure that attention is focused on key points or facts.

7. Use numbers selectively. People who are comfortable with a large array of numbers (particularly accountants) seem to be fond of including voluminous spreadsheets in presentations. Most readers recoil at pages of numbers, particularly precise numbers (like, $10,371,286.37).

Remembering these points will help you produce concise, punchy reports that both inform and convince your readers.

Production Considerations in Written Presentations

Production problems are the downfall of many well-written reports. Scheduling production is important in order to avoid errors, omissions, and other embarrassments that mar the effectiveness of the report. You should estimate in advance how long it takes to type, proofread, correct, duplicate, and bind the report you are planning. Planning this time into your overall schedule can help you avoid some very uncomfortable problems.

The good news in report production is the proliferation of microcomputer-based word processing equipment in consulting offices. This has substantially shortened the time required from rough draft to final report. Consultants increasingly bypass the typing and revision steps by drafting their reports at a word processor and going directly to the finished product.

Techniques for Presenting Written Reports

The critical moment is when your creation is actually transferred to the client. The transfer is an important event that always has a "moment of truth" aura. There are several methods of transferring the report, some more effective than others.

One way is simply to send your report by mail or messenger. This is generally the least effective approach because you can't control when and how your client receives the report. It may get stuck in an "in" box for several days or may get read just after a stack of customer complaint letters. Presumably, your report has something important to say, and it's likely that your client paid handsomely for it. Delivery by mail means you can't be there to explain points, gauge reactions, and make adjustments if necessary. You rely on the written document to convey emphasis, intonations, and subtleties that are simply beyond the capability of the written word.

A second method of presentation is to hand deliver the report and discuss it with the client before leaving it to be read. This is the method that I have found most successful. A variation of this approach is to deliver the document to be read, leave the client alone long enough to read it, then immediately return and discuss it face to face. This approach is very effective, but timing is critical. The important thing is not to let time elapse between the reading and the discussion.

A third method is to have a brief presentation, covering the major points in the report, then distribute the report for your client to read. This method can be effective if the presentation is in-depth and if time is allowed for discussion and questions. The difficulty in this approach, however, is that your clients will often be eager to get their hands on the report before you finish speaking. It is almost always a mistake to hand out a report during a presentation because the audience is reading the report rather than listening to you.

Closing Note on Written Presentations

A final point about written presentations: In my opinion, written reports should be archival in nature. Ideally, they simply record and document what has already been discussed and agreed to by you and the client. Written reports should never surprise your client. Good consulting practice requires that all information contained in a report should already have been conveyed to and discussed with your client. "No surprises" should be the rule.

IN-PERSON PRESENTATIONS

This is the other major presentation category to be discussed in this chapter. Some form of in-person presentation takes place in almost all consulting engagements unless a report is written and mailed to the client.

If the concentration is on an oral report, the written presentation may be coincidental or entirely absent. An oral presentation can be more difficult to carry out satisfactorily than a written report because it involves more considerations. Presenting an oral report requires that you assemble your thoughts, define scope, and develop wording, much like a written presentation. In addition, you must consider such factors as location of the presentation, equipment needed, and the preparation of visual aids. All in all, in-person presentations are more demanding than written presentations; however, they have some significant advantages.

When presenting in person, you are able to add your own emphasis and inflection, which allows you greater smoothness and subtlety. You are able to see and interact with your audience, allowing you to adjust emphasis as needed. You can deal with questions and concerns, immediately ensuring that communication is achieved and problems are solved. Presenting in person requires that your clients deal with you face to face, which reduces their tendency to be critical. Finally, the in-person form gives you an opportunity to project your personality and persuasiveness to a far greater extent than you can do on paper.

How to Prepare an In-Person Presentation

An in-person presentation is really a combination of a speech and a training session. The process begins in a way very similar to preparing written presentations: You define the objectives, consider the audience, prepare an outline, etc. It is not necessary, or even desirable, to write out your presentation as if it were a report. You need only to list the major points to be communicated.

Beyond the material to be presented, there are further considerations for your in-person presentation. The major ones are listed below:

1. *Length of time for the presentation:* How long do you need to get your points across, and how much time is the client willing to make available?

2. *Timing:* You should try to be presenting at a time when your client is receptive and unencumbered by other considerations. What time of day is best? Are Mondays peak work-load days? Is the client preoccupied with closing the books the first week of the month? Can you keep the client's attention on the afternoon before a holiday?

3. *Size of the audience:* Presenting to two people is vastly different from presenting to fifty. Tailor your presentation to the size of the group. If the presentation needs to be given to a small group, try to schedule several presentations to smaller groups of a large audience.

4. *Composition of audience:* This is extremely important but often

overlooked. To whom will you be talking? What are their points of view, their level of knowledge about your subject, their receptivity to what you will say, etc.? Everything about the presentation should be planned with some consideration for the composition of the audience.

5. *Atmosphere:*   Where will you be presenting? At a resort? In an office? In a restaurant or dining room? Will the atmosphere be casual or formal?

6. **Dress:**   How should you look? On some occasions you will want to look authoritative and conservative. Other times you may want to appear relaxed and casual. Consider that your effectiveness may be increased by dressing one way for the senior partners of a law firm and another way for a group of first-line supervisors in a maintenance operation.

Visual Aids

Visual aids could have been listed above as a planning point, but I consider them important enough to be dealt with separately. Remember, you are the most important visual aid in any presentation and you should only use auxiliary aids to complement your presentation. Often, you will be presenting complex or abstract material in reporting to your clients. Visual aids used properly can help get your message across to the client. Key points or critical comparisons can sometimes be brought out with great impact through the use of visual aids.

Visual aids come in many forms. Consultants most often use flip charts, overhead transparencies, and slides. Occasionally, you will see chalk boards or magic marker boards. I have occasionally seen blow-up photographs and even physical models used with great effectiveness. Whatever form you choose to use, keep several key points in mind to ensure that your visuals will help, not hinder, your presentation:

1. *Clarity:*   Each visual should express a clear point or thought. Be sure to hone and polish the points expressed in your visuals so they are logical, evident, and easily understood.

2. *Brevity:*   Too many thoughts are often loaded into one visual. Keep visuals simple and short.

3. *Readability:*   The person in the last row should easily be able to read and see all of your visuals. If you see the people in the first row squinting at your transparencies, you know you're in trouble.

4. *Quantity:*   Use enough to get your major points across, but don't overdo it. Too many visuals can clutter up your presentation, taking the focus off you and the points you're trying to make.

Some of the most effective visual aids I have seen are extremely simple: sometimes a few words on a slide, often nothing more than a picture. The easy preparation of effective visual aids is another area in which computer technology and the spread of microcomputers are vastly helpful.

Making the Presentation

When you have written your outline, considered and dealt with all the additional factors surrounding the presentation, developed effective visual aids, and rehearsed enough to be comfortable, you are ready to meet your audience. Table 13.2 lists some points to assist you. You might review these just before you make a presentation. They are simple, straightforward suggestions and they work.

Closing Note on In-Person Presentation

Effective presentation is an increasingly important skill in the consulting profession. It takes time, dedication, and a certain amount of hard knocks to become skillful and polished. I strongly recommend that you

Table 13.2 Making the Presentation

Before presenting
• Be confident, emphasize positive thoughts.
• Look your best.
• Remove distractions such as keys, coins, and pens from your pockets.
• Arrive early.
• Check out room, equipment, podium, lights, etc.
• Arrange for a signal when your time is almost up.

Presenting
• Stand tall.
• Command your audience.
• Make eye contact (one person at a time); avoid "panning" the audience.
• Speak up, enunciate clearly.
• Vary your pace.
• Pause periodically.
• Move naturally.
• Watch the audience, and adjust as needed.
• Finish on time (no exceptions).

attend to this area of professional development because your competitors certainly will be improving their skills.

Speaking of competition, be aware that you are going up against electronic media every time you speak. Today's audiences are conditioned to seeing presentations on television, at the movies, and on videocassettes. Their expectations will be high, and their comparisons can be harsh. Be sure to prepare yourself adequately.

MISTAKES TO AVOID

No one makes deliberate errors in presenting results to clients. Even so, mistakes are frequently made and often are fatal to the consultant-client relationship. A good report or a smooth presentation won't paper over poor-quality consulting work. Even the best consulting work, however, can be ruined by a poor presentation. If the client-consultant relationship is weak, presentation mistakes can often be the "last straw" that severs the relationship.

Here, for your quick reference, is a catalog of the more common errors I have observed. Some are so obvious as to appear almost trivial, but they can and do occur with unnerving frequency.

Common Mistakes Made in Presenting Results

1. Failing to address the client's primary concerns, key issues, or pet peeves

2. Answering the right questions but failing to provide enough background on the basis for your conclusions

3. Failing to obtain concurrence on conclusions and recommendations from members of the client's staff who must support them or carry them out

4. Ignoring the significance of timing and emotional considerations when delivering a report or presentation

5. Producing a report that seems cheap by comparison to the amount of your fees (which refers to the quality and usefulness of your report, not to its volume or weight)

6. Allowing inadequate time to prepare your presentation

7. Making the client feel silly, naive, negligent, or undeserving of your respect in either the tone or content of your presentation

8. Showing sloppiness, inattention to detail, or superficiality in your presentation

9. Surprising your client, especially in a group meeting or in a written report that cannot be retracted

10. Trying to sell future services via your presentation

CONCLUSION

Business organizations are becoming more sophisticated and discriminating in their use of consultants. As this occurs, their expectations will be raised concerning the level of service rendered by consultants. To succeed, you must be prepared to perform high-quality work. Doing good work is not enough; you must also effectively communicate the results of your efforts.

Success in consulting will not be guaranteed by the ability to present results effectively, but quality presentations can enhance your professional reputation. Consultants who can get across to their clients what they did, what it means, and how it can be used, will have an increasing edge over the good technician who falls short in communication.

Management of the Practice

14

Practice Planning and Administration

MYRON A. FRIEDMAN
Myron A. Friedman & Company
Palos Verdes Estates, California

INTRODUCTION

Management advisory services is a very broad and ill-defined term. Those of us who are consultants are attempting to say, "We can help you." We have expertise in certain areas of activity. We can provide knowledge gained from experience. We can stand off to the side and provide an independent, objective point of view. This viewpoint, however, is generally not unbiased.

If you wish to be a consultant, you must first evaluate your own talents and expertise. In addition, you need to review your communication skills, both oral and written; sales ability; ability to focus on a project and carry it to conclusion; and ability to maintain objectivity. You also must evaluate your business and professional judgment.

The scope of a consulting practice is defined by the expertise and experience of the consultants within the practice. Many practices start with a single individual, and the management consulting they offer is the area of the individual's expertise. This can be technical consulting in engineering, in industrial management, in marketing, in business management, or in financial areas. There is no limit to the potential for consulting activity. Consulting services can be provided to businesses, to governmental agencies, to nonprofit organizations, and certainly to individuals.

The scope of the consulting practice needs to be well defined so that it can be properly communicated to the potential users (clients). Often, it is unclear what consulting services are being provided or to whom those services might apply. Sometimes consultants are willing to provide services in many areas, but the scope of these services should be based upon expertise if the firm is going to be successful. It is extremely important to recognize the firm's background and expertise and not attempt to "oversell" these abilities or accept work outside the firm's capabilities.

ESTABLISHING OBJECTIVES AND STRATEGIES

Market Research and Economic Statistics

Prior to entering into a consulting practice, you should conduct market research to identify opportunities in the marketplace. For many types of consulting activities, it is relatively apparent that there is a market for services and a ready acceptance of such services. Some areas of the country appear to be accepting and interested in using consulting services, whereas other areas are less attuned to the benefits and use of such services.

Some highly specialized types of consulting services have not been established and accepted in the marketplace. Those types will require considerable effort for cultivation and development of markets. A clue to the market potential of consulting services can be gleaned from studying the listings of management consultants or surveying local CPA firms to determine which ones offer consulting services.

It will be much easier for an individual or firm to embark on a successful practice if there is an established marketplace. You must evaluate whether there is an oversaturation of consultants in your specialty area. A related issue is the competitive edge that new services would provide in a less penetrated marketplace.

Economic statistics and financial information concerning consulting practices are generally not readily available. Most of this information comes from word of mouth discussions with other consultants and knowledge of the local marketplace.

Quite frequently a consultant gets started because one or two clients indicate that they would be happy to use his or her talents as a consultant. This limited number of clients will provide a sufficient base for the individual to get started and maybe even keep busy on a full-time basis.

Follow-up work and referrals frequently will provide sufficient opportunities in these instances. If the practice is based upon relatively short engagements that require numerous contacts, or if staff is going to be hired right away, the need for market research is more important. In any case, a practice development program needs to be initiated to target potential clients. One of the biggest challenges is to keep productive time at a sufficiently high level and at the same time carry on an active program of building new contacts. New and old contacts are necessary to ensure a constant flow of new work. The classic balancing problem is overwork for periods of time and droughts for periods of time. Part of this problem results from the inability to stimulate additional business when you are really busy and the necessity of concentrating on stimulating business when you have finished projects.

Market research is important both for the new firm and the established consulting practice. Every practice needs to have a continual flow of work. No consulting engagement lasts forever, so there has to be a steady stream of new opportunities and new contacts for the consulting practice to survive. Some effort has to be made to reach out, contact potential clients, and make them aware of your services. You need to keep your name before the potential clients and, more important, before referral sources. Market research will help you focus your efforts as well as target organizations you should join to find potential clients.

Market Service Objectives

The previous section addressed the practice from a market research point of view, assessing the market potential for specific services. Armed with necessary information, you need to establish an operating plan for the practice—to set goals and objectives. These goals and objectives should include a desired income level, potential clients, and strategies to obtain those clients.

One of your most difficult tasks is to develop a picture of what you do that can be understood by potential clients and referral sources. It is often a significant challenge to educate potential clients about their problems and the way you can effectively solve the problems. In any event, it is important to develop both a story about what you do and a picture that others can understand—what service you are providing and how those services are applicable. Obviously, you should not overstate your capability and you should not accept projects for which you might not be able to deliver a quality service.

It is important to be imaginative and creative in your approach to marketing professional services. You should address your effort toward the individual who has the authority to hire a consultant. You can waste valuable time with a decision influencer who has to sell the idea to a superior, especially when the individual does not fully understand the capabilities and services being offered.

You need to attain "stature" in your field and establish that you are qualified to carry out the work that is proposed. This may involve participation in professional organizations, speaking engagements, writing articles, or related activities. These outside activities are frequently also excellent sources of contacts for new engagements.

The important point is that you must identify what services you propose to provide, the types of potential clients that could benefit from those services, and the potential amount of work. Based on these assumptions, you can identify staffing requirements and financing needs. All of these issues are somewhat interrelated.

Implementation Strategies

The crucial aspect to developing a consulting practice is obtaining clients. The challenge of obtaining clients is ongoing as long as you are in business and separates the successful practice from the ordinary practice.

Every consulting firm goes through periods of very good business and very little business. In the good periods new business seems to come in the door without any effort being made. In periods of slow business it is difficult, no matter what you do, to generate sufficient additional work. Clients and projects are really the critical elements in any consulting practice. Accordingly, you must direct a meaningful portion of your time toward the development of new business opportunities and the retention of existing clientele. If you are just getting started, this problem may be even more critical since your initial client base may not be sufficient to provide you with a satisfactory level of earnings.

Embarking on a new practice requires an inordinate amount of time spent in forming potential contacts. Contacts can made by letter, but in-person meetings and visits (perhaps lunch, breakfast, or dinner) to describe the practice are probably more effective. Keeping a log of contacts, referred to on a regular basis as a reminder to cultivate relationships, is one technique. Even the strongest contacts should be renewed continually. This is particularly true of business acquaintances whom you may not see on a regular basis but who can help the growth of the practice if they are made aware of recent projects.

You may want to develop a small brochure to send or give to people. Such a brochure could fit inside a standard business envelope when folded. It would describe the capabilities of your organization and the background of the principals. Some firms go into much greater detail in their brochures. The purpose of the brochure is to provide tangible information regarding the organization that can be retrieved at a later time when the potential client has a need to reach you. Newsletters are effective; they can be mailed on a monthly or quarterly basis to inform clients and potential clients about recent events in the practice or other special interest areas.

ORGANIZING THE PRACTICE

Financing Requirements

A consulting practice is a business and, like all businesses, must have financing. Financing can be provided by capital invested by you (or the initial group of consultants) or by funds borrowed from banks and others.

Capital requirements include the need for working capital to pay basic monthly operating expenses such as rent, telephone, utilities, stationery, and perhaps secretarial services. In a new consulting practice, operating expenses may also include your living expenses during the early stages of practice development. Working capital will be needed to fund accounts receivable that represent time billings to clients. In some instances, you may provide services over a lengthy period of time before you are able to bill for those services. Invoice payments may be delayed for any number of reasons. In any event, all of the expenses are ongoing. Accordingly, working capital is required to smooth out the fluctuations in cash flow and keep the practice going.

The next step in the process of establishing a new consulting practice is to realistically evaulate what facilities will be required, including office space and its accoutrements. Initially, you may work out of your home, limiting the out-of-pocket expenses. You will still need stationery, some type of telephone answering service, and some type of secretarial service. When you are ready for office space, monthly costs are going to increase substantially. If the consulting practice is growing and you hire staff, there will be salary costs as well.

You need to carefully determine what these monthly costs and expenses are going to be and budget for them. Next, determine how many months it will take to generate a level of income equal to or exceeding these monthly costs. You also need to determine how much income you require to cover normal living expenses.

It is prudent to have at least three or four months' expenses available as the initial capital funds, either invested or borrowed funds. Many consultants obtain retainers at the beginning of a consulting assignment to help finance the burden of monthly expenses. Retainers can create a financial trap if the funds are received and spent before the work is actually performed.

One critical aspect to consider is the establishment of fees for services. It is also necessary to make a projection of consulting practice income and how much time will be required to generate that income.

There are approximately 2040 hours in a standard work year. Most consultants expect to invest some overtime, but you must also consider holidays, vacations, illness, administrative time, practice or business development time, and nonproductive time. Many consultants figure that if they are productive as much as 60 percent of the total available time, they have done very well. Table 14.1 shows one approach to determining available hours and projected revenues.

Legal Form of the Practice

The actual legal form of the practice is an issue to consider. You can operate as a sole proprietor with or without employees; as a partnership; or you can form a corporation that will employ you and other employees.

Determination of the legal form is based on a number of factors including legal liability, income tax aspects, and personal objectives. You should seek proefessional counsel in making this determination and review each form's various benefits. Regardless of which structure you choose, you should not commingle personal finances with business finances. A good basic business rule is to establish and maintain careful records of time expended, expenses incurred, billing, collections, and other information pertinent to the practice.

Table 14.1. Revenue Projections for Single Practitioner

Assumption		Result
Total available hours		2,040
Less: Holidays	80	
Vacation	40	
Administration	180	
Practice development	500	
Professional development	80	880
Available chargeable time		1,200
Revenue at $75.00 per hour		$90,000.00

Office Facilities and Equipment Requirements

If you are an individual practitioner or are just beginning to build a practice, you may not need to have a formal office. You may initially operate your practice out of a room in the home, and you may not have any office equipment or secretarial service. When you are in business, however, it is important to act as if you are in business. Specifically, this means establishing a professional and businesslike image for your basic business operations through: the stationery utilized, the telephone answering procedures employed, and the quality of typed material that is presented to a client.

As the practice begins to grow and the need arises for full- or part-time secretarial help, you will also need to consider more conventional office facilities. A very practical option for a start-up firm is leasing an office in a professional suite that provides many facilities including secretarial services, telephone answering, library, and copy machine. Options include single or multiple offices and can involve renting office furniture and fixtures. As the firm continues to grow, the next step is leasing office facilities and employing a permanent secretary/receptionist, multiple employees, and other consultants. Each of these steps requires a business decision as to the viability of the practice and the capacity to handle the additional overhead expenses.

The location of your office will be of prime concern if clients will frequently visit. Issues such as availability of parking, ease of finding the location, aesthetic appearance of the office are important when the public comes to you. If you usually travel to the client, location becomes particularly important relative to the geographic target market. All of these factors translate into significant cost differentials.

Of prime concern to your consulting practice are the costs of operation. The greater the operating costs, the greater the overhead and the more revenues must be generated before profit will be realized. Accordingly, the break-even point is greater and the chargeable time goals may have to be higher. Careful consideration must be given to equipment and facility requirements because they can have a long-term impact on the practice profitability.

Time Scheduling

Once you begin to develop mutliple consulting engagements, you will have a problem of time scheduling—figuring out how to perform all of the work both profitably and on time.

This problem exists both for the individual consultant and for the consulting practice with multiple staff. Planning time utilization is a key to success, both from a financial standpoint and from a client-service standpoint. While exact time schedules are difficult to maintain, it is important to have a time-utilization plan several weeks in advance. This may include time spent with various clients on various projects; time for administrative responsibilities; and time for continuing education or practice development. Meetings and breakfast, lunch, and dinner appointments should also be reflected on a personal schedule.

You should plan and schedule your time in advance for a period of 1 to 6 weeks, allowing some flexibility in the event of emergencies or new opportunities. You need a good bit of self-discipline to profitably utilize the available time by seeking work to fill that time, or to use unscheduled time for administrative responsibilities, practice development, or continuing education. Getting maximum profitability from your consulting practice is directly related to the optimum use of available time. A balance can be maintained between effort and reward through proper time utilization.

For the larger practice, the problem of time utilization increases geometrically. Larger practices often require the use of multiple consultants on a single engagement and there is often contention for staff time among multiple jobs. The nature of the engagement and its duration also play a part in time scheduling. Potential chargeable time lost is never recoverable. Time must be looked upon as a very perishable commodity to be carefully preserved and utilized. It is very important to properly plan the use of available time and not rely on overtime to correct errors in time scheduling.

The cost of employees or associates exists regardless of whether they are generating appropriate revenues. It is up to the administrator/manager of the consulting practice to make certain that there are appropriate utilization controls. One technique is to review the schedule of the professional staff or consultants at least once weekly, generally late on Thursday or Friday, to be certain they are utilized for the ensuing week. It's usually too late on the day that an individual is unassigned to find a productive activity for him or her. It is also important to make certain the client understands the consultant's time is very valuable and that appointments need to be kept. The client and the consultant waste time if appointments are canceled at the last minute.

Billings and Collections

Certainly one of your most important considerations is how you establish professional fees. For example, some consultants bill services on an hourly basis. Some bill on a daily, or per diem, basis. Some add out-of-pocket expenses and attempt to identify as many out-of-pocket expenses attributable to the client as possible, while others absorb out-of-pocket expenses. Some consultants charge for professional services and for support staff, such as secretarial assistance. Some charge for telephone calls, photocopying, postage, and similar expenditures; others absorb these costs. Similarly, billing rates vary from very high levels to relatively low levels. Staff billing rates are often a multiple of the salary paid to the employee. Multiples of 2.5, 3, and 3.5 the actual hourly rate of pay are very common.

If an employee is being paid $42,000 a year, which is $3500 a month (close to $20 an hour based on a 2040-hour standard work year), the billing rate will perhaps be calculated at a multiple of 3, or $60 an hour. The actual rate should be tied to the productivity (billable hours) of the staff member. There are certainly other costs for the employee in addition to salary: payroll taxes for social security and unemployment taxes, insurance costs, including workers' compensation, and perhaps medical insurance. There are additional benefit expenses that may be incurred: vacation, holidays, and some sick-leave allowance. All of this probably results in actual available time amounting to perhaps only 80 to 90 percent of the year.

The consultant-entrepreneur can readily base potential revenues on the number of projected revenue-generating hours times the billing rates. The total revenue compared to the projected salary expense plus other expenses can determine if this level of activity produces a satisfactory result. Billing rates must also be considered within the competitive environment and within the framework of the potential productive hours that can be reasonably expected.

Another billing approach is on a project basis. Here the fee is determined for the project, and you have to get the work completed within a reasonable time. No matter what the method of billing, time keeping is of prime importance. In fact, all record keeping is of prime importance. For the sole practitioner, good time utilization is important in maintaining a satisfactory level of productivity. There is nothing worse than working 60 to 70 hours a week and discovering that you have little to show for it. Be sure you are not spending too much time on nonproductive assignments and administrative matters. Also, there should be an appropriate mix between practice development and productive chargeable time.

If you have a multiperson firm, the need for time and record keeping is even greater and the information must be maintained on a timely basis. A lot of this information is for billing purposes; if billings aren't rendered on time, collections will not be on time. Clients tend to respond promptly to invoices rendered close to the time services have been provided. There will be fewer disputes when invoices are sent as in-progress billing or the month following project completion.

Follow-up on unpaid invoices is important. Statements should be sent as a reminder of outstanding invoices. It is usually appropriate to send statements when invoices have been outstanding 60 to 90 days depending upon the individual circumstances. Aggressive invoice collection is important to cash flow and survival of the practice.

Timely maintenance of all accounting records is just as important for your practice as it is for any other business. Accounting records are the primary source for managing the cash position and profitability of the consulting practice. Management information is even more important in a larger practice and, in addition to basic accounting records, productivity data are a must. Comparison of chargeable hours to standard hours—and comparison of fees collected or collectible compared to labor costs—are probably the significant standards for measuring profitability. It is also extremely important to have established budgets and targets to monitor the performance of the practice. If you continually establish targets for the firm and budget expenses and time, you will be far more successful than the competition.

BUILDING THE PRACTICE

Initial Client Base

The starting point for a new consulting practice is usually one or more clients who provide the base. As the practice grows, you should develop a base of clients to serve and use for referrals. To begin building the base, it is important to define the marketplace. This includes types of potential clients, size of potential clients, and type of services to be provided. It also involves identifying the decision maker in each target organization and its buying patterns. Each practitioner needs to define a particular niche or market and develop a game plan and marketing effort to penetrate the target market.

To a degree, the definition of that market will depend on the services you are capable of providing. Of course, you need to evaluate the potential of the marketplace in terms of type and size of clients, geographic area, and the opportunity to establish market visibility and presence.

Positioning the Practice

Every successful business enterprise understands its reason for existence in the business world. Perpetuating that existence requires some form of positioning through unique capabilities, unique experiences, or ability to deal with specific problems. It is important to identify these competitive advantages and use them to establish and maintain market share.

You also need to be aware of your competition: what they do, how they do it, what they do well and why. This information can help you adjust and refine your approach to developing a practice. By being aware of your competition, you can learn from them or establish your own uniqueness.

Consulting work is primarily obtained from two sources: people you know and people who know you. Your contacts provide a direct opportunity to sell yourself and your services.

The people who know you provide an opportunity for referrals and new contacts to build your network. One of the best uses of your time is to develop and maintain a network of contacts. If developed properly, these contacts will inevitably lead to business. A third-party recommendation is probably the most important sales tool for the professional consultant.

A marketing plan should be developed, implemented, and maintained to structure the building effort. This is difficult if you are working on your own or with a limited staff; it means balancing between carrying out assignments and prospecting for new ones. The best advice is to plan, pay attention to detail, and carefully allocate your most important resource—time. It is axiomatic that marketing must be done on a continuous basis and not when you are suddenly in need of assignments.

If you have a staff, it is important that they be trained and encouraged to develop consulting opportunities for the firm. If it extremely rewarding when the staff member obtains an assignment that helps to keep him or her busy and productive.

Practice Development Network

The development of an ongoing source of revenues is critical to the success of the consulting practice. Work loads that routinely go from feast to famine are both impossible to deal with and often unprofitable. Accordingly, there must be a reasonably regular source of new business so that the work load can be balanced over the entire year.

As with any business, a consulting practice is going to be somewhat seasonal. Aside from holiday periods, however, a consulting practice does not suffer from seasonal highs and lows. Generating work on a continuous basis is a continuous problem. In a one-person operation you have to contend with allocating time for performing work and carrying out practice development activities. If you have a staff, everyone should be expected to participate in the business development activities. There are usually one or more individuals who seem to be adept and capable of generating new business.

Business comes to a practice through people: people you know who have a need for your services and people you know who refer you to others. This is commonly referred to as a "network" of contacts and resources. Professionals working in related areas will often have opportunities to refer work to one another. Certain types of professionals such as CPAs, attorneys, and bankers are in a particularly good position to make referrals. These relationships have to be developed over time and cultivated to make them personally and professionally rewarding. You also have to be aggressive enough to let people know you are interested in referrals and that in appropriate instances you will reciprocate.

To develop a meaningful and worthwhile network, you must establish quality contacts and educate your network as to the type of services you offer. People making referrals must have an understanding of what you do and what types of consulting engagements you are seeking.

If you have built a quality network, some contacts will continually refer work to you. These productive contacts develop and grow based on a solid personal relationship and your commitment to providing excellent service.

Building a successful network requires keeping your name in front of clients and contacts. This can be done through client newsletters, articles, seminars, entertainment, or even periodic phone calls. In any event, there need to be consistent, intermittent reminders to the network about you, your firm, and your services.

Community Involvement

Considerable emphasis has been placed on the need to develop referral networks and establish contacts generating new business. One important aspect of network building is community involvement both for you and other staff members. Large consulting firms encourage their people to become active in various organizations because this is a means of establishing contact and participating in the community. Because there is a significant cost involved, in terms of time and expenses, you should evaluate the quality of the participation and the quality of results.

Business development does not necessarily produce results immediately, and contacts may not produce results for an extended period of time. Accordingly, it is frequently difficult to measure the results of professional, community, and charitable involvement. Results also require aggressiveness on your part in ensuring that the people you associate with have some idea of what you do, how your service might be beneficial, and what talents you can apply to their activities. It is far better to participate in something that you can do well than to take on responsibilities for something in which you have little interest or ability. Community involvement is one of the better ways to broaden your network of contacts and display some of your professional capabilities. As with all other activities, the results of this involvement need to be evaluated.

MONITORING RESULTS

Performance Measures

Every business needs to maintain some type of scorecard to determine whether or not it is achieving its goals and objectives. A consulting practice is no different. One of the basic practice administration requirements is to maintain the financial and accounting records that provide a financial scorecard. Objectives established prior to the beginning of the practice year are necessary for evaluation of actions taken to achieve desired results.

The financial scorecard typically compares actual gross revenues against projected revenues and net profits against projected profits. Other measures or scorecards should also be kept. These include: the productive hours as a percentage of total hours; average fee generated per hour worked and per chargeable hour; the ratio of expenses to revenues; profit as a percentage of revenue. In addition, other measures include the number of new clients obtained during a year; the amount of dollars generated from new business; and the increase in business from one year to the next. Other accounting information to monitor includes collected fees versus uncollected fees; amount of bad debt write-offs; and amount of time charges that are not billable.

The relationships between revenues generated and total hours expended, between chargeable hours and total hours, and between revenues and chargeable hours are key ratios for a consulting practice. Year-to-year comparison of these figures can indicate whether the practice is improving, becoming more efficient, obtaining more profitable work and quality clients. The objectives you establish will set the expectations, and monitoring key figures will help achieve desired results. Comparing your results with those of other consultants is also a good way of measuring the relative success of the practice. A standard for chargeable time should be 60 to 70 percent of total available hours. Nonchargeable time should be composed of administrative time, business development time, holidays, vacation, sick leave, and nonproductive time. The performance figures become much more critical as the consulting practice adds staff and at this point they need to be monitored on a constant basis.

Other information that is pertinent to monitoring the overall results of the practice include the actual completion date of a project as promised, and the actual time expended per job and per person. Tracking promised completion dates is a good technique for effectively managing quality control. By closely monitoring the practice performance, you can make changes that will improve efficiency and profitability.

Quality Control Standards

An important part of any consulting practice is establishing quality control standards to ensure that the work is properly performed. Quality work includes properly communicated results and minimal errors and omissions. Maintaining quality control requires discipline. You must rely on discipline and a sense of care and caution to ensure that projects meet professional standards.

In a consulting practice with two or more individuals, quality control takes on a different aspect. Individuals within a consulting practice can review and evaluate each other's work. You can discuss the engagement with your colleagues to ensure that the project is on the right track; you can review reports written by one another to see that they are complete, hang together, and provide the client with understandable results. As the consulting staff grows and there are projects involving multiple staff, the problem of quality control becomes much greater. Younger, less experienced consultants may not be aware of the need to be thorough; the potential for omissions and errors may increase.

In a practice that involves many consultants you should establish a formal quality control program to review the work being performed by the consultants, and to review reports issued in connection with the consulting engagement. Each consulting organization deals with this requirement a little bit differently. Generally, a senior staff member reviews the work being performed throughout the course of the engagement and a partner reviews the formal report before it is issued.

The supervisory review may consist of nothing more than discussion between the consultant performing the engagement and the manager on the job. In addition, the review may cover the approach the consultant is using on the assignment, the findings to date, and an evaluation of the consultant's thought process and judgment on key issues. This type of quality control is beneficial to everyone. It protects the firm from errors and omissions and helps teach and train the individual performing the work. Someone else who is a professional in the field serves as sounding board for the consultant's ideas, conclusions, and thought process. The manager broadens his or her knowledge base because of the exposure to multiple projects and a variety of issues. Ongoing supervision helps to focus staff time on the necessary areas and to control actual time as compared to the project budget. The larger the consulting practice or the more stratified the staff at the lower level, the greater the need for periodic review and supervision of the engagements. Engagements carried out by highly experienced consultants would require less review and supervision and might be limited to brief discussions on the progress of the engagement.

The written document provides both a threat and an opportunity to a consulting practice. The written document tends to be permanent because, depending on how the client uses the report, it can be referred to and read by many people. As a result, it is critically important that the document be well written from the standpoint of content, presentation, use of language, spelling, and punctuation. Small, insignificant errors that would be overlooked or forgotten in oral presentations are recorded forever in a written document. A written document must be carefully reviewed before submission and every effort must be made to ensure accuracy and quality. Even when the actual consulting engagement is extremely well performed, the client may remember flaws in the written document.

If you are an individual practitioner, it is extremely difficult to establish quality control over the written document. Although you can personally review the document after typing, you really need a second party to review it technically for accuracy and clarity. In a multiperson consulting firm, it is a good practice for reports to be read by someone other than the writer. There should also be a procedure for a partner to review the finished product prior to delivery to the client.

A strong stimulus for establishing internal quality control procedures is the potential liability from incomplete or improper conduct of a consulting engagement. Word travels fast, and low-quality projects can affect existing and prospective clients.

15

Marketing Professional Services

LARRY WHITE
CRAIG MINBIOLE
White Communications Corporation
Birmingham, Michigan

INTRODUCTION

For most professional service organizations, new business opportunities are created through activities in four major areas. Whether an organization has a formalized marketing plan or pursues opportunities on a less structured basis, research has shown that most new business flows, as indicated in Figure 15.1, through: present client activities, nonclient relationships, public relations or promotional activities, and potential client activities. Specific marketing efforts in each of these areas may be undertaken by individuals, by a firm as a whole, or by any segment within the firm such as an office or industry group.

PRESENT CLIENT ACTIVITIES

Present clients form the core of most new business activities for all firms except those in a completely new, start-up situation. In the professional environment a start-up situation usually means initially working with a single client or small group of clients and almost always precedes a decision to "start" a consulting, accounting, or law practice.

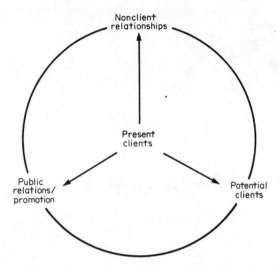

Figure 15.1   Practice development framework.

The three primary purposes of business development activities directed toward present clients are (1) retention, (2) expansion of services, and (3) generation of referrals for new business.

Retention

Most professional service firms subscribe to the maxim that it is easier to keep a current client than to attract a new one. Firms that aggressively pursue new clients while taking client retention for granted have often experienced unexpected losses and decreasing profitability that are not offset by gains from new clients. Perhaps of greatest importance, emphasis on new client acquisition over client retention overlooks the way most professional firms have grown—through referrals from satisfied clients and by meeting a full range of present client needs.

Many professional service firms espouse quality service to current clients and active, ongoing monitoring of client satisfaction. Few firms, however, have established a systematic approach for ensuring that these goals are met. Specific activities such as those listed below have been effective:

- Client satisfaction letters, surveys, or meetings in which evaluations of personnel and performance can be gathered
- Partner/colleague programs which ensure that more than one key professional maintains regular contact with significant clients
- Client service planning in which detailed plans for providing additional services to key clients are developed

Client satisfaction/retention can often be a priority marketing goal for younger members of a professional service firm who want to meet management's expectations regarding business development. Many younger, ambitious professionals tend to equate marketing with bringing new clients in the door, which sometimes results in less than ideal situations. While attracting new desirable clients is a key goal of any firm's business development efforts, a somewhat wider definition of marketing needs to be promulgated so there is full understanding of all aspects of the firm's program. Most important, young professionals will learn how to sell to new prospects when they learn how to keep a present client satisfied.

Expansion of Services

The second purpose of present client marketing is the "cross-marketing" of services to current clients. Many firms have realized the substantial potential in providing further services beyond those originally proposed to the client. Most firms find that the $1000 client of today can become the $10,000 client of 3 years from now. For example, accounting firms of all sizes learned early on that clients using accounting and auditing services also needed tax planning expertise. The full range of consulting services being provided by accounting firms to clients is a further example of the development of new business within the current client base. Law firms have only begun to tap the potential of cross-selling. Professional firms will find growth easier if they build on their present clients. Personnel recruiting firms, for example, may find that adding a training function would add more profits.

There are three important reasons why effective cross-selling should be a marketing goal for all professional service firms. First, the profit margin on additional services is usually greater because they are more specialized (tax research is less a "commodity" than an audit) and require less start-up time to know the client.

Second, increased attention to cross-selling more services to current clients reduces vulnerability to client loss. A client who has an unmet need and is aware that the needed expertise is available from his or her current firm will probably ask for the assistance. A client who is not fully aware of the additional expertise will go outside seeking assistance, and a firm may find itself competing to retain the client. Worse yet, if the client is simply not aware of a need (e.g., compliance with a tax regulation) and the professional service firm doesn't raise the issue, the unmet need may result in a problem that could endanger the firm-client relationship.

Several studies have shown that the decision-making process regarding the selection of outside professional service assistance is greatly influenced by direct experience. The trust and confidence that develops because of a satisfactory service relationship is often cited as the key criterion in the selection of a professional service firm. Thus, the current provider of a service tends to be in a much stronger position to provide additional services than another firm with whom the buyer has had little or no experience. For this reason, effective cross-marketing to develop more business is usually an easier "sell."

To be able to take full advantage of cross-marketing opportunities, a professional service firm needs to be sure there is proper internal communication. Specialists in one area should be aware of the services available from their own colleagues down the hall. Too often one professional shies away from a client question in an unknown area rather than encouraging and facilitating a meeting with a fellow partner-specialist who could address the client need. Until such barriers can be removed, a firm is really marketing individuals and not the firm as a whole.

Generation of Referrals

Almost without exception, professional service firms will categorically state that present clients are their best single source of referrals for additional clients. Firms tracking the sources of new business report that 50 to 75 percent of new clients come from the direct or indirect referral of a current client. Regardless of statistics, it would appear safe to assume that current clients provide the best single source for referral of new clients.

It is important for a professional service firm to develop and cultivate service and personal relationships with clients that will encourage referrals when an opportunity arises. Clearly, satisfaction of the client is critical to his or her willingness to serve as a sponsor with business colleagues. Beyond ensuring clients' satisfaction, many firms have developed specific programs to take the fullest possible advantage of current clients' referral potential. For example, a CPA firm cosponsoring a seminar with a restaurant wholesaler was found to be effective both in strengthening the relationship with the client and in establishing new contacts. Making sure clients are aware of the firm's full range of services is an important dimension of such programs; brochures, newsletters, and seminars have been used effectively in this regard. Attending trade association meetings with current clients can also provide opportunities for formal or informal referrals to business colleagues.

A professional service firm has to be conscious of the image it creates in the community regarding its interest in new business. Rarely is a professional considered "too aggressive" or too interested in new work. Usually, a more neutral or even "not interested" image is conveyed. A large number of current clients, when surveyed, have indicated that they don't know if their professional service firm is interested in new business. This perception often results from the professional's failure to indicate interest forthrightly by asking for the additional work or for the referral. Less direct indicators include failure to return phone calls promptly or frequent comments about how busy the firm is. To a great extent, marketing and business development represent a frame of mind—a recognition that business development is an integral part of one's professional life. Opportunities to convey an impression of sincere interest in providing service must not be lost.

Overall, marketing to current clients to retain them, expand services, and generate new business should be the foundation of a professional service firm's efforts to develop new business opportunities. Without a strong commitment to present client marketing and equally strong programs to carry out the commitment, other marketing activities will be less fruitful in the long run.

In addition, as shown in Figure 15.1, present clients provide a key link to the other three marketing activity areas. For example, an effective way to develop relationships with third-party referral sources is to meet with the other professionals (attorneys, bankers, insurance people) who serve current clients. Opportunities for speeches, articles, and other public relations/promotional activities are often generated by professionals via current clients' membership in trade associations or civic groups. Finally, the link between present and potential clients has typically been the most lucrative source of new business for professional service firms.

THIRD-PARTY REFERRAL SOURCE ACTIVITIES

The Importance of Relationships

A second important activity to facilitate building a consulting practice is the development of relationships with significant third-party referral sources. Most often, these referral sources are fellow professionals who serve mutual clients; however, third parties are by no means restricted to other professionals. For example, any consultant building a computer software development practice would do well to maintain a strong liaison with computer brokers, dealers, and sales representatives. Attorneys, accountants, investment personnel, insurance brokers, bankers, and financial planners are frequently cited as significant third-party referral sources. Clearly, the relative importance of any particular group of referral sources will depend on the nature of a firm's practice as well as its goals for the future. Other referral sources of potential influence include firm alumni and client alumni (i.e., former client personnel). Although it is often very difficult to maintain contact with the two alumni groups, those who have had direct experience with a firm's services and personnel are in the best position to serve as a source of referrals. Former clients are a particularly good source for new business if you are just starting a practice. Such contacts take time to develop—plan on a year or more—but need to be cultivated from the start.

The primary purpose of developing relationships with significant third-party referral sources is to build a communications network that provides significant information about clients and potential clients. Many professionals put too much emphasis on the second agenda—generation of referrals—without recognizing the importance and long-range value of the primary objective—building the communications network. For example, the sharing of information and the discussion of common problems between accountants and attorneys working in the tax area can create the foundation for a long-lasting relationship among individual professionals and their firms. This dialogue is not only a valuable source of knowledge but a necessary prerequisite to mutual referrals. Often, referrals are made solely on the basis of a personal relationship rather than a rigorous search for the "right" firm. Studies have reportedly shown that referral sources rarely know what various professionals actually do for their clients. Bank loan officers may know what an audit is, but they rarely understand how management information systems or cash management programs work. Unfortunately, loan officers rarely know when their clients need such assistance and would appreciate referrals. Finally, most professionals indicate that they refer more to a specific individual with whom they have a relationship than to a firm as an institution.

Strategies for Building Relationships

Specific strategies for developing relationships with third-party referral sources can be implemented by a firm as a whole, by individual officers, and by individual professionals. For example, some accounting firms have developed specialized brochures or newsletters for bank loan officers outlining their expertise in conducting cash flow studies and management reviews. These brochures are used to make it clear that the firms can do more than audit historical financial data. At the local office level, organized programs for periodic mailings, social events, or roundtable luncheons have become standardized parts of many contact development programs. However, since the foundation for strong relationships among professionals is personal contact, successful programs use publications and group meetings as a tool to get the ball rolling. The primary focus of the program is follow-up by key individuals to build the types of relationships that will be mutually beneficial to the individuals and the firm.

Several studies have suggested that professionals prefer personal contact and direct experience as the media for learning about another professional service firm's expertise. Traditional activities such as seminars and brochures/newsletters are also cited as being important and valuable but still do not have the same impact as direct and indirect personal communication. Advertising, as such, is not typically perceived by professionals to be an effective medium for communicating about specific expertise. Even though the emphasis is on the personal dimension of third-party referral relationships, there should be coordination between the firm's efforts and those of individual professionals to ensure a meaningful program. To ensure that all significant third-party groups are exposed to consulting or other services being offered, an organized, coordinated plan is important. On the other hand, research shows far too often that individual professionals do not consciously work on relationship development because they think a firm program such as educational seminars for bank loan officers will do the job. Follow-up is important in formally monitoring as closely as possible which third-party referral groups and individuals have been important sources of new business. It is equally important to investigate and evaluate which groups may be most helpful in referring the types of clients a firm may be targeting for the future. The increased competition among professional service firms of all types has given added significance to the term *reciprocal referrals* as firms and individuals have become less reticent about directly asking each other for referrals. In fact, many professionals will define the ideal professional as one "who services my clients well and refers work to me."

Building the Target List

One of the most common misconceptions in building a consulting practice is that developing a mailing list focusing on third-party relationships is unnecessary until the practice is started. Developing a list of third-party contacts may often be a good way to determine if marketing a particular service will be effective. If few third-party relationships exist, starting a consulting practice should probably be postponed until these contacts can be developed. In today's world of computers, any consultant can build a segmented contact list with minimal investment that will help him throughout his career. The development of relationships with fellow professionals is typically seen as an activity area in which both senior and junior members of a firm can become effectively involved. Generally speaking, specific relationships will be based on mutuality of interest or area of expertise among peer groups of similar age, experience, and position. For example, the founder of a computer software consulting practice will typically be familiar with owners/

managers of hardware dealers. However, because it is important to establish and maintain a contact base with fellow professionals over time, younger consultants ought to be encouraged to develop their own relationships with sales representatives and others who work for the owner/manager. Such relationships may not provide short-term immediate referrals of potential clients, but they will contribute to developing a communications base and building individual involvement in an overall firm program.

Finally, professionals must remember that the quality of relationships is more important than the quantity. While relationships need to be built continually, a natural "weeding out" process will also occur. Out of every ten contacts a professional makes, perhaps only one or two will be important referral sources over the long term. When building a consulting practice, the key is to make sure the "pipeline" of third-party relationships is continuously being expanded. This ensures that the very best contacts are identified and cultivated over the years.

PROMOTIONAL AND PUBLIC RELATIONS ACTIVITIES

Scope of Public Relations

The third general area for marketing professional services involves promotional and public relations activities and includes a wide range of traditional as well as innovative strategies. Historically, professional service firms have used public relations activities such as membership in a country club or making a speech as their major effort in business development. In today's world, focusing on such activities is too general and can cause frustration for a firm which believes that public relations or promotional activities will lead directly to new business. Because professional services are highly personal, most authorities agree that promotional activities should be viewed primarily as vehicles for creating and enhancing awareness of the firm. This awareness can be leveraged so that it builds a contact base to be cultivated on a personal basis through follow-up.

Special activities that would fall under the heading of public relations/ promotion range from advertising to the sponsorship of golf tournaments to giving a speech at an appropriate trade organization. An all-inclusive list of standard promotional activities would be impossible to create, but the following might be considered representative:

• Institutional advertising

• Product and service-oriented advertising

- Newsletters
- Seminars and workshops
- Speeches
- Articles in professional or industry publications
- Press relations
- Trade shows
- Participation in community trade and professional organizations
- Symposia and panels

Effective Promotional Activity

The effectiveness of public relations/promotion depends in large part on targeting. While the development of strong name recognition is an important overall goal, establishing contacts with key influencers or decision makers at selected businesses is more likely to produce new business in the long run. It is more important, for example, for a law firm with a strong labor practice to be recognized by construction companies, which have frequent need of legal assistance in labor-related matters, than it is for the general business community to recognize the firm's name. Similarly, a consulting firm that wishes to market software development assistance to small retailers should probably become active in downtown and regional business associations. As a result, many professional service organizations are now producing specialized brochures, newsletters, and seminars targeted at specific audiences among which the firm hopes to expand its business.

Perhaps most important, all public relations/promotional activities should be designed to establish contacts that can be enhanced on a personal basis as a follow-up to the activity. If a seminar is conducted, an attendance list should be maintained so follow-up mailings and telephone calls can be made to establish and enhance personal relationships. A professional on a fund-raising committee for a community activity should make a point of getting to know other committee members. Far too often, professionals see the public relations activities as the goal rather than pursuing the opportunities the activity creates. In fact, the follow-up yields the real benefits in marketing a professional service.

Seminars

Seminars remain a popular tool for many professionals primarily because they offer an opportunity to meet a large number of people and to demonstrate indirectly the quality of the firm's people and expertise. Both business executives and other professionals acknowledge seminars to be an effective medium for the communication of expertise. Seminars that are designed for a specific audience on a topic of interest, that are short (2 or 3 hours), and that provide the participants with practical suggestions are typically the most successful. Seminars or symposia cosponsored by two groups of professionals offer the opportunity for enhancing relationships between the cosponsors as well as between participants. A CPA firm and a bank might cosponsor a seminar on cash-flow planning aimed at the clients of both organizations.

Community Involvement

Community involvement in civic or charitable organizations continues to be an important dimension of many professional service firms' promotional programs. From an idealistic standpoint, such activities offer professionals the opportunity to "repay" their communities; more pragmatically, they also meet fellow professionals and future business contacts. Participation in such activities should be based primarily on the individual professional's interests and desire to contribute to the community. Enhancing the firm's image and generating contacts, while secondary, will be a fairly natural occurrence if those who participate really like what they are doing. The involvement of a firm's professionals needs to be planned, coordinated,and monitored, however, for maximum benefits to be derived. If a firm is developing a practice in executive search, for example, it would be a serious omission not to become actively involved in local trade groups made up of personnel managers. In all cases, leadership in such activities—or at least maintenance of a very high profile—is highly recommended if good results are to be achieved.

Because reputation is among the most important criteria in the evaluation and selection of a professional service firm, all public relations or promotional activities should be evaluated for their impact on the firm's reputation. Although name recognition and reputation are not synonymous, a long-term objective of promotional activities should be to make the firm's name synonymous with quality people providing quality expertise and service.

POTENTIAL CLIENT ACTIVITIES

The ultimate objective of all business development activities is to attract new clients. Because of the combined long-term/short-term nature of professional services marketing, a wide variety of strategies involving present clients, third-party referral sources, and promotional activities is required for aggressive pursuit of specific prospects. The fourth general activity, which focuses on "real" potential clients, is perhaps the most critical but complex component of an effective overall program. Even the most sophisticated professional service firms have difficulty targeting and acquiring specific clients.

Potential Client Profiles

Generally speaking, the purpose of potential client activities is to identify potential clients, to position the firm or individual for an opportunity, and to ultimately acquire the clients. In some instances this process occurs quickly and without a great deal of overt effort on the part of the service firm. In most instances, however, the process is longer term and requires ongoing monitoring and evaluation.

It is important for the firm to define its potential client profile. To accept any client who will pay a fee is not necessarily in the firm's long-term best interest. Although the acceptance criteria will vary widely from firm to firm, two factors deserve special consideration:

1. Be sure that the potential client has needs that are related to the firm's expertise and service capabilities.
2. Be sure that the potential client is able to enhance the firm's practice.

By pursuing any and all projects, some firms have mistakenly sold services to a prospective client that the firm cannot really deliver. This can create substantial problems and the decreased profitability that comes with learning a new service area. For example, the computer consulting firm that always does work for banks may find trying to provide the same services for retailers less profitable and frustrating. Selling a service the firm does not normally deliver can create problems beyond the immediate project with the individual client. On the other hand, a new client who provides opportunities for expanding expertise, developing the firm's reputation, and increasing its base can have a beneficial effect that transcends the specific project. In either case, the issue is making an intelligent choice based on overall goals rather than simply pursuing new clients without any predetermined criteria for acceptance.

Targeting Potential Clients

Once a potential client profile has been established, the firm should analyze the overall marketplace in order to identify specific potential clients who meet the criteria. Such an analysis would include examining the market in terms of industry groups, size of companies, geographical areas of growth, and the fee potential of desirable companies. Analysis of competition must also be considered in establishing the realistic potential for attracting specific new clients. To the extent possible, such an analysis might also include examining the types of services currently being received and needed by potential new clients. Relationships among potential clients and their current providers of other professional services should also be considered.

An effective bridge between identification and positioning can be built by attempting to determine existing relationships with potential clients through the firm's own professionals, current clients, and referral sources. Knowing a potential client's attorney and banker may enhance opportunities, especially if other mutual client relationships already exist. Because businesses in similar industries develop their own relationships and thus share information about providers of professional services, leveraging off the current client base can be very effective. In addition, matching on the basis of current relationships helps a firm to build on its strengths and work as a team in the positioning effort. Most important, firms must classify prospects realistically in terms of their potential so they pursue realistic opportunities and use their resources wisely.

Establishing a Monitoring System

Establishing a system for monitoring progress on target prospects is perhaps the most critical factor in successful programs. Goals should be realistic and based on a limited number of potential prospects. Responsibilities for establishing and maintaining contacts should be assigned to individuals or teams so that effective ongoing monitoring of progress can take place. Internal communication regarding progress helps to motivate those who are responsible for implementing the contact program and to ensure that significant opportunities don't "slip through the cracks." Part of the monitoring process should be periodically adding or deleting prospects from the list.

To help monitor their activities and progress with potential clients, many firms have created marketing data bases with information about clients, prospects, referral sources, services, fees, current relationships, and status. Such an information system helps track progress, assists the internal communication process, and provides an external stimulus for active participation by members of the firm.

CONCLUSION

Table 15.1 is a checklist that should provide some assistance in helping a firm building a consulting practice determine which of the four types of activities discussed in the chapter requires the most attention.

Table 15.1 Marketing Checklist

Present clients

- Have key clients been identified?
- Have client retention plans been developed?
- Has client service planning for expansion of services to key clients been undertaken?
- Has information about clients been communicated across departments?
- Have client-centered communications been devised and implemented?
- Have present client referrals to potential clients been sought and pursued?
- Have the causes for losing clients been determined and corrected?

Third-party referral sources

- Have alumni, client alumni, attorneys, bankers, and other key referral source contacts been identified?
- Has information for establishing, maintaining, and enhancing relationships been implemented?
- Have all members of the firm been encouraged to participate in programs?

Public relations/promotion

- Have key civic organizations, social groups, and trade associations been identified?
- Have participation in groups and activities been planned, implemented, and evaluated?
- Have leadership roles in key organizations been pursued?
- Have opportunities for speeches and articles been targeted and pursued?
- Have contacts with the local press been made?

Potential clients

- Has an ideal potential client profile been defined?
- Have potential clients been identified and prioritized?
- Have specific programs for strengthening relationships and "positioning" been implemented?
- Has the responsibility for maintaining contact and monitoring progress been assigned?
- Have timely, client-centered proposals been developed?

Staff Selection and Development

JAMES BUCK
James L. Buck and Company
Nashville, Tennessee

STAFF SELECTION

Matching Staff to the Needs of the Practice

Type of practice. This chapter deals with the subject of selecting and developing the consulting staff. In my opinion, this is the single most critical function of management in building a successful consulting practice. The people you select to represent your consulting firm, provide services to your clients, and develop future business will determine the level of success, the rate of growth, and the future of your consulting practice. These are your assets, but they are not constant like machinery or inventory: They change. A consultant who does not grow in knowledge and expertise will soon become obsolete in the fast-paced world of management consulting. Consultants are composites of training and experiences. Your consultants will have strengths and weaknesses, good days and bad days. Not everyone is suited to the consulting business, and as owner of a consulting practice you cannot afford the luxury of allowing would-be consultants to use your practice and your clients as a testing ground.

Some basics must be considered prior to selection of the consulting staff:

1. What kind of consulting practice do you plan to build—specialist or generalist?
2. What is your principal market: corporate (big business) or proprietorship (small business)? Product or service related?
3. What kind of image do you plan to project, and what kind of reputation do you plan to develop? (You will develop a reputation, so don't leave it to chance: Plan and develop a positive one.)
4. What are your long-range plans for your consulting practice? Do you anticipate maintaining a local client base, or is your objective to be a national firm with branch offices?

These questions must be asked and properly answered before you begin the process of hiring and training staff personnel. Your business objectives will be achieved through your staff, and staff selection should be based on criteria stemming from your stated business objectives. If you plan to target the Fortune 100 companies as your primary market, you may need a staff of technical specialists with the ability to conduct in-depth assessments and critical analyses leading to decisions and recommendations to be implemented by your client's professional staff. On the other hand, if you plan to carve your niche in the small business market, you will want to carefully select a staff of consultants with general business experience who possess excellent people and communications skills. In the small business arena you will be working with a more entrepreneurial management style and fewer professional staff members to successfully implement your recommendations. For this type of client you need a mature and experienced consultant with the personal characteristics to develop a working relationship with the client. Empathy and communication are key traits for any consultant.

Practice and staff profiles.   The first step in staff selection is to develop a profile of the type of person you need to achieve your business objectives. These consultants are your corporate tools and should be chosen very carefully. Select only people fitting the profile you have developed, and do not be tempted to accept less qualified candidates just because they may be available.

Let's assume you have only recently developed your business plan. You will have determined your corporate objectives and developed your action plan accordingly. You are now ready to select your staff consultants. This will require the development of three profiles to use during the recruiting, evaluating, and hiring process.

With a clear understanding of what your consulting practice will be, write out a formal description (profile) of the *company* as you see it developing. This will include periods of (1) start-up and infancy, (2) rapid growth, and (3) establishment and maturity. The profile is sometimes difficult to develop, and you may be tempted to skip this activity.

This process will ensure that you have clarified your plans in your own mind and will save time in presenting your company to the potential candidates during the interview process. Most important, this written profile of your company will serve as a bench mark against which you can measure your growth and make course corrections.

The company profile should be general enough to present the philosophy behind the business, the markets to be developed, and the long-range plans. It should be specific enough to show how the functional parts of the organization will fit together and how the daily business activities will be carried out.

The second profile should be the *position* profile. This will be a two-part description of the specific position you wish to fill. A position profile should be developed for each position to be filled. The first part of this two-part profile should be general in nature, describing the overall role of the position in the organization. The second part should include the specific responsibilities and duties of the person in this position.

We are basically talking about a job description. You must decide whether you want the job description to be tight and well defined or loose and somewhat informal. This may depend in part on your personal style of management: a tight ship emphasizing personal control versus a flexible system that allows experimentation and innovation.

It is not my intent to advise you on management style, though that is a part of every consulting practice. My intent is to make you aware that your style of management will play a major role in how effective your consultants will be as they work for you. Your style of management will determine the culture of your organization and, to be effective, your staff must feel comfortable with the company's environment and its culture. As you select each member of your staff, you must determine whether that person will fit into your organization.

The third profile is a *person* description. What kind of person do you want to have on your staff? What kind of person will be required for you to accomplish the goals of your action plan and achieve the objectives in your business plan? There are three parts to this profile: (1) academic credentials, (2) experience, and (3) personal traits and characteristics. All are equally important and must be weighed carefully in making your decision to hire.

The academic credentials requirement will be the easiest to evaluate. The nature of your consulting practice will determine what educational credentials your staff must have. Keep in mind that the more specialized a person's education the more limited his or her capability in a general consulting practice. Also, education will never make up for lack of common sense and practical experience; yet the right education is an absolute must. You must decide what is *right* for your practice.

Experience is a common characteristic of successful consultants. The experience factor must be evaluated carefully because it is from the experiences of the past that your consultant will draw knowledge to solve problems and direct the activities of junior consultants. You will need to carefully evaluate the experience of each prospective staff member. Does this person have a proven track record as an individual contributor? Have this person's previous experiences shown progression in terms of responsibility and project management? Have previous positions and experiences refined this person's analytical and decision-making abilities? Has this person been tested and proven as a problem solver or only functioned as an implementor of other people's decisions? And certainly you want to consider this person's failures. We learn from our failures and the failures of others. Has this potential consultant ever experienced failure? If not, what will be his or her reaction to failure? Does this mean the person has never fully been tested (good or bad)? Failure gives a strong manager sensitivity and helps refine skills. Failure can also take the starch out of a once capable manager leaving an impotent decision maker. The successes and failures of previous experiences must be considered and weighed carefully.

Personal traits and characteristics are critical factors because they determine how well this person will perform in the role of consultant. Quality education and experience are of little value to a person who is lazy and unmotivated. Exceptional analytical and conceptual skills will never have a chance to be productive if the consultant is abrasive, conceited, or an ineffective communicator. A consultant needs to be perceptive, strong-willed, and persistent while, at the same time, being practical and having a great deal of finesse and empathy.

Required skills.   The effective and successful consulting practice will have people with consulting skills and technical skills. To be valuable to the firm, a person does not necessarily have to possess both skills. Because each of us starts out in the business world as a specialist—an engineer, accountant, salesperson, etc.—we take that specialty with us as we move into the ranks of management. The higher in management we go, the less we use our technical skills and the more we develop and use management skills (conceptual and people management). Once you have defined the focus of your practice and selected your market, you can determine the specific technical skills you will need to deliver a quality service. It is critical that the senior members of your staff have technical skills as well as the management experience. The management experience is *most* important in selecting the senior consultant because this person will be the contact with your client, manage the project, and make decisions critical to your client's business.

Your senior consultant is your income producer, so leverage the consultant's time (for income generating) with junior technicans who can provide technical support and perform less demanding activities. Leveraging will allow each senior consultant to manage several ongoing projects at the same time while maintaining a certain amount of business development activity.

Technical versus Consulting Skills

In a small practice you are likely to have more senior than junior consultants. Those senior consultants should be experienced professionals who possess technical skills as well as executive maturity. They will manage projects while developing new business. Typically, this type of consultant will generate new client business and complete most of the consulting activity personally. Technical support staff will be limited or not available until the practice has revenues to justify and support them. The initial staff members will often be cofounders of the firm, or capable individuals known by the founder, who can be relied upon to share the responsibilities for developing the practice. As the practice grows and the staff becomes larger, you will want to leverage the time and effectiveness of your senior consultants by bringing into the firm technical specialists and junior support people.

First, let us differentiate between a consultant and technical specialist. The consultant, because of experience and track record, will oversee a consulting project and will direct the activities of others in conducting problem analysis and researching a client's needs. The consultant is the key person who will conceptualize and put the pieces of the puzzle together and also see the big picture. This person should be a leader. The technical specialist, by reason of training and experience, usually functions as an individual contributor providing input and recommendations on a specific or limited number of subjects. The technical specialist is generally less experienced, has limited or no managerial experience, and works in a support role to the consultants. Both are necessary components in a successful consulting practice, and they should be selected to complement each other.

As you continue to develop your practice, you will add staff to further leverage the capabilities of your senior consulting staff. You may have as few as two or as many as five technical specialists per consultant depending upon the kind of service you provide and the management abilities of your senior consultants. Use the same procedures in selecting both technical people and consultants.

Recruiting Sources

You have clearly determined the nature of your practice and your market. You have developed the three profiles needed to recruit competent staff with the desired technical and consulting skills. Now, where do you find candidates from whom to select and hire?

You have two tasks before you. First, you must identify a group of possible candidates who are recruitable and meet the requirements of your profile. Second, you have the task of interviewing, making an assessment, and then trying to hire the candidate you have selected. There are two ways to find viable candidates. One, you can retain the services of a professional search consultant to seek out, screen, and bring to you a candidate meeting your requirements. Two, you can undertake this project yourself. Either way, the cost will be approximately the same. A professional search consultant's services will cost you an amount equal to approximately one-third of your newly hired consultant's first year's salary. Using this method of recruiting means that you are not investing your time in the search and screening process; you only spend time in the interviewing process with a qualified candidate of known quality and verified credentials. The search consultant does the bulk of the work for you. By paying the search consultant to do the front-end screening, you hope to save time, and time is money. This should let you spend your time producing income for your business.

Now let's say you decide to recruit a senior consultant yourself. (The process is the same for any staff position.) Where do you begin? First, review your position profiles until you know by memory the requirements for the position and the type of person you want to hire. Once again you have two options. One, you can take a very active approach by identifying the best candidates and conducting a direct recruiting campaign. First, make a list of all the companies and organizations in which potential candidates may be found. Next, find out who the potential candidates are and begin to make direct contact.

The second option is a reactive approach where you rely on luck or some indirect action to bring a potential candidate to your attention. Using this approach, you first make a list of everyone you know personally or indirectly who may be a candidate. Next, you make a list of everyone you know who may know someone else who may be a candidate. This process is known as "working the network." While you are waiting for leads to come in from the network, you make contact with the people on your first list. One additional activity, which is still used in a limited fashion, is to run a series of classfied ads. Beware of the time cost that this method involves.

Interviewing Techniques

Getting started.   There are many books on the subject of interviewing. Some have been written for the job seeker who wants to make the right impression by saying and doing all of the right things. Others have been written to help the employer distinguish the real from the facade when interviewing candidates who have read the effective interviewing books. Interviewing is usually a hard chore made bearable by the pleasure of meeting and getting to know another individual. The first lesson in effective interviewing is: Always conduct a structured interview.

To begin with, I suggest you read several how-to books on interviewing to get a general idea of how other people think it should be done. I have listed several potentially helpful sources at the end of this book. You should not be surprised to learn that each how-to book will suggest a different method. There is no absolutely right or wrong way. What is effective for one person may be quite uncomfortable for another. You will develop your own style. As you do, remember the objective and purpose of the interview: to gather information, to confirm or clarify data, and to make a decision about whether or not a candidate is acceptable.

Objective/subjective components. Once again, you will be conducting a two-part exercise—one part *objective* and one part *subjective*. The objective part of the interview begins long before you meet face to face with the candidate. You begin by collecting information that will tell you whether or not the candidate meets the requirements of the position as measured against the position and person profiles. Much of this information can be weighed objectively because it either is or is not a match with the profiles. Specifically, you will want a detailed résumé; but since this contains only limited information, you should request additional information about prior experiences, accomplishments, successes and failures, attitudes and philosophies on certain subjects important to your practice. You should ask for a written paragraph detailing concisely what practical experiences the candidate has had in every functional area that your position profile covers. You should certainly request a cover letter from the candidate clearly stating career goals and how joining your firm will lead to their accomplishment. If the candidate has trouble meeting your request, you may have saved yourself time because this person may not be successful in a business that demands attention to details, critical analysis, and concise presentation of facts. This part of the evaluation covers the objective assessment of academic and experience credentials.

The subject evaluation takes place during the personal interview. You will be required to make personal decisions about this candidate before making a "go or no-go" decision. Here you are studying personality, style of management, communication skills, characteristics and traits required in a consultant—including such things as executive presence and leadership.

The accurate assessment of these qualities in a candidate is difficult for the most skilled interviewer, so it is wise to use whatever tools are available to help you. Our firm uses psychological evaluation as an assessment aid, and we have been quite pleased with the results. You may want to consult with an industrial psychologist about the many types of instruments available and what they will tell you. The use of certain psychological instruments is helpful in creating a profile of the candidate; however, do not make any decision based solely upon the results of these instruments. They are viewed as effective tools to be used with other techniques and processes in evaluating candidates.

Interview phases.   The interview itself should include four phases. The first phase is preparation. You should list every subject you wish to discuss, including items in the written material needing clarification. Plan to take notes and record bits of information for review later. Prior to the interview, you should already have sent complete information about your firm and your plans for the future to the candidate. During the personal interview, you will want to review the candidate's current pastimes, personal values, and life goals. If you don't prepare for the review ahead of time, you probably won't get it done during the interview.

The second phase, the personal interview itself, should be very straightforward and open. Since you have initiated the meeting, you should politely define the ground rules. The candidate will appreciate this and should feel more relaxed knowing what to expect. After opening pleasantries you may thank the candidate again for all of the information furnished and for meeting with you. Restate the importance of this hiring decision to your firm and identify those items about which you wish to talk. Take notes as you talk because you don't want to rely on your memory. Take time to answer the candidate's questions, but try not to ramble. Be pleasant, but remember that you are here to collect information and form some opinions that are important to the future of your consulting practice. This is not the time to discuss last week's ball game or to become involved in idle chitchat.

The third phase of the interview is writing up the personal meeting. This should be done immediately while information and impressions are fresh in your mind. Decision time: Continue to the fourth and final interview phase, or break off discussions at this point?

The fourth phase of the interview process is the casual or social meeting. The objective here is to assess the candidate's behavior in an informal, social setting. Does the candidate exhibit proper social graces, and will you be proud to have this person represent you and your firm in the business community?

If you have followed these procedures in evaluating each candidate, you will be rewarded with more successful staff members and fewer employee casualties after the hiring decision is made.

STAFF DEVELOPMENT

Initial Assignments

Regardless of how well-credentialed a new staff member may be, every consultant should go through a period of orientation. Every organization has a culture—sometimes described as "the way we do things around here"—and it takes a while for a new staff member to settle into this culture.

During the orientation period you will want to assign the new staff member to work with a senior member of the firm, or possibly even yourself, for a few weeks. Teammates and specific assignments should be selected with some forethought because the initial experience will indicate to the new staff member what you expect in terms of performance and behavior. Are projects handled in a timely and professional manner? Do the consultants utilize their time well and display genuine interest in the client's welfare? What does management expect in the way of reports and business development? Teach your new consultant all of your firm's good habits. This is the time for the new consultant to modify behavior patterns (habits) that do not fit the new culture.

As your new consultant becomes familiar with your clients, your market, and your current projects, he or she should work under the supervision of the senior staff member. It may be advisable initially to assign the new staff member to the less complicated assignments. Settling into a new career carries enough anxiety without the additional pressures of critical assignments. Do not create problems for yourself by putting a new consultant to the acid test too quickly.

After a few weeks of getting his or her feet wet, if your observations reinforce your hiring decision, you should move the new consultant into the mainstream of your regular practice.

Exposure to the Different Facets of Consulting

A senior consultant is a valuable asset. This is the person who develops clients, manages projects, and supervises and trains junior consultants and technicians. This person should be experienced and well rounded. The concern to you as a manager is: How do you manage the development of your entire staff to maximum effectiveness? The demands of your practice will require various levels of talent and expertise. You may not want, nor be able to afford, a large staff composed only of senior staff consultants. No matter how sophisticated a project may be, there will always be some very critical activities along with various routine support activities and a certain amount of busywork. The critical analysis, conceptualization, and decision-making activities will be the responsibility of your senior consultants, and a lot of the data collection may be done by a junior consultant. Remember the importance of leveraging the productive time of your key income generators—the senior consultants.

The title of senior consultant implies a number of years experience and practice that give the person the competence to be a manager and a consultant. The individual has been tried and proven and his or her past performance and track record speaks for itself. Your junior consultants and trainees should be working at developing a sound track record of successes that will provide them the backgrounds to be senior consultants.

As owner and manager of a consulting practice, you will have two responsibilities to face in developing your staff and exposing junior members to the many facets of consulting. One responsibility will be to yourself and your practice. You should have a balanced staff in terms of positions and responsibilities based upon expertise and experience. You must plan for growth and expansion by developing your in-house talent. You may want to develop a unique specialty to capture a select market, and you want to ensure adequate replacement strength when you lose a valued senior consultant. You will want to develop clients that will provide training opportunities and experience for your staff. You should assign projects with discretion, to provide training experience while balancing the work load.

Your second responsibility as a manager in developing your staff is to your employees. As an employer you are responsible for providing each of your employees with the environment and opportunity for personal growth and development. As an employer you also bear the responsibility of encouraging and motivating your staff toward growth and personal development. The employee gains experience, expertise, and earning power and grows by contributing to the practice.

Consultants wear several different hats in solving the multifaceted problems of a business client. They gain competence through their experiences. As a manager make sure your staff members are diverse in experience and plan your projects to give them adequate exposure in areas needed for personal improvement.

Continuing Education

New demands.   Fifty years ago a person graduating from college with a bachelor's degree in a technical field could expect to remain relatively current throughout a career with only moderate continuing education. Today technology is cycling at such space-age speed that many technologies learned in college are obsolete even before graduation. How can a consultant stay current? This can be accomplished only by understanding the need for, wanting, and personally committing to a structured program of continuing education throughout one's career.

Continuing education 50 years ago meant an annual 2-week seminar to update you on new developments, a possible 3-day convention to see what your competitors were doing, and a fair amount of reading from a few select trade journals. An adequate continuing education program today will include as many specialized seminars as you can make time for, at least one convention, and a reading schedule that will be comparable to that of a good doctoral program. If you are not reading one major book per month, three of four monthly trade publications (technical in nature), one credible management development periodical (*Harvard Business Review* or *Sloan Review*, for example), and the usual business magazines (*Fortune*, *Inc.*, *Venture*, etc.), you are probably not current in your field or aware of business trends.

All of the items mentioned are valuable components of a quality continuing education program, and additional degrees, certifications, and new skills development are also important. If you can maintain this kind of continuing education program, you will be a known leader in your field.

Because you are the owner/manager of your consulting practice, you will be setting the example for your staff (establishing the culture). You must insist that your staff stay current in their respective specialized fields and business in general. You must provide them with support and encouragement by having a stated program to reimburse employees for all or part of the cost incurred in this continuing education program. Obviously, this could become a significant expense item, so you should include this program with your yearly budget and your business plan.

One word of caution—research has indicated that unless a positive reinforcement activity immediately follows an intensive training seminar, participants retain less than 80 percent of the information learned at the seminar. Try to schedule seminar training to coincide with work projects that will provide participants with an opportunity to put their new skills to immediate practical application.

Training programs.   Your staff continuing education program will require more than a moderate amount of in-house training to be complete. In fact, the major thrust of an excellent training program will be an in-house program designed by management, taught by management, and augmented with external seminars and training courses. The training required to develop a competent staff—one that can grow a successful practice—must be structured to fit the specific needs of your staff as determined by your practice. And the person to design and implement that training program is you, the owner/manager.

The continuing education program should be a part of your business plan. The program should be structured with forethought and time tables to ensure that training gets its share of management's attention. A productive continuing education/training program can be structured and managed without being overwhelming. It requires that you practice a bit of internal consulting for yourself in the same disciplined way you would for a client.

The training program must be developed by management because you are in the best position to know the long-range needs of the practice as well as the needs of your individual staff members. The training program must be relevant and closely tied to how things are actually done in your practice. Employees must understand that training will be done systematically and will be scheduled as a continuing effort. As Andrew S. Grove, President of Intel Corporation, has said many times, training should be a process, not an event.

There are two types of training to plan for as your practice grows. The first type is teaching new staff members the skills and processes needed to perform their jobs. In other words, provide them with an explanation including demonstrations of the culture or "how we do things around here." The second type of training is new skills and concepts. This includes technical skills as well as management skills. Your involvement is important in both types of training if the program is to meet your objectives of consistency and quality. You must continue to set the standard.

Once you are committed to a formal continuing education/training program you, the manager, should develop the format. Make a list of those subjects in which your staff will need to maintain high levels of competence to build their future and your practice. Your list should be broad and include subjects ranging from daily activities to specific technical skills required by your practice. As you make this list, solicit input from your staff members. Your staff will feel better toward the training program and will work harder at developing new skills if they both understand the purpose and have a say in what they will be learning. Training is a partnership arrangement and requires commitment from both parties.

With your list at hand, take stock of what materials and training aids are available. Do not rely solely on external sources. You should structure your program to utilize your own talents as well as those of your senior staff members. The external training should be plugged in to support your in-house training. Your list should be prioritized and balanced so that the most important subjects are taught first. The overall program should be diverse and provide variety to maintain a high level of interest on the part of participants. Do not become too ambitious in the beginning. Attempting too much at one time can reduce the quality of the training and may result in bogging down of the program. Take one subject at a time and build on small successes. Once you have a particular training lecture perfected, you can repeat it often with little additional effort.

As to who should do what training, as mentioned before, use and develop your in-house talents. This kind of participation by staff members builds their camaraderie, confidence, skills, and expertise. One important fact to remember, as you use and develop your in-house training skills, is the benefit to the instructor. The preparation work and the questions and discussion during the course will sharpen the instructor's skills and understanding of the subject.

Specialist versus Generalist Training

The kind of training you prescribe for your staff will depend upon whether your practice specializes in specific areas of business and technology or is a general practice. This is analogous to a doctor's being a surgeon, specifically a heart bypass surgeon, rather than a general practitioner (a family doctor). Regardless of the particular nature of your practice, however, you may have both specialists and generalists on your staff.

As you determine what kind of training your staff should have, keep in mind your business objectives. In contemplating a particular seminar or training activity for you or your staff, ask yourself, "Will this help me reach my objective?" If the answer is not a definite yes, look for another training activity that will satisfy a need in meeting your business plan. This decision-making process is more pertinent to the area of technical training than to management skills development.

CAREER PATHS

The consulting industry is somewhat unusual in that people can move into and out of the consulting world without changing their basic skills or careers. Many people see their entry in and exit from consulting as part of a personal career development plan. Others leave the profession with the realization that consulting does not meet their personal or professional needs as well as expected. Let us consider this situation briefly because you should be aware of the positive and negative impact of staff turnover.

Career versus Training Ground

Many people select consulting as a lifetime career and begin early preparation by acquiring the academic credentials to give them a fast start in the challenging field of consulting. Such a person may solicit guidance from a professional consultant in structuring an undergraduate curriculum to prepare for a consulting career with a specialty in finance or engineering. This person may go on to graduate school to get an MBA or other advanced technical degree to better prepare for a career in consulting. This person may have visions of getting onto a fast track into management with hopes of an early invitation into the partnership. The results can be a long and rewarding career in professional consulting.

Another person's objective may be to gain as much broad experience as possible in the shortest time frame. The exceptional experiences gained as a consultant might provide an entrée to private industry and a higher management position. Because experience is the best teacher, many corporate boards prefer a senior manager to have a track record of accomplishments and diverse experiences. Theoretically, the firm is getting a much higher-quality executive and the individual uses the consulting as a springboard.

The reverse is also true. Many exceptionally qualified managers leave a productive career in private industry to become professional consultants. They desire the challenge of diverse and demanding problem-solving situations that consulting can offer. They may have become bored with the routine of one industrial setting and may see the consultant's role as a way to put excitement back into their careers. Using previously acquired skills and experiences to solve other people's business problems can be stimulating. They can be valuable assets to a practice, providing they can adapt to a vastly different culture, adjust to the change in life-style, and providing they have the traits and character-istics required of senior management consultants.

Not everyone is suited for a career as a consultant. Selling and deliver-ing a service is quite different from selling and delivering a product. Not everyone can adjust to the varying levels of stress, anxiety, and uncer-tainty that are periodically associated with management consulting. Some people perceive consulting as an exciting and often glamorous profession but do not realize that a large part of the profession is grinding out the work.

Your first objective should always be to attract, train, and retain the most qualified and competent people possible for your practice. A good entry-level person is one with excellent academic credentials plus a few years of practical experience in a specific field prior to moving into consulting. The person should understand the basics of daily activity in business and should also have a high energy level, ambition, and willingess to work hard.

The person using your practice as a stepping stone should clearly understand what you expect and should bring specific skills and talents to your practice during a period of growth. The contribution might be to carry part of the work load while you build up permanent staff. A mature and experienced executive coming into your practice from a senior managerial position in industry can be a valuable asset. This type of person has the combined credentials of seasoned technical skills and managerial maturity. This person can bring to your practice an element of refined problem-solving skills, leadership, and executive presence in the form of role model and mentor for junior consultants.

Degree of Commitment

Every staff member represents an investment in the future of your practice. Each time a new staff member comes into the company, you make a sizable investment in terms of orientation, initial training, and increased overhead prior to the new member's contributing to the earnings of the practice. Your investment will continue with each year's training and development while at the same time you will be recovering your investment through the personal contribution of the consultant to the practice. Naturally, you want to protect your investment. You can do this only by actions that will lead to and ensure a strong and growing sense of commitment from each staff member to the firm.

As the manager of the practice, you must effectively manage every part of the organization including those elements that provide the security, enjoyment, satisfaction, and commitment of employees in your practice. By understanding and employing the fundamentals of participative management, you can mange commitment. The things you do in running your company can increase or decrease commitment of staff members to the practice.

The general rules of thumb are to:

1. Select people who share your values and business philosophies.
2. Provide an environment that people are comfortable with and enjoy working within.
3. Demonstrate your personal interest in each individual employee.
4. Provide opportunity for career growth and personal development.
5. Involve your staff in decisions and commitments that affect them.
6. Maintain open lines of communication within the organization.

If you are determined to build a quality professional consulting practice, the development of good management techniques can lead to personal satisfaction and a feeling of exhilaration as the practice and the employees grow.

Career Path Progression

As you develop your business plan and the corresponding action plan, consider the long-term structure of your consulting practice. How will the organization will be structured to maintain proficiency and quality as your practice grows in volume, clients, and staff? Fast-track companies sometimes collapse under their own weight because no one has planned for the firm's infrastructure to grow in proportion to sales and staff growth. Consider the growth problems you will experience and be prepared to solve them. Perhaps it is more positive to think of this as growth strategy rather than potential problem solving; however, the end result is the same.

One important strategy necessary for smooth and uninterrupted growth is a well-defined career path for staff members. The demands of your practice will increase and take on more complex dimensions as your practice grows, so you should plan career progression opportunities in advance of demand. Part of a satisfying work environment is a clear understanding of promotion opportunities. What advancement can a trainee expect during a 20-year career with your firm? Is management an option, and what are the possibilities for becoming a partnership member?

These are logical questions that every employee will ask. From your perspective, you have two reasons to have a clearly defined plan for staff progression within your practice. One, you must devise a workable plan for promoting competent individuals into positions of increasing responsibility as the demands of your growing practice dictate. Second, you want to retain valued staff members by meeting their needs for personal achievement and self-actualization.

The number of professional and management positions in your firm should be the result of need and firm growth. As you plan for growth, project the levels of talent needed to do the work and run the company. Do not allow your management to become top-heavy. The possibilities are numerous: trainee, junior consultant, associate consultant, senior consultant, technical specialist, project coordinator, project manager, unit manager, partner, managing partner, and on and on. The best rule of thumb is to keep the title and position simple and representative of responsibilities and management authority. As far as organization structure goes, always let form follow function. Design the structure to fit the actual needs of the workplace. Do not design a structure and then try to make everything fit into the little squares. The structure is right when it goes unnoticed and everything gets done with harmony.

Career Path Planning

In the not-too-distant past a person who was considered prudent and stable prepared for a career, went to work for a good company, and stayed with that same company until retirement. That is certainly not the case today, as we all know, for many reasons. The changes in our society during the past 2 decades have been most noticeable in our changing sense of values, our living habits, and our expectations for satisfaction from work.

Today a person may change companies several times during a career and, in fact, may change careers several times. The writings of John Naisbitt in *Megatrends* and Daniel Yankelovich in *New Rules* are examples of the shifts taking place in our culture and of how we are changing the way we do things.* The phrase "quality of work life" has come to stand for the element of satisfaction that we seek in our work environment. Not only are we looking for quality in our work life, we are actively seeking a greater level of quality in our lives as a whole. This new striving for quality of life is bringing about new ways of assigning value to work in selecting careers, employers, and work environments. Meaningful work is once again becoming an important part of our lives. We need to work to satisfy a human need for accomplishment and are, therefore, choosing our work more carefully.

As you select your staff (they will also be selecting you) and create continuing education/training programs and career paths for advancement, your success as a business will ultimately rest upon your hiring decisions. In considering candidates, carefully analyze their professional goals as well as their personal goals. If the two are not closely parallel, the candidates may not be sure of what role they want work to play in their lives. If their professional goals are part of their personal goals, you have people who know what they want out of life and will work hard to get it.

One last word on personnel development. An important part of your action plan is the employee performance appraisal. This is a valuable communication tool and it serves as an excellent navigational chart. Workers have the right to know how their work and their personal contributions are perceived by management. The periodic performance review is a time for clarifying goals and expectations. Performance appraisals are effective tools for good management. Use them well.

---

*John Naisbitt, *Megatrends*, Warner Books, New York, 1977; Daniel Yankelovich, *New Rules*, Random House, New York, 1981.

Practice Economics

TERRY NUGENT
Touche Ross and Company
Nashville, Tennessee

INTRODUCTION

The consulting business demands a great deal from the individual but also offers great rewards. In order to provide financial rewards, a consulting practice must be built on a solid, profitable financial plan. This chapter will address the basic economics of a consulting practice. The key issues to be discussed include:

- Fee structures
- Importance of leverage
- Productivity measures
- Budgeting
- Engagement economics

Two separate approaches to budgeting a consulting practice will be examined. The first approach is incorporated into a budget model developed for a small consulting practice. This practice is typical of first- and second-year Big Eight consulting operations in a new location. The model was developed using Lotus 1-2-3.

The second budget model is more typical of mature consulting practice. The model was developed using a mainframe financial modeling language called EMPIRE. The model displays a gross margin plan for a practice with twenty-eight professionals. This plan stops at the gross margin before nonpayroll level. Overhead costs shared by audit and tax divisions were budgeted on an office basis and are therefore omitted.

LEVERS OF PROFITABILITY

Staff Pyramid and Fee Structures

A simple way to look at staffing a consulting practice is to break the practice into pyramids of from five to fifteen people. Depending upon the practice specialty and the particular firm's philosophy, the size but usually not the structure of the pyramid may vary.

The top or narrow part of the pyramid contains the partner, principal, or director. This individual is typically the most experienced, highly paid professional and is normally responsible for the successful completion of engagements dealing directly with clients and for selling work.

The next tier of the pyramid is made up of senior managers, managers, and supervisors. These individuals perform the week-to-week management of the engagements and are responsible for identifying new client prospects and assisting in the sales process.

The third tier of the pyramid is made up of seniors or senior consultants. These individuals typically have 2 or 3 years of consulting experience and are capable of supervising the daily work of the younger staff. This staff level is the "bread and butter" of the consulting business. They possess the right combination of experience and dedication to complete difficult projects with limited supervision. Seniors are normally in short supply in most firms.

The final layer of the pyramid consists of young or new staff. Depending upon the firm, these individuals usually have less than 2 years of consulting experience and may have been hired directly out of graduate or undergraduate school. Some firms require prior business experience and an advanced degree, while others prefer to train their own personnel and hire some undergraduate students.

Figure 17.1 is a graphic depiction of the consulting pyramid. As shown, each pyramid is built around one partner, principal, or director. Each firm seems to develop its own special version of the pyramid. A pyramid rarely exceeds fifteen professionals per partner. The narrowest pyramids have a total of about five personnel per partner. This width of the pyramid depends on the type of consulting work performed by the firm. Systems consulting lends itself to a wider pyramid and greater

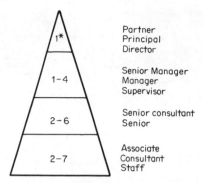

1*	Partner Principal Director
1-4	Senior Manager Manager Supervisor
2-6	Senior consultant Senior
2-7	Associate Consultant Staff

*Each pyramid is built around a signal partner, principal, or director. In large practices, there will be multiple pyramids. The numbers in the pyramid refer to the typical number of personnel at each level (per pyramid).

Figure 17.1   Staffing pyramid.

utilization of inexperienced staff. Strategic and business planning consulting requires more experienced personnel, closer supervision, and a narrower pyramid. The width of the pyramid is often referred to as the leverage of the practice.

Figure 17.2 shows the typical billing rates of the four pyramid levels. These rates vary by geographic location. The larger cities (New York, Los Angeles, Chicago, and Houston) typically rate a $10 to $15 per hour premium. Billing rates are normally adjusted annually when promotions are given and salaries are changed. Within each pyramid level there may also be multiple billing codes relating to salary and experience levels.

Leverage

Leverage may appear to be a simple concept, but it is a key ingredient to a profitable consulting practice. Leverage consists of delegating engagement tasks to the very lowest-level person capable of successfully completing the task. Standardized work approaches and staff training support greater degrees of leverage through reduced supervision requirements.

Leverage allows the most profitable use of the more experienced professionals' time. It provides a growth environment for the staff members by stretching their capabilities. By leveraging the work, the partner and manager can free up time to develop additional engagements. Indeed, in some firms the partners spend as little as 30 percent of their time on client engagements. In a practice with more narrow pyramids, a partner may spend 70 percent of his or her time on client work.

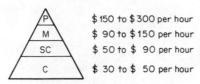

Figure 17.2   Billing rate ranges.

Utilization and Gross Services

Every firm has a particular name for utilization. It represents the percent of each professionals' time chargeable to a client engagement. Since this chargeable percentage or utilization ratio is usually based on a year of 2080 hours, it is possible (and normal) for certain levels of staff (seniors) to exceed 100 percent utilization due to overtime. Fully utilized or 100 percent chargeable staff means profitable operations. Utilization is an excellent performance indicator for the staff. Staff members who do the best work and work the hardest usually have the highest utilization ratios.

Gross services or gross fees are simply the total chargeable hours worked by a professional times his or her billing rate. They are gross since they represent the total fee value for the actual time required to complete a project. The difference between gross fees and the amount paid by the client is the allowance, fee adjustment, or write-off. The percentage of the allowance to gross services is a critical management indicator. This so-called allowance ratio or fee adjustment percentage indicates how well projects are being estimated, planned, and controlled.

Just as high utilization is a good performance measure for a staff member, low allowance ratios are measures of good performance for the partners and managers. Low allowance ratios suggest effective use of the staff. Large write-offs waste effort and severely hurt profits. A good target allowance percentage is in the 12 to 16 percent range.

Realization and Net Services

Realization is a measure of the fees actually received from an engagement. Realization percentage is the ratio of net services to gross services. If a client paid $10,000 for a project that took 100 hours to complete at $100 per hour, the realization would be 100 percent since the gross services would equal the net services at $10,000. If the same project took 115 hours to complete at the same billing rate, and it was not possible to bill any additional fees, the realization would be 87 percent and the allowance rate 13 percent.

Net services or net fees are another critical planning measure in a consulting practice. They represent the dollar value of what has actually been sold to the client and what will be received as revenue. Gross services, on the other hand, represent a measure of capacity: what could be sold or collected if better estimating, project planning, and control or client negotiating had occurred. Some firms look at gross services as an interim performance measure only to find later on in the year that higher than expected allowances or fee adjustments severely impact their profitability. By concentrating on net services, you gain a clear picture of what cash will be paid for the firm's services. If the practice is profitable using net services as a planning tool during the year, it will be profitable at the end of the year.

FINANCIAL MANAGEMENT

Gross Margin

Gross margin is a measure of a consulting practice's potential profitability. It is normally defined as net services less payroll expenses. Some firms use gross margin per partner as a performance measure to compare operations at various geographical locations. Gross margin is a good measure of each individual's direct contribution to the bottom line of the practice. Theoretically, positive gross margin on an individual staff basis indicates a proper staffing level; however, the consulting business tends to be feast or famine. Therefore, a practical staffing level is less than the theoretical number.

Collectible Fees

Fee collection is among the most important elements of a consulting practice's financial management. The older the fees get, the less likely they are to be collected. Poor fee collections may be an indicator of other more severe problems. Happy clients pay bills, assuming they are presented on a timely basis.

Each project manager should be required personally to follow up receipt of payments from his or her clients. The project manager knows the client personnel, is aware of any engagement difficulties, and should know the best way to expedite collections. By making collections a monthly ritual, a consultant can avoid potential cash flow problems and lost fees due to lack of follow-up.

A key concern on every project is that (1) the scope of the project remains as originally agreed upon or (2) a new arrangement is reached so that additional fees may be billed and collected. The engagement manager should be responsible for controlling the project scope and should always work to negotiate fee increases for any project scope changes. It is very unlikely that the practice can maintain a low allowance ratio if engagement scope is not closely controlled on every project.

Profit Contribution and Overhead Billing and Collections

Overhead items should be budgeted for and worked into the original profitability plan. A consulting practice by its very nature requires an investment in items that cannot be directly charged to projects. Impressive offices, libraries containing current technical and business periodicals, and participation in professional and civic organizations are essential investments if one plans to build a successful consulting practice. Care must be taken, however, to develop a reasonable budget, and control must be exercised to live within certain limitations. Expenditures for all overhead items should be challenged regularly to ensure that they are contributing positively to the practice.

Obviously, reductions in overhead contribute directly to increases in profits. Without investment, however, sales can be lost and gross margin reduced.

ENGAGEMENT ECONOMICS

Fee Estimation

As already mentioned, practice profitability begins with the engagement. Before an engagement can begin, a fee must be determined and the project sold to the client. In many situations—especially those involving competitive bids that result in fixed fee engagements—the fee is fixed and therefore needs to be very carefully estimated.

Estimating a consulting engagement is like estimating a construction contract. The more you know, the better job you can do. This implies that before a fee can be established you had better know what the result will look like. It is very important to develop a project work plan and to establish time estimates at the detail level of the work plan. This means considering the environment under which the project will be performed and the complexity of the individual tasks.

Figures 17.3 through 17.10 represent an engagement estimating model developed to prepare a competitive bid for a data processing effectiveness review project. Figure 17.3 is the summary fees by project phase in which the overall estimated project time is converted into fees for the total project. This particular data processing effectiveness review utilized a joint venture with a specialized hardware and technical software

Figure 17.3 Data processing effectiveness review fees by project phase.

Task	Activity	Firm A project fees	Firm B project fees	Total project fees
1.0	Project organization, planning, and review.	$12,600		$12,600
2.0	Evaluate the effectiveness of the data processing organization and administration.	18,400		$18,400
3.0	Evaluate the effectiveness of computer hardware and systems software.	2,025	$33,387	$35,412
4.0	Survey the effectiveness of major application systems.	81,050		$81,050
5.0	Evaluate computer operations work flow.	8,125		$8,125
6.0	Review the effectiveness of the data transcription function.	5,600		$5,600
7.0	Present effectiveness review results.	10,300	1,113	$11,413
	Total project	$138,100	$34,500	$172,600

consulting firm. Firm A, the primary consulting organization on the project, hired firm B to perform specialized tasks. As shown, the total fees for the project were $172,600.

Figure 17.4 is a project work hour break-out by major task or project phase for the overall project. As shown, firm A's time is broken out into a partner, two managers, and two senior consultants' time for the seven major project task headings. Firms B's time, amounting to 248 hours, is not broken out by individual. Figures 17.5, 17.6, and 17.7 show a detailed project work plan with detailed hour estimates by person and by project task. Each work hour estimate was developed considering the probable number of people to be interviewed, the quantity of documentation to be reviewed, or the scope of a particular operation. It is generally a good idea to break down the fee estimates into task detail requiring less than 3 days to accomplish. The clearer the estimator's understanding of the project, the more accurate the estimate. Therefore, any tools that the estimator can use to define the work more clearly will eliminate potential future problems with the project. On this particular project, the fourth major task—*survey the effectiveness of major applications systems*— was to be largest single task activity. To better analyze and estimate this major task, we broke task 4.3—*perform detailed application effectiveness review for selected systems*—into six subtasks shown on Figure 17.8. As shown, this estimate summarized the time by project subtasks, by person for task 4.3. These individual task estimates were developed using an actual assessment of the complexity of the applications that were to be reviewed. Figure 17.9 shows the list of twenty-seven applications systems to be reviewed and the complexity assessment. As

Figure 17.4 Data processing effectiveness review fees by project phase.

Task	Activity	Estimated project work hours Firm A & Co.							Firm A project fees
		Total Firm A	Partner	Mgr 1	Mgr 2	Senior 1	Senior 2	Total Firm B	
1.0	Project organization, planning, and review.	82	32	40	6	2	2		$12,600
2.0	Evaluate the effectiveness of the data processing organization and administration.	144	16	40	56	32	0		18,400
3.0	Evaluate the effectiveness of computer hardware and systems software.	15	4	2	4	5	0	240	2,025
4.0	Survey the effectiveness of major application systems.	833	17	88	263	74	391		81,050
5.0	Evaluate computer operations work flow.	83	4	4	24	12	39		8,125
6.0	Review the effectiveness of the data transcription function.	60	4	4	16	0	36		5,600
7.0	Present effectiveness review results.	96	8	16	28	8	36	8	10,300
	Total project	1313	85	194	397	133	504	248	$138,100

Figure 17.5 Data processing effectiveness review project work plan estimate (page 1 of 3 pages).

Task	Activity	Firm A total	Estimated project work hours Firm A & Co.					Firm B total
			Partner	Mgr 1	Mgr 2	Senior 1	Senior 2	
1.0	Project organization, planning, and review.							
1.1	Establish Metro effectivenss review committee.	2		2				

1.2 Finalize scope, work plan, and project schedule.	6	2	2	2		
1.3 Conduct initial project team meeting.	10	2	2	2		
1.4 Schedule and conduct initial effectiveness review committee meeting.	6	2	2	2	2	2
1.5 Project review and supervision.	58	26	32			
	82	32	40	6	2	2
2.0 Evaluate the effectiveness of the data processing organization and administration.						
2.1 Assess the position of data processing in the organization.	52	4	24	24	24	
2.2 Evaluate the organizational structure of the data processing department.	60	4	8	24	8	
2.3 Review data processing administrative control procedures.	32	8	8	8		
	144	16	40	56	32	0
3.0 Evaluate the effectiveness of computer hardware and systems software.						
3.1 Analyze current environment.	0					40
3.2 Review plans and strategy for delivering data processing sevices.	4			4		40
3.3 Assess the suitability of systems software complement.	2				2	32
3.4 Perform a capacity assessment including required modeling.	2		2		2	80
3.5 Formulate recommendations, strategies, model scenarios, attendant action plans, and submit final report.	7	4			1	48
	15	4	2	4	5	240

Figure 17.6 Data processing effectiveness review project work plan estimate (page 2 of 3 pages).

Task	Activity	Firm A total	Firm A & Co.					Firm B total
			Partner	Mgr 1	Mgr 2	Senior 1	Senior 2	
4.0	Survey the effectiveness of major application systems.							
4.1	Develop and distribute an application effectiveness survey questionaire.	25		3	6		16	
4.2	Assess application survey results.	30	2	6	6		16	
4.3	Perform detailed application effectiveness review for selected systems	778	15	79	251	74	359	0
		833	17	88	263	74	391	0
5.0	Evaluate computer operations work flow.							
5.1	Analyze physical layout.	17			6	2	9	
5.2	Review computer operations production scheduling.	22			6	2	14	
5.3	Evaluate machine room operations.	9			5	4		
5.4	Review output distribution management.	3			3			
5.5	Document operations effectiveness and review with effectiveness committee.	32	4	4	4	4	16	
		83	4	4	24	12	39	0
6.0	Review the effectiveness of the data transcription function							
6.1	Evaluate data entry equipment.	16			4		12	
6.2	Review input control procedures.	6			2		4	
6.3	Evaluate transcription productivity.	6			2		4	

Estimated project work hours

	Firm A total	Partner	Mgr 1	Mgr 2	Senior 1	Senior 2	Firm B total
6.4 Review physical environment.	10		2	4		4	
6.5 Summarize transcription review results and present to effectiveness committee.	22	4	2	4		12	
	60	4	4	16	0	36	0
7.0 Present effectivness review results							
7.1 Develop draft of management report.	48	4	8	16	4	16	

Figure 17.7 Data processing effectiveness review project work plan estimate (page 3 of 3 pages).

| | | Estimated project work hours | | | | | |
| | | | Firm A & Co. | | | | |
Task	Activity	Firm A total	Partner	Mgr 1	Mgr 2	Senior 1	Senior 2	Firm B total
7.2	Develop management presentation.	12		4	4		4	
7.3	Review report draft and presentation with effectiveness review committee.	10	2	2	2	2	2	4
7.4	Review management report.	8			4		4	
7.5	Conduct management presentation.	10	2	2	2	2	2	4
7.6	Issue management report.	8					8	
		96	8	16	28	8	36	8
	Total project	1313	85	194	397	133	504	248

Figure 17.8 Data processing effectiveness review project work plan estimate.

Task	Activity	Firm A total	Estimated project work hours Firm A & Co.				
			Partner	Mgr 1	Mgr 2	Senior 1	Senior 2
4.3.1	Interview key user personnel.	226		23	79		124
4.3.2	Review system documentation.	92		9	32		51
4.3.3	Evaluate system control processes.	40		4	14		22
4.3.4	Analyze cost effectiveness.	66		7	23		36
4.3.5	Evaluate technical efficiency.	208		21	52	52	83
4.3.6	Develop detailed application recommendations.	146	15	15	51	22	43
	Total all applications	778	15	79	251	74	359

Figure 17.9 Data processing effectiveness review.

Applications	Complexity assessment		
	Complex	Moderate	Simple
Automated Inquiry Management System			
Dept of Health			1
Mayors Office			1
Public Works			1
Billing System (Dept of Health)			1
Clinical Services			1
Administrative System (Dept of Social Services)			1
Payroll (Dept of Finance)			1
Current Property Tax Accountant			1
Accounts Receivable (Emergency Ambulance and			
Rescue Service)			1
Newspaper Subject Index System			1
Motor Vehicle Registration			1
LIB Mapping Section			1
Employee File			1
Voter Registration			1
Motor Vehicle Management		1	
Billings and Collections (Water and Sewer)		1	
Financial Management and Control		1	
Housing Management		1	
Financial Reporting		1	
Scheduling (Metro Transit Authority)		1	
LIB Permits		1	
LIB Land Information System	1		
Patient Accounting	1		
Tax Reappraisal	1		
LIB Tax Assessment	1		
On-Line Accounting	1		
Budget System	1		
Total applications	6	7	14

shown, there were six complex applications, seven moderate applications, and fourteen simple applications to be reviewed.

Estimating Model

The estimating model used the estimated work hours per application review task summarized in Figure 17.10 to calculate the total estimated application review time for all the applications. The model counted up the number of complex, moderate, and simple applications; multiplied each quantity by the individual hours per subtask shown in the complex, moderate, and simple columns of Figure 17.10; and dropped them into the subtask hour estimated by person table, which is Figure 17.8. Using

Figure 17.10 Data processing effectiveness review project work plan estimate.

| | | Estimated work hours per application | | |
| | | Application complexity | | |
Task	Activity	Complex	Moderate	Simple
4.3 Detailed application effectiveness review				
4.3.1	Interview key user personnel.	12	6	8
4.3.2	Review system documentation.	6	4	2
4.3.3	Evaluate system control processes.	2	2	1
4.3.4	Analyze cost-effectiveness.	4	4	1
4.3.5	Evaluate technical efficiency.	16	8	4
4.3.6	Develop detailed application recommendations.	8	6	4
	Total per application	48	30	20

this procedure, the estimator could modify the individual task hour estimates for complex, moderate, and simple systems and change the individual application complexity assessment, rerun the model, and then analyze the fee impact. This "what if" analysis was a critical part of establishing the final bid price and project scope in this competitive bid situation.

Other types of projects, such as system design of installation projects, could use similar estimating techniques in which individual design or development units would replace the applications systems reviewed on this project and the appropriate work program tasks descriptions would replace the ones shown on this work plan.

Important features of this estimating model are the ability to sub-estimate higher-level project tasks utilizing project-specific environmental or complexity assumptions. When that is accomplished, the hours are split out by project team member and each team member's billing rate is incorporated into the model to determine automatically the project fees for various engagement scope assumptions.

CONSULTING PRACTICE BUDGET MODELS

Small Practice Budget Model

The financial plan for a consulting practice should include an annual, by-month projection of planned net services, operating expenses, overhead, and contribution.

Chargeable hours should also be estimated by person and used to determine the feasibility of achieving the financial plan. Salaries and other known expenses should be estimated as accurately as possible and incorporated into the budget.

Figures 17.11 through 17.14 show a budget model example developed for a start-up consulting business. As shown on the figures, net services for the year were projected to be $338,624. This amount represents the total sales of consulting projects during the planned year of operation. This number was projected from the gross services number, assuming an allowance or fee adjustment of 20 percent. The gross services number was calculated from the planned chargeable hours (utilization ratio times 2040 hours). The allowance percent, shown in the last line of Figure 17.11, was a planning variable that could be adjusted to analyze the sensitivity of the practice's profitability to increased or decreased allowance. Operating expenses were estimated using actual anticipated expenditures for items such as salaries planned on a monthly basis. Overhead items spread monthly for the plan in reality are incurred on a quarterly basis.

Figure 17.12 shows the monthly gross services plan for this consulting practice. Note that target utilization, total projected hours, billing rates, and assumed number of days are used in the model. Notice also that the total gross services figure of $423,280 ties to the gross services on the prior figure. Figure 17.12 was used to develop the gross services number that plugged into the projected contributions statement shown in Figure 17.11. Figure 17.13 is a projected overhead summary showing projected monthly expenditures by overhead line item. Most of these items were planned on an annual basis and then split out by month to provide a budget for monthly financial reporting purposes. Notice again that line 84 (total local overhead, $70,300) ties to the projected contributions statement, local overhead.

The final part of this budget model is Figure 17.14, which shows the salary assumptions, target utilization, planned billing rate, gross and net services, annual salary, bonus, and project gross margin for each consulting staff member. In the case of midyear hiring, the portion of the staff member's annual salary and bonus applicable to the planning period is shown in the fiscal year salary column. Again notice that each of these numbers ties to the projected contribution statement, Figure 17.11. Throughout this budget model, changes to any of the planning assumptions—including salary, overhead, projected hours, billing rates, and utilization percentages—automatically readjust all the related numbers and create a new projected contribution and overhead statement.

The capability of performing "what if" analysis when preparing your annual budget is a very valuable tool. A key profitability indicator is line number 24 on the practice contribution statement, Figure 17.11. Departmental direct contribution as a percentage of net services (23.6 percent) was the number that each iteration of the budget model attempted to improve. As shown, this particular budget called for a solid profitable financial plan.

Figure 17.11 Example of small consulting practice annual budget projected contribution statement.

	Line no.	Annual plan	Percent of net services	Sept.	Oct.	Nov.	Dec.
Gross services	2	$423,280		$27,200	$27,200	$32,980	$32,980
Allowances	12	84,656		5,440	5,440	6,596	6,596
Net services	13	338,624	100.0%	21,760	21,760	26,384	26,384
Operating expenses							
Staff salary	15	155,417	45.9%	9,987	9,987	12,109	12,109
Staff bonus	16	15,542	4.6%	999	999	1,211	1,211
Total (staff only)	18	170,959	50.5%	10,986	10,986	13.320	13,320
Typists and off. sal.	19	17,500	5.2%	1,458	1,458	1,458	1,458
Total ben. and sal.	20	188,459	55.7%	12,444	12,444	14,778	14,778
Local overhead—direct	21	70,300	20.8%	5,373	5,373	5,720	5,720
Interest penalty	22	0	0.0%	0	0	0	0
Total direct oper. exp.	23	258,759	76.4%	17,817	17,817	20,498	20,498
Department direct contrib.	24	79,865	23.6%	3,943	3,943	5,886	5,886
Chargeable hours	35	5,074		221.0	221.0	365.5	365.5
Equivalent people	40	3.4					
Allowance percentage		20.0%					

Figure 17.12 Example of small consulting practice annual budget.

Personnel	Category	Target util.	Projected hours	Billing rate	Gross services	Sept.	Oct.	Nov.
Director		60%	1,224	$150	$183,600	$15,300	$15,300	$15,300
Manager		70%	1,428	100	142,800	11,900	11,900	11,900
Staff 1	*	165%	1,445	40	57,800			5,780
Staff 2	*	82%	977	40	39,080			
			5,074		$423,280	$27,200	$27,200	$32,980
Total: Hours		2040						
Days		255.00						
Avg rate		$83						

*Assumes entry level staff brought in or transferred in. Staff would have 2 to 3 years' audit or consulting experience.

Jan.	Feb.	March	April	May	June	July	Aug.	Total
$32,980	$38,563	$38,563	$38,563	$38,563	$38,563	$38,563	$38,562	$423,280
6,596	7,713	7,713	7,713	7,713	7,713	7,713	7,710	84,656
26,384	30,850	30,850	30,850	30,850	30,850	30,850	30,852	338,624
12,109	14,159	14,159	14,159	14,159	14,159	14,159	14,162	155,417
1,211	1,416	1,416	1,416	1,416	1,416	1,416	1,415	15,542
13,320	15,575	15,575	15,575	15,575	15,575	15,575	15,577	170,959
1,458	1,458	1,458	1,458	1,458	1,458	1,458	1,462	17,500
14,778	17,033	17,033	17,033	17,033	17,033	17,033	17,039	188,459
5,720	6,055	6,055	6,055	6,055	6,055	6,055	6,064	70,300
0	0	0	0	0	0	0	0	0
20,498	23,088	23,088	23,088	23,088	23,088	23,088	23,103	258,759
5,886	7,762	7,762	7,762	7,762	7,762	7,762	7,749	79,865
365.5	505.1	505.1	505.1	505.1	505.1	505.1	504.9	5,074.0

Dec.	Jan.	Feb.	March	April	May	June	July	Aug	Total
$15,300	$15,300	$15,300	$15,300	$15,300	$15,300	$15,300	$15,300	$15,300	$183,600
11,900	11,900	11,900	11,900	11,900	11,900	11,900	11,900	11,900	142,800
5,780	5,780	5,780	5,780	5,780	5,780	5,780	5,780	5,780	57,800
		5,583	5,583	5,583	5,583	5,583	5,583	5,582	39,080
$32,980	$32,980	$38,563	$38,563	$38,563	$38,563	$38,563	$38,563	$38,562	$423,280

Figure 17.13 Example of small consulting practice annual budget projected overhead summary.

	Line no.	Annual plan	Percent Services	Sept.	Oct.	Nov.
Pensions	51	5,500	1.6%	353	353	429
Grp life and medical insur.	52	4,700	1.4%	302	302	366
Payroll taxes	53	15,200	4.5%	977	977	1,184
Total supplimentary benefits	54	25,400	7.5%	1,632	1,632	1,979
Rent	55	10,000	3.0%	833	833	833
Depreciation and amortization	57	3,300	1.0%	275	275	275
Total occupancy	58	13,300	3.9%	1,108	1,108	1,108
Stationery and office supplies	61	0	0.0%	0	0	0
Subscription and services	63	7,000	2.1%	583	583	583
Total office	66	7,000	2.1%	583	583	583
Other staff expense	68	5,000	1.5%	417	417	417
Educational expense	69	0	0.0%	0	0	0
National training	69A	7,300	2.2%	608	608	608
Total staff expense	71	12,300	3.6%	1,025	1,025	1,025
AICPA state society dues	75	500	0.1%	42	42	42
Other dues and expenses	77	6,000	1.8%	500	500	500
Contributions	78	0	0.0%	0	0	0
Total other expenses	79	6,500	1.9%	542	542	542
Insurance	80	5,800	1.7%	483	483	483
Interest	81	0	0.0%	0	0	0
Taxes	82	0	0.0%	0	0	0
Total insur. interest, and taxes	83	5,800	1.7%	483	483	483
Total local overhead	84	70,300	20.8%	5,373	5,373	5,720
Total controllable overhead		51,200	15.1%			
Total direct overhead		25,800	7.6%			

Figure 17.14 Example of small consulting practice annual budget salary assumptions.

Name	Target util.	Projected hours	Billing rate	Gross services	Net services	FY 198X salary	FY 198X bonus	Gross margin	Annual salary
Director	60%	1,224	$150	$183,600	146,880	$70,000	$7,000	$69,880	$70,000
Manager	70%	1,428	100	142,800	114,240	50,000	5,000	59,240	50,000
Staff 1*	85%	1,445	40	57,800	46,240	20,833	2,084	23,323	25,000
Staff 2*	82%	977	40	39,080	31,264	14,584	1,458	15,222	25,000
Total hours 2040		5,074		$423,280	$338,624	$155,417	$15,542	$167,665	$170,000

Dec.	Jan.	Feb.	March	April	May	June	July	Aug.	Total
429	429	501	501	501	501	501	501	501	5,500
366	366	428	428	428	428	428	428	430	4,700
1,184	1,184	1,385	1,385	1,385	1,385	1,385	1,385	1,384	15,200
1,979	1,979	2,314	2,314	2,314	2,314	2,314	2,314	2,315	25,400
833	833	833	833	833	833	833	833	837	10,000
275	275	275	275	275	275	275	275	275	3,300
1,108	1,108	1,108	1,108	1,108	1,108	1,108	1,108	1,112	13,300
0	0	0	0	0	0	0	0	0	0
583	583	583	583	583	583	583	583	587	7,000
583	583	583	583	583	583	583	583	587	7,000
									0
417	417	417	417	417	417	417	417	413	5,000
0	0	0	0	0	0	0	0	0	0
608	608	608	608	608	608	608	608	612	7,300
1,025	1,025	1,025	1,025	1,025	1,025	1,025	1,025	1,025	12,300
42	42	42	42	42	42	42	42	38	500
500	500	500	500	500	500	500	500	500	6,000
0	0	0	0	0	0	0	0	0	0
542	542	542	542	542	542	542	542	538	6,500
483	483	483	483	483	483	483	483	487	5,800
0	0	0	0	0	0	0	0	0	0
0	0	0	0	0	0	0	0	0	0
483	483	483	483	483	483	483	483	487	5,800
5,720	5,720	6,055	6,055	6,055	6,055	6,055	6,055	6,064	70,300

Medium-Sized Practice Budget

A slightly different approach to budgeting a consulting practice is to budget chargeable hours by billing class by month for all staff billing classes. The budget is planned in hours with special attention to target chargeable percentages. Once the chargeable hour plan is determined, the annual fees and expenses are calculated.

Figures 17.15 through 17.19 show several budget reports resulting from this process. The first report, Figure 17.15, shows division margin before nonpayroll expenses. As shown in this figure, chargeable hours have been converted into fees-chargeable time, which is equivalent to gross fees or gross services in the previous model. Fee adjustments are subtracted from the top line to give net fees or, in our previous model, net

Figure 17.15   Division margin before nonpayroll.

	Amount	Percent
Fees—chargeable time	2,891,835	100
Fee adjustments	404,857	14
Net fees	2,486,978	86
Chargeable payroll	726,828	25
Nonchargeable payroll	697,807	24
PM overtime credit	(33,619)	(1)
Gross payroll	1,391,016	48
Charged to firmwide activities	(26,127)	(1)
Net payroll expense	1,364,889	47
Margin before nonpayroll	1,122,089	39

Figure 17.16   Gross fees—chargeable time.

	Total generated	Per person	Per chgble hour
Ptr	370,575	123,525	183
Mgr	867,100	173,420	116
Sr	655,040	131,008	71
St	999,120	66,608	48
Subtotal	2,891,835	103,280	73
Ad	0	0	0
Total	2,891,835	103,280	73

services. As shown, the realization in this budget (shown as net fees) is 86 percent and the allowance rate is only 14 percent. This is more aggressive than the previous model, in which I used a 20 percent allowance rate. Payroll expenses are then subtracted from net fees to provide margin before nonpayroll expenses. In this particular example, note that the credits available to the local office for firmwide projects and adjustments for payroll cost are not actually incurred since partners and managers were not compensated for overtime hours.

Figure 17.16 summarizes the gross fees by personnel category, showing total fees, average fees per person, and average fees per chargeable hour. Figure 17.17 summarizes projected hours by personnel classification for the upcoming year. It includes both chargeable and all nonchargeable time classifications. This report results from the detailed monthly plan by individual billing rate class. Figure 17.18 summarizes total, chargeable, local nonchargeable, and firmwide project payroll

Figure 17.17 Total hours by classification.

	Total	Vacation	Holiday	Overtime	Regular available	Chargeable	Local Nonchg.	Firmwide	Chargeable percent
Ptr	6,915	432	168	627	5,688	2,025	4,038	252	32
Mgr	11,526	720	280	1,046	9,480	7,475	2,931	120	71
Sr	11,526	720	280	1,046	9,480	9,200	1,086	240	87
St	34,577	2,160	840	3,137	28,440	20,700	10,757	120	66
Subtotal	64,544	4,032	1,568	5,856	53,088	39,400	18,812	732	62
Ad	4,610	288	112	418	3,792	0	4,210	0	0
Total	69,154	4,320	1,680	6,273	56,880	39,400	23,022	732	62

Figure 17.18 Payroll distribution—budget preparation.

	Total	Chargeable	Local Nonchg.	Firmwide	Chg. pay as a percent of gross fees	Chg. pay as a percent of total payroll	Total payroll as a percent of gross fee
Ptr	483,109	141,224	237,883	17,575	38	29	130
Mgr	301,130	194,963	48,458	3,836	22	65	35
Sr	157,966	125,874	668	3,163	19	80	24
St	443,024	264,767	97,447	1,553	27	60	44
Subtotal	1,385,229	726,828	384,456	26,127	25	52	48
Ad	65,532	0	4,484	0	0	0	0
Total	1,450,761	726,828	388,940	26,127	25	50	50

Figure 17.19 Hours per person (annualized).

	Total	Per ptr	Chargeable	Local Nonchg.	Firmwide	Overtime
Prt	3	1	675	1,346	84	209
Mgr	5	2	1,495	586	24	209
Sr	5	2	1,840	217	48	209
St	15	5	1,380	717	8	209
Subtotal	28	9	1,407	672	26	209
Ad	2	1	0	2,105	0	209
Total	30	9	1,407	822	26	224

costs by personnel category. It also represents these items as a percentage of gross fees total and total payroll.

The final figure in this budget model, Figure 17.19, summarizes hours per person on an annual basis showing chargeable, local nonchargeable, firmwide, and overtime hours by personnel category.

18

Micros for the Consulting Practitioner

SAM W. BARCUS III
Barcus Nugent Group
Nashville, Tennessee

INTRODUCTION

The microcomputer revolution is under way. Computer power is shifting from those who understand the giant computers to "the rest of us." The instrument of this revolution is the microcomputer.

What can you do with this power? You and your clients can put it to work producing answers to professional and personal questions—questions about investments, taxes, housing costs; questions about files and records; questions about business management, budgeting, and forecasting; questions about history, economic statistics/mathematics, languages—all types of research. Questions about almost anything. More important, questions about how to run your consulting practice more effectively.

You don't need to be a technician to get started. Instead, you simply answer a few basic questions: What is a microcomputer? What will one do for me and my practice? How do I shop for one? How do I run it? What will it cost?

The first question may be the simplest to answer. What is a microcomputer? It's a tool for finding solutions, just as a telephone is a tool for talking to other people. To understand the microcomputer's usefulness, this commonsense description is all you need to know.

In fact, common sense is the best approach to the other four questions and to computers in general. Try not to focus too much on computer jargon and technical arcana. Focus on understanding how the microcomputer can be used as a tool.

WHAT WILL A MICROCOMPUTER DO FOR YOU?

Like an automobile, a microcomputer can get you to places quickly and take you to places you've not been before. More important, the microcomputer does this for your professional and intellectual interests. Of equal significance is the microcomputer's adaptability, which lets you use the micro for a number of the activities in the practice.

I've identified seven areas where the computer can be put to use in your practice. I will use these categories as a guide in discussing and showing you some examples of programs for professional use.

Education

The microcomputer is a potent tool in education. The computer is adaptable, never tires, and provides a different way to learn. The computer can be used with subjects that require drill and practice, such as math and accounting. A microcomputer can combine text, music, and graphics to add impact to the learning environment. Lectures on a particular topic combined with computerized drill and practice and quizzes can improve results, facilitating evaluation and review.

Using a microcomputer is education in itself. The widespread use of computers in business and the home means that everyone needs to know how computers can be used. Colleges, technical schools, and local computer stores usually offer introductory courses and specific training for complex computer programs. A number of the software programs that apply to your practice have educational tutorials that provide basic instruction for the program. Some of the tutorials are interactive, which allows you to problem solve and learn more about the program's features and capabilities.

Accounting and Finance

The microcomputer is a useful tool for managing business finances. Handling numbers is a basic capability for a computer, which is why so many computers are used for accounting. The computer can also perform business analyses including financial projections, forecasts, and statistical analyses. Many of the functions available on the microcomputer have been available until recently only on large computers. A single microcomputer can handle accounting, inventory control, accounts receivable, accounts payable, payroll, word processing, and financial projections. If used properly, a computer can save money and improve productivity for the growing practitioner.

The language of accountancy is numbers. Many items in a business can be identified by some type of number. Items (e.g., inventory) can be broken into components, and each component can be assigned a number. All the pieces of paper that flow in a business can also be tracked by numbers: check numbers, invoice numbers, purchase order numbers, employee numbers, voucher numbers, client numbers, etc. Computers are designed to capture, store, and retrieve all these business numbers.

You can analyze long-term investments, follow the stock market, monitor interest rates, and calculate the return on IRAs if you have the right software. Almost any type of financial analysis can be performed on the microcomputer, including feasibility studies and financial projections for all types of projects. Personal and corporate tax planning is another aspect of financial planning on the microcomputer.

A general purpose program that is very popular with accountants and consultants is the electronic spreadsheet. This program is a computerized version of a columnar pad and lends itself to analyzing similar types of problems. The major difference is that once the problem is defined and entered onto the spreadsheet, many variations of the problem can be analyzed by changing parameters on the sheet and pressing a key for recalculation. The better spreadsheets provide simple command structures, data formatting, manipulation of work sheet segments, mathematical functions, tutorials, good documentation, and powerful print/graph capability. Spreadsheets can be used for tax calculations, trial balances, consolidations, financial statement analysis, depreciation schedules, lease computations, LIFO computations, EPS computations, loan amortizations, trend analysis, and bad debt analysis.

With the success of the spreadsheet program Lotus 1-2-3, software vendors have developed clones and enhanced financial projection and business planning programs. All these programs are designed to be run by the person wanting the analysis, not assigned to someone to "run these numbers through the computer." This direct contact with the computer leads to a higher quality analysis because your idea for analysis can be translated directly into action. Working directly with the computer encourages fiddling, changing, experimenting, trial and error—all the creative things that contribute to a better result.

Accounting packages for microcomputers are also becoming very popular. Features and capabilities that used to be available on large computers are being offered on micro packages. Some of these packages can be used for write-up work and for generating all of the various financial reports, both monthly and year-end. Accounting software is the most intricate, expensive, and difficult set of programs you can buy. There is probably also accounting software written especially for your client's organization, just as there is specific software for accounting and consulting firms. Most of the programs offer modules for each of the accounting areas: general ledger, accounts receivable, accounts payable, inventory. Automated accounting systems can improve the accuracy of record keeping, reduce the time it takes to maintain the records, control finances, and improve cash flow.

Correspondence

Word processing is a perfect application for microcomputers. Word processing works like an electronic typewriter, with many more capabilities. The computer will let you rearrange whatever you've written and display the results on your screen. You can correct typos and syntax; you can even experiment with new page formats. A word processing program instantly adjusts the entire document to reflect all your changes. When your writing is complete, the computer stores the results on a disk for review or further revision. When you connect your computer to a printer, you can print the documents automatically.

Because word processing makes changes easier, you can improve your writing. You can compose as you go, deleting parts that don't fit in and stitching together parts that really say what you want to say. Word processing lets you write the way you think—spontaneously trying things out and pasting together all the best ideas. Even short documents are easier to compose and read because of the power and speed of word processing.

All forms of correspondence that pertain to the practice can be generated on a microcomputer with word processing software. You will need one of the more powerful software packages with such features as word wrap, text underline, insert/delete, search/replace, cut/paste, merge, and powerful print control for: margins, headers, footers, pagination, justification, and formats. You will also need a letter quality printer if you are going to produce client documents on your microcomputer. Proposals and reports are particular candidates for word processing because they usually have so many revisions and you often want to pull parts from earlier documents to create a new version. You can add a spelling checker to your word processor that will scan your finished document and call your attention to words that are not in its dictionary. Matched with a mailing list program, the word processor can be used for client and nonclient mailings.

Although word processing software is powerful, the practice will still require a typewriter for some correspondence. The stand-alone typewriter is still more efficient for typing envelope addresses, specialized forms, and reports requiring unique symbols. Some of the newer typewriters can function as computer printers and as stand-alone typewriters.

Electronic Lists

Besides numbers, long lists are among the things that computers can keep track of easily. Using the right program, it's possible to file and retrieve almost anything. This includes client files, target client lists, tax tickler files, reference materials, almost anything that would fit a card file or Rolodex.

The real power of the microcomputer is evident when you want to cross-reference topics. List programs will allow you to retrieve almost any combination of topics that you want to examine. There are two types of electronic lists programs: data base managers and file managers. A file manager is the more limited of the two, storing data as a single file of individual records. For example, each book in your professional library would become a record on your electronic filing system. Data base managers tend to be more flexible than file managers. This means that additional information can be added readily and different data bases linked together. You may have a data base of target clients and a data base of practice development time and expenses. A data base manager could link these together and generate reports for marketing analysis and tax purposes.

Data base management systems are the computer's way of keeping track of information. Working with computer-stored files, you can store, sort, collect, and summarize information about your practice that you couldn't keep up with by hand. You can keep track of mailing lists and targeted mailings; sales summaries by service/partner/client/department; contents of professional journals and magazines; client portfolios; price lists; and other pertinent data. Information is stored so that you can retrieve it by different codes or cross-references. In your client file you can locate your client by last name, first name, company, title, zip code, city, state, project type, service code, annual billings—by any code you specify.

When you are evaluating data base systems, you should look for certain features in addition to matching your specific needs to the capabilities of the program. The system should let you set up your own forms for entering and updating information. You should be able to retrieve information according to your specifications and combinations of various criteria. Updating capability should be for specific records or for the entire file based on changing all records that meet a certain criterion. You should be able to change the format of the file both to add additional fields and to change the definition of existing fields. The better data base managers will exchange information with other programs in particular spreadsheets and word processors. Finally, you should be able to define various types of reports with tailored formats and computed values that are printed on the reports but not maintained on the file.

Data Banks

Not only can microcomputers communicate with you, they can talk to other computers and data banks. Data banks gather, store, and distribute data. Microcomputers talk to data banks by using a modem and the telephone line. This opens up other possibilities such as working at home, following stock prices, checking on the commodities market, or calling another computer to send a message or a report. You can also browse through specialized libraries, complete your banking, check airline schedules, or access statistical and economic data bases.

First, you have to find the right data bank. There are currently over 1700 available. Some popular ones include The Source, Dow Jones News, Mead Data Central, CompuServe, BRS/After Dark, Dialog's Knowledge Index, and NewsNet. Nearly all data services charge a one-time hookup fee plus user fees for the amount of time you are attached to the system. These fees are in addition to phone charges. The surface has only been scratched because there are so many new areas to explore with your microcomputer linked to the outside world.

Practice Management

The microcomputer can be used as a practice management tool. In simply helping to organize the practice, the micro's word processing capability can record the initial business plan and then recall that plan when it's time to make changes. A data base system can list the current client base with all the appropriate detail, capture economic statistics, save market research, and store valuable data about competition. A spreadsheet can do the initial financial projections and then be saved and recalled at a later date for comparison of actual results with the plan. On a monthly basis, the micro can be used to analyze the financial performance of the practice: utilization, gross services, operating costs, net services, realization, and contribution to profit. A staff-skills profile can be developed and placed on the micro for staff planning, performance evaluation, and proposal preparation.

For individual engagements the micro can be an effective productivity tool. The work plan section of a proposal can be used as the basic input for using a project management package or a spreadsheet to manage a project. Milestones would be identified and responsibilities assigned along with time estimates. Additional detail could be added to the tasks and they could be resequenced if necessary. The job could also be costed out as initially planned and recosted as actual hours are incurred and as the staff mix changes.

The micro can be used to facilitate engagement documentation and control. Work paper content forms can be maintained on the micro and printed as required. Generalized forms for gathering background information, interviewing, summarizing data, and documenting key events can also be designed and saved on the micro for retrieval as necessary. Checklists for diagnostic reviews or additions to regular work programs are easy to develop and maintain on the micro. Memos on client meetings and progress reports can be prepared using a word processor or the limited word processing capability in one of the integrated packages. For more sophisticated and complex jobs, there are software packages that can prepare Gantt charts and network diagrams.

Marketing, Business and Community

The micro can play a role in developing the practice and helping it grow. Once the business plan has been developed, a specific marketing plan can be devised. Some of its components can be pulled directly from the practice business plan and used to develop specific marketing activities. Various marketing data bases created from research are useful for focusing the marketing activities. Word processing can be used as the recording device for the marketing plan, though idea processing software is invaluable for "brainstorming." Recommendations from satisfied clients can be captured on a data base, used to develop additional projects, and included in proposals. Target clients can be tracked via a data base "tickler file" with all the appropriate information for follow-up and sales tracking. The micro can be used to develop promotional material, speeches, and workshops and to write articles for publications. Keeping track of business and professional activities is another use for the microcomputer.

Micros are particularly important for the proposal process. Proposals can be letters of understanding, oral presentations, or more extensive formal documents. Besides the obvious use of word processing to prepare documents, micros can substantially improve and expedite the proposal process. Background research can be stored on the micro and recalled for a particular situation. Results of a bidder's conference can be recorded and used as input to the proposal. Information gathered from initial meetings with the potential client can be entered on the micro and retrieved to fulfill specific requirements for a proposal. Work plans can be developed using spreadsheets and modified for "what if" analysis. If an integrated package is being used to develop the project time estimates, these can be automatically moved into the written document with graphics to enhance the proposal. If an oral presentation is required, the micro can be used to develop overheads, graphics, or slides.

QUESTIONS TO ASK BEFORE BUYING

What Do I Want to Do with a Computer?

Establish priorities. You first need to spend some time deciding what you want your computer to do. Consider present and future applications. This means that the first step may be finding out what computers can do. Remember, a computer is a tool that manipulates dots and the dots must be available.

What Will It Cost to Do the Things I Want to Do?

Consider the costs to get started in addition to hidden costs. A "bargain" computer may be great for learning but probably needs enhancements to run business and productivity software.

Is It Expandable?

The power of some microcomputers can be expanded and other devices hooked to the computer as new uses are discovered. The key is understanding the limitations of the particular machine you are considering and thinking about both its immediate and future uses. The important question is: How much can the machine be expanded and how much will expansion cost?

Where Can I Get Service If the Computer Breaks Down?

Manufacturers and/or retailers frequently offer 90-day warranties on equipment. For a fee, some will extend the warranty for the remainder of the year. You can also get a service contract to cover the machine after the warranty expires. This may mean taking the computer back to the dealer or shipping it back to the factory.

Where Can I Get Moral Support and Technical Advice?

Computers are still complex business tools. Manufacturers sometimes offer toll-free hot lines to answer questions. Dealers will provide some free training and additional training for a fee. Workshops and seminars provide additional information, and user groups, books, and magazines help minimize problems.

Where Am I Going to Put the Computer?

Microcomputers are small, but they do require some table or desk space. They also require cables that hook together all the parts (monitor, disk drive, printer, modem, plotter, etc.) and power outlets. You will need to consider lighting and seating in order to ensure a comfortable environment for operating your computer.

Who Will Use the Computer?

If the computer is for the entire staff, guidelines should be established for allowing access to people interested in using the machine. Some systems—such as accounting packages—allow access to more than one person, but most microcomputer programs are oriented toward exclusive individual use.

SELECTING THE RIGHT COMPUTER

Evaluate Software

Software determines what the computer can do. It is very much like records for your stereo: Without software, the computer can't do anything. Again, as with records, it is important to consider software first or you may not be happy with what you "hear" on your computer. As mentioned earlier, you first ask yourself what you want to do with your computer and then look for software that fits your need. Now you are ready to begin evaluating the various software options. There are over 20,000 software packages on the marketplace, so the search can be frustrating. Here are a few suggestions that will help you narrow the search:

1. Look for quality both in the program and the instruction books that are included with the program. You can begin to assess this by asking for a demonstration. Be sure the person showing you the program knows something about the program.
2. Ask about compatibility. A program disk will usually only run on one type of computer or that computer's clones. Compatibility has to do with the type of computer and the computer's operating system. The operating system is like the conductor of an orchestra: It makes

all the parts work in harmony. Your software has to be compatible with both the computer hardware and the operating system.

3. Find out about the power of the program. This means assessing what the program can actually do. It also means looking at the features of the program to determine how it stacks up against competition. For example, some word processing programs are little more than text editors that don't show you how your letter will look when it's printed. Power also has to do with the speed of the program. Some list programs are slow if the list is excessively long.

4. Try out the program to see if it is easy to use. It should have menus or command windows that are straightforward. Screens should have a consistent look, and interaction with the program should be smooth and consistent. Help should be available on the screen and should relate to where you are in the program. Most of the functions should be intuitive and easy to remember when you use the program irregularly.

5. Determine if the program is competitively priced based on its features and capabilities.

6. Ask what type of support is provided. This can range from local dealer support to an 800 number. Also ask about the publisher's return policy for disks that develop flaws and for programs that really don't meet your expectations. Is there any type of warranty?

Select Hardware

You start by asking: What do I want this computer to do for me? This is where jargon can often get in the way. You're not so much concerned with RAMS and ROMS, bits and bytes as you are with what the computer is capable of doing. Four factors are of concern: power, ease of use, cost, and service/support.

Power. A computer's power has to do with several elements. One is the central processing unit (CPU). The CPU is the brain of the computer and does the "thinking" for the machine. One measure of a computer's power is the bit structure of the CPU, which is something like the difference in car engines and horsepower (6-cylinder versus 8-cylinder). The first personal computer CPUs were 8-bit, and the newer ones are either 16-bit or 32-bit. For your purpose, the major difference is speed and the size and complexity of computer programs that the more powerful CPUs will handle. Also, the type of CPU will determine the operating system (conductor) that the machine will support. Remember that the operating system determines which programs will operate on the machine.

The internal memory also determines a computer's power. The internal memory is where programs reside when the computer is operating. The amount of internal memory determines the knowledge that the computer has while it is working on a problem. This knowledge is comprised of the operating system, the program you are running (e.g., word processing), and your information (e.g., proposal). Memory is usually called RAM and ROM. ROM is the part of memory that helps get the machine started and stays there even when the machine goes off. RAM is the part of the machine where the operating system resides with your program and your data. This memory goes blank when the electricity is turned off. Memory's capacity is measured in thousands of characters (bytes is the jargon) and might range from 64K RAM up to 640K RAM. The more RAM, the more the computer can do. RAM can also be saved on a floppy or hard disk (external) memory for future use. External memory capacity ranges from around 360K up to 30 or 40 million characters.

Expansion is another aspect of power. This is important because as you get comfortable with your computer, you will begin to find a variety of new things to do with it. Look for a system with expansion slots that will let you add telecommunications equipment, printers, graphic plotters, and control devices for operating other kinds of equipment. An expandable machine will be able to grow with your interests and offers a better value.

Ease of use. This may be the most important criterion. The instruction manuals that come with the personal computer are a good indicator of how easy the system will be to learn and use. At first, you will need these books to learn the basics, so be sure they are easy to follow and comfortable to work with and find things in. Later on, these books will be returned to when something new occurs or you try to do something you have not done in a while. If you can't make sense of the books, you are going to have a difficult time with the machine. Manuals can be fairly intimidating, but remember you don't have to absorb them all at once. The instruction books should have the following qualities:

- They should be plain and clear and free of jargon.
- They should be well organized and show a sensible progression.
- They should give you a feel for the machine so that you begin to understand its components.

Look at the manuals to see if they are readable and straightforward; you will have to live with them for a long time.

The keyboard is probably the next most important aspect related to ease of use. Keyboards should be detached and have separate keys rather than a pressure-sensitive surface. Keyboard "feel" like that on a good quality typewriter is important. Layout is critical, too, because placement of function keys and special purpose keys can make a big difference.

Monitors also make a difference. Although you can hook your computer to a TV, the resolution will be fuzzy for numbers and words. To test image sharpness, look at a display of upper- and lowercase text both in standard and inverse modes. If you are going to use the system for graphics, be sure to test it with different graphics packages.

Cost.   Do not inadvertently buy a system that cannot do all the things you want just to save a few dollars. There is a big difference between the cost of a computer and the cost of a usable computer system. Also, remember that the costs can add up when you identify all the components you need to get started. Some computer consoles start at $1000; but when you add the cost of the other necessary items, the cost can go to $5000 quickly.

Service.   When the computer does not work, what happens next? The dealer from whom you purchased the computer will usually service your machine. The level of service that dealers will and can provide varies. Some have full-fledged service centers with trained technicians and an inventory of parts. Others maintain a limited inventory of parts and part-time or contracted technicians. In some cases, you may have to ship your computer back to the manufacturer to have it fixed. If you bought your computer from a mail order operation, you may have a problem getting any service. If you are technically oriented, fixing your own computer may be the least expensive approach—but most people want service that is established, accessible, and competent. One other approach is a protection plan that covers all repair and maintenance for a yearly fee. Such plans usually cost about 10 percent of the system's purchase price.

Hardware Specifics

Disk drives.   Disks and disk drives are like records and record players. The main purpose of a disk is to store programs and/or data when you turn your computer off. Disks store data magnetically and can be erased by magnet and metal detectors. The current standard is 5¼ inch with data stored on one or both sides. These disks can store the equivalent of 125 to 500 single-spaced pages of information. Disks have to be placed into disk drives to feed information to the computer. Disk drives are the record player portion of the system, and they have to be compatible with your computer. If you work with lots of data, you may need a hard disk drive, particularly with accounting programs. The hard disk drive is about 10 times faster than the floppy drives and stores from

10 to 100 million characters of information. These drives cost more ($2000 to $3000 each), and you will still need at least one floppy with your system. Micro floppy disks (3½ inch) are new and are beginning to be used on portable computers because of their size and durability.

Monitors.   You can always use a TV as the system's monitor; but if you are going to work with words and numbers, you are better off with a real monitor. Monitors produce much sharper images than TV screens. There are basically three types:

1. Composite color, which are best for graphics
2. RGB (red, green, blue), which produce truer colors and sharper images
3. Monochromatic, which are best for words and numbers

You will want a monitor that can display 25 lines and 80 columns. A monitor's resolution is measured by megahertz and pixel count. The higher the MHz and the more pixels, the sharper the resolution. A monitor with a nonglare screen will minimize eyestrain.

Modems.   These devices let one computer talk to another over the phone lines. The modem takes the computer's digital signal and converts it to a tone that the phone system understands. With a modem you can "talk" to computers anywhere in the world and tap into all sorts of commercial data bases. There are two types of modems: acoustic and direct connect. Direct connect modems work better because they hook directly to the phone line. Modems plug into one of the computer's ports or snap into a slot in the back of the computer. They transfer data at rates of from 30 to 240 characters per second. Be sure your modem can answer calls as well as make them. Full duplex modems can send and receive data at the same time. There are "smart" modems that can automatically dial phone numbers and be programmed to place calls at certain times. You will also need some communications software to make your modem and computer work together harmoniously.

Printers.   Most of the computer interaction will be between the keyboard and screen, but you will also need a printer. The basic trade-off is between quality and speed. Dot matrix printers are faster (100 to 400 cps) than letter quality and also cost less. They use tiny pins that strike an inked ribbon to print clusters of dots that form characters (like the bank's time-and-temperature sign). Look for printers that can form characters in a denser matrix than the usual 5 × 7 grid. Letter quality printers, though slower (10 to 60 cps) and more costly, can achieve typewriterlike print quality. Most letter quality printers use a daisy wheel with a raised letter on each "petal." Type fonts can be changed by putting on a new daisy wheel. Laser and ink jet printers are expensive but produce superb quality printing. Laser printers scorch images on the paper, and ink jet printers spray characters on the paper. Other printer features to consider include proportional spacing, buffer capacity, baffles, and bidirectional printing. Also, be sure to match the capabilities of your software to your printer.

Other Considerations

The amount and quality of help you get after you bring the computer back to the office will determine whether or not the computer really becomes part of the practice. To get the benefits of computers, you need front-end learning time. You have to know your computer and the software before you can begin to enjoy computing and before it benefits your practice. There are plenty of sources of help, so take advantage of them. Books, manuals, courses, and user groups all help, but remember that each takes an investment of time. As in any new learning experience, you have to make a commitment and invest adequate time or you will be disappointed.

To assist your effort to evaluate software and hardware configurations for your practice, I have developed software/hardware critique sheets (Figures 18.1 and 18.2). The purpose of the work sheets is to add some objectivity to the selection process. First, review each feature on the work sheet and assign a weight based on your particular needs. Then review the software and/or hardware system you are considering and rate the system's performance. Calculate an overall score by multiplying the weighting factor times the rating and summing for an overall total. When working on a software and hardware evaluation use the following weighting and rating scales to complete the sheets. A pricing work sheet is also included (Figure 18.3).

Weighting factor	Rating
1 = Unimportant	1 = Poor
2 = Somewhat important	2 = Below average
3 = Mildly important	3 = Average
4 = Important	4 = Above average
5 = Moderately important	5 = Excellent
6 = Very important	
7 = Extremely important	

DEALING WITH COMPUTER VENDORS

Even though computers are getting easier to use and understand, they are still a complex product and are difficult to buy in a retail environment. To help you make the right decision, the salespeople have to know their products in intricate detail. They also have to understand what you want

Figure 18.1 Software critique sheet.

Characteristics	Weighting factors	Rating	Score
Program			
Ease of start-up	————	————	————
Screen layout	————	————	————
Meaningful prompts	————	————	————
Input protection	————	————	————
Error recovery	————	————	————
Help screen	————	————	————
Consistency	————	————	————
Ease of use	————	————	————
Restart/terminate ability	————	————	————
User flexibility	————	————	————
Originality	————	————	————
Limited use of jargon	————	————	————
Use of color	————	————	————
Use of sound	————	————	————
Use of graphics	————	————	————
Content quality	————	————	————
Proper performance	————	————	————
Overall usefulness	————	————	————
Subtotal			————
Documentation			
Clarity	————	————	————
Style	————	————	————
Completeness	————	————	————
Organization	————	————	————
Graphics	————	————	————
Subtotal			————
Overall total			═══════

Package title: ————————————
Publisher: ————————————

and help you find the right system. After you've bought your computer, they still need to be there for service and support. As with other kinds of products and vendors, there is a wide range of offerings from very good to very bad.

Types of Dealers

There are basically four types of computer resellers:

1. Independent dealers who run their own businesses
2. Franchise dealers

Figure 18.2   Hardware critique sheet.

Characteristics	Weighting factors	Rating	Score
Hardware			
Keyboard layout	_____	_____	_____
Video display	_____	_____	_____
Graphics	_____	_____	_____
Color capability	_____	_____	_____
Sound/music capability	_____	_____	_____
Language capability	_____	_____	_____
Memory capacity	_____	_____	_____
System expansion capability	_____	_____	_____
Interfacing capability	_____	_____	_____
Peripheral devices	_____	_____	_____
Execution time	_____	_____	_____
Communications capability	_____	_____	_____
Flexibility	_____	_____	_____
Service support	_____	_____	_____
Software availability	_____	_____	_____
Warranty	_____	_____	_____
Subtotal			_____
Documentation			
Clarity	_____	_____	_____
Style	_____	_____	_____
Completeness	_____	_____	_____
Organization	_____	_____	_____
Graphics	_____	_____	_____
Subtotal			_____
Overall total			_____

Model: _____

Manufacturer: _____

3. Department stores with computer centers

4. Chain computer stores

Each outlet has its advantages and disadvantages. Some dealers concentrate on a few major brands and attempt to know those brands inside and out. This approach works well if the salespeople really know their product. Other dealers try to carry most of the brands on the market, but this really spreads even the best salespeople thin. Some dealers try to mass merchandise computers in the same way as appliances. This works only for the very simple, limited machines.

Many dealers do not specialize in business accounting applications; they focus more on high-volume, low-end systems. Salespeople in these

Figure 18.3   System-pricing work sheet.

Hardware		Accessories and Supplies	
Processor, disk drive, and keyboard	$ _____	Floppy discs	$ _____
		Paper	$ _____
Additional memory	$ _____	Forms	$ _____
Additional disk drive	$ _____	Disk storage case	$ _____
Monitor	$ _____	Disk cleaner	$ _____
Printer	$ _____	Furniture	$ _____
Expansion cards	$ _____		
Interface cards	$ _____	Total accessories	$ _____
Graphics	$ _____	(B)	
Modem	$ _____		
Other peripherals	$ _____		
Total hardware	$ _____		
Software		**Miscellaneous**	
Operating system	$ _____	Service contract	$ _____
Utilities	$ _____	Training	$ _____
Spreadsheet	$ _____	Installation	$ _____
Word processing	$ _____	Insurance	$ _____
Graphics	$ _____		
Data base management	$ _____	Total other costs	$ _____
Other software:		(C)	
_____	$ _____		
_____	$ _____		
_____	$ _____		
Total software	$ _____		
Total hardware/software	$ _____	Total estimated costs	$ _____
(A)		(A+B+C)	

stores are not accustomed to solution selling and may emphasize product availablity rather than needs. Do your homework and find out whether the computer dealer specializes in particular industries and systems. The best approach is to find a computer dealer who has experience with a specific type of business.

Salespeople

The salesperson becomes a critical element in the process of buying a personal computer. The better ones focus on your needs first rather than on the particular computer they are trying to sell. Find a salesperson with whom you are comfortable, one who seems to be interested in meeting your needs and who seems to know the store's products and capabilities. A good salesperson can give you a complete demonstration of both hardware and software with a little hands-on practice to ensure that you are selecting the right system.

Service and Support

Even after you have found a good dealer and salesperson, there is one other critical area: the dealer's service and support policies. The better dealers will have the capability of fixing most minor computer problems and will stock replacement parts. Some dealers may even loan you a machine when yours has to be shipped away for repairs. Support is also important. This means doing all the things necessary to get you up and running: assembling hardware, loading software, and making sure everything works together. The dealer should spend time with you going over setup and operating procedures. When problems do occur, someone should be available (at least over the phone) to solve problems. Really good dealers offer training programs and seminars that get you up to speed on your machine and on the different software packages you have purchased. Even if there is a cost involved, it is money well spent.

There are a multitude of computer systems available and many types of computer dealers selling systems. This chapter has explored ways in which you might put a microcomputer to use in your practice and grow professionally at the same time. Before you buy a micro, or add to your current system, consider the questions raised in the chapter and study the suggested evaluation and selection steps. If you do your homework—think about how you will use the computer, consider mainstream computer systems, and survey competent dealers—the end result will be productive and profitable. Remember, it is your responsibility to think about your needs and keep the dealer focused on configuring a system that matches those needs.

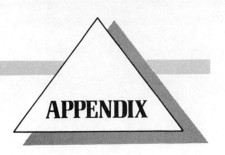
APPENDIX

Checklists and Work Plans in Key Practice Areas

A. Business Planning

INTRODUCTION

Business planning is forecasting developments for a specific period of time in order to formulate a course of action. The course of action is spelled out in a document called the business plan. Effective planning enables the organization to control its direction and stabilize it. Planning is an effective way of guiding the organization through a changing environment. Planning enables the company to achieve results on a broader scale rather than constantly reacting to events on a day-to-day basis.

Planning in an entrepreneurial business means two or three people sitting together and discussing where the business is going. Formal long-range planning systems are unnecessary in a small firm. The entrepreneur usually does not have training or experience in planning. Plans for the smaller firm have to be flexible because of the potential impact of external events.

THE PLANNING PROCESS

The planning process should be viewed as two stages. Initially, during the *strategic planning* phase, the long-term goals of the organization are established. During this phase, the organization should address major issues, such as the markets in which it will compete or long-term facilities requirements. The second stage, *tactical planning*, is the allocation of production, financial, and manpower resources to achieve established goals. In general, tactical planning is the process by which management will direct the company's growth toward its objectives; the budgeting process is the link between today's operational capabilities and the objectives derived from tactical planning.

On a broad basis, planning can be viewed as the process by which management focuses on influences that can impact a company. Those influences can be classified into three categories: external, internal, and management.

1. External—largely beyond the company's control
   a. Development of new or improved competitive products with an advantage in cost, quality, or availability
   b. Changes in the volume or type of business of present or potential customers, which in turn affect the supplier's volume of sales or alter the specifications required from the supplier
   c. Additional competitors furnishing the same goods or services
   d. Changes in industry credit policies
   e. Improvements in materials or parts available from competitive suppliers
   f. Improvements in machinery and equipment
   g. Development of new packaging and transportation methods
   h. Changes in economic and market conditions for the industry or business as a whole
2. Internal—established by the characteristics of the company
   a. Financial resources
   b. Capabilities of managerial, technical, and other staff and employees
   c. Capabilities of present machinery and equipment
   d. Size and location of plant
   e. Costs of producing goods and services
3. Management—reflecting the desires of the owner and management
   a. Desire to diversify or to shift dependence from a product with uncertain demand
   b. Desire to grow in order to produce greater profits, more opportunities for employees, etc.

c. Desire to raise the quality of products and services

d. Desire to move into additional geographic markets

e. Desire to increase profitability of money invested

IMPORTANCE OF PLANNING TO AN ENTREPRENEURIAL FIRM

While planning is necessary for all firms, it can be particularly important for entrepreneurial businesses since:

1. Planning helps smaller businesses to identify and allocate scarce resources to move the company in the desired direction. Without an explicit plan, resources may be used to meet immediate needs that may conflict with long-term objectives.
2. Smaller businesses cannot absorb mistakes as well as larger firms; therefore, risks must be continually identified. Planning helps small businesses to identify these potential hazards earlier and to prepare a contingency plan.
3. The flexibility common to many small firms enables easier implementation of plans. Small firms can make major changes in direction. Therefore, a smaller firm can often quickly capitalize on economic or market shifts if it has developed the appropriate plans.

ELEMENTS OF GOOD BUSINESS PLANNING

The Business Plan

1. A brief description of the company's present practices in all important areas, including products, purchasing, quality control, labor relations, channels of distribution, and production
2. A list of the principal external factors—government regulation, the economy, competition, the community environment, technology, and the labor markets
3. A list of changes expected in present practices and external factors over the next few years
4. An assessment of the strengths and weaknesses of the firm and its products
5. A forecast of expected financial results for the next 2 years
6. A financial analysis identifying anticipated problems (cash shortage, low profits, etc.) or potential actions (investment of cash, expanded advertising, etc.)
7. Performance projections under alternate assumptions such as decline in sales, shortage of material, and increase in labor costs
8. Contingency plans for action under various scenarios
9. If the business plan is for starting a new venture or raising additional financing, it includes the following:
   a. Financing requirements
   b. Detailed marketing information
   c. Relevant technical factors
   d. Sensitivity analysis indicating the critical factors
   e. Resumes for key personnel
   f. Bank and investor relationships
   g. Past and potential problem areas

Common Characteristics

A significant aspect of planning for small business involves evaluating and deciding upon such changes to the business as capital investment, new products, or the acquisition of a computer. Plans include not only a solid economic evaluation but also an assessment of the risks involved. While the methods of individual organizations may vary, common characteristics would include the following:

1. Plans are kept as simple as possible.
2. Plans are flexible enough to change with unexpected events.
3. Plans are supported by information that is complete, accurate, and usefully organized.
4. Planning is approached in an organized manner.
5. The plan includes the actions to be taken and not just the desired results.
6. The managers who will be responsible for these actions participate in their planning.
7. The planning horizon is clearly defined.
8. Plans are effectively communicated and monitored.
9. Motivation and controls exist within the organization so that it will operate according to plans.
10. The plan relates to the financial statements.

Role of the Consultant

The assistance rendered by the consultant is not necessarily any different from the results that could be produced by the internal planning process of the company itself. Consequently, a consultant could be effective in a situation in which there is no current planning process. In addition, the consultant might provide input to the existing planning efforts if an outside and independent opinion might be useful. Finally, a consultant can work closely with the individuals having planning responsibilities and, through this interaction, enhance the organization's planning capability.

In a planning engagement, a consultant can render assistance in a number of different areas.

1. *Develop the methods for planning:* Where a company does not have a formal planning approach and does not have the staff or the capability of developing an approach, the consultant can develop the features of a good planning system.
2. *Evaluate the methods for long-range planning:* If the company is capable of developing plans with its own planning function, then the consultant can evaluate the various aspects of the planning methods.
3. *Instruct members of management about planning:* While a company may have a planning capability, chances are the resources will be limited. One of the tenets of planning is to have the individuals who will be responsible for the fulfillment of the plans actually prepare the plans themselves. Planning staffs should be small and should not be charged with preparing the plans. Outside assistance can instruct the members of top and middle management in proper planning techniques.
4. *Suggest techniques to be used in the planning process:* Consultants should be familiar with techniques that could be utilized to implement the goals and objectives of the planning process. Financial reporting systems, financial projection systems, and other subsystems of the planning process can be suggested. The purpose of these subsystems is to mechanize the process of capturing data and to provide feedback to management. Effective reporting systems can improve the quality of the planning process.
5. *Play the "devil's advocate":* Perhaps the most effective role for the consultant would be playing devil's advocate with regard to the goals and objectives of the company. The consultant can suggest additional factors to be considered in the development of goals and objectives.
6. *Conduct sessions to determine the cause of variances:* As a follow-on to the development of and instruction in a planning methodology, the consultant can conduct a series of sessions aimed at exploring the causes of variances from the plans. This activity takes place after the fact rather than before. As a result of this interaction, the company should be able to reset its goals and objectives and explore additional alternatives.

B. Emerging Business Management Analysis

INTRODUCTION

As the consultant gains knowledge and understanding of the client's business he or she is in the position to develop substantial recommendations that should contribute to the client's economic success. For entrepreneurs the business usually represents their major source of income, the annuity for their retirement, and possible inheritance for their children. They are therefore interested in the profitability and success of the business.

The need for sound management techniques, including adequate organization, good planning, and good operational information do not vary by the size of the business. Small businesses rarely have the management personnel to handle all the necessary functions. Owners of small business have to apply limited resources to a variety of needs in order to achieve their business objectives. Leverage in this process is timely and adequate information to assess the status and direction of the business. The following checklist can be used to interview the entrepreneur, assess the management practices and make recommendations on items that are of major importance to the client.

A. BUSINESS PLANNING

1. Has the company developed clear and formal objectives for the business?
2. Are the objectives quantified in terms of rate of return, growth, market share, product or service development?
3. At what stage are the company's products/services in their life cycle?
4. Are there clear objectives for each function in the company?
5. Do the functions have quantified objectives?
6. Is the company planning expansion into new products or markets?
7. Has management defined the critical success factors for the business?
8. Does the company have a formal business plan including:
   a. Description of the business?
   b. Market?
   c. Competition?
   d. Location?
   e. Management?
   f. Key personnel?
   g. Key financial data:
      (1). Financial projections?
      (2). Cash flow projections?
      (3). Break-even analysis?

B. FINANCIAL PLANNING AND CONTROL

1. Are annual operating budgets prepared?
2. Are the budgets consistent with the objectives of the company?
3. Are individual functional area managers responsible for preparing their own sections of the budget?
4. Are budgets based on detailed assumptions that are evaluated each year?
5. Do budget assumptions consider:
   a. Changes that may impact revenues or costs?
   b. Capacity?

    c. Manpower requirements?

    d. Market trends?

    e. Sales mix?

    f. Contribution by product/service?

6. Are budgets sufficiently detailed to provide a measure of control:

    a. By time period?

    b. By area of responsibility?

    c. By line item?

7. Are budget assumptions consistently and thoroughly documented to provide the capability for variance analysis?

8. Does financial reporting provide:

    a. Reports comparing actual performance to budgets?

    b. Basic financial reports:

        (1). Balance sheet?

        (2). Statement of income?

        (3). Sources and uses of funds?

    c. Exceptions?

    d. Percentages of revenue for major line items?

    e. Statistics and ratios that focus attention on the "critical success factors"?

    f. Measures of profitability by:

        1. Product/service?

        2. Customer group?

        3. Geographic area?

        4. Salesperson/account executive?

9. Are the financial reports produced on a timely basis?

10. Are variances documented and plans adjusted accordingly?

11. Is cash flow monitored on a routine basis?

12. Is there a linkage between budgets and cash flow analysis?

13. Does the company have an adequate credit line?

14. Has the company made adequate use of leverage?

C. MANAGEMENT

1. Does the company have sufficient numbers of qualified people at the right levels to perform the following functions:

    a. Marketing?

    b. Finance?

    c. Production?

    d. Technical development?

    e. Personnel and administration?

2. Do the managers have the appropriate background and skills to manage these functions?

3. Is the organization structure defined?

4. Are the responsibilities of each job defined?

5. Does the company use procedure manuals so that:

    a. Many decisions can be handled on a routine basis?

    b. New people can be trained easily?

6. Are managers given authority for decisions and results?

7. Are individuals aware of their duties and responsibilities?

8. Does the company have a formal management program including employee appraisals?
9. Is employee turnover a problem?
10. Is there excessive overtime?
11. Does employee morale appear high?
12. Is the company people-oriented?

D. MARKETING/SALES AND ACCOUNTS RECEIVABLE

1. Does the company know its share of the market?
2. Does the company know the size of the total market?
3. Does the company have a formal price structure?
4. Does the company analyze the relationship of volume changes to changes in price?
5. Does the company know the stage of growth in the product cycle for each of its products?
6. Is the company aware of new trends?
7. Does the company evaluate the competition?
8. Does the company assess the performance of its products relative to customers' needs?
9. Does the company analyze the profitability of its products?
10. Does the company review the effectiveness of its marketing and distribution activities?
11. Does the company review the effectiveness of its marketing support?
12. Does the company evaluate the adequacy of its customer service?
13. Does the company monitor sales performance?
14. Are substantial variances from the sales forecast adequately analyzed and explained?
15. Does the company consistently review back orders?
16. Does the company have a formal credit policy?
17. Does the company calculate the number of days sales in receivables?
18. Is firm action taken against excessively late payers?

E. PURCHASING AND INVENTORY

1. Is company purchasing tied to sales forecasts and current inventory levels?
2. Does the company know the correct purchasing points for its inventory items?
3. In planning inventory purchases, are the following taken into account:
   a. Demand patterns?
   b. Usage?
   c. Lead time?
4. Are stock levels consistent with operating needs?
5. Does the company maintain historical purchase information?
6. Does the company evaulate vendor performance?
7. Are payments made to take advantage of available discounts?
8. Does the company produce to stock and/or to order?
9. Has management analyzed inventories (ABC or 80/20 rules) to determine which items represent the major investment?

10. Is there a report that combines:
    a. Inventory on hand, by item?
    b. Goods on order?
    c. Goods in process?
    d. Unfilled sales orders?
11. Do reports include a calculation of inventory turnover by item or in total?

F. PROFITABILITY ANALYSIS

1. Does the company use a costing system to:
   a. Develop product costs to be used in setting selling prices?
   b. Valuing inventories?
   c. Provide a basis for developing a profit plan by pricing the sales forecast?
2. Does the costing system provide management with each product's contribution to company profit?
3. Does the costing system identify fixed and variable costs?
4. Does the costing system identify direct costs?
5. In establishing selling prices, are direct costs and contribution margin considered?
6. Are reports generated showing products or classes of products with the highest contribution margins?
7. Does management use contribution analysis to:
   a. Select the products to purchase/manufacture and sell?
   b. Decide whether to make or buy?
   c. Select the most profitable use of capacity?
   d. Optimize the use of limited resources?
   e. Add new product lines and eliminate old ones?
   f. Develop promotions to meet competition or move inventory?

C. Evaluating and Selecting a Computer System

INTRODUCTION

As computers become increasingly common in business, many executives are asking themselves, "What computer should I buy?" Before this question can be answered, a business person should ask a different question, "Do I need a computer?" With the advent of microcomputers, prices have dropped dramatically and many smaller organizations have installed a computer system. However, each business should assess its specific accounting and information requirements before purchasing a computer system.

There are two major activities in acquiring a computer system. The first activity is to understand the needs of the business and match the computer system to those needs. The second activity is to properly install the computer system with new procedures and training. An effectively installed computer system can translate into benefits:

Order processing—quicker deliveries and more accurate order statistics
Accounts receivable—faster routine billing and collection
Inventory—reduced investment and faster availability

Purchasing—better cash management and vendor analysis
Payroll—timely processing and labor cost analysis
General ledger—timely financial reporting and exceptions analysis
Production planning—efficient use of production facilities

The following work plan provides the basis for a methodical evaluation and selection of a computer system to ensure a successful installation.

TASK I: CONDUCT A FEASIBILITY STUDY.

A. Perform a preliminary review of the business.
1. What are the business plans? In what direction is the company going?
2. What are management objectives? Are there business problems?
3. Is there something in the plan that makes it difficult to predict the company's needs?
4. Can a computer offer benefits to the organization? Are there areas that should be computerized? Can the computer provide a competitive edge?
5. Can the organization afford a computer? Does management have time for the project?

B. Gather pertinent data for analysis. The data you need to gather for the client analysis include:
1. Budgets
2. Organization chart
3. Job descriptions
4. Business plans
5. Financial information and projections
6. Marketplace information

C. Determine how a computer can benefit the business. In order to determine the value of a computer to the organization, you have to examine the business plans and objectives.
1. Where is the company positioned in the marketplace, with competition, financial performance?
2. Is the company growing or declining? Is the company entering new markets or developing new products?
3. How will the company reach its objectives and plans? What resources will be needed?

D. Determine which application systems offer potential benefits for the business. Based on the fact finding and your understanding of the business priorities, help decide which computer applications would best support the business. Focus on the major applications as a starting point for the discussion.

E. Assess the business climate and organization. Can this business implement a computer successfully?

F. Estimate approximate costs. The cost estimate is determined by the size of the computer needed by the business. Computer needs can be classified by number of work stations:
1. Single work station (a single microcomputer)
2. Several simultaneous work stations (several microcomputers or a single small minicomputer with terminals)
3. Multiple high-volume work stations (standard minicomputer with terminals)

The internal resources required to select and implement the computer also represent a cost and should be quantified.

G. Determine the areas in which a computer could benefit the business and evaluate the approximate costs involved in acquiring a system.

TASK **II**: DEFINE REQUIREMENTS.

A. Review the results of task I.

B. Identify the application systems for which you will define computer requirements. For each application on this list, go through the activities that follow. As you gather data or perform an activity, put the related information in the appropriate section of your work papers.

C. Review and analyze the current operations. The detailed definition of requirements begins with a review of the existing business applications. The current system provides the basis for understanding and defining the new system. In this activity, review the current system, its inputs, its outputs, its major functions, and the operation of the system. List major strengths and weaknesses, keeping desired changes for the new system in mind.

The review and analysis should involve the following tasks for *each* application system:

1. Conduct interviews with appropriate supervisory and clerical personnel.
2. Review existing documentation.
3. Review procedures manuals.
4. List problems, concerns, and issues.
5. Document transaction flow.
6. Obtain transaction volume estimates on average and peak use.

D. Gather examples of all input documents. A copy of each current input document should be gathered (preferably a copy of a completed document). Any new input documents or changes to current documents should be defined also.

E. Gather examples of all reports. A copy of each current report should be gathered. Any new reports or changes to existing reports should be defined also.

F. Define the system requirements. Based on the strengths and weaknesses of the current system, the major functions and features of the new system should be defined. Highlight or identify separately any requirements that are unique to the client's operation.

G. Specify system control requirements. Identify the basic requirements for software controls and general operating procedures. These requirements should address both automated and manual controls for each application system. Control considerations are an important part of the system requirements and should address the following:

1. Data entry error detection
2. Access to and security over processing data and output through reports or on-line inquiry
3. Processing control—verification, balancing, limit checks
4. File maintenance—backup and run-to-run controls

TASK **III**: SELECT VENDORS AND ISSUE A REQUEST FOR PROPOSAL.

A. Review the results of tasks I and II.

B. Identify potential vendors. Based on the requirements defined in task II, identify potential vendors. Initially assess vendors by briefly contacting them and performing limited research.

Begin investigating potential vendors using the following list of hardware and software reference sources. Research and vendor contact should be performed on a broad, overview basis.

1. Industry and association contacts
2. Computer stores
3. Computer directories
4. Advertisements
5. Computer magazines
6. General and industry-specific trade shows and conferences
7. Software listings

     8. Computer-related organizations

     9. Hardware manufacturers

   10. Value-added resellers

   11. Professional publications

Review the list of potential vendors, and determine whether each vendor satisfies initial screening criteria.

     1. Does the vendor offer the basic application systems?

     2. Can the vendor handle the level of needs indicated by the requirements?

     3. What is the approximate cost range of such a system?

   C. Narrow the vendor alternatives. Determine which vendors meet the criteria. The objective is to narrow the choice of vendors to between three and five. Review the selection with management and explain the methodology used to arrive at the final group of vendors.

   D. Prepare the RFP or a checklist. The RFP should contain five sections:

     1. *Introduction*: Briefly describe the company and the project.

     2. *Instructions*: Include the proposal due date, timetable for evaluation, and other related information.

     3. *Deliverables*: Define the content to include in the proposal. The proposal should include the following sections:

       a. Executive summary

       b. Hardware configuration

       c. Application software

       d. Itemized costs

       e. Vendor support and references

       f. Warranties and system acceptance criteria

       g. Implementation approach

       h. Sample contracts

       i. Supporting documentation

     4. *Evaluation criteria*: Define how proposals will be reviewed and evaluated. The criteria for evaluating the proposals are:

       a. Ability to satisfy requirements

       b. Vendor quality and support

       c. System capacity and flexibility

       d. Contract terms and product warranties

       e. Costs and financing arrangements

     5. *Requirements*: Attach the system requirements to the RFP as supporting information.

If a simplified checklist is being prepared, use the basic categories from the RFP as a guideline for developing the checklist.

   E. Send the RFP or checklist to the appropriate vendors.

TASK **IV**: EVALUATE ALTERNATIVES AND SELECT A SYSTEM.

   A. Review the results from task III.

   B. Evaluate each alternative against the system requirements. This activity is very important. Basically, you are determining whether each system can meet the client's needs. To determine whether a system meets requirements, request detailed documentation of the system's features, functions, and processing. Read through the documentation and the vendor's proposal and identify requirements that are met by the system.

   This activity requires significant client involvement. The client is essential in determining whether the vendors' systems satisfy the requirements.

   C. Evaluate vendor quality and support. Try to determine which vendor(s) will provide good support both before and after the sale. Factors to consider include:

1. Number of installations the vendor has completed
2. Hardware and software maintenance facilities, including 1-800-numbers, technical people, user groups, and newsletters
3. Vendor references

D. Evaluate the system capacity and flexibility. Several factors that should be considered in evaluating hardware and software include:

1. *Growth capability*: Can the hardware be expanded as the business grows?
2. *Upward compatibility*: Can software still run if the system is upgraded?
3. *People features*: Look for differences in the ease of use and convenience of various systems.

E. Evaluate contract and product warranties. If the system is expensive, there should be a contract that provides for guarantees and warranties. For a less expensive single work station system, standard manufacturer warranties and maintenance contracts are generally used. Factors to consider in this evaluation include:

1. Acceptance periods
2. Maintenance response time
3. Hardware backup

F. Contact vendor references. Contact the references to discuss in detail:

1. Whether the system met expectations
2. Whether the vendor provided promised support
3. Whether the system was easy to implement
4. Whether the system had any "bugs"
5. What pitfalls/problem areas should be avoided

G. Evaluate costs and financing arrangements. Calculate the costs of each system, including costs for all hardware, software, installation, and maintenance.

H. Make a summary evaluation, rank the alternatives, and review results with the client. Prepare a detailed evaluation of each alternative's ability to meet requirements, vendor support and references, system capacity and flexibility, contract and product warranties, and costs. Make a summary evaluation comparing and ranking alternatives.

I. Attend an in-depth demonstration of the top-ranked alternatives. It is preferable to attend a demonstration at a customer location. For smaller purchases, the hardware and software are commonly demonstrated at the store or vendor location. The demonstration should show how each of the requirements is met by the system.

Encourage management to attend the vendor demonstration. Inclusion of both top and middle management will result in broader and more extensive questioning of the vendor. In addition, middle management participation will result in better acceptance of the computer during the installation.

Work with vendors *prior* to the actual demonstration to specify what should be demonstrated and discussed. Prior planning ensures that the demonstration focuses on covering system requirements.

J. Make the final decision. Given the analyses performed in prior tasks, the client should be in a position to make a decision.

D. Software Package Evaluation

INTRODUCTION

The costs of in-house application system development continue to climb steadily, and the retention of competent programmer analysts is more difficult. It is understandable that proprietary software packages are receiving so much attention from management. Substantial savings can be realized by using generalized software wherever practical and allowing the in-house EDP staffs to concentrate on the more specialized projects that cannot be addressed by using software packages.

In addition to the potential for reduced cost, other advantages of software packages over tailored systems (e.g., reduced risk, faster implementation) should continue to favor the use of packages in a large number of situations. As a general rule, if a software package meets a user's needs, the package alternative is more frequently selected than tailored systems. The challenge becomes one of the determining user needs and finding the software package(s) that most closely match those needs.

The following work plan will assist the consultant in appraising an application package's processing features, controls, technical efficiency, other users' experience, and the vendor's reputation.

TASK I: DEFINE USER REQUIREMENTS.

A. Develop a profile of the business.
   1. Describe the business and the potential growth in transaction and file volumes.
   2. Review the data processing organization, staffing, and equipment.
   3. Prepare an organization chart including the data processing department.
   4. Assess the role of data processing in the company.

B. Define system requirements.
   1. Define the basic objectives for each application.
   2. Define each application's processing requirements and processing features.
   3. For each application output, define report media, selection criteria, and report headings and summarizations.
   4. Define file contents for master and transaction files.
   5. Identify the validity checks and error correction edits for input data.
   6. Determine transaction and master file controls and audit trail requirements necessary to provide adequate processing controls.

C. Estimate the application work load.
   1. Number of master file records
   2. Number of update and file maintenance transactions
   3. Number and size of reports, the number of copies and report production frequency
   4. Number of input/output file records
   5. Processing schedule requirements—frequency of update and processing runs, response time and deadlines.
   6. Other volumes and timings that affect the evaluation of the software package

D. Assess the capacity of the EDP operation.
   1. Determine, based on the volume estimates, whether additional computer equipment will be required to support the processing requirements of the application system.
   2. Determine whether the business has the personnel skills to modify, implement, and operate the system.

TASK II: EVALUATE THE SOFTWARE PACKAGE'S FEATURES/BENEFITS.

A. Compare package features to user requirements.
   1. Determine whether the software package meets the required processing needs.
   2. Perform a detailed comparison of the application requirements to the capabilities of the package.
   3. Evaluate the package's capability to provide the desired functions.

4. Review the adequacy of input, processing, and output controls.
5. Estimate the cost/benefit of adding desired features that are not available.

B. Determine hardware/software requirements for operation.
  1. Hardware
    a. Memory requirements
    b. Number of disk and/or tape drives
    c. Disk space requirements
    d. Terminals
    e. Other peripheral equipment
  2. Software
    a. Operating system
    b. Compilers
    c. File access methods
    d. Communications software
  3. Off-line equipment
    a. Key entry
    b. Sorters
    c. Bursting and decollating equipment
    d. Mircofilm processors and readers
  4. Operating personnel
    a. Data control
    b. Data entry
    c. Computer operations
    d. Off-line areas
    e. Distribution

C. Evaluate the technical efficiency of the package.
  1. System design
  2. Program structure
  3. Programming techniques
  4. Job stream command structure

D. Evaluate the package's documentation.
  1. Complete and understandable
  2. Comparison to documentation standards

TASK **III**: CONTACT CURRENT USERS.

Visit current users of the package, preferably similar organizations that have comparable processing requirements. The primary purpose of the visit is to determine the user's experience with implementing and using the system. Use the following questions as a guideline.

A. What portion of the system is implemented and how is the system being used?

B. Ease of installation
  1. What problems were encountered in adapting the package to the user's needs?
  2. How much time was spent installing the package?
  3. How were files converted?
  4. How long was parallel operation maintained?

C. Training
   1. How much training was required?
   2. How effective was the training?
   3. Who conducted the training?
   4. Where was the training conducted?

D. Documentation
   1. How useful was the documentation supplied by the vendor?
   2. Did the vendor provide user, operations, and system documentation?

E. Ease of use
   1. Is the package easy to use?
   2. Is much clerical effort required?
   3. Were there many "bugs" in the system?
   4. Have there been many program updates and enhancements?

F. Throughput/efficiency
   1. At reasonable usage, what are response times?
   2. Does the system perform as promised by the vendor?

G. Vendor support
   1. Did the vendor meet schedule commitments?
   2. Did the vendor promptly respond to correct errors?
   3. Rate the vendor's attitude, cooperation, and willingness to help.
   4. Is there a users' association for this vendor?

H. Overall satisfaction
   1. What is the worst experience encountered in implementing and installing the package?
   2. What are the overall strengths and weakness of the package?

TASK IV: EVALUATE THE VENDOR.

A. Vendor profile
   1. Number of years in business
   2. Software sales per year
   3. Number of technical, development, and support personnel
   4. Number of customers

B. Vendor support
   1. Ratio of support personnel to customers' supported
   2. Support specialists' level of expertise
   3. Range of products that the support specialist has to support
   4. Level of implementation assistance provided
   5. Policy toward upgrades and enchancements to the product

TASK V: PREPARE A COST ANALYSIS.

A. Start-up costs
   1. *Package purchase/lease*: Costs involved in acquiring the package.
   2. *Modification*: Costs of modifying the package prior to implementation.
   3. *Hardware/software*: Costs for additional hardware and software required to implement and operate the system.

4. *Documentation*: Costs for supplementing the documentation supplied by the vendor.

5. *Conversion*: Costs of converting data to load the files.

6. *System testing*: Costs for personnel and processing to perform all levels of testing required to make the system operational.

7. *Training*: Costs for training all the personnel that will use the system.

8. *Other costs*: Costs associated with the acquisition and implementation of the system.

B. Operating costs
   1. Data collection
      a. Cost of the number of employees required to perform data preparation, collection, key transcription, and control balancing.
      b. Cost of collection and entry equipment needed to support the package.
      c. Other costs—such as forms, supplies, space, and utilities.
   2. System processing
      a. Cost of computer usage based on estimated processing time, including computer operations personnel.
      b. Cost of file storage.
      c. Cost of allocated computer operations such as space and utilities.
      d. Other costs.
   3. Programming support
      a. Cost of personnel, including programmers, analysts, and supervision.
      b. Cost for computer resources required for testing.
      c. Other associated costs, for supplies, space, data entry, etc.
      d. Other identifiable costs, such as additional terminals.

E. Computer System Security Evaluation

INTRODUCTION

Security is critical to the longevity and health of an enterprise. Unless the enterprise can safeguard its assets, including its data and information, it will not prosper or perhaps even survive over the long run. With the advent of on-line computer-based information systems and networks, however, security has become more difficult to maintain at an effective level. Not only must an enterprise secure itself from theft or carelessness by employees, but it must be wary of computer "hackers" and professional intruders who attempt to break into its data base.

The following checklist provides guidance with respect to several areas in which weaknesses can give rise to security violations. For convenience, these areas are somewhat arbitrarily identified as personnel, organizational, physical, data, software, documentation, operational, backup, development, and disaster prevention.

PERSONNEL

1. Is each new applicant for employment checked, within the confines of state and federal law, with respect to:
   a. Past and present employment?
   b. Friends and acquaintances who are employees within the company?

    c. Proof of citizenship?

    d. Problems that might have an adverse effect on the security of the computer system?

2. Is each new applicant for a position involving trust required to be bonded?

3. Is each newly hired employee given an identification card with photograph?

4. Is each terminated employee given an exit interview in which the identification card, credit card, keys, and company documentation of procedures are retrieved?

5. Is an agreement signed with each new employee concerning the nondisclosure of proprietary information?

6. Are employees required to take periodic vacations?

7. Are employees who are assigned to critical or sensitive positions rotated on a periodic and regular basis?

8. Is a policy established with respect to potential conflicts of interest, and is it strictly enforced?

9. Are employees closely supervised, in order to detect those:

    a. Who are in possible financial difficulties?

    b. Who are disgruntled or a threat to company property?

    c. Who are drinking or using drugs on the premises?

    d. Who might be performing unauthorized actions?

    e. Who might be careless about leaving confidential materials unlocked?

10. Are employees well trained to perform their assigned responsibilities in a capable manner?

11. Are employees cross-trained, so that one employee can substitute for another who may suddenly be unable to perform his or her job?

ORGANIZATIONAL

1. Are personnel and organizational units so divided with respect to responsibilities that:

    a. Those having custody over assets do not perform data processing or recordkeeping duties with respect to the assets?

    b. Those having custody over assets do not have operating duties?

    c. Those having authorization responsibilities are not directly involved in transaction processing?

2. Are responsibilities so divided that fraud cannot be perpetrated without the collusion of two or more persons?

3. Are proof and control functions performed by persons other than those involved in data processing or system development?

4. Are computer operators and programmers separated with respect to duties, functions, and physical work locations?

5. Are all transactions authorized by persons who are not involved in transaction processing or the maintenance of master files?

6. Does an internal audit department exist that:

    a. Reports to the board of directors?

    b. Reviews the organizational arrangements in all departments involved in the inputting, processing, and outputting of information?

    c. Reviews all controls and security measures pertaining to the safeguarding of assets and the reliability of data?

PHYSICAL

1. Is access to the computer facilities restricted to all except authorized operating and management personnel?

2. Are visitors to the buildings housing data processing facilities required to log in and out?
3. Are employees who enter buildings housing data processing facilities after scheduled hours required to log in?
4. Do guards check credentials of visitors and badges of employees?
5. Are closed circuit television monitors employed to survey key points of entry and sensitive areas such as data vaults?
6. Are detectors employed at points of entry to data processing facilities to detect:
   a. Magnets for erasing tapes or disks?
   b. Metal objects, such as firearms or bombs?
7. Is the data center patrolled during nonworking hours by guards whose rounds are recorded by check-in stations?
8. Do guards have access to telephones in case of emergencies?
9. Is a burglar alarm system in operation and tested regularly?
10. Are at least two persons on duty at all times in the computer center?
11. Is the computer center located in an area that is not in plain sight of the public?
12. Are doors to the computer center controlled by badge-operated locks?
13. Are locks or lock codes changed periodically?
14. Are fire and smoke detection systems located in the computer center and data library?
15. Are the computer center and data library protected by an automatic fire extinguishing system employing a nondamaging substance such as Halon gas?
16. Is the fire extinguishing system checked periodically?
17. Are portable fire extinguishers readily available in the data processing facility?
18. Is the space below raised computer center floors free of combustible debris?
19. Is the computer center constructed of noncombustible materials?
20. Are computer operators instructed how to respond in case of a fire emergency?
21. Are fire instructions posted in all data processing areas?
22. Are fire alarm boxes mounted and clearly marked?
23. Are computer operators familiar with emergency power switch locations and procedures?
24. Is there an emergency power supply for the computer center?
25. Is smoking prohibited in the computer center?
26. Is a complete set of backup tapes and files stored in a location remote from the computer center?
27. Does the company carry adequate insurance with respect to such disasters as:
   a. Fire?
   b. Windstorm?
   c. Flooding?
   d. Power failure?
   e. Sabotage or other criminal acts?
   f. Fraud?
28. Is the building housing data processing facilities sufficiently sound to withstand strong winds and other natural forces?
29. Are inspections conducted regularly of all cabling and electrical junctions and boxes?
30. Is the electrical system inaccessible to unauthorized persons?
31. Is first-aid equipment readily available?
32. Are emergency exits well located, well marked, and free of obstructions?
33. Is the building housing data processing facilities located on high ground and protected by a drainage system to avoid possible flooding?

34. Is the building housing data processing facilities correctly grounded for protection against lightning?
35. Is the electrical system protected by a voltage regulator from sudden surges?

DOCUMENTATION, INCLUDING DATA AND SOFTWARE

1. Are documentation standards established and available in writing, including those pertaining to:
   a. Systems design?
   b. Programs?
   c. Sample outputs?
   d. Record and file layouts?
   e. User procedures?
2. Are all production programs fully documented, including:
   a. Program listings?
   b. Narrative descriptions?
   c. Program flowcharts?
   d. Setup instructions?
   e. Control checks?
   f. Halt and restart and checkpoint procedures?
3. Are documentation and programs stored in a location that is secure from unauthorized access?
4. Is specific responsibility assigned to a librarian for the custody and maintenance of documentation, data tapes or disks, and programs?
5. Is access to the data library restricted to authorized persons and prohibited to computer operators and programmers?
6. Is a log maintained with respect to the issue and return of documentation, data, and programs?
7. Is an up-to-date catalog of computer programs maintained?
8. Are program changes logged in a change register?
9. Are important programs, records, securities, checks, preprinted computer forms, sensitive data, etc., stored in a fireproof vault within the data library?
10. Are periodic inventories (and, occasionally, surprise inventories) taken of the data library contents?
11. Are external and internal labels provided on all tape and disk files?
12. Is program testing performed on a copy of the production program, using copies of live data, rather than on the original program and data?
13. Is a distribution catalog of reports maintained, showing those who are to receive each report from computer processing?
14. Are signature plates stored in a secured place and equipped with nonresettable counters to register the number of signature impressions, including the handling of spoiled and voided checks?
15. Are blank check forms imprinted with sequential numbers?
16. Are confidential reports destroyed by burning or shredding?
17. Is a records retention plan in effect?
18. Are desks locked during nonworking hours and all desk tops cleared of papers?
19. Are data encryption techniques employed to transmit confidential data over communications lines?
20. Is a listing of data files maintained in the data library?

21. Are changes to data files and programs initiated in user departments outside the data processing department?
22. Are changes numbered and recorded in a register?
23. Are user departments that initiate changes to data files or programs provided with printouts that reflect the actual changes made?
24. Are documentation standards reviewed periodically for completeness and up-to-dateness?

OPERATIONAL

1. Are written and up-to-date computer center operating procedures available?
2. Is adequate documentation available to facilitate running computer applications?
3. Is an operating console log maintained to record all actions taken by computer operators, as well as halts, malfunctions, and so forth?
4. Is the console log inaccessible to the computer operators?
5. Is the console log inspected daily by the internal auditors or data processing managers?
6. Are computer hardware and/or software monitors employed to check equipment utilization?
7. Are programmers and other nonoperator personnel prohibited from operating the computers in the center?
8. Are computer operators denied access to program documentation?
9. Are all computer operations authorized by work requests?
10. Are all computer runs scheduled?
11. Are data received for processing logged in by a control group?
12. Are reports transmitted from the computer center logged out by a control group?
13. Is preventive maintenance of all equipment performed as scheduled?
14. Are temperature and humidity controlled by automatic thermostats and checked by charts?
15. Are protective devices, such as "file protect rings," employed to protect files?
16. Are computer operators prohibited from making changes to programs?
17. Are passwords, encoded badges, or other access restriction devices required for use on terminals and microcomputers that are connected to an on-line network?
18. Are passwords changed frequently?
19. Does the data entry device, e.g., a terminal, lock after three attempted accesses?
20. Does the system automatically log all attempted accesses and produce reports showing these attempts?
21. Are security authorized levels established within the data bases, so that each user of the system gains access only to limited areas and functions on the basis of his or her password?
22. Are checks received by mail or over the counter:
    a. Stamped "for deposit only" as received?
    b. Kept in a locked safe if held overnight before being deposited?
    c. Deposited intact?
23. Is a stamped deposit slip obtained from the bank and returned to the internal audit department?
24. Are credit approvals, credit memos, and adjustments to customers' account balances authorized by suitable managers?
25. Are amounts in suspense accounts monitored on a regular basis?

26. Are differences between inventory balances, as shown in the accounting records and found by physical counts, verified by the internal audit department or by external auditors?
27. Does the internal audit department periodically distribute paychecks and verify the existence of employees who do not personally claim paychecks?
28. Does the internal audit department periodically test production programs on a surprise basis?
29. Does the internal audit department periodically verify cash in cash registers and petty cash funds on a surprise basis?

BACKUP AND DISASTER PREVENTION

1. Does the company have a written disaster prevention master plan that describes operational responses to disasters for periods of 1 day, 1 week, and 1 month?
2. Is the disaster plan reviewed periodically?
3. Does the disaster plan cover:
   a. Responsibilities of specified individuals?
   b. Procedures for protecting personnel from injury?
   c. Procedures for protecting property from damage?
   d. Emergency phone numbers?
   e. Fail-safe and override provisions for alarms and doors in case of emergencies?
4. Is a procedure established for processing at an alternate facility in the event of a breakdown of the organization's computer or related equipment?
5. Are the backup facilities tested on a periodic basis, to assure that processing is compatible and that procedures are sound?
6. Is the backup procedure for the reconstruction and recovery of destroyed files tested on a periodic basis?
7. Are copies of all master files, transaction files, and programs stored in an off-premises location?
8. Does the company have insurance that covers costs of reconstructing destroyed files or programs and payments for backup facilities?
9. Has the company installed an uninterruptible reserve or backup power supply?
10. Is the power supply tested periodically?
11. Has a security officer been appointed, with the responsibility of searching for and correcting security weaknesses?
12. Has a safety committee been appointed, with the responsibility of searching for and correcting safety hazards?

DEVELOPMENT

1. Are all requests for new programs and changes to existing programs reviewed and approved by an information systems manager?
2. Must all changes be initiated by or agreed to by the affected user departments?
3. Are formal testing procedures employed to check the accuracy of all new programs and changes to programs?
4. Is a special file of test data prepared and maintained for each new or changed program?
5. Are final program listings and the results of tests reviewed by information systems management and discussed with affected user departments?
6. Are all work papers, coding sheets, test printouts, and other documentation pertaining to new programs and changes to programs kept on file?

7. Does the internal audit department receive copies of all systems and program documentation, including changes and updates to the programs themselves?

8. Does the internal audit department perform tests of production programs and obtain listings of the programs on a surprise basis?

9. Are systems specifications for new systems and for major changes to current systems reviewed by the internal audit department?

10. Are final systems and programs tests procedures and results reviewed by the internal audit department?

F. Computer Department Effectiveness Review

INTRODUCTION

There have been major changes in data processing and data processing departments in recent years. Substantial changes have usually occurred with respect to equipment, software, and people resources. In response to this change, a systematic review can produce recommendations for short-term enhancements and provide the basis for a 3-to-5-year EDP plan. A comprehensive effectiveness review can benefit in a number of ways. It can:

1. Improve short-term management decision making
2. Identify new application systems
3. Prioritize system development efforts
4. Improve EDP resource requirements allocation
5. Identify opportunities for cost savings
6. Improve communications between DP and user departments

The following checklist provides the basis for a methodical examination of EDP, which can contribute to management effectiveness and operational performance.

TASK I: ESTABLISH PROJECT ORGANIZATION, PLAN, AND REVIEW PROCEDURES.

The purpose of this task is to provide guidance and structure to the overall project. This will include project management, technical review, and periodic status meetings. A key work step in this task is the establishment of an effectiveness review committee to consist of key personnel from the organization who would meet with the project team on a regular basis. The project team would present the results of each major task to the EDP effectiveness review committee to obtain their guidance, input, and direction.

TASK II: EVALUATE EFFECTIVENESS OF DATA PROCESSING ORGANIZATION AND ADMINISTRATION.

A. The purpose of this task is to evaluate how well the resources currently available to the data processing department are utilized. This includes an assessment of the service level provided to the user departments. Interviews would be conducted with the major department heads and key data processing personnel, including:

- Information systems coordinator
- EDP administrator
- Assistant director of data processing
- Data systems manager
- Computer operations manager

The results of the interviews would be an assessment of the perceived strengths and weaknesses of the data processing services provided as well as an evaluation of the organizational structure of the data processing department.

B. The remainder of Task II involves a detailed assessment of the administrative control procedures used by the data processing department, including:

- Standards, policies, and procedures
- Project planning and control procedures
- Data processing status and performance reporting
- Hardware and system software selection procedures
- Disaster recovery plans and procedures

Key areas to address in this task include:

1. Reporting relationship of EDP within the company
    a. Organization structure
    b. Areas serviced by EDP
    c. EDP objectives
    d. EDP decentralization
2. Structure of the EDP department
    a. Job descriptions
    b. Job context, responsibility, and authority
    c. Resource balance
    d. Span of management
    e. Systems plan
    f. Executive capability
3. Level of administrative control
    a. System development priorities
    b. System development process
    c. Change control procedures
4. Approach to management control
    a. Effectiveness of operating reports
    b. System and programming reports
    c. Accounting controls
5. Determination of staff requirements
    a. Development plan with manpower requirements
    b. Definition of skill requirements
6. Staff skill base
    a. Staff backgrounds
    b. Level of EDP sophistication
    c. Key staff members
7. Personnel policies and procedures
    a. Recruiting sources
    b. Selection criteria
    c. Recruitment results
    d. Employee training
    e. Salary scales and benefits
    f. Performance appraisal
    g. Personnel security

8. Opportunities for career development
   a. Criteria for advancement
   b. Activities rate
   c. Formal training courses
   d. OJT
   e. Training plan

C. The results of Task II would be summarized and then reported to the EDP effectiveness review committee. These results would be incorporated into the final report.

TASK III: EVALUATE THE EFFECTIVENESS OF THE COMPUTER HARDWARE EQUIPMENT AND SYSTEMS SOFTWARE CONFIGURATION.

A. The purpose of this task is to identify both short- and long-term recommendations for EDP hardware equipment and system software. The review should be structured to address the following six specific questions:

1. Have all key factors been considered in the data processing strategy?
2. Is the present computer equipment being adequately measured and utilized?
3. Are the projected requirements for processor resources reasonable in light of expected transaction volumes, present and planned applications, and anticipated technological advances during the planning period?
4. Which equipment strategy will best provide the flexibility for growth, establish an appropriate technological base for present and future applications, and provide a cost-effective solution?
5. What future applications are recommended to help improve equipment planning and capacity management?
6. What changes (if any) to the system control software could improve performance, reduce overhead, and provide the best foundation for future growth?

Answers to these questions will provide independent assurance that all reasonable alternatives have been considered, that the strategic direction is economically and technically sound, and that any recommended future actions are clearly documented.

B. The approach combines rigorous analysis of measurement data and technical issues together with an understanding and appreciation of organizational and management issues. The major work steps in this section include:

1. Gathering and reviewing utilization statistics
   a. Accounting data
   b. CPU utilization
   c. Main storage utilization
   d. Idle time
   e. Program test time
   f. System software maintenance
   g. Rerun time
   h. On-line response time
   i. Multiprogramming impact

2. Analyzing the equipment configuration
   a. Tape and disk units
   b. Data access patterns
   c. Internal memory
   d. CPU options

    e. Operations procedures

    f. Unit record devices

    g. Printing devices

    h. Job and production mix

  3. Analyzing the software configuration

    a. Operating system release

    b. Operating system configuration

    c. Program libraries and data files

    d. Level of multiprogramming

    e. Utilities

    f. Efficiency software packages

    g. Programming languages

    h. Programming techniques

    i. Software techniques including file organization

  C. The output should include a concise summary together with preparation of specific action plans for any recommended performance improvements. Recommended priorities are assigned to the action plans based on their relative costs and benefits. The action plans should include detailed work task information as well as estimated levels of effort.

TASK **IV**: SURVEY THE EFFECTIVENSS OF MAJOR DATA PROCESSING APPLICATIONS SYSTEMS.

  A. The purpose of this task is to assess the current applications systems running on the data processing facility. Detailed application effectiveness questionnaires should be distributed to users of all of the applications. The application questionnaires collect background information on each data processing system from the user's perspective. Information collected should include:

- Purpose and scope of the application
- Importance of the application to the user department
- Key system features
- Adequacy of the system reports and inquiry screens
- Operating costs
- Benefits received from the systems, including tangible dollar benefits and other intangibles
- Efficiency of data input editing and correction procedures
- User satisfaction with the system
- Known problems in the system
- System modifications implemented during the past year

  B. The next step is the detailed technical review and evaluation of selected application systems. Review the highest priority systems and address the following:

  1. Satisfaction of user requirements

    a. Primary business purpose of the system

    b. Frequency of use

    c. Number of processing functions

    d. Processing bottlenecks

    e. Unnecessary work steps

    f. Processing schedules

    g. Mixture of on-line versus batch

    h. User's manual

    i. Quality of input elements
    j. Effectiveness of output reports
    k. Level of user confidence
  2. System reliability
    a. Accuracy and timeliness of data
    b. Effectiveness of data security
  3. Cost-effectiveness
    a. Operating costs
    b. Transaction processing costs
    c. Implementation costs
    d. Manpower and machine utilization costs
    e. Maintenance costs
  4. Technical efficiency
    a. Efficient system design
    b. Efficient use of computer equipment
    c. Number of files and programs
    d. File-processing techniques
    e. Flexibility for expansion and modification
    f. Efficient operating procedures
    g. Efficient programming practices
    h. On-line response time and availability

  C. The results of the detailed review should be documented, including an assessment of the long-term viability of the applications. Short-term recommendations should be developed and, where necessary, applications prioritized for future replacement.

TASK **V**: EVALUATE COMPUTER OPERATIONS WORK FLOW.

  A. In running a computer organization, it is important to have a physical environment that is adequate in terms of hardware, software, people, and procedures. In this task, evaluate the operations of the data center.
  The focus of the review should be:
  1. Physical arrangements
    a. Layout of functional areas
    b. Adequate work space
    c. Adequate storage space
    d. Backup facilities
  2. Scheduling
    a. Standard production schedule
    b. Changes to the schedule
    c. Special job requests
    d. Job mix
    e. Production reports
  3. Operations
    a. Run books for production jobs
    b. Job staging
    c. Job setting up and tearing down
    d. Staffing
    e. Job mix
    f. Restart procedures

4. Distribution
   a. Written instructions
   b. Control checks
   c. Output controls

B. The purpose of the review should be to develop recommendations for achieving more effective utilization of the data processing resources. This includes an assessment of the scheduling process, the physical flow of work to, through, and from the operations center, as well as the actual physical layout of the facility.

TASK **VI**: REVIEW THE EFFECTIVENESS OF THE DATA TRANSCRIPTION FUNCTION.

A. Even the most effective and efficient data processing operation is still extremely dependent upon the data transcription function for accurate entry of information into its data processing systems. This function is typically very labor intensive and therefore subject to cost savings when productivity improvements can be made.

B. Perform interviews and observe the data transcription operation. Also review daily application transaction volumes, staffing and scheduling procedure, and validation processes for the high-volume application systems. Determine the cost-effectiveness of the current data entry equipment. Factors considered in this review would include hardware maintenance costs, personnel costs, and the cost of acquiring more efficient equipment.

C. Review and evaluate the controls over input documents and transactions in the data transcription area. Typical controls used in the data transcription area include:

• Well-documented instructions
• Job status
• Job sign-off
• Verifications
• Control figures
• Cover sheets with sign-off
• Log books

Focus attention on items that would result in cost-effective recommendations in improving the data transcription function.

D. The final area of the review should be evaluation of data transcription productivity. This review would include an evaluation of the scheduling and work distribution procedures, the use of premium rate entry such as overtime or temporary help, and evaluation of entry operator performance. You should compare operator performance in typical measures—such as keystrokes per hour—with those of other data processing organizations in the local area. Also review data transcription error rates and evaluate the physical environment for conditions that could impact productivity.

Summarize the results of the review and discuss them with the effectiveness review committee.

TASK **VII**: PRESENT EFFECTIVENESS REVIEW RESULTS.

The final task involves consolidating the results of the review and presenting to the effectiveness review committee as well as to key management personnel who can take action on the recommendations submitted. Both the management presentation and management report should be cleared with the effectiveness review committee prior to their release to management.

G. Office Management and Automation Review

INTRODUCTION

Whether an enterprise sells a product or provides a service, it must maintain an office. Office management is the coordination and direction of the resources—personnel, machines, facilities, supplies, funds— involved in office-based work. The management of an office can have a critical bearing on the efficiency and profitability of the entire enterprise. If the office is not well managed, the costs in resources and losses in effective services can be extremely damaging.

Dramatic changes are occurring within the office setting. White-collar office labor is the fastest-growing component of the work force. In order to improve the productivity of office workers, automation is being rapidly introduced. This office automation is making use of sophisticated computer system technology. It is being increasingly integrated to form networks of work stations, each with a variety of word processing as well as data processing services.

The following checklist addresses areas of office management pertaining to organization, facilities, activities, and personnel. It also includes a section pertaining to specific aspects of office automation. The consultant should use the checklist as a guide to conducting an office management audit and to developing recommendations that are intended to enhance the client's performance.

MANAGEMENT OF OFFICE ORGANIZATION

1. Is the office organization established on the basis of sound organizational principles that consider:
   a. Objectives of the enterprise?
   b. Establishment of clear lines of responsibility and authority?
   c. Concept of simplicity?
   d. Concept of unity of command?
   e. Concept of span of control?
   f. Need for adequate motivation?
   g. Provision for effective leadership?
2. Is an organization chart of the office organization prepared and kept up-to-date?
3. Are the lines of communication and coordination between the office function and the other functions of the enterprise clearly established?
4. Has careful consideration been given to the centralization of such services as:
   a. Mail handling?
   b. Communications?
   c. Filing?
   d. Typing?
   e. Purchasing?
   f. Utilities?
   g. Duplicating?
   h. Computing and cost analysis?
   i. Reception?
   j. Graphics?

k. Supplies?

l. Methods and procedures?

m. Forms control?

n. Planning and scheduling?

o. Personnel administration?

MANAGEMENT OF OFFICE FACILITIES

1. Is the location of the office function:
    a. In a building with adequate ceiling heights, space, floor live loads, windows, lighting, ventilation, heating, elevator service, janitor service, and fire protection apparatus?
    b. In an area that is convenient to customers and others in the same business, transportation facilities, shopping centers, restaurants, hotels, and mail facilities?
    c. In a portion of the building that is free from excessive dust and noise?
2. If the building in which the office function is located is leased, is the lease favorable with respect to renewing, rental payments, maintenance, and provided services?
3. Does the office layout follow sound principles, such as:
    a. Large working areas for better lighting, ventilation, and access?
    b. Partitioned and clustered work stations within the large work area?
    c. Location of files and equipment close to the work stations?
    d. Simplified work flows, with no backtracking and crisscrossing?
    e. Grouping of related departments and sections?
    f. Convenient rest-room facilities and lounging areas?
4. Is lighting adequate, allowing for the special needs of such activities as accounting and drafting?
5. Are the colors pleasant and harmonious?
6. Are humidity, temperature, and ventilation controlled to provide comfortable working conditions?
7. Is acoustic tile material used in sufficient quantity to reduce noise to acceptable levels?
8. Are desks of adequate height and desk tops of adequate dimensions to accommodate the needs of occupants?
9. Is a clean-desk-top rule encouraged to increase efficiency and security?
10. Are posture chairs provided for secretarial and clerical personnel?
11. Does filing equipment include the following, as appropriate to particular files and tasks:
    a. Vertical filing cabinets?
    b. Visible files?
    c. Rotary files?
    d. Reciprocating files?
12. Are office aids in use, including:
    a. Sorting devices?
    b. Copyholders?
    c. Desk trays?
    d. Calculators?
    e. Notched cards and needles?
13. Are machines employed that are not electronically tied into office automation, such as:
    a. Accounting machines or computers?

    b. Duplicating machines, e.g., Xerox machines?

    c. Addressing machines?

    d. Cash registers?

    e. Autoregisters?

    f. Recording and dictating devices and tapes?

MANAGEMENT OF OFFICE ACTIVITIES

1. Is each record cost justified?
2. Does each record and report have a clear and recognized purpose?
3. Are duplicate records and reports reviewed and eliminated if possible?
4. Are managers encouraged to prepare written narrative reports that follow principles of good communication, such as:

    a. Having a definite purpose?

    b. Following a logical order?

    c. Using simple words and short sentences?

    d. Stating and interpreting factual findings?

    e. Making specific recommendations?

5. Are all forms controlled by a central group with respect to:

    a. Format?

    b. Information included?

    c. Adequate identification, including assigned title and number?

    d. Number of copies?

    e. Weight and grade of paper?

6. Does a central mail room perform such functions as:

    a. Receiving all mail?

    b. Sorting envelopes and packages by class?

    c. Opening all mail (except personal mail)?

    d. Sorting contents?

    e. Stamping time and date of receipt?

    f. Listing remittances and totaling?

    g. Stamping all checks with restrictive endorsements?

    h. Collecting outgoing mail?

    i. Grouping outgoing mail by destination?

    j. Sealing and stamping outgoing mail, using a postage meter?

7. Does the company use standard-size envelopes and paper?
8. Does the company use a 9-digit business zip code to speed the receipt of correspondence?
9. Are the principles of good letter writing followed, such as:

    a. Definite purpose for each letter?

    b. Clear and simple style?

    c. Friendly tone?

    d. Clear conclusion?

    e. Simplified block-style for the form of the letter?

10. Are form letters and paragraphs used as frequently as feasible?
11. Is typing performed by trained typists, using error-correcting typewriters or word processing machines?
12. Is material cross-filed when suitable, using:

    a. Alphabetic arrangement?

    b. Numerical arrangement?

    c. Chronological arrangement?

    d. Geographical arrangement?

13. Are file indexes employed to indicate the arrangements by which materials are filed?

14. Are guides, colored tabs, and folders used when filing material in file drawers?

15. Is microfilming employed whenever feasible?

16. Are retention periods established to encourage the review and disposal of inactive material?

17. Are substitution cards used when materials are removed from a file for a period of time?

18. Are the top drawers of a filing cabinet used for current filing, while the bottom drawers are for relatively inactive materials?

19. Is there one person in charge of all filing who establishes standardized filing procedures and prepares reports on filing output?

20. Are only authorized personnel allowed access to centralized files?

21. Is a messenger service employed to distribute written materials within the office and to outside points?

22. Do the messengers have preestablished routes and times?

23. Are telephones available to authorized personnel?

24. Is telephone usage limited to authorized personnel and to business calls?

25. Are communication services (in addition to the telephone) available, such as:

    a. Intercommunication systems?

    b. Paging systems?

    c. Mobile radio-telephone service?

MANAGEMENT OF OFFICE PERSONNEL

(For a more detailed checklist, see Appendix L, Personnel Management Review.)

1. Does the company employ and train supervisors who provide effective supervision of office employees?

2. Are office jobs analyzed and described in job descriptions?

3. Are office employees evaluated with respect to job performance periodically (at least once each year) and by means of a systematic procedure?

4. Do supervisors discuss job evaluations with employees?

5. Does the company have a sound office salary administration plan?

6. Does the salary administration plan include merit pay increments based on merit ratings?

7. Does the salary administration plan include provision for bonuses and other financial incentives?

8. Are the policies and procedures of the salary administration plan carefully explained to office employees?

9. Does the company explore all reasonable sources when hiring new office employees?

10. Are applicants for office jobs required to complete formal application forms?

11. Are applicants for office jobs interviewed by trained interviewers in the office personnel department?

12. Are applicants for office jobs required to take tests to reflect:

    a. Aptitude for office work?

    b. Achievements in office duties, e.g., preparing letters?

    c. Personality for office work?

    d. Interest in office work?

13. Are new office employees carefully and thoroughly trained in the skills and knowledge needed for assigned duties?
14. Is one person delegated to be in charge of office safety?
15. Is a safety committee appointed to advise on safety matters?
16. Has the safety committee established safety rules?
17. Is safety promoted by means of:
    a. Posting of safety rules on bulletin boards?
    b. Safety contests?
    c. Reported safety statistics and indexes?
18. Are work areas checked for safety hazards?
19. Are work areas made safer through the use of physical safeguards and good housekeeping practices?
20. Has a suggestion system been established?
21. Are employees given exit interviews upon termination of employment?
22. Are adequate employee benefits provided with respect to:
    a. Insurance?
    b. Pension plans?
    c. Recreational facilities?
    d. Credit union facilities?
    e. Parking?
    f. Counseling?
    g. Profit-sharing plans?
23. Are office employees kept well informed through:
    a. Newsletters?
    b. Meetings?
    c. Films?
    d. Bulletin boards?

OFFICE AUTOMATION

1. Has an office automation strategic plan been developed that reflects the realities of the enterprise's business operations and management environment?
2. Does the office automation strategic plan specify the functional scope of the office automation project, i.e., which of the capture, processing, storing, retrieving, and communicating functions are to be automated?
3. Does the office automation strategic plan specify the degree of integration of the office systems, i.e., the extent to which systems resources and data bases are to be shared, and which departments are to have stand-alone systems?
4. Does the office automation strategic plan specify the level of resources, e.g., the sizes of processors, and the quantity of word processing units per department?
5. Have the present office systems been analyzed to determine the existing problems, overloads, needed improvements, etc.?
6. Has a detailed analysis been prepared to show the requirements in terms of system capabilities with respect to:
    a. Word processing?
    b. Textual inputs?
    c. Electronic mail?
    d. Electronic filing and retrieval?
    e. Graphics?
    f. Voice input and conversion?

g. Data processing?

h. Teleconferencing?

i. Microfilming?

j. Voice outputs?

k. Hardcopy outputs?

l. Softcopy outputs?

7. Has a request for proposal, which contains the above requirements, been sent to all likely office automation vendors?

8. Have the proposals from vendors been evaluated to determine that they meet all stated requirements?

9. Have those proposals meeting all requirements been compared to rank such factors as:

a. Performance of equipment in terms of productivity, quality of outputs, ease of use, timeliness, etc.?

b. Cost of equipment and payment terms?

c. Reliability of equipment?

d. Extent of training provided?

e. Maintenance service?

f. Vendor's reputation, financial strength, etc.?

10. Has a comprehensive implementation plan been developed for guidance in installing selected equipment?

11. Does the implementation plan cover such aspects as:

a. Delivery schedule?

b. Preparation of work station sites and processing centers?

c. Selection and preparation of local area network for data communications?

d. Installation schedule?

e. Testing of new equipment?

f. Conversion from old files and equipment to new files and equipment?

g. Removal of old equipment?

h. Preparation of job descriptions for new positions in the word and data processing centers?

i. Recruitment of new personnel?

j. Training of new personnel and current office personnel?

k. Conduct of acceptance tests of new equipment and network?

12. Is the new implemented office automation system evaluated by means of post-implementation reviews?

H. Production Planning and Control Review

INTRODUCTION

Production consists of transforming raw materials into finished goods. In other words, it is a process that creates form utility. This process is generally quite complex, since it involves (a) the use of direct labor and overhead and (b) a sequence of numerous steps in order to accomplish this transformation. Moreover, specific production processes can vary widely in their physical arrangements and bases of demand. Four differing physical arrangements are: (1) process production, which involves the continuous production of standardized products; (2) mass production, which involves the production of discrete and relatively similar products on an assembly line; (3) batch production, which involves the production of batches or job lots of distinctly differing products; and (4) custom production, which involves the production or construction of individual complex product units. Production may be initiated either (a) on the basis of forecasted demand or (b) on the basis of firm customer orders.

The following checklist addresses both the planning and control functions pertaining to production. While it does not attempt to differentiate precisely among the various arrangements and bases of demand, the checklist does include questions that highlight key problems raised by one or more of the optional arrangements or demands. The consultant should use the checklist as a guide in conducting a survey of production planning and control practices and in developing recommendations intended to enhance the client's performance.

PRODUCTION CHARACTERISTICS

1. Does the company manufacture products:
   a. On the basis of customer orders?
   b. On the basis of forecasted demand?
2. Is the production process best characterized as:
   a. Process production?
   b. Mass production?
   c. Batch production?
   d. Custom production?
3. What is the average production lead time from the beginning of manufacture of a product to its final operation (including packaging)?
4. Are finished products stored as inventory in a warehouse before shipment?
5. Are finished products shipped to remote warehouses for storage as inventory before shipment to customers?
6. What is the average time of storage before shipment?
7. What is the percent loss due to aging of products being stored as inventory?
8. What is the percent loss in the manufacturing process due to:
   a. Scrapped and spoiled units?
   b. Production yield loss?
   c. Production start-up?

PRODUCT CHARACTERISTICS

1. What are the major product lines?
2. What are the individual finished goods item numbers associated with each product line, and what unique characteristics (if any) pertain to the products?
3. What is the average number of component parts per product?
4. What is the maximum number of manufacturing levels in the production process?
5. What is the current level of product technology?
6. How many new products were introduced last year, and how many major changes were made to existing products?
7. What is the extent of outside contracting in dollars and units by type of product?
8. Are alternate material substitutions allowed in place of standard materials?
9. Is printing of packaging materials done in-house?
10. Does a work-in-process identification number remain the same through the final operation?

11. How are work-in-process identification numbers assigned and controlled through the production process?
12. What is the average value of the following per year:
    a. Number of work orders?
    b. Number of raw materials items?
    c. Number of work-in-process item numbers?
    d. Number of finished goods items?
13. What is the average number of production operations for each major product?

PRODUCT STRUCTURES AND ENGINEERING DATA

1. Are the following defined for all products:
    a. Product item masters?
    b. Bills of material?
    c. Routings?
    d. Work centers?
2. What is the maximum number of levels associated with bills of material?
3. What is the typical product life cycle?
4. How many engineering methods and materials changes are introduced during a typical year:
    a. To products?
    b. To the production process?
5. Do manufacturing bills of material aid:
    a. Product planning?
    b. Master production scheduling?
    c. Planning of subassembly priorities?
    d. Order entry?
    e. Final assembly scheduling?
    f. Product costing?
6. To what extent is computer processing employed in this function?
7. Is the effectiveness of the engineering function and production functions measured by:
    a. Bill of materials accuracy?
    b. Lead times accuracy?
    c. Materials usage?
    d. Labor efficiency?
    e. Scrap and rework?
8. Which departments/individuals are responsible for developing and maintaining:
    a. Product item masters?
    b. Bills of materials?
    c. Routings?
    d. Work center activity?
9. Are all manufactured and purchased items assigned specific codes?
10. What coding structures are employed?
11. Is the bill of material computerized?
12. What items are included on the:
    a. Product item master?
    b. Bill of material?

13. What is the typical number of components in an assembly?
14. Are the following available via the information system:
    a. Maintenance audit reports?
    b. Phantom/psuedo items and structures?
    c. Engineering changes?
    d. Single-level bills of material?
    e. Single-level where-used reports?
    g. Indented where-used reports?
    h. Missing data reports?
15. Do production routings exist for all items?
16. Do manufacturing routings include:
    a. Operation number?
    b. Operation description?
    c. Work center number?
    d. Operation run time standard?
    e. Tooling data?
    f. Standard cost by operation?
    g. Alternate process steps?
    h. Inspection requirements?
    i. Setup operation standard?
    j. Standard scrap or yield percentage?
17. Do tool records include:
    a. Tool number?
    b. Tool drawing number?
    c. Tool description?
    d. Stores location?
    e. Date last inspected?
    f. Remaining tool life?
    g. Estimated tool life?
18. Are tools classified by inspection, maintenance, and usage codes?
19. Are the planned assignments of tools to particular jobs indicated by:
    a. Work center?
    b. Order number?
    c. Requirement date?
20. Are the following elements defined for each work center:
    a. Work center number?
    b. Name of center?
    c. Location code?
    d. Machine number?
    e. Supervisor number?
    f. Codes for all grades of labor utilized within the center?
    g. Machine-hour or labor-hour rate?
    h. Overhead distribution basis?
21. Do records and reports concerning work centers reflect:
    a. Machine capacity and load projections?
    b. Labor capacity and load projections?
    c. Available capacity?

    d. Machine status?

    e. Preventive maintenance?

    f. Performance?

22. Are setup, test, and inspection operations adequately defined?

23. Is standardization widely used in the product design process to minimize redundancy of components?

24. Is computer aided design (CAD) used extensively in the design process?

25. Are the following standards maintained in the engineering and production data base:

    a. Static standard costs?

    b. Standard material, labor, and overhead rates?

    c. Revised or recalculated standard costs?

DEMAND FORECASTING AND PRODUCTION PLANNING

1. Is a valid forecasting methodology consistently used, such as:

    a. Intrinsic forecasting?

    b. Extrinsic forecasting?

    c. Combination of expert opinion?

2. What is the time frame of the demand forecasts?

3. How detailed are the demand forecasts?

4. Are seasonality and/or trends in demand reflected in the forecast?

5. Are statistical and/or econometric models used in preparing the forecasts?

6. How large are forecast errors?

7. Are control limits and tracking signals used to identify "out of control" forecasts, so that corrective actions may be taken promptly?

8. Are the causes of forecast errors analyzed regularly in order to improve future forecasts?

9. Does the company track its share of the market in all products sold?

10. If product life is limited, are forecasts projected beyond the expected product life?

11. How extensively is the computer system employed in the forecasting activity?

12. How well are the demand forecasting, production planning, and master production scheduling activities integrated?

13. Is a production plan prepared that:

    a. Requires approval by all functional departments?

    b. Receives periodic updates to reflect current economic conditions?

    c. Includes appropriate time horizons and time buckets?

    d. Provides a breakdown by product lines?

    e. Integrates with the business plan, capacity planning, inventory planning, and master production scheduling?

    f. Is based on written policies?

14. Which departments/individuals are responsible for:

    a. Preparing forecasts related to product demands?

    b. Measuring variances between forecasts and actual demands?

    c. Reviewing and approving forecasts and production plans?

    d. Executing production plans?

    e. Preparing master production schedules?

15. Are key assumptions made during forecasting and production planning processes, such as possible plant shutdowns and strikes, clearly documented?

16. What key inputs are used in developing the production plan?

17. Are various conditions—such as a high level of customer service, peaks and valleys in demand, capacity bottlenecks, inventory turnover, and profit targets—carefully evaluated in developing the production plan?
18. Is actual performance measured against the production plan to determine variations, so that corrective action may be taken?
19. Is the production plan used to formulate and update the annual profit plan (budget)?
20. Are the financial impacts of alternative production plans determined before selecting the optimal plan?
21. Is the production plan used to provide financial outlooks of dollarized sales, production, inventories, costs, profits, and return on investment for future years?

PRODUCTION SCHEDULING

1. Is the master production schedule established in accordance with production levels for each product, as specified by the production plan?
2. Is master scheduling performed at:
   a. The product level?
   b. The work order level?
   c. The work center level?
3. Is master production scheduling integrated with a sound shop floor reporting system to monitor and control production?
4. Is the master production schedule used to:
   a. Set expected delivery dates?
   b. Validate plant capacity at a gross level?
   c. Assist in resource planning?
   d. Determine options requirements?
   e. Drive material requirements planning?
5. Does the master production schedule take into consideration such data as:
   a. Customer orders?
   b. Dealer orders?
   c. Finished goods warehouse requirements?
   d. Service parts requirements?
   e. Demand forecasts?
   f. Safety stock levels?
   g. Other?
6. Does the master production scheduling system provide notification when changes are required to accommodate earlier-than-scheduled orders, etc.?
7. Is the effectiveness of master scheduling measured by:
   a. Percent attainment of the schedule?
   b. Percent on-time deliveries?
   c. Percent machine utilization?
   d. Percent labor efficiency?
   e. Percent labor utilization?
8. Do shop floor supervisors use the production schedules and dispatch lists provided by production planning and control?
9. Which departments/individuals are responsible for:
   a. Releasing orders?
   b. Establishing order priorities?
   c. Establishing sequences of operations?

    d. Dispatching?

    e. Expediting?

10. How effectively is capacity planned to assist in production scheduling?
11. How effectively are shop order priorities planned?
12. Is backward scheduling or forward scheduling performed?
13. Do order release procedures differ by type of shop orders?
14. Are procedures for order release clearly established with respect to:
    a. Numbering orders?
    b. Identifying rush orders?
    c. Assigning priorities?
    d. Issuing shop packets with appropriate documents?
    e. Preparing requisitions?
    f. Assigning needed tools?
15. Are procedures established with respect to:
    a. Engineering changes?
    b. Special shop orders?
16. Are priorities established for available jobs?
17. Do production lead times include allowances for:
    a. Set-up times?
    b. Movement times?
    c. Run times?
    d. Waiting times?
18. Are dispatch lists prepared for all work centers?
19. Are the capacities and work loads of all work centers balanced to ensure steady flows of work through the production lines?

PRODUCTION MONITORING AND CONTROL

1. Are shop floor supervisors and production managers provided with information concerning:
   a. Machine utilization?
   b. Labor efficiency?
   c. Material yield?
   d. Average number of orders in production this period?
   e. Average number of operations per routed order this period?
   f. Number of direct and indirect labor personnel on the job?
   g. Overtime hours as a percent of regular hours?
   h. Scrappage as a percent of standard material costs?
   i. Rework costs as a percent of standard labor costs?
   j. Work-in-process inventory turnover?
   k. Average queue time for key orders?
   l. Overdue shop orders?
   m. Cost variances?
2. Are supervisors and managers well trained in production scheduling and controlling procedures?
3. Are the systems for collecting and reporting production control information integrated, computer-based, and cost-effective?
4. Are discrepancies promptly investigated and corrected?

5. Have the following been established:
   a. Normal loads for all work centers?
   b. Load control limits, based on capacities?
6. Does production planning and control maintain continuous knowledge of:
   a. Current load in each work center?
   b. Inflows and outflows from each work center?
   c. Expected average rates of inflows and outflows from each work center during coming weeks?
7. Are reasons for machine downtime specified?
8. Is machine monitoring used to perform:
   a. Piece counts?
   b. Checks on production rates?
   c. Checks on machine status?
   d. Changes to tool schedules?
9. Is labor reporting by work order and operation number integrated or reconciled with attendance reporting?
10. Are effective procedures employed for:
    a. Reporting labor times by job orders and operations?
    b. Transferring personnel between work centers?
    c. Authorizing overtime?
    d. Recording arrivals, departures, breaks, elapsed times between operations, etc.?
11. Are the same transactions used to capture data concerning labor efficiency, piece counts, and operations on jobs in process?
12. How are labor charges for rework operations reported?
13. How is indirect labor reported?
14. Are indirect labor standards used to evaluate actual performances and to compute variances for control purposes?
15. Are raw materials inspected before being entered into production?
16. Is the quality control function formally organized?
17. Are quality control inspectors fully trained?
18. Are acceptable quality levels established for all products?
19. Are specifications and tolerances clearly specified?
20. Are statistical inspection procedures utilized?
21. Is information concerning rejects available on a timely basis?
22. Are records maintained on rejections, showing quantities, causes for rejection, lot size, vendor data, inspector, etc.?
23. Are quality circles used to enlist ideas for better quality?

MANUFACTURING METHODS AND PROCESSES

1. Does the general plant layout minimize handling and allow work to flow smoothly all the way from receiving to shipping?
2. Does material handling play a major role in productivity and in production costs?
3. Are automated process design, manufacturing, and material handling techniques applicable to this company?
4. Are plant utilization measures employed?
5. Is space planned effectively to streamline work flow, maximize space utilization, and allow for expansion?

6. What departments/individuals perform each of the following tasks:
   a. Product design development?
   b. New product introductions?
   c. Process design and selection?
   d. Standard operating procedures documentation?
   e. Methods design and development?
   f. Value engineering?
   g. Plant layout?
   h. Materials handling?
7. In process design are alternative processes examined with a view toward minimizing production costs while meeting product performance needs?
8. Does engineering match specifications and tolerances for products at different operations to the capabilities of the manufacturing process?
9. Are current processing methods and equipment periodically evaluated for cost reduction and quality improvement opportunities?
10. When designing standardized work methods, are the following considered:
    a. Materials specifications?
    b. Tolerances and inspection requirements?
    c. Process capabilities?
    d. Tooling?
    e. Equipment speeds, feeds, depths of cuts?
    f. Work place layout?
    g. Working conditions and safety?
11. Are robotic systems employed?
12. Are numerical control machines employed?
13. Does plant layout design include:
    a. Continuous flow from receiving to shipping?
    b. Efficient space utilization, with no congested areas?
    c. Anticipated facilities requirements?
    d. Well-marked aisles?
    e. Effective use of overhead areas?
    f. Provision for vendor containers, in-process handling containers, and shipping containers?
14. Do materials handling systems provide for:
    a. Planned and orderly flows of materials, equipment, and personnel?
    b. Adaptability to changes in product mix and production volumes?
    c. Controlled flows and storage of materials?
    d. Integrated processing, inspection, handling, and storage of materials?
    e. Minimized manual handling of materials?
    f. Scheduled deliveries of parts to work centers in predetermined quantities and physically positioned to allow automatic transfer and parts feeding to machines?
    g. Deliveries of tooling to machines in controlled positions that allow automatic unloading and tool changes?
15. Are automated storage and retrieval systems employed in order to improve space utilization, lower operating costs, reduce inventories, reduce pilferage, lower energy consumption, and reduce product damage?
16. Does the plant employ preventive maintenance schedules for all machines?

I. Materials Requirements Planning

INTRODUCTION

Most businesses maintain an inventory of product to sell or materials for manufacturing products to build. Few operations can produce products entirely made to order. Customers expect quick delivery, and slow order fulfillment means lost business. To the extent that excess stock is maintained, the company suffers a drain on resources (interest cost on capital invested plus carrying charges). Insufficient stock can mean reduced customer service or the slowing down of production, which eventually impacts customer service.

The appropriate level for materials and inventory is a function of numerous factors: turnover rate, time needed for replacement, and purchase price as a proportion of total inventory investment including carrying cost. The following checklist should assist the consultant in evaluating the client's materials planning to enhance this area of resource management.

A. MATERIALS PLANNING PROFILE

1. Examine inventory categories per the following measures: dollars, percentage value, and inventory turnover statistics.
2. Are items in different inventory categories stratified through an ABC grouping for planning and control?
3. Are inventory variances monitored and is action taken to control inventories?
4. What is the amount of inventory write-offs over the past few years for obsolete inventories?
5. Is the inventory subject to a limited shelf life?
6. Are the company's products: made/purchased to stock; assembled to order; made/purchased to order; engineered to order?
7. Is master production scheduling (MPS) integrated with the production plan of the company?
8. Is material requirements planning (MRP) used?
9. Is the MRP system supported by accurate bills of material and accurate inventory records?
10. Does the MRP system establish and maintain valid due dates?
11. Is materials planning complicated by excessive and/or unpredictable yield losses?
12. Examine inventory goals by category and compare them to past performance and current performance.

B. MATERIALS ORGANIZATION

1. Who has the overall responsibility of materials planning?
2. Who is responsible for the following functions and how effectively are they managed?
   a. Finished goods inventory planning
   b. Work in process
   c. Raw materials and purchased parts
   d. Purchased products for resale
   e. Operating supplies

3. Are there materials planning systems policies and procedures?
4. Do personnel in materials planning and support functions fully understand the systems and procedures?
5. Select a sample of critical orders that have materials shortages and examine the reason for the shortages.
6. Select a sample of orders on the shop floor. Examine their due dates and compare with customer/ stocking requirements.
7. Analyze selected key raw material, work in process, and finished goods item inventories and compare to required inventory levels based on customer needs and safety stocks.

C. FINISHED GOODS PLANNING

1. What are the sources of demand for individual items?
2. How are the forecasts for each of these demand sources consolidated into a single, combined forecast?
3. Are there families of products that are most economically produced together?
4. What order point rules are used in making replenishment decisions for finished goods?
5. What procedures are used to handle special items or promotional items in finished goods inventory?
6. Does the computer system monitor actual customer orders against forecasts, actual receipts from production against scheduled receipts to provide proper control of finished goods inventory?
7. Are policies clearly defined for inventory planning and control of all categories of inventories?

D. MASTER PRODUCTION SCHEDULING (MPS)

1. Is master scheduling done at the most appropriate product level?
2. Is the MPS used for:
    a. Establishing delivery to sales/customers?
    b. Committing plant capacity?
    c. Assisting in resource planning?
    d. Driving material requirements planning?
3. Does the MPS take into account all the following sources of demand:
    a. Customer orders?
    b. Dealer orders?
    c. Finished goods warehouse requirements?
    d. Service parts requirements?
    e. Forecasts?
    f. Safety stock?
4. Does the MPS system include the following:
    a. Planning horizon?
    b. Time periods?
    c. Ability to update frequently?
5. Do all of the following functions provide input to MPS: marketing, manufacturing, materials management, finance, master production scheduling?
6. Does the MPS system exhibit the following:
    a. Overload?
    b. Excessive past due?

    c. Instability?

    d. Incompleteness?

    e. Horizon too short?

7. Does the MPS system indicate when action is required for discrepancies such as an item required earlier or later than scheduled, one not required but scheduled, a production plan imbalance, etc.?

E. MATERIAL REQUIREMENTS PLANNING (MRP)

1. Does the current MPS system provide the following features:

    a. Net change or regeneration method?

    b. Time period and planning horizon?

    c. Firm planned orders?

    d. Pegged requirements?

    e. Component availability check?

    f. Engineering change effectivity?

    g. Action notices?

    h. Sensitivity filters?

    i. Material availability projections?

    j. Order planning?

    k. Order release?

2. How frequently are the MRP reports updated?

3. Are the MPS modified and MRP rerun to reflect material shortage?

4. Is the MRP system integrated with a shop floor control system that can take MRP due date changes and reflect revised shop floor priorities?

5. Are there informal systems of expediting such as hot lists used by the company?

6. Are spares and distribution warehouse requirements handled by the system?

7. Are lead times calculated meaningfully using queue, move, setup, and production lead times?

8. What percentage is production and setup time of the total lead time?

9. Is the calculated lot size increased for expected losses?

10. Is the effectiveness of MRP limited because of:

    a. Lack of a well-managed MPS?

    b. Poorly defined or inaccurate bills of material?

    c. Poorly defined or inaccurate inventory records?

    d. Wide differences between planned and actual lead times?

    e. Items not being recorded as going into and out of stock?

    f. Bulk issues of component materials?

    g. Inadequate attention paid to capacity planning?

J. Project Monitoring and Control

INTRODUCTION

Project control is concerned with the planning and monitoring of resource utilization to ensure that a project will be completed on time, will be within cost, and will produce quality results. Some basic practices will ensure effective project control:

• Establish standards for recording results.

- Subdivide each project into clearly distinct tasks.
- Prepare estimates and target completion dates for each task.
- Be specific in job assignments.
- Compare progress in each task against its predefined schedule.
- Control project changes.
- Establish a quality assurance function.

Effective project control means developing an overall project control framework (Figure J.1). The purpose of the framework is to:

1. Establish the mechanism to monitor the status of each task
2. Establish the methodology for collecting status information on a regularly scheduled basis using a standard format
3. Organize the project team in the most effective manner for collecting status information and for monitoring and controlling specific aspects of the project

Emphasis on project planning and control contribute to a number of benefits:

1. Improved understanding of project scope and objectives
2. Improved understanding of requirements for completing objectives
3. Improved organization of the overall project into manageable pieces
4. Improved definition of project outputs by tasks
5. Improved monitoring of the status of specific project activities and their associated outputs
6. Improved ability to track overall project status
7. Improved management of project resources
8. Improved documentation of project work completed

The real key to effective project management and control is monitoring projects and consistent status reporting. By understanding the "blocking and tackling" issues and applying solid tools and techniques, you can develop strong project management skills.

BASIC TOOLS AND TECHNIQUES USED TO MONITOR PROJECT STATUS

1. Preparation of project budget by task and resource
2. Collection of actual costs by task and resource
3. Reporting on status of individual project tasks
4. Comparison of actual cost and status to budgeted cost and projected status
5. Reconciliation after completion of project to amount of budget expended
6. Analysis of budget and results variances

MONITORING PROJECT STATUS ON AN OVERVIEW AND ON A DETAILED BASIS

1. Overview basis should include review of overall project status and total level of effort by major task or phase only and a brief discussion of the status of milestones and major problem areas.
2. Detailed basis should include review of specific level of effort by individual for detailed project tasks and subtasks and should include comprehensive explanations of problem areas by task.

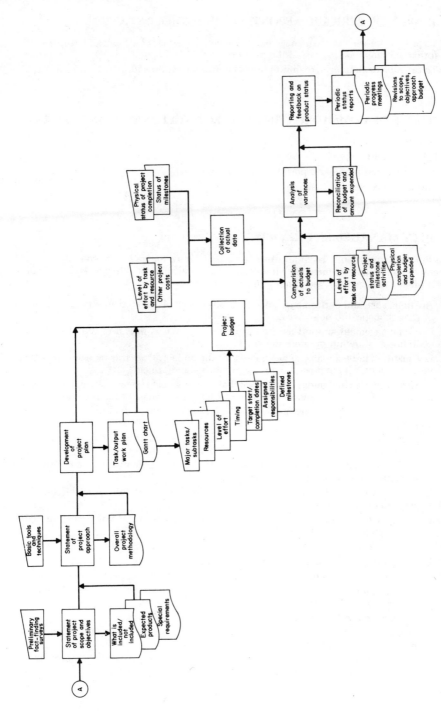

Figure J.1 Project-monitoring-and-control framework, overview block diagram.

PURPOSES OF PERIODIC REPORTING ON PROJECT STATUS

1. To provide information to management on a regularly scheduled basis and in a standard format on the overall status of the project
2. To provide for an interim review of project outputs and allow for revisions, as required

METHODS OF COMMUNICATING PROJECT STATUS TO MANAGEMENT

1. Oral status reports
2. Brief highlights reports
3. Formal written progress reports
4. Formal project review meetings

PROJECT MANAGEMENT REVIEW

The following questionnaire should provide a framework for reviewing the client's approach to project management. The questionnaire can also be used to assess the consultant's project management techniques and identify areas for improvement.

1. Are time, cost, and performance specifications clearly defined in an initial statement of project scope and objectives?
2. Is top management support assured through an initial approval of the project and continuing follow-up progress meetings?
3. Is a qualified project manager designated for the project? Does this manager have the necessary authority and responsibility to manage the project?
4. Are a project plan and budget developed that define tasks to be performed, milestones for measuring progress, and deliverable results at each stage of the project?
5. Are resources committed by management for the project based on the project scope and objectives?
6. Is there a project status reporting system, so that actual schedules and costs can be monitored against plans, with corrective actions taken as needed?
7. Is there exception reporting for the early identification of potential problems through an exception reporting methodology?
8. Do project team members actively cooperate and apply their collective skills in the implementation process?
9. Is senior management kept informed of overall progress and major issues through summary progress reports and periodic meetings?
10. Are computerized project management systems used to plan and control projects?
11. Does the project control system have the following features:
    a. Project results monitored on a basis consistent with how projects are planned.
    b. Original budget maintained in addition to the current approved budget to monitor performance.
    c. Projects controlled on an hours or dollars time-frame basis.
    d. Project control reporting used as a tool to improve the reliability of adjusted resources and completion dates.
    e. Product costs information generated in the cost accounting system compared to product development estimates.
    f. Ongoing resource estimates for completion, schedule estimates for completion, and authorized budget revisions kept up-to-date throughout the project.

12. Are systems development projects logically organized through activities (with management checkpoints) such as:

    a. Project selection

    b. Feasibility study

    c. Project initiation

    d. Analysis and definition

    e. Design

    f. Implementation

    g. Start of operations

    h. Post-implementation review

K. Productivity Improvement Review

INTRODUCTION

Productivity is defined as total output divided by total input, or total results achieved compared to resources consumed. In other words, it is a measure of the effectiveness and efficiency with which resources are used to accomplish desired results. The highest level of productivity can be equated with the maximum performance achieved for the minimum expenditure of resources. Productivity is relevant to every aspect of an enterprise, from white- and blue-collar employees to office machines and plant capacity. It is important to the success of every enterprise. In particular, productivity is the vital concern of business firms since it has a direct effect on the level of their profits and hence their longevity.

The following checklist addresses the means of improving productivity via the various human and nonhuman resources. The consultant should use the checklist to conduct a productivity audit and to develop recommendations intended to enhance the client's overall productivity.

PRODUCTIVITY PLANNING

1. Has a written productivity plan been prepared to guide the enterprise's productivity improvement effort?

2. Does the productivity plan have the full support of top management?

3. Is the productivity plan in accordance with the objectives of the enterprise and its functions?

4. Does the productivity plan integrate with the other plans of the enterprise, such as the operational budget, capital budget, and information system strategic plan?

5. Does the productivity plan define or specify:

    a. The meaning of productivity?

    b. The quality of work life?

    c. An acceptable level of productivity and quality of work life?

    d. The priority to be attached to productivity improvement?

    e. The method(s) of measuring productivity?

    f. The responsibility of individual employees for improving productivity?

    g. The authority and responsibility of the individual who is appointed to direct the productivity improvement program?

6. Have managers and employees:
   a. Participated in developing the plan?
   b. Been fully informed of all aspects of the approved plan?
   c. Been trained in techniques for improving productivity at the various levels of the organization?

PRODUCTIVITY MEASUREMENT SYSTEMS

1. Have standards of performance been established?
2. Have these standards been objectively determined by means of engineering work measurement techniques?
3. Have techniques been established for measuring actual results against the standards of performance?
4. Have productivity data been translated from physical terms to dollar terms, so that they can be related to short-term and long-term budget amounts?
5. Does the productivity measurement system include elements related to:
   a. Profitability?
   b. Price recovery?
   c. Physical and nonphysical productivity?
6. Do the profitability measures show the change in profitability, i.e., the relative change in the output value compared to the relative change in one or more of the input resource values?
7. Do the price recovery measures show the relationship between the change in the unit price of the output and the change in the unit cost of an input?
8. Are these measures expressed both as improvement ratios and dollar effects, e.g., sales per payroll dollar or sales dollars per employee?
9. Are these measures adjusted for inflation effects?
10. Which of the following physical productivity measures are employed:
    a. Number of orders processed?
    b. Number of lines processed?
    c. Order output per labor hour?
    d. Line output per labor hour?
    e. Number of units (e.g., cars) produced per hour?
    f. Average number of hours of direct labor consumed per unit produced?
    g. Average number of indirect hours of labor consumed per unit produced?
    h. Average miles driven per gallon?
    i. Average quantity of materials consumed per unit produced?
    j. Average percent of rejects?
    k. Average number of complaints from customers?
    l. Average time to answer a request?
    m. Actual daily output to planned daily output?
    n. Average number of potential customer contacts per sale?
    o. Average percent of equipment downtime?
11. Do the nonphysical (dollar) productivity measures include measures of all major activities, such as:
    a. Costs of purchased materials and services to sales?
    b. Total storage and retrieval expenses to total documents processed?
    c. Total managerial recruiting costs to number of managers hired?
    d. Total bad debt write-offs to total number of sales?
    e. Total first-year savings to number of hours required to develop a new system?

12. Is each of the measures computed:
    a. Monthly?
    b. Weekly?
    c. Daily?
13. Is each of the measures compared with industry averages?
14. Which of the measures are reported to the owners of the enterprise through appropriate channels, e.g., the stockholders' annual report?

PRODUCTIVITY IMPROVEMENT ACTIONS

1. Are employees given cash payments through a productivity improvement program?
2. Are "work smarter" procedures developed and taught to employees?
3. Are employees allowed to participate in the establishment of productivity standards?
4. Do employees view the established productivity standards as fair?
5. Do productivity standards pertain to quality as well as time quotas?
6. Are employees evaluated with respect to productivity, and do supervisors discuss the evaluations with the employees?
7. Are employees awarded merit pay on the basis of productivity evaluations?
8. Does the company have an incentive pay system?
9. Are employees placed in positions for which they are best suited, on the basis of both aptitude and interest?
10. Are microcomputers, computer terminals, or other tools provided to employees to enable them to perform their duties more quickly and accurately?
11. Are adequate capital investments made in order to provide needed support to operations employees?
12. Are all jobs and projects carefully planned before beginning, so that needed resources will be available without delay?
13. Are peaks and valleys in work loads minimized in order to avoid excessive overtime?
14. Are research and development functions supported vigorously?
15. Are job methods studied by industrial engineers, so that the most efficient methods can be instituted?
16. Are work assignments enriched (i.e., increased in content) to provide variety, increased interest, and added challenge?
17. On the other hand, has simplification been applied to:
    a. Physical work procedures?
    b. Paperwork procedures?
18. Is healthy competition between departments and other work units encouraged?
19. Are employees fully trained to perform assigned tasks?
20. Are "refresher" training sessions and courses provided from time to time?
21. Are meetings of employee groups held on a regular basis, in order to provide full communication and to promote productivity?
22. Does the company sponsor social events on a regular basis, in order to improve morale and cohesiveness?
23. Are employees helped to overcome drug, alcohol, and other personal problems that interfere with productivity?
24. Is a suggestion box provided in a conspicuous place?
25. Are employees awarded a percentage of cost savings or added profits gained by the implementation of their suggestions?
26. Are time-management techniques employed, such as:
    a. Careful scheduling of appointments and activities, using PERT diagrams when suitable?

    b. Setting of targets to be achieved during a specified time period?

    c. Managing by exception?

    d. Performing the more difficult tasks during personal periods of high energy?

    e. Delegating tasks to the extent feasible?

    f. Limiting the times of phone and face-to-face conversations?

27. Are consultants engaged to perform specialized tasks of limited duration?

28. Are machines kept in good working condition through preventive maintenance?

29. Has a quality control program been established?

30. Are supervisors carefully selected for their people-oriented skills and given adequate training in areas of employee concern, i.e., grievances, communication?

31. Does the information system provide adequate information to managers concerning:

    a. Productivity trends?

    b. Costs per jobs?

    c. Costs per function?

    d. Level of product quality?

    e. Level of materials spoilage?

32. Are productivity audits performed on a regular basis?

33. Are conditions not conducive to productivity corrected as soon as possible after discovery?

L. Personnel Management Review

INTRODUCTION

Personnel management is concerned with the human resources of an organization. Suitable personnel policies can lead to satisfied and highly motivated employees who identify with the organization's objectives while gaining a measure of self-fulfillment and receiving adequate compensation for their contributions. Personnel management spans a wide range of activities, including planning, hiring, training, career development, compensation and benefits, labor relations, industrial relations, and safety and health services.

    The following checklist addresses these key areas within the area of personnel management. The consultant should use the checklist as a guide in conducting a personnel audit and developing recommendations intended to enhance the client's performance.

PERSONNEL PLANNING AND CONTROL

1. Does the company have a separate personnel department that is organized to provide staff services, that counsels top management concerning personnel matters, and that receives an adequate budget?

2. Are personnel policies clearly established by top management in all areas affecting the employees?

3. Has the company prepared a personnel manual that incorporates all personnel policies and procedures?

4. Does the company disseminate the policies and procedures to employees by other means, e.g., meetings and newsletters, that ensure their clear understanding?

5. Does the company review the policies and procedures on a regular basis?

6. Does the personnel department employ sound planning practices, including the written statement of plans for review and approval by top management?

7. Does the company perform periodic personnel audits by individuals, e.g., consultants, who are independent of the personnel department?
8. Does the personnel department prepare periodic reports that reflect its achievements in the various areas of personnel management?
9. Has the company established a personnel committee for recommending changes in policies and procedures, and does the committee membership include a cross-section of employees?

RECRUITMENT

1. Has the company developed clear sources of personnel, such as:
   a. Universities?
   b. Newspaper ads?
   c. Professional journal ads?
   d. Union hiring halls?
   e. Employment agencies?
2. Are there clear, written job descriptions for all jobs, including specific requirements in terms of knowledge, skills, experience, aptitudes, and attitudes?
3. Are applicants required to complete written application forms?
4. Are applicants interviewed by trained personnel interviewers?
5. Are applicants required to take:
   a. Aptitude tests?
   b. Achievement tests?
   c. Interest tests?
   d. Physical examinations?
6. Are references requested and carefully checked, preferably in person or by telephone?
7. Does the personnel department perform follow-up checks after employees have been placed?
8. Is each new employee provided with an employee handbook?
9. Are key personnel policies, procedures, benefits, and hazards explained to each new employee?
10. Are affirmative action programs established and followed consistently?

TRAINING

1. Has a formal training program been established?
2. Is the formal training program designed to meet the particular needs of positions such as:
   a. Clerk?
   b. Laborer?
   c. Supervisor?
   d. Department head?
   e. Professional?
   g. Manager?
3. Does the training program provide special accommodation for handicapped employees?
4. Are those responsible for conducting training programs given special instruction in effective teaching techniques?

5. Are suitable training aids employed in the programs, such as:
   a. Charts or projected slides?
   b. Sound films?
   b. Computer-assisted instruction?
6. Are outside speakers included in the training programs?
7. Are formal courses at universities encouraged via tuition subsidies?

CAREER DEVEOPMENT

1. Are career paths for various categories of personnel clearly defined?
2. Are employees informed and counseled with respect to suitable career paths?
3. Are employees counseled with respect to their life careers, including retirement?
4. Is a promotion-from-within policy established and followed consistently?
5. Are employees assigned duties that enrich the content of their jobs and thus create greater job interest?
6. Are formal performance evaluation procedures established, including reviews of all employees at least yearly?
7. Are formal performance evaluations based, to the greatest extent possible, on objective measures rather than subjective opinions of the supervisors?
8. Are supervisors required to discuss each employee's performance evaluation with the employee in a private conference?
9. Are careful progress reports of all employees maintained in their personnel folders?
10. Are exit interviews held with all employees who leave the organization?
11. Are employees who are terminated without cause aided in finding new jobs?

COMPENSATION AND BENEFITS

1. Are all jobs and positions analyzed, evaluated, and classified according to level of difficulty, required skills and education, and so forth?
2. Are wages and salaries based on formal job analysis, evaluation, and classification?
3. Are wages and salaries in line with those for similar jobs elsewhere, allowing for differences in localities, etc.?
4. Does the organization perform periodic surveys of wages and salaries in comparable organizations?
5. Does the compensation plan provide for incentives based on performance?
6. Is a reasonable severance pay policy established?
7. Are bonus plans established?
8. Which of the following fringe benefits are provided:
   a. Stock option plan?
   b. Group health insurance?
   c. Life and disability insurance?
   d. Use of company car?
   e. Company-provided uniforms?
   f. Educational tuition subsidy?
   g. Paid sabbatical leaves?
   h. Paid vacation?
   i. Sick leave?
   j. Reduced work week?
   k. Flex time?

    l. Company-sponsored sports events?

    m. Company-sponsored picnic or other social events?

    n. Cafeteria with reduced prices?

    o. Retirement pension plan?

    p. Credit union?

    q. Payroll savings plan?

    r. Employee profit-sharing plan?

    s. Guaranteed minimum annual wage or salary?

9. Does the company provide shift premium differentials?

10. Does the company provide hazardous duty differentials?

LABOR AND INDUSTRIAL RELATIONS

1. Has the company signed a contract with one or more trade unions?

2. Does the company have a formal grievance procedure?

3. Does the company conduct collective bargaining with the trade unions in good faith?

4. Do employees participate in decisions concerning working conditions and other matters of direct concern to them?

5. Does the company have a suggestion plan, with payments for adopted suggestions?

6. Are periodic employee morale surveys conducted?

7. Are employees kept informed through:

    a. Bulletin boards?

    b. Newsletters?

    c. Magazines?

    d. Loudspeaker announcements?

    e. Meetings?

8. Is music piped throughout work areas?

9. Are washrooms kept clean and sanitary?

10. Are locker rooms clean and convenient for employees?

11. Are no-smoking rules established for offices and plants?

12. Are cafeterias kept clean, sanitary, and open for all shifts?

13. Are athletic facilities provided?

SAFETY AND HEALTH SERVICES

1. Is an infirmary available to employees at all major sites?

2. Is an accident prevention program established and promoted on a continuous basis?

3. Are all accidents investigated and corrective actions taken so that the accidents will not be repeated?

4. Are employees given or encouraged to obtain annual physical checkups?

5. Are health records maintained for all employees?

6. Are the following checked on a regular basis for safety or health hazards:

    a. High walkways?

    b. Gas vents?

    c. Ventilation systems?

    d. Lighting systems?

    e. Open machinery?

    f. Fan belts?

M. Marketing Audit

INTRODUCTION

The essence of entrepreneurship is to convert an idea into a product that people will buy. Brilliant and innovative ideas are useless unless someone can turn them into a marketable product. Marketing encompasses much more than sales. Marketing is the act of identifying and satisfying a need. The marketing function touches all parts of the company. A company's success is tied to the potential market for the product, the market forces affecting the company, the segmentation of the market, and the company's ability to sell and distribute the product.

The following checklist addresses the key areas of the company's marketing activities. The consultant should use the checklist as a guide to conducting a marketing audit and developing recommendations to enhance the client's performance.

A. MARKETING PLANNING

1. Does the company have an analysis of its strengths and weaknesses?
2. Has the company defined its objectives in marketing terms?
3. Has the company determined growth potential for the current market and new markets which the company might enter?
4. Does the company analyze customer demographic, government, economic, social, technological, and competitive factors affecting marketing strategy?
5. Has the company identified customer needs to be fulfilled by new products and services?
6. Has the company determined the feasibility of enhancing current product features?
7. Has the company identified resources needed to enter new markets?
8. Has the company established criteria for introducing new products and product improvements into the marketplace?
9. Has the company determined time requirements involved in effecting market strategy?
10. Has the company developed strategic alternatives for accomplishing market objectives?
11. Has the company assessed the likelihood of accomplishing various strategic plans?

B. PRODUCTS

1. Has the company defined its products in marketing terms?
2. Does the company know the stage of growth or decline in the product cycle for each of its products/services?
3. Does the company know the new product trends?
4. Does the company evaluate competitive products that are direct substitutes?
5. Does the company know the extent of market coverage provided by its products?
6. Does the company analyze the quality of its products as they relate to the competition?
7. Does the company assess the performance of its products in terms of its customers' needs?
8. Does the company constantly review the need for new products and product improvements?
9. Does the company analyze the profitability of its products?

10. Does the company know what type of image its products have with customers? Salespeople?
11. Does the company review product guarantee or warranty results?
12. Does the company analyze the cost-to-value relationship of its various product designs?

C. PRICES

1. Does the company have a formal price structure?
2. Does the company have information on competitors' price structure?
3. Does the company review and respond to deviations from list prices?
4. Does the company capture information regarding the relationship of volume changes to changes in price, quality, or other factors?

D. MARKETS

1. Does the company know its share of the market?
2. Does the company know the competition's share of the market?
3. Does the company know the size of the total market?
4. Does the company understand the forces determining the size and nature of the market?
5. Does the company develop sales forecasts?

E. MARKETING AND DISTRIBUTION

1. Does the company review the effectiveness of its marketing and distribution methods?
2. Does the company review the effectiveness of its competitors' marketing and distribution methods?
3. Does the company analyze the effectiveness of its marketing support including advertising and promotion and technical service?
4. Does the company evaluate the adequacy of its customer service including delivery performance?
5. Does the company evaluate the adequacy of its competitors' customer service?
6. Does the company review the effectiveness of its salespeople?
7. Does the company capture information regarding sales performance including:
   a. Sales versus forecast or budget
   b. Incoming orders
   c. New account analysis
   d. Lost account analysis
   e. Lost order analysis
   f. Return sales analysis
   g. Customer complaint analysis
8. Does the company calculate profitability by
   a. Type of distribution?
   b. Type of customer?
   c. Geographical area?
9. Does the company have expense control information for marketing and distribution activities?

10. Does the company survey its dealer organization?
11. Does the company maintain information on customer inventories?
12. Does the company have information on reciprocal sales?

F. SALES FORECASTING

1. Does the company have a formal sales forecasting activity?
2. Does the company utilize quantitative sales forecasting methods and techniques?
3. Does the company utilize qualitative sales forecasting methods?
4. Are quantitative and qualitative approaches to sales forecasting combined?
5. Is consideration given to external factors including
   a. Competition?
   b. Technological change?
   c. Economic conditions?
6. Are sales forecasts monitored for accuracy and effectiveness?
7. Are sales forecasting methods and techniques and sales analyses performed on the computer?

G. SALES REPORTING AND ANALYSIS

1. Does the company utilize various forms of sales information (units, revenue, etc.)?
2. Does the company report sales information by product in various product groupings?
3. Does the company report sales by responsibility center
   a. Geographic territory?
   b. Division?
   c. Branch?
   d. Sales region?
   e. Salesperson?
4. Does the company have reporting by market
   a. Class of customer?
   b. End user?
   c. Distribution channel?
5. Does the company have sales reporting by major customers?
6. Does the reporting system include comparisons to internal measures of performance, i.e., budget, last year, etc.?
7. Does the company develop market share analyses including served market and served industry market?
8. Does the company utilize various measures of selling activity?

N. Financial Management Review

INTRODUCTION

Financial management is concerned with the inflows and outflows of funds, both in the short run and the long run. Suitable financial management policies and procedures help to acquire funds as needed, to conserve invested and earned capital, to avoid cash shortages and excessive surpluses, to optimize the capital structure, to minimize doubtful accounts, to make sound investments and appropriate expenditures, to safeguard assets, to provide financial information for decision making, and to disseminate financial reports to the owners and creditors and public.

The following checklist addresses these key aspects of financial management. Although the accounting function is closely related to financial management, guidelines pertaining to accounting activities, such as financial reporting, are generally covered by other checklists. The consultant should use this checklist as a guide in conducting an audit of the financial management function and in developing recommendations intended to enhance the client's performance.

FINANCIAL PLANNING AND CONTROL

1. Does the company have a separate finance department that is organized to provide financial services, that counsels top management concerning financial matters, and that receives an adequate budget?
2. Are financial policies clearly established by top management in such areas as:
   a. Acquisition of capital funds?
   b. Capital structure?
   c. Cash management?
   d. Credit management?
   e. Short-term expenditures?
   f. Long-term capital expenditures?
   g. Financial reporting and budgeting?
3. Are financial policies and procedures clearly specified in a financial manual?
4. Does the finance department follow sound planning practices, including the statement of short- and long-term plans in writing for review and approval of top management?
5. Does the company perform periodic financial audits by internal or external auditors who are independent of the finance department?
6. Does the company perform periodic financial appraisals by independent financial consultants?
7. Does the finance department prepare periodic reports on its achievements in the various areas of responsibility?
8. Has the company established a high-level finance committee for recommending changes in policies and procedures, and does it include members from all major functions and an outside consultant?

ACQUISITION OF INVESTED FUNDS

1. Has the company developed a sound strategy for attracting capital?
2. Does the company meet all legal and stock exchange regulations?
3. Does the company have a capital structure that is appropriate to its form of ownership?
4. If the company is a partnership, does it have a partnership agreement?
5. If the company is a corporation, has it considered including the following types of equity and debt:
   a. Cumulative preferred stock?
   b. Noncumulative preferred stock?
   c. Participating preferred stock?
   d. Nonparticipating preferred stock?
   e. Convertible preferred stock?

   f. Common stock with par value?

   g. Common stock with no-par value?

   h. Common stock with stated value?

   i. Secured bonds?

   j. Debenture bonds?

   k. Convertible bonds?

6. Does the company maintain an adequate amount of capital for its activities, so that it is neither undercapitalized nor overcapitalized?

7. Does an appropriate balance exist between equity capital and debt capital, based on the type of industry in which the company is located?

8. Does the company employ sufficient financial leverage, in order to reduce its overall cost of capital?

9. Does the company earn several times the interest owed on long-term debt?

10. Does the company earn a return on equity that is at least as high as the industry average?

11. Does the company earn a return on total assets that is at least as high as the industry average?

12. Is a stock dividend declared on occasion, instead of a cash dividend, in order to conserve cash?

WORKING CAPITAL MANAGEMENT

1. Does the company have a sound strategy with respect to the management of working capital—cash, marketable securities, receivables, and inventories?

2. Is a long-term cash forecast prepared on a regular basis?

3. Is a short-term detailed cash budget prepared and kept updated on a regular basis?

4. Is petty cash controlled by an imprest system?

5. Is an open line-of-credit maintained with at least one bank?

6. Does the company take full advantage of bank float?

7. Does the company analyze all bank accounts on a continuing basis for activity and balances?

8. Does the company keep the overall amounts in non-interest-bearing bank accounts to the minimum needed for effective daily operations?

9. Are cash funds above the minimum needed for effective daily operations invested in marketable securities?

10. Is all cash received each day deposited the same day intact in a bank account?

11. Is short-term financing arranged in advance when cash is expected to be short?

12. Does a policy exist with respect to credit management?

13. Does the company evaluate the credit policy periodically, especially with respect to credit limits, discounts, and due dates?

14. Does the company have a collection procedure that includes:

   a. Periodic reviews of aged accounts receivable?

   b. Past due collection notices?

   c. Follow-up telephone calls to severely delinquent customers?

   d. Factoring of accounts receivable?

15. Does the company carry credit insurance?

16. Are all purchase discounts taken?

17. Are payments to vendors delayed to take full advantage of the discount period?

18. Are prenumbered checks written for all except petty disbursements?

19. Is the cash dividend carefully considered before each declaration date with respect to:

   a. Availability of and impending need for cash?

    b. Need to retain and attract stockholders or to maintain level of stock price?

    c. Substitution of stock dividend or stock split?

20. Is optimal inventory management employed, in order to minimize total inventory costs?

21. Is an appropriate inventory valuation method employed on a consistent basis?

22. Does the company continually review such ratios as:

    a. Current ratio?

    b. Quick ratio?

    c. Inventory turnover?

    d. Dividend payout ratio?

    e. Receivable turnover?

    f. Debt/equity ratio?

CAPITAL INVESTMENT EXPENDITURES

1. Does the company have a policy and procedure with respect to the acquisition of capital investments?

2. Does the company prepare and maintain a capital budget?

3. Does the company diversify its capital investments among such possibilities as:

    a. Real estate?

    b. Ownership in another business?

    c. Research and development?

    d. Marketable securities?

    e. Joint ventures?

    f. Leaseholds?

    g. Insurance?

    h. Productive capacity?

    i. Treasury stock?

4. Is a conceptually sound technique, such as the net present value technique, employed in the evaluation of capital investments?

5. Are proposed investments approved at a sufficiently high level of management before being acquired?

6. Is an accelerated depreciation method employed with respect to new depreciable assets?

7. Are all tax effects considered in the evaluation of alternative types of capital investments?

8. Are the elements of risk and uncertainty taken into account when evaluating potential capital investments?

FINANCIAL INFORMATION

1. Are the financial implications of alternative strategies considered before adoption?

2. Are financial analyses prepared when two or more alternative courses of action are being weighed with respect to a resource allocation decision?

3. Are financial analyses provided in support of proposals for new capital investments?

4. Are financial statements prepared in sufficient detail to be effectively used by managers at varying levels for purposes of planning and control?

5. Are comparative financial statements provided to management?

6. Are financial ratio analyses prepared and distributed to appropriate managers?

7. Are financial statements prepared appropriately and transmitted to the following when due:
   a. Creditors?
   b. Stockholders?
   c. Government agencies?

O. Operations Management: Billing Through Collecting Cycle and Purchasing Through Disbursement Cycle

INTRODUCTION

Although it is true that no enterprise can succeed without a salable product/service, managing a business requires operating procedures and systems that address order entry, customer service, billing/collections, purchasing, inventory management, and cash management. The accounting system and financial reporting are the vehicles by which the data to run the company are gathered, stored, and reported. Once these systems and procedures are in place, the ability to monitor the results means the difference between success and failure.

The following checklist provides guidance for reviewing each of the key operational areas. The consultant should be able to use the findings to develop meaningful recommendations for enhancing the client's operations.

A. Order entry
   1. Does the company have detailed policies regarding:
      a. Minimum order?
      b. Credit requirements?
      c. Classification of customers?
      d. Pricing?
      e. Discounts?
      f. Shipping terms and requirements?
      g. Special orders?
   2. Does the company have detailed procedures regarding:
      a. Customer account analysis?
      b. New customer setup?
      c. Order editing: item number, quantity, specifications, price?
      d. Specification of delivery dates?
   3. Does the computer system provide the following:
      a. Open order summary?
      b. Back-ordered items?
      c. Credit rating?
      d. Current inventory report?
      e. Projected inventory report?
      f. Summary of customer order status?
      g. Competitive product data?

4. Gather the following order statistics:
   a. How many orders are processed per day (week, month, etc., as appropriate)?
   b. What is the average dollar value of orders?
   c. What is maximum dollar value?
   d. What are the average and maximum number of line items per order?
5. Calculate the following ratios:
   a. Phone orders to total orders?
   b. Salesperson orders to total orders?
   c. Reorders/back orders to total orders?
   d. Mail orders to total orders?
   e. Number of complaints to total orders?

B. Shipping and receiving
1. Does the company have detailed procedures regarding:
   a. Verification of orders and shipments?
   b. Customer service?
   c. Partial shipments?
   d. Receipt and shipment of goods?
   e. Damage and shortage reporting?
2. Are the following documents in place and used:
   a. Customer order?
   b. Pick lists?
   c. Packing lists?
   d. Shipping order?
   e. Bill of lading?
   f. Invoice?
   g. Receiving report?
   h. Shipping summary?
3. How are pack lists generated?
4. Are processing times excessive?
5. What procedure is used for reconciling packing lists to invoices?
6. Are packing procedures current and state-of-the-art?
7. Are innovative transportation methods being used?

C. Accounts receivable and credit/collections
1. Does the company have an established credit policy?
2. Does the company control and measure accounts receivable?
3. Does the company periodically review payment terms, discounts and due dates?
4. Does the company emphasize collecting past due accounts?
5. Does the company look at ways to speed up collection?

D. Cash management
1. Does the company have a cash flow plan or forecast?
2. Is the planning interval short enough to predict changes in cash balances?
3. Does the forecast address longer-range cash needs?
4. Does the company have agreements with outside lenders?
5. Is full advantage taken of services offered by commercial banks to improve cash in-flows?
6. Does the company utilize lock boxes and wire transfer facilities?
7. Does the company analyze bank accounts for activity and compensating balance levels?

8. Does the company utilize electronic funds transfer services?

9. Does the company charge divisions for the use of working capital?

E. Purchasing

    1. Does the company have a purchasing function?

    2. Does the company have detailed policies for:

        a. Competitive bidding policies?

        b. Purchase specifications?

        c. Purchase authorization?

        d. Completed purchase orders?

        e. Physical control of purchased items (inspection, frequency of inventory)?

        f. Annual contracts?

        g. Order quantity considerations?

        h. Segregation of duties?

        i. Enforcement of conflict of interest policy?

    3. Does the company have detailed purchasing procedures regarding:

        a. Use of requisitions?

        b. Use of purchase orders?

        c. Approval procedures for requisitions and purchase orders?

        d. Analysis of purchase prices?

        e. Verification of physical receipt of items: quantity, price, quality, timeliness?

        f. Prompt processing of damage and shortage claims?

        g. Responsibility reporting system and budgetary controls for expenses?

    4. Does the purchasing function determine when to purchase?

    5. Does the purchasing function determine how much to purchase?

    6. Does the purchasing function decide on vendors?

    7. Does the computer system provide the following:

        a. Purchase price variance?

        b. Vendor evaluations for reliability, technical capabilities, after-sale service, availability, buying convenience, sales assistance?

        c. Value analysis for purchased items?

        d. Listing of alternative vendor sources?

    8. How many purchase orders are written per week (month, day, other, as appropriate)?

        a. What is the total dollar value?

        b. How many line items per order?

        c. Are there peaks and troughs in the frequency?

    9. What percentage of orders are subject to competitive bidding?

   10. What percentage of orders are subject to quantity discounts?

F. Inventory

    1. Does the company have a formal inventory management process?

    2. Does the company plan inventory levels?

    3. Is inventory planning based on policy or guidelines?

    4. Are individual inventory levels set for:

        a. Finished goods?

        b. Work in process?

        c. Raw materials?

    5. Are inventory levels measured by units or dollars?

    6. Are inventory levels measured:

        a. Daily?

      b. Weekly?

      c. Monthly?

      d. Quarterly?

      e. Annually?

7. What are the current inventory levels of:

      a. Finished goods?

      b. Work in process?

      c. Raw materials?

8. Are inventory levels consistent with customer service objectives?

9. Is a physical inventory taken?

10. Are variances noted? What is their average dollar value?

11. Is someone responsible for reconciling variances?

12. How is inventory forecasting performed?

13. Does the company determine safety stock levels?

14. Are demand characteristics of items considered when establishing safety stock levels?

15. Are lead time characteristics of items considered when establishing safety stock levels?

16. How frequently are safety stock levels updated?

17. Is the timing of inventory replenishment consistent with the value of the item, lead time required, and anticipated seasonal needs?

18. Are there policies regarding obsolete, slow-moving inventory?

19. Is an obsolescence review performed regularly, with items identified as obsolete?

20. Are there documented inventory stock control procedures?

21. Are perpetual inventory records maintained?

22. Is there a stock status report?

23. Is the product coding structure effective?

24. What type of inventory costing is used:

      a. LIFO?

      b. FIFO?

      c. Average costing?

25. Is the costing system used to transfer cost of inventory consumed to products being manufactured?

26. Does the finished product involve multiple manufacturing levels?

27. Are there multiple uses of components and subassemblies, with significant value attached to each?

28. Are there numerous custom features added to a standard product?

29. Is the finished-product manufacturing cycle relatively long?

30. Are raw materials and/or semifinished components stocked, and how long are lead times?

P. Operational Budgeting and Financial Reporting

INTRODUCTION

An enterprise must plan for the short-range future. This type of planning is known as tactical planning. Among the key concerns to be faced in the short-range future is the allocation of such resources as personnel, materials, machines, and money. The instrument that reflects the allocation of these resources over a coming quarter or year is the operational budget. Operational budgeting, one of the most important and time-consuming tactical planning processes, generally involves managers at all levels of the enterprise.

Operational budgets serve as one basis for evaluating the performances of managers, as well as reflecting the operational results of the overall enterprise and its principal operating segments. When the dollar amounts in the operational budgets are compared with the actual operating results expressed in dollars, they produce the variances that indicate favorable or unfavorable performances and results. Much of the financial reporting of an enterprise is concerned with presenting the actual operating results and these dollar variances.

Approaches employed in developing operational budgets and in forecasting financial results have undergone dramatic transformation in recent years. Computer technology and financial modeling techniques have greatly enhanced the sophistication of the operational budgeting and financial reporting processes; they are now accessible to almost every business enterprise.

The elements and levels of business planning are discussed in the appendixes entitled Business Planning and Emerging Business Management Analysis. Therefore, this appendix focuses on the concepts and techniques related to operational budgeting, financial reporting, and financial modeling. As is the case with most of the appendixes, it provides a checklist for use by the consultant.

OPERATIONAL BUDGETING

1. Does the company have a formal operational budgeting system that serves such purposes as:
   a. Making and coordinating short-range plans?
   b. Establishing standards for controlling ongoing operations?
   c. Communicating the short-range plans to the various managers throughout the company in the form of budgets?
   d. Motivating managers to achieve the objectives of their respective responsibility centers?
   e. Evaluating the performances of the managers and their respective responsibility centers?
2. Are the operational budgets consistent with the objectives of the company and its responsibility centers?
3. Do operational budgets fit into a master budget that includes a cash budget and a capital expenditure budget?
4. Do operational budgets coordinate closely with the cash and capital expenditure budgets?
5. Do operational budgets include component responsibility budgets for:
   a. Sales revenue?
   b. Sales expense?
   c. Advertising?
   d. Research and development?
   e. Inventory?
   f. Purchases?
   g. Personnel?
   h. General and administrative functions?
   i. Other areas suitable to the type of company?
6. Do operational budgets include program budgets that arrange estimated revenues and costs by:
   a. Product lines?
   b. Sales territories?

    c. Channels of distribution?

    d. Markets?

    e. Projects?

7. Are operational budgets based on assumptions with respect to such factors as:

    a. Sales forecasts, by product and sales mix?

    b. Inflation rate?

    c. Interest rate?

    d. Standard unit costs for materials, labor, and overhead?

    e. Production levels and capacities?

    f. Availability of resources?

    g. Customer attitudes?

    h. Cash inflows and outflows?

    i. Seasonal factors?

    j. Irregular events, such as strikes and floods?

8. Are responsibility-type operational budgets sufficiently detailed to provide control with respect to:

    a. Cost element?

    b. Activity?

    c. Time period?

    d. Line item?

9. Are flexible budgets used for responsibility centers having a high proportion of engineered costs?

10. Is the management by objectives (MBO) approach employed for those responsibility centers in which monetary measures are relatively unimportant?

11. Are operational budgets adapted to reflect suitable performance measures when responsibility centers are:

    a. Cost centers?

    b. Profit centers?

    c. Investment centers?

12. Are responsibility center managers responsible for participating in the preparation of the operational budgets for their respective responsibility centers?

13. Is a budget committee formed that:

    a. Consists of members of top management?

    b. Recommends budgetary guidelines to the president?

    c. Disseminates the approved budgetary guidelines to the various responsibility-center managers?

    d. Coordinates the various budgets prepared by the responsibility-center managers?

    e. Submits the final coordinated budget to the president and/or board of directors for approval?

14. Has a budget director been appointed with responsibility for assisting in the preparation of the budget?

15. Is the operational budget broken down by:

    a. Quarters?

    b. Months?

16. Is a so-called rolling-budget approach employed?

17. Is the zero-based budgeting concept employed?

18. Can the standards employed to compute the budget values be described as:

    a. Tight?

    b. Loose?

    c. Attainable (i.e., between tight and loose)?

19. Is the operational budget revised during the year to reflect significant changes in conditions?

FINANCIAL MODELING

1. Is a computer system employed to aid the budgeting process?
2. Does the company use computer-based financial models to aid in the development of operational budgets?
3. If financial models are used, do they employ:
   a. Simulation techniques?
   b. Optimization techniques?
   c. Forecasting techniques?
4. Are sales or demands forecasted by means of such statistical techniques as:
   a. Exponential smoothing?
   b. Trend extrapolation?
   c. Regression analysis?
   d. Input-output analysis?
   e. Econometric modeling?
5. If simulation is used via financial models, does it involve:
   a. "What if" analysis?
   b. Goal-seeking analysis?
   c. Sensitivity analysis?
   d. Monte Carlo (risk) analysis?
6. If optimization is used via financial models, does it involve:
   a. Linear programming?
   b. Dynamic programming?
   c. Simultaneous equations?
7. Are the financial models used in a mode known as:
   a. Interactive?
   b. Batch?
8. Does the company gather environmental data for use in financial models, such as:
   a. Inflation rate?
   b. Interest rate?
   c. Construction indexes?
   d. Labor rates?
   e. Competitors' prices?
   f. Materials' unit costs?
   g. Index of industrial activity?
9. Are the data used by the financial models:
   a. Entered specially for processing by the models?
   b. Drawn by the computer system directly from the company's "live" data base?
10. Do managers who have responsibility for developing budget estimates:
    a. Use the financial models directly themselves?
    b. Use the financial models through staff assistants?
    c. Assist in constructing or modifying the models?
11. Has a staff function been established with the responsibility of developing and maintaining financial models?
12. Do the financial models for operational budgeting integrate with financial models for cash budgeting and capital budgeting?

FINANCIAL REPORTING

1. Does financial reporting include the following:
   a. Balance sheet?
   b. Income statement?
   c. Statement of sources and uses of funds?
   d. Responsibility accounting reports?
   e. Profitability accounting reports?
2. Are comparative balance sheets and income statements provided, with differences between this period and last for each line item being expressed in dollars and percentages?
3. Are key financial statement ratios provided in an analysis?
4. Do the responsibility accounting reports reflect variances between the budgeted and actual values, in terms of dollars and percentages, for each responsibility center?
5. Do the profitability reports reflect variances between the budgeted and actual values, in terms of dollars and percentages, for each:
   a. Product?
   b. Geographical sales territory?
   c. Customer class?
   d. Channel of distribution?
   e. Market?
   f. Salesperson?
6. Are exceptional events highlighted in financial reports and explained by narrative notes?
7. Are the financial reports provided:
   a. On a timely basis?
   b. On the basis of an approved distribution list?
   c. In a graphic as well as tabular format?
   d. In a soft-copy form (on the screen of a terminal) as well as a hard-copy form?
   e. In a summarized form, with details available if requested?
8. Are financial reports prepared by a computer system?
9. Can managers request displays of financial reports prepared "on demand" in accordance with specifications provided by the managers?

Q. Capital Investment Planning and Budgeting

INTRODUCTION

An enterprise must plan for the long-range future. This type of planning is known as strategic planning. Among the key concerns to be faced in the long-range future are the investments that should be made in such capital assets as machinery, plants, product research, and executive development programs. Decisions relating to these types of investments are known as capital investment decisions. In some cases these decisions may affect planning horizons of as long as 30 years.

Generally, an enterprise has a limited supply of funds available for investment in capital assets. Thus, it must develop a procedure for allocating these funds among the array of investment opportunities. A procedure for this purpose is known as capital budgeting. It forms a part of the overall budgeting procedure of the enterprise and is facilitated by means of the management information and decision system.

The elements and levels of business planning are discussed in the appendixes entitled Business Planning and Emerging Business Management Analysis. Therefore, this appendix focuses on the concepts and techniques of capital investment analysis and budgeting.

BASIC CONCEPTS OF CAPITAL INVESTMENTS

Types of Investment Opportunities

Capital investments are defined as investments having expected economic lives of longer than 1 year. Within this definition, investment opportunities can be classified according to such categories as the following:

1. Investments that replace current investments, e.g., machines or trucks
2. Investments that expand capacity, e.g., extension to present plants or new plants
3. Investments that are financed by capital funds, e.g., from retained earnings or from the issue of stocks or bonds
4. Investments that are financed by leasing, e.g., building that is leased
5. Investments that have relatively short planning horizons, e.g, typewriters
6. Investments that have relatively long planning horizons, e.g., plants
7. Investments that are tangible, e.g., machines
8. Investments that are intangible, e.g., executive development programs, sales promotion campaigns.

Relevant Factors in Capital Investment Analysis

Certain factors are not relevant in the analysis of an investment opportunity, such as the expected physical life of the investment, the book value of the asset (if any) that is to be replaced by the investment, and the nominal rate of interest on current long-term debt. Among the relevant factors are the following:

1. The expected economic life of the investment
2. Aquisition value of the investment (i.e., the invoice price plus all costs required to put the investment into effective operation)
3. Salvage value of an asset (if any) that is to be replaced by the investment
4. Expected salvage value of the investment at the end of its expected economic life
5. Required rate of return on the investment, as established by management
6. Investment tax credit, if applicable
7. Marginal income tax rate
8. Expected rate of obsolescence of the investment, as measured by its yearly decline in salvage value
9. Expected rate of increase in replacement value of the investment, as measured by the yearly increment in invoice price
10. Method by which the investment is to be depreciated
11. Cost savings and/or revenue enhancements that are expected from the investment, relative to the present situation and existing set of capital assets
12. Probability distributions with respect to future costs, revenues, tax rates, salvage values, economic lives, etc.

Administrative Aspects of Investment Analysis

A management review and approval procedure should be performed before an investment decision is made. This procedure involves preparing a request for capital expenditure form, which is then submitted by the requestor to higher management. After adequate review, the request is either approved, deferred, or rejected. In many enterprises the approving authority is established by reference to the dollar amount of the investment. For instance, investments of less than $1,000 may be approved at the department level, of less than $10,000 at the division level, and over $10,000 at the corporate level. After an investment has been acquired, a postacquisition review should be conducted by the internal audit department to determine whether the estimates were reasonable and the investment decision was sound.

BASIC CONCEPTS OF CAPITAL BUDGETING

The relevant factors listed above pertain to single investments or capital investment projects. Additional concepts and factors must be considered when budgeting rationed capital funds, including the following:

1. Budgeted program of investments, listing the dates when each investment is to be acquired, its amount, and its expected economic life
2. Overall cost of capital to the enterprise (representing the minimum rate of return that can rationally be accepted on a single investment) based on a weighting of equity and debt capital plus retained earnings
3. Method of financing the portfolio of investments, through either (a) purchasing the investments by the use of retained earnings or borrowed funds or (b) leasing the investments by means of financial-type leases
4. Diversification of available funds among the various types of investments listed above (e.g., among replacement-type investments and capacity-expansion investments)
5. Attitudes toward risk, as exhibited by management

TECHNIQUES FOR EVALUATING CAPITAL INVESTMENTS

Payback Period

To compute the payback period in years, divide the total cost of the investment by the net cash inflow or return, assuming the net cash inflows to be uniform for all years. (If the net cash inflows are not uniform, subtract the net cash inflows from the total investment; the payback period is obtained when the cumulative net cash inflows equal the total investment). If the payback period is within the span viewed as being acceptable to management, the investment is considered to be economically feasible. The payback period technique is simple to understand and compute. It ignores the time value of money, however, and thus is not conceptually sound.

Internal Rate of Return

To compute the internal rate of return, find (by trial and error) the rate of discount that exactly equates the total cost of the investment and the net present value of the cash inflows. If the internal rate of return is viewed as being acceptable to management, the investment is considered to be economically feasible. While this technique recognizes the time value of money, it is often difficult to compute without the aid of a computer program.

Net Present Value

To compute the new present value, find the difference between (a) the total cost of the investment and (b) the sum of all net cash inflows, discounted to present value at the required rate of return. (Note that cash inflows include cost savings, revenue enhancements, and salvage values.) If the net present value is positive, the investment is considered to be economically feasible. This technique recognizes the time value of money and is easier to compute than the internal rate of return. Its main drawback is that it requires management to specify a required rate of return.

Risk Analysis

When the environment reflects the degree of uncertainty known as risk, the risk analysis technique may be employed. As noted in Chapter 8, in the risk environment the values of key factors can be expressed by probability distributions. The risk analysis technique, also known as the Monte Carlo simulation approach described in the same chapter, can be applied within the framework of the net present value technique. Thus, after repeated trials using probabilistic values, the results will consist of (a) an expected value for the net present value and (b) a value for the standard deviation of the net present value.

SAMPLE COMPUTATIONS USING NET PRESENT VALUE TECHNIQUE

The net present value technique, with or without risk analysis, is generally accepted as the single best technique for individual investments. A simple replacement investment example will illustrate its use:

Assume that an enterprise currently owns a machine that has a salvage value of $3,000 and an expected physical life of 10 more years. (The book value is equal to the salvage value.) Each year it requires an outlay of $10,000 to operate and maintain. A new machine that performs the same functions has just become available and will cost $19,000 to buy and install; however, it is so efficient that it will only cost $4,000 each year to operate and maintain. It has an expected economic life of ten years, with a salvage value of $3,000 at the end of its life. If the marginal income rate is 50 percent and the required rate of return is 18 percent, is the new machine economically feasible at this time? (Assume for the sake of simplicity that the investment tax credit is zero and the machine will be depreciated on the straight-line basis).

The investment in the new machine is economically feasible, as the following computations show:

Total investment	($19,000)
Less: Salvage value,	
current machine	3,000
Net investment	($16,000)

Before-tax annual cost savings on new machine:
$10,000 − 4,000 = $6,000
After-tax annual cost savings on new machine:
$6,000 × (1 − .50) = $3,000
Present value of after-tax cost savings:
4.494 × $3,000 = $13,482
Depreciation tax shield of new machine:
(19,000 − $3,000)/10 × (1 − .50) × 4.494 = 3,595
Present value of salvage value of new machine:

0.191 × $3,000 =		573
Present value of returns from new machine		$17,650
Net present value of returns from new machine		$ 1,650

CAPITAL BUDGETING TECHNIQUES

A capital budgeting technique is necessarily more complex than a capital investment technique such as net present value, since capital budgeting involves a set of investments within a budget ceiling over a finite capital planning horizon. Because of the complexities, the technique most frequently employed is trial and error.

A more systematic and mathematical sound technique to employ is linear programming, or a variant of linear programming such as integer programming or goal programming. Linear programming seeks to maximize the total net present values from the feasible set of investments, given a budget ceiling. It is a mathematically sound technique and has been applied in a variety of real-world situations. The following constraints, however, cause difficulties in attempting to apply the technique to capital budgeting:

1. The package of best investments may not fit neatly within the budget ceiling. For instance, if the ceiling is 1 million dollars, but the best package would cost somewhat more than 1 million dollars, a less optimal package may have to be selected.

2. Some investments may be contingent upon other investments that are not feasible, or barely feasible, themselves.

3. Criteria other than dollars may provide a better overall return. An example is the profitability index, which is computed by dividing the present value of all returns from an investment by the amount of the investment.

4. The management may have an aversion to risk that dictates the use of an approach such as the minimax approach (described in Chapter 8).

5. The method of financing generally interacts with the cost of capital and hence with investment decisions. This interaction is difficult to incorporate into the linear programming technique.

R. Merger and Acquisition Analysis

INTRODUCTION

An enterprise may grow in several ways. It may grow internally through product development, marketing expansion, new processes and applications, and technological advancements. Alternatively, it may grow externally through corporate mergers and acquisitions. Mergers join together enterprises with mutual interests. They may be instigated due to a desire to pool resources and talents, or they may be motivated by tax considerations. Acquisitions are normally undertaken (a) to accelerate expansion by immediate entry into a new marketing area or (b) to obtain new facilities. A temporary type of combination, a joint venture, is formed when two or more enterprises desire to share the financial risks of some undertaking. Joint ventures are not directly considered in this appendix.

A main concern during merger and acquisition analysis is to determine the valuation of the entities being merged or acquired. The following checklist addresses the key facets of the valuation process and then surveys the variety of capabilities and resources that affect the total valuation amount. The consultant should use this checklist as a guide to conducting the evaluation of entities being considered for merger or acquisition and to developing recommendations for the client's management.

OVERVIEW OF VALUATION PROCESS

1. Is the valuation process to be initiated by:
   a. Negotiation meetings between the parties?
   b. Computation of a "fair and reasonable amount" for shares of the enterprise to be acquired, with the acquiring enterprise advertising the amount in a public offer to acquire shares from current stockholders?
   c. Computation of a "fair and reasonable amount" for shares of the enterprise to be acquired, with the acquiring enterprise advertising for tenders of stock on a bid basis?

2. Is the net valuation amount for the purpose of the merger or acquisition transaction to be considered as:
   a. The economic value, i.e., the value of the enterprise as an ongoing entity?
   b. Liquidation value, i.e., the net amount realizable from the sale of assets after allowance for the liabilities?
   c. Book value, i.e., the net worth of the enterprise as shown on the balance sheet?
   d. Replacement value, i.e., the cost of the same or similar assets, less depreciation of the present assets?
   e. Market value, i.e., the price the market will pay for the assets?
3. Are the assets to be appraised by one or more licensed appraisers?
4. Will appraisal include at least the following:
   a. Detailed listing of all property items at date of appraisal?
   b. Inspection and detailed analysis of the present condition of the property items?
   c. Pricing of all items inventoried?
   d. Calculation of the amount of accrued depreciation?
   e. Final determination of the equitable net value of the assets at the date of appraisal?
5. Is the goodwill of the acquiring enterprise to be added to the valuation of assets, where goodwill represents the incremental benefits (and hence future profits) that an established enterprise may enjoy due to special relationships with the markets, among its employees, and with outside organizations such as governmental agencies?
6. Is the goodwill to be evaluated as the present value of the future stream of incremental profits, or by some other method?

EVALUATION OF MARKETS

1. What are the major business segments of the enterprise?
2. What are the major products marketed in each segment?
3. What are the major marketing channels used to sell the products?
4. What are the market shares of the major products?
5. What is the percentage of domestic to international sales?
6. What are the major marketing strategies of the enterprise?
7. What is the competitive environment within the industry?
8. What has been the trends of sales and profitability within the industry during the last several years?
9. What are the major innovations or technological advances seen within the industry during the past 2 years?
10. What changes within the industry are foreseen in the future?
11. What are the key financial operating performance indicators usually applied within the industry?
12. What market distribution methods are used within the industry?
13. What are the main problems and pressures faced by the industry?
14. Do population growth, new competition, or competitive change in methods justify new ways of serving the markets?
15. Has the character of the population in the markets changed, aside from general growth or decline?
16. Has the ratio of population to number of firms in these markets changed since the enterprise was established?
17. If the ratio in question 16 has changed, how successfully has the enterprise adapted to the changes?
18. When was the last market survey undertaken by the enterprise?

19. What have been the recent trends for the enterprise with respect to:
    a. Sales volume in each relevant market?
    b. Profitability in each relevant market?
    c. Market share in each relevant market?
    d. Return on investment for each major product?
20. How do these trends compare to industry trends?
21. What factors determine the showing of trends, both for the enterprise itself and for its relative standing with respect to industry trends?

EVALUATION OF SALES DEVELOPMENT ACTIVITIES

1. Does the enterprise distinguish between established demand and created demand for its products?
2. Does the enterprise engage in direct and indirect sales promotion activities?
3. Is the present advertising program checked for effectiveness?
4. Do customers generally reflect a feeling of satisfaction in doing business with the enterprise?
5. What is the image of the enterprise in the community?
6. Do the employees engage in sound personal sales practices?

EVALUATION OF PRICING POLICIES

1. Do prices produce an average gross margin consistent with the sales volume for this type of enterprise?
2. Is the enterprise's pricing policy influenced by fair trade laws, nationally advertised prices, or market prices?
3. Does the enterprise adopt less-than-average markup prices when the situation dictates their use?
4. Are prices lowered when necessary to move aged merchandise?
5. Is style a factor in merchandise markups and markdowns?
6. Do original markups reflect normal markdowns, employee discounts, damaged merchandise, and shortages?
7. Are markups based on costs or retail prices?
8. Are loss leaders employed?

EVALUATION OF CREDIT POLICIES

1. Is the enterprise financially able to carry its own accounts receivable?
2. Does the enterprise make available a suitable range of types of credit accounts?
3. What is the cost of administering the credit program?
4. Are credit sales being efficiently collected?
5. Should the enterprise discount its receivables?
6. Is the bad debt rate realistic?

EVALUATION OF ASSET ADEQUACY

1. Are the present assets (e.g., store fixtures, office fixtures, machines, equipment) consistent with the floor plan, available space, and customer needs?
2. Are the present assets reasonably new and modern?

3. What is the list of present assets, including for each:
   a. Acquisition cost?
   b. Depreciation method?
   c. Accumulated depreciation?
   d. Estimated remaining economic life?
   e. Net asset value?
   f. Replacement value?
4. Does the enterprise lack any assets that would improve its capacity for service or profitability?
5. Could the enterprise expand sales or profits by acquiring more assets?
6. What would be the approximate cost of such assets, as compared to the added benefits?
7. Does the enterprise employ a satisfactory asset acquisition procedure, including the following:
   a. Formal proposals?
   b. Detailed descriptions of needed assets?
   c. Analysis of the application of the needed assets, showing designs, installation steps, plant rearrangements, testing steps, and prototype development?
   d. Time phasing of required investments, recurring costs and cost savings, and other benefits?
   e. Forward and backward integration considerations (e.g., how this asset affects related operations in the production process)?
   f. Documentation of major assumptions?

EVALUATION OF THE ACCOUNTING SYSTEM

1. Does the enterprise have a complete accounting system?
2. Is the accounting system computerized?
3. Does the system provide financial statements on a monthly basis?
4. Does the system identify the behavior of costs in relationship to volume and other independent variable changes?
5. Does the system enable the managers of the enterprise to determine:
   a. Amounts owed by credit customers, aged by overdue periods?
   b. Balances due to creditors?
   c. Sales, broken down by departments, products, channels of distribution, geographical areas, etc.?
   d. Profitability, broken down by the same segments as above?
6. Are monthly adjusting entries complete and promptly entered?
7. Are all expenses, revenues, assets, and equities properly classified?
8. What information needed for decision making is not currently provided by the accounting system?

EVALUATION OF FINANCIAL CONDITION

1. What is the ratio of total assets to total liabilities?
2. What is the ratio of current assets to current liabilities?
3. What are the cash and working capital amounts?
4. Does the enterprise have adequate capital in relation to the volume of sales?
5. Does the enterprise have the necessary capital to finance its own receivables?
6. Is the enterprise trading on a adequate level of equity?

7. Does the enterprise have difficulty in paying current bills?
8. What proportion of current profits is being employed to acquire fixed assets?
9. Are creditors withholding credit because of the enterprise's debt-paying habits or other financial problems?
10. Does the enterprise need additional investment capital, and if so how much?
11. What financing sources are available?
12. Is gross margin percentage equal to that of comparable enterprises?
13. What is the likely trend with respect to financial condition?

EVALUATION OF LEGAL FORM OF ORGANIZATION

1. Under what legal form of organization is the enterprise now operating?
2. What are the major risks to which the enterprise is subjected?
3. Does the legal form of organization provide adequate protection against these risks?
4. Does the enterprise supplement its legal form of protection with public liability insurance?
5. Does the present legal form of organization limit financial needs in any way?
6. Are tax advantages available if the legal form of organization were changed?
7. Are the features of a Subchapter S corporation suitable to the enterprise?
8. Is the enterprise utilizing all advantages afforded by the present legal form of organization?

EVALUATION OF EXPENSES

1. Are expenses regularly separated into their fixed and variable components?
2. Does the enterprise prepare break-even charts?
3. What is the effect upon the break-even volume of:
   a. A 10 percent increase in sales?
   b. A 10 percent decrease in sales?
   c. A 10 percent reduction in fixed costs?
   d. A 10 percent reduction in unit variable costs?
4. Can any of the fixed costs be converted into variable costs?
5. Is the enterprise approaching 100 percent of capacity?
6. Are operating expenses as a percent of sales in line with the industry average?
7. Is inventory turnover adequate for the type of enterprise?
8. Is each expense dollar providing a productive return?
9. Does the enterprise prioritize the areas of highest cost reduction potential?
10. Are cost reduction and technological improvement proposals prepared on a frequent basis?

EVALUATION OF PURCHASING AND INVENTORY CONTROL

1. What sources of supply are currently being employed?
2. Does the enterprise take advantage of all purchase discounts?
3. Are safety stock levels, reorder points, and minimum reorder quantities determined by engineering methods?
4. Does the enterprise suffer from stockouts of finished goods or raw materials?
5. Are suppliers satisfactory with respect to:
   a. Quality of goods?
   b. Lead times and other services?

    c. Dependability?
    d. Unit prices?
6. What is the monthly cost of carrying inventory in stock until needed?
7. Are the purchasing and inventory control procedures in need of improvement?

EVALUATION OF RISK PROTECTION

1. Does the enterprise analyze all major risks to which it is subject?
2. What protection is provided against each of these risks?
3. Is the incidence of risk properly considered, in light of protective actions taken?
4. Is self-insurance suitable for the enterprise?
5. Is coinsurance suitable for the enterprise?
6. Can risks be protected in a more economical manner than presently provided?

EVALUATION OF PERSONNEL ACTIVITIES

1. What is the turnover of desirable employees?
2. Does the enterprise provide adequate training for new employees?
3. Are incentives provided for employees to seek advancement?
4. Do opportunities exist for employees to work in different types of positions?
5. Does the enterprise have a good image with prospective employees?
6. Are employee pay levels and benefits consistent with comparable enterprises in the area?
7. What improvements in employees policies and procedures are currently needed?

EVALUATION OF LOCATION

(Note: The questions below pertain only to retailers. Similar lists could be developed for wholesalers, manufacturers, and service organizations.)
1. Is the enterprise located in a high-rent area?
2. How good is the location for attracting customers?
3. Is the traffic volume adequate?
4. If located in a low-rent area and competing with enterprises in high-rent areas, how does the enterprise compensate in attracting customers?
5. Do neighboring stores draw off potential customers?
6. Does a parking problem exist?
7. Does a better site exist in the area?
8. Is the location near a community with desirable payrolls, population trends, living habits, and attitudes?
9. Are there other disadvantages of the present location?

EVALUATION OF LAYOUT

(Note: The questions below pertain only to retailers. Similar checklists could be developed for wholesalers and manufacturers.)
1. Does the present layout encourage sales by reflecting the buying habits of customers?
2. Is merchandise attractively displayed?
3. Does displayed merchandise facilitate easy comparisons and examinations?
4. Are associated lines of merchandise displayed in adjacent areas?

5. Does the layout reflect optimal use of light, ventilation, and heat?
6. Is selling space used efficiently?
7. Are selling and nonselling activities separated?
8. Are convenience, shopping, and specialty goods suitably located to accommodate customers?
9. Does the layout reflect the image of the store in colors, fixtures, displays, lounges, and other comforts that are compatible with the type of customers sought?

Bibliography

CHAPTER 1

American Institute of Certified Public Accountants, *Definitions and Standards for MAS Practice*, Statement on Standards for Management Advisory Services No. 1, New York, 1981.

Business Week, "The New Shape of Management Consulting," May 21, 1979.

Chenok, P. B., "The Exciting Challenges of Management Advisory Services," *The Journal of Accountancy*, June 1981.

Greiner, Larry E., and Robert O. Metzger, *Consulting to Management*, Prentice-Hall, Englewood Cliffs, New Jersey, 1983.

Klein, Howard, M., *Other People's Business: A Primer on Management Consultants*, Mason/Charter, New York, 1978.

Kubr, M. (ed.), *Management Consulting: A Guide to the Profession*. International Labour Office, Geneva, 1976.

Paget, Richard M., "The Future of Management Consulting," *MAS Communication*, March 1982.

CHAPTER 2

AICPA, *Professional Standards for Management Advisory Services*, AICPA, New York, 1984.

Association of Consulting Management Engineers, *Professional Practices in Management Consulting*, New York, 1984.

Carpenter, Robin L., "Get Close to Your Consultant, "*Managerial Planning*, November–December 1982.

Czarnecki, G. W., "Case for Internal Consulting," *Journal of Systems Management*, November 1981.

Fuchs, Jerome, *Making the Most of Management Consulting Services*, AMACOM, New York, 1975.

Ibid, *Management Consultants in Action*, Hawthorne Books, New York, 1975.

Kelly, Robert O., "Should You Have an Internal Consultant?" *Harvard Business Review*, November–December 1979.

Marshall, Thomas R., "How Do You Spell Relief? C-O-N-S-U-L-T-A-N-T," *Managerial Planning*, May–June 1982.

Ibid, "Use and Misuse of Consulting Services," *Journal of Systems Management*, April 1982.

Sawyer, Lawrence B., "Consultant to Management: the Internal Auditor," *The Internal Auditor*, June 1981.

Schein, Edgar H., *Process Consultation: Its Role in Organization*, Addison-Wesley, Reading, Massachusetts, 1969.

Turner, Arthur N., "Consulting Is More than Giving Advice," *Harvard Business Review*, September–October 1981.

Weinshall, Theodore D., "Help for Chief Executives: The Outside Consultant," *California Management Review*, Summer 1982.

CHAPTER 3

Institute of Management Consultants, *Body of Knowledge in Management Consulting*, IMC, New York, 1979.

Kuttner, Monroe S. (ed.), *University Education for Management Consulting*, AICPA, New York, 1979.

Summers, E. L., and K. E. Knight, *Management Advisory Services by Certified Public Accountants: A Study of Required Knowledge*, AICPA, New York, 1976.

CHAPTER 4

AICPA, *Statements on Standards for Management Advisory Serivces*, AICPA, New York, 1983.

Association of Consulting Management Engineers, Inc., *Personal Qualifications of Management Consultants*, ACME, New York, 1971.

Kennedy, James H., "Management Consultants and Conflict of Interest," *Dun's Review*, March 1978.

Shay, Philip W., *Professional Responsibilities of Management Consultants: Ethics and Professional Conduct*, Association of Consulting Management Engineers, New York, 1973.

CHAPTER 5

AICPA, *Documentation Guides for Administration of Management Advisory Services Engagements*, AICPA, New York, 1971.

Andersen, Anker, V., *Graphing Financial Information*, New National Association of Accountants, 1983.

Arevalo, Claire B., *Effective Writing: A Handbook for Accountants*, Prentice-Hall, Englewood Cliffs, New Jersey, 1984.

Carnes, William T., *Effective Meetings for Busy People: Let's Decide and Go Home*, McGraw-Hill, New York, 1980.

Ewing, David, *Writing for Results in Business, Government, the Sciences, and the Professions*, 2d ed., Wiley, New York, 1979.

Golen, Steven P., C. Glenn Pearce, and Ross Figgins, *Report Writing for Business and Industry*. Wiley, New York, 1985.

Ibid, Ross Figgins, and Larry R. Smeltzer (eds.), *Readings and Cases in Business Communications*, Wiley, New York, 1984.

Lanham, Richard A., *Revising Business Prose*, Scribners, New York, 1981.

Morrisey, George L., *Effective Business and Technical Presentations*, 2d ed., Addison-Wesley, Reading, Massachusetts, 1983.

Pearce, C. Glenn, Ross Figgins, and Steven P. Golen, *Principles of Business Communication: Theory, Application, and Technology*, Wiley, New York, 1984.

Sides, Charles H., *How to Write Papers and Reports About Computer Technology*, ISI Press, Philadelphia, 1984.

Skees, William D., *Writing Handbooks for Computer Professionals*, Lifetime Learning Publications, Belmont, California, 1982.

Skopec, Eric W., *Business and Professional Speaking*, Prentice-Hall, Englewood Cliffs, New Jersey, 1983.

Snell, Frank, *How to Hold a Better Meeting*, Cornerstone Library, New York, 1979.

Stewart, Charles J., and William B. Cash, Jr., *Interviewing: Principles and Practices*, 2d ed., William C. Brown, Dubuque, Iowa, 1978.

Strunk, William Jr., and E. B. White, *The Elements of Style*, 3d ed., Macmillan, New York, 1979.

Sullivan, Jeremiah J., *Handbook of Accounting Communications*, Addison-Wesley, Reading, Massachusetts, 1983.

CHAPTER 6

Ackoff, Russell L., *The Art of Problem Solving*, Wiley, New York, 1978.

Lippitt, Gordon L., and Ronald Lippitt, *The Consulting Process in Action*, University Associates, La Jolla, California, 1978.

Rapp, John, "Discovering and Evaluating Client Problems," *CPA Journal*, October 1976.

Pounds, William F., "The Process of Problem Finding," *Industrial Management Review*, Fall 1969.

CHAPTER 7

Bramson, R., and N. Parlette, "Methods of Data Collection for Consultancy," *Personnel Journal*, May 1978.

Burch, J. G., F. R. Strater, and G. Grudnitski, *Information Systems: Theory and Practice*, 3d ed., Wiley, New York, 1983.

CHAPTER 8

Bartee, E. M., "A Holistic View of Problem Solving," *Management Science*, December 1983.

Caws, P., "The Structure of Discovery" *Science*, December 1969.

Churchman, C. W., *The Systems Approach*, Delta, New York, 1968.

FitzGerald, J. M., and A. F. FitzGerald, *Fundamentals of Systems Analysis*, Wiley, New York, 1973.

Hayes, J., *The Complete Problem Solver*, The Franklin Institute Press, Philadelphia, 1978.

Mayer, R. E., *Thinking, Problem Solving, Cognition*, W. H. Freeman, New York, 1983.

Olson, R. W., *The Art of Creative Thinking*, Barnes & Noble, New York, 1978.

Simon, H., *The New Science of Management Decision*, Prentice-Hall, Englewood Cliffs, New Jersey, 1977.

CHAPTER 9

Andersen, Arthur & Co., *Method/1 Information Systems Methodology*, Arthur Andersen & Co., Chicago, 1983.

Davis, William S., *Systems Analysis and Design*, Addison-Wesley, Reading, Massachusetts, 1983.

Kolle, Michael, "Going Outside for MIS Implementation," *Information and Management*, October 1983.

Kotter, John P., and Leonard A. Schlesinger, "Choosing Strategies for Change," *Harvard Business Review*, March–April 1979.

Zaltman, Gerald, and Robert Duncan, *Strategies for Planned Change*, Wiley, New York, 1977.

CHAPTER 10

Corban, Douglas M., and Robert F. Shriver, *EDP Engagement: Software Package Evaluation and Selection*, AICPA, New York, 1984.

Lehmann, Robert S., *Successful Expansion Techniques for Small and Medium-Sized Accounting Firms*, Chapter 3, Prentice-Hall, Englewood Cliffs, New Jersey, 1970.

Whiteside, Conan D., *Accountant's Guide to Profitable Management Advisory Services*, Prentice-Hall, Englewood Cliffs, new Jersey, 1969.

Documentation Guides for Administration of Management Advisory Services, AICPA, New York, 1981.

CHAPTER 12

Baumgartner, John Stanley, "Documentation," *Project Management*, Chapter 10, Richard D. Irwin, Inc., Homewood, Illinois, 1963.

Cleland, David I., and William R. King, "Network Techniques in Project Management," by Joseph J. Moder, *Project Management Handbook*, Chapter 16, Van Nostrand Reinhold, New York, 1983.

Kindred, Alfred R., *Data Systems and Management*, Prentice-Hall, Englewood Cliffs, New Jersey, 1973.

Kelley, Albert J., "New Dimensions of Project Management," *The New Project Environment*, Chapter 2, D. C. Heath, Lexington, Massachusetts, 1982.

Martin, Charles C., "Project Management: How to Make it Work," AMACOM, New York, 1976.

Peart, A. T., "Design of Project Management Systems and Records," *Executing the Project*, Chapter 4, Cahners, Boston, Massachusetts, 1971.

Price Waterhouse, "Effective Engagement Management," Price Waterhouse, New York, 1983.

CHAPTER 13

Professional Practices in Management Consulting, Association of Consulting Management Engineers, Inc., 1966.

deMare, George: *Communicating for Leadership: A Guide for Executives*, Ronald Press, 1963.

Diehart, Ligita, and E. Melvin Pinsel, *Power Lunching—How You Can Profit from More Effective Business Lunch Strategy*, Turnbull and Willoughby, Chicago, 1983.

Kelley, Robert E., *Consulting: The Complete Guide to a Profitable Career*, Scribner's, New York, 1981.

Koberg, Don, and Jim Bagnall, *The Universal Traveler: A Soft-Systems Guide to Creativity and the Process of Reaching Goals*, William Kaufman, Inc., Los Altos, California, 1976.

Strunk, William Jr., and E. B. White, *The Elements of Style*, 3d ed., Macmillan, New York, 1979.

White, Jan V., *Graphic Idea Notebook*, Watson-Guptill, New York, 1980.

CHAPTER 15

Bell, Chip R., *Influencing: Marketing the Ideas that Matter*, Learning Concepts, Austin, Texas, 1982.

Dunn, D. T., et al., "Pitfalls of Consultative Selling," *Business Horizons*, September–October 1981.

Goldsmith, Charles, *Selling Skills for CPAs: How to Bring in New Business*, McGraw-Hill, New York, 1985.

Kotler, Philip, and Paul N. Bloom, *Marketing Professional Services*, Prentice-Hall, Englewood Cliffs, New Jersey, 1984.

Levitt, Theodore, *The Marketing Imagination*, The Free Press, New York, 1983.

Mahon, James J., CPA, *The Marketing of Professional Accounting Services*, Wiley, New York, 1978.

Ries, Al, and Jack Trout, *Marketing Warfare*, McGraw-Hill, New York, 1986.

Webb, Stan G., *Marketing and Strategic Planning for Professional Service Firms*, AMACOM, New York, 1982.

Wilson, Aubrey, *The Marketing of Professional Services*, McGraw-Hill, New York, 1972.

CHAPTER 16

Blanchard, Kenneth, Ph.D., and Spencer Johnson, M.D., *The One-Minute Manager*, Morrow, New York, 1982.

Boll, Carl R., *Executive Jobs Unlimited*, Macmillan, New York, 1965.

Bolles, Richard N., *What Color Is Your Parachute?*, Ten Speed Press, 1983.

Chapman, Elwood N., *Scrambling: Zig-Zagging Your Way to the Top*, J. P. Tarcher, Inc., 1981.

Deal, Terrence E., and Allen A. Kennedy, *Corporate Cultures*, Addison-Wesley, Reading, Massachusetts, 1982.

Freudenberger, Herbert J., and Geraldine Richelson, *Burn-Out*, Bantam, New York, 1981.

Hall, Jay, *The Competence Process*, Teleometrics, Intl., 1980.

Kanter, Rosabeth Moss, *The Change Masters*, Simon and Schuster, New York, 1983.

Maccoby, Michael, *The Gamesman*, Simon and Schuster, New York, 1976.

Ibid, *Leader: A New Face for American Management*, Simon and Schuster, New York, 1981.

Naisbitt, John, *Megatrends*, Warner Books, New York, 1982.

Peters, Romas J., and Robert H. Waterman, Jr., *In Search of Excellence*, Harper & Row, New York, 1982.

Shtrogren, John A. (ed.), *Models for Management: The Structure of Competence*, Teleometrics, Intl., 1980.

Yankelovich, Daniel, *New Rules*, Random House, New York, 1981.

CHAPTER 18

Blank, Hannah I., *Mastering Micros*, Petrocelli, 1983.

Blumenthal, Howard J., *Everyone's Guide to Personal Computers*, Ballantine, 1983.

Bolek, Raymond W., Michael J. Berkery, and Irwin T. David, *Government Executives' Guide to Selecting a Small Computer*, Prentice-Hall, Englewood Cliffs, New Jersey, 1984.

Bunnel, David, and Adam Osborne, *An Introduction to Microcomputers: Volume O The Beginner's Book*, Osborn/McGraw-Hill, 1982.

Gibson, Barbara, *Personal Computers in Business: An Introduction and Buyer's Guide,* Apple Computer, Inc., 1982.

Lundstrom, Peter, *A Guide to Personal Computers,* Apple Computer, Inc., 1982.

McWilliams, Peter A., *The Personal Computer Book,* Prelude Press, 1983.

Ibid, *The Personal Computer in Business Book,* Prelude Press, 1983.

Ibid, *The Word Processing Book,* Prelude Press, 1983.

Microcomputer Literacy Program: For Executives, Managers and Professionals, McGraw-Hill, New York, 1982.

Microcomputers: Their Use and Misuse in Your Business, Price-Waterhouse, 1983.

Needle, Sheldon P., *A Guide to Accounting Software for Microcomputers,* Computer Training Services, Rockville, Maryland, 1984.

The Insider's Guide to Small Business Computers, Data General Corporation, 1980.

GENERAL

Altman, Mary Ann, and Robert I. Weil, *Managing Your Accounting and Consulting Practice,* Matthew Bender, New York, 1978.

Atkins, William, Charles L. Briggs, and Susan G. Birks, *Managing the Systems Development Process,* Prentice-Hall, Englewood Cliffs, New Jersey, 1980.

Bell, Chip R., and Leonard Nadler, *Clients and Consultants,* Gulf Publishing Company, Houston, Texas, 1985.

Cohen, M. Bruce, and Seymour Jones, *The Emerging Business: Managing Growth,* Wiley, New York, 1983.

Computer Installation Effectiveness Review, Price Waterhouse, New York, 1983.

Davis, Keagle W., and William E. Perry, *Auditing Computer Applications: A Basic Systematic Approach,* Wiley, New York, 1982.

Engle, Norman L., *Management Standards for Developing Information Systems,* AMACOM, New York, 1976.

Greiner, Larry E., and Robert O. Metzger, *Consulting to Management,* Prentice-Hall, Englewood Cliffs, New Jersey, 1983.

Hunt, Alfred, *The Management Consultant,* Ronald, New York, 1977.

Levoy, Robert P., *The Successful Professional Practice,* Prentice Hall, Englewood Cliffs, New Jersey, 1970.

Raising Venture Capital: An Entrepreneur's Guidebook, Deloitte Haskins and Sells, New York, 1984.

Shelley, Gary B., and Thomas J. Cashman, *Business Systems Analysis and Design,* Anaheim Publishing Co., Fullerton, California, 1975.

Silvers, Gerald A., and Joan B. Silvers, *Introduction to Systems Analysis,* Prentice Hall, Englewood Cliffs, New Jersey, 1976.

Walley, G. H., *Management Services Handbook,* Business Books, London, 1973.

PRACTICE AIDS

Management Advisory Services Staff Studies, *Management Advisory Services Practice Aids,* American Institute of Certified Public Accountants, New York.

DIRECTORIES

Consultants News, *Directory of Management Consultants,* 2d ed., Fitzwilliam, N.H.: 1980.

Wasserman, Paul, and Janice McLean, *Who's Who in Consulting,* 2d ed., Gale Research Co., Detroit, 1972.

Index

ABOUT THE AUTHORS

Sam W. Barcus III received his B.B.A. degree from the University of Texas and his M.B.A. degree from the University of Houston. He joined Price Waterhouse in Memphis as a computer consultant, working on a variety of computer-related projects, including system design. In 1983 he joined Touche Ross in Nashville to establish a microcomputer consulting practice serving small businesses. Today he is a partner in the Barcus Nugent Group, which provides management consulting to professionals and small business executives. Mr. Barcus is a certified public accountant and has held leadership positions in a number of professional organizations, including the National Association of Accountants. He has written many articles and has conducted workshops and seminars on topics relating to the computer industry.

Joseph W. Wilkinson is professor of accounting at Arizona State University, where he teaches an introductory course in management advisory and consulting services. Before earning his doctorate at the University of Oregon, Dr. Wilkinson worked as an industrial engineer, systems analyst, and accountant in such organizations as Price Waterhouse and Hughes Aircraft. Dr. Wilkinson is the author of numerous articles and four textbooks, including *Accounting and Information Systems*.